PENGUIN CLASSICS

REFLECTIONS ON THE
REVOLUTION IN FRANCE

CONOR CRUISE O'BRIEN, Consultant Editor with the *Observer* since
1981, has been Pro-Chancellor of the University of Dublin since 1973.
Born in 1917, he gained his B.A. and Ph.D. degrees from Trinity
College, Dublin, and entered the Department of External Affairs of
Ireland in 1944. In 1955 he was Counsellor in Paris, and from 1956
until 1960 he was head of the United Nations section and a member of
the Irish Delegation to the U.N. In 1961 he represented the Secretary–General of the U.N. in Katanga, and at the end of that year he
resigned from his appointments. He was Vice-Chancellor of the
University of Ghana from 1962, to 1965. Albert Schweitzer Professor
of Humanities at New York University from 1965 to 1969, a Fellow
of St Catherine's College, Oxford from 1978 to 1981 and Visiting
Professor at Dartmouth College, USA, from 1984 to 1985. He was a
member of the Dail for Dublin North-East from 1969 until 1977 and
of the Senate of the Republic of Ireland for the following two years.
He joined the *Observer* in 1978, where he was Editor-in-Chief until
1981. His books include *Parnell and His Party* (1957), *To Katanga and
Back* (1962), *Writers and Politics* (1965), *The United Nations: Sacred
Drama* (with drawings by Feliks Topolski; 1968), *States of Ireland*
(1972), *Herod* (1978), and *Neighbours: the Ewart-Biggs memorial lectures
1978–79* (1980).

EDMUND BURKE

REFLECTIONS ON THE REVOLUTION IN FRANCE

AND ON THE PROCEEDINGS IN
CERTAIN SOCIETIES IN LONDON
RELATIVE TO THAT EVENT

*

EDITED WITH AN INTRODUCTION BY
CONOR CRUISE O'BRIEN

PENGUIN BOOKS

PENGUIN BOOKS

Published by the Penguin Group
27 Wrights Lane, London w8 5TZ, England
Viking Penguin Inc., 40 West 23rd Street, New York, New York 10010, USA
Penguin Books Australia Ltd, Ringwood, Victoria, Australia
Penguin Books Canada Ltd, 2801 John Street, Markham, Ontario, Canada L3R 1B4
Penguin Books (NZ) Ltd, 182–190 Wairau Road, Auckland 10, New Zealand

Penguin Books Ltd, Registered Offices: Harmondsworth, Middlesex, England

First published 1790
Published in Pelican Books 1968
Reprinted 1973, 1976, 1978, 1979, 1981
Reprinted in Penguin English Library 1982
Reprinted 1983, 1984
Reprinted in Penguin Classics 1986, 1987, 1988

Made and printed in Great Britain by
Hazell Watson & Viney Limited
Member of BPCC plc
Aylesbury Bucks
Set in Linotype Pilgrim

CONTENTS

ACKNOWLEDGEMENTS

I AM indebted to Professor Thomas Copeland, the general editor of *The Correspondence of Edmund Burke* (see Bibliographical Note) for much valuable advice both in conversation at Sheffield and in correspondence; to Mrs Valerie Jobling for generous and painstaking help in connexion with documents at Sheffield; to Professors David Erdman, R. B. McDowell and Edward P. Thompson, and to Mr William Vanech and Miss Eileen Sheerin, my colleagues in the Schweitzer Programme at New York University during all or part of the academic year 1967–8, for comments, corrections and assistance of many kinds; to Professor William Todd and Messrs Holt, Reinhart & Winston for permission to use their authoritative text (see Bibliographical Note); to Earl Fitzwilliam for permission to use the Burke papers in the Fitzwilliam Wentworth Collection; to Mr John Babbington, Chief Librarian, and Miss R. Meredith, Librarian, Central Public Library, Sheffield, for facilitating access to these papers. Finally and especially, my thanks are due to my wife for her invaluable work on the annotation. The notes as they stand are our joint work. Professor Todd in presenting his definitive edition of the text of the *Reflections* spoke of 'peculiarities ... condoned by the author', which of course have been preserved in the text. If any additional peculiarities have been condoned by the editor he alone is responsible for these.

C.C.O'B.

The footnotes to this text are indicated by asterisks, daggers, etc.

The superior numbers (thus: [48]) refer to the notes by the editor of this Pelican edition. They are to be found on p. 378ff.

INTRODUCTION

'THE MANIFESTO OF A COUNTER-REVOLUTION'

I

THE spectre haunting Europe in *The Communist Manifesto* (1848), and haunting the world today, walks for the first time in the pages of Burke:

... out of the tomb of the murdered monarchy in France has arisen a vast, tremendous, unformed spectre, in a far more terrifick guise than any which ever yet have overpowered the imagination, and subdued the fortitude of man. Going straight forward to its end, unappalled by peril, unchecked by remorse, despising all common maxims and all common means, that hideous phantom overpowered those who could not believe it was possible she could at all exist, except on the principles, which habit rather than nature had persuaded them were necessary to their own particular welfare, and to their own ordinary modes of action.*

The revolution which Burke feared is not of course identical with Marx's Communist revolution, but has much essential in common with it, and in some ways more in common with it than with the actual French

---

* First of the *Letters on a Regicide Peace* (1796); *Works* V, p. 155; Marx may have known the passage; he did know some of Burke's writings. There is a bitter footnote about Burke in *Capital*: 'The sycophant – who in the pay of the English oligarchy played the romantic *laudator temporis acti* against the French Revolution just as, in the pay of the North American colonies at the beginning of the American troubles, he had played the liberal against the English oligarchy, was an out-and-out vulgar bourgeois.' (*Capital* I, Moscow, 1954, p. 760, n2.) Earlier he had described Burke as the man whom both Parties in England regard as the model of a British Statesman (*N.Y. Daily Tribune*, December 1855). From a Marxian point of view there is of course no contradiction between the two descriptions.

Revolution of Burke's day. Burke would have been likely
to see in the principles of the Communist revolution the
emergence in even purer form of all that he most
detested in the contemporary revolution whose progress
he watched with horror and fascination in France, and
sought with eloquence and skill to check in England. The
spirit of total, radical innovation; the overthrow of all
prescriptive rights; the confiscation of property; destruction of the Church, the nobility, the family, tradition,
veneration, the ancestors, the nation – this is the cata-
logue of all that Burke dreaded in his darkest moments,
and every item in it he would have discovered in Marx-
ism. In the personality of Marx himself he would have
seen incarnated that energy which he regarded as most
dangerous to ordered society: the energy of ability without property.* In Engels he would have seen a prime
representative of a category whose activities he found
both noxious and incomprehensible: the category of the
men of property who encouraged the spread of principles
inimical to the rights of property.† Like Burke, Marx and
Engels long and anxiously scrutinized the French Revolution, seeking in its course the secret of the future
development of European and world politics.‡ Like his,
their imagination was deeply penetrated by the energies
which the Revolution let loose, deeply impressed by the

* 'But as ability is a vigorous and active principle, and as property
is sluggish, inert and timid, it never can be safe from the invasions
of ability unless it be out of all proportion, predominant in the
representation.' (*Reflections*, p. 140.)

† See *Letter to a Noble Lord* (1796); *Works* V, pp. 110–51. See also
p. 384, n.42.

‡ Marx in his earlier years applied the lessons of the French Revolution too schematically as in his writing for the *Rheinische Zeitung*
and *The Civil War in France*. But in *The 18th Brumaire of Louis
Bonaparte*, in chastened and deliberate language he gives an extraordinary sense of how, and in what ambiguous shapes, the great
Revolution weighs on his own time.

contrast between the scale of these events and the routine of politics in a world that hoped the Revolution could be ignored, or treated as a purely local and exceptional event, isolated in space or time. Like him they looked through the political surface of the Revolution towards its economic and social substance: Burke provides, in the *Reflections** and elsewhere, some of the best examples of that aristocratic critique of the bourgeoisie, to which the *Communist Manifesto* allows a provisional and sardonic welcome. Burke and Marx both sought to understand the revolutionary principles at work in France – Burke in order to stop them from spreading, and to destroy the nucleus of infection; Marx in order to hasten the victory of a new revolution, bringing with it the triumph of all that for Burke had been most hateful – though not of that which had been most contemptible – in the old one.

The great revolutions of our own time, those of Russia and China, came, under Marxist leadership, in lands which had never known an equivalent of the French Revolution. France, itself, and those other Western countries most exposed to the Enlightenment, and – like Britain and the United States – least resistant to those principles of political democracy which Burke abhorred, are not among the most revolutionary in the world today. The country which was the fulcrum of counter-revolution in his day – the country whose Empress he praised†

---

* See for example the passage (*Reflections*, pp. 311–313) about the ascendancy of financial speculators, with its peroration: 'Here end all the deceitful dreams and visions of the equality and rights of men. In the "Serbonian Bog" of this base oligarchy they are all absorbed, sunk and lost for ever.' See also (p. 130) the discussion of the membership of the Tiers État and its implications: 'From the moment I read the list I saw distinctly, and very nearly as it has happened, all that was to follow.'

† *Letter to the Empress of Russia* (1791), *Corr.* VI, pp. 441–5, 448. Privately he had his reservations.

was to become for our time that nucleus of revolutionary infection which France was for his. We have lived to see Russia itself, through its revolutionary gains, cease to be a revolutionary force, superseded by a power which had clung even longer than Russia to the ancestral ways, which had furnished the supreme example in the world of long adherence to the social contract in the form that Burke conceived it – 'a partnership not only between those who are living but between those who are living, those who are dead and those who are to be born.'* If, as Burke desired and passionately urged, the European monarchies had whole-heartedly and successfully combined to crush the Revolution early and utterly in France, while ruthlessly suppressing every incipient manifestation of potential revolutionary character in their own countries, one wonders what results such success would have produced in a longer term. Might not the revolutionary forces, not so much suppressed as compressed, have burst out at a later date, with far greater violence, under more disciplined, consistent and determined leadership; and with even more radical effects on the structure of society? Merely to pose the question is I think to raise doubts about the degree of enlightenment in the self-interest of international counter-revolutionary com-

* *Reflections*, pp. 194–5. The long passage which contains these words still has a profound appeal to lovers of all forms of traditional society. A brilliant young East African writer, Ali al 'Amin Mazrui, has said that, in this passage, Burke is at his most 'African' – closest, that is, not to the University-trained African, but to 'the African who is steeped still in traditional ways'. (*Comparative Studies in Society and History*, vol. 1, no. 2, Jan. 1963.) Mazrui's contention about the compatibility of Burke's doctrine in this passage with African traditional thought is surely sound; his attempt to apply Burkian principles to the Congo was, however, vitiated by the inadequacy of the information then available to him. The Tananarive agreement of 1960 was not, as he assumed, an inter-tribal settlement but an internationally sponsored attempt at a compromise between international forces.

bination. I shall return to this topic, in considering the relevance of Burke to the militant anti-communism of our own day. First, however – since Burke's own attitude to the Revolution was not all at once a crusading one – it is necessary to discuss the actual development of his opinions, emotions and apprehensions about the Revolution, to the extent to which these are revealed in his surviving writings.

2

From the very beginning, just after the fall of the Bastille, events which seemed to so many a new dawn of liberty aroused Burke's forebodings, without however yet drawing down a general condemnation.

'As to us here', he wrote to Lord Charlemont on 9 August 1789,*

our thoughts of everything at home are suspended, by our astonishment at the wonderful Spectacle which is exhibited in a Neighbouring and rival Country – what Spectators and what actors. England gazing with astonishment at a French struggle for Liberty and not knowing whether to blame or to applaud! The thing indeed, though I thought I saw something like it in progress for several years,† has still something in it paradoxical and Mysterious. The spirit it is impossible not to admire; but the old Parisian ferocity has broken out in a shocking manner. It is true this may be no more than a sudden explosion. . . . But if it should be character rather than accident, then that people are not fit for Liberty, and must have a **Strong** hand like that of

* *Correspondence* VI pp. 9–12. This is Burke's earliest known comment on the Revolution.

† The editors of *Corr.* VI comment: 'As early as 1769 Burke after describing the financial difficulties of France wrote "No man, I believe, who has considered their affairs with any degree of attention or information, but must hourly look for some extraordinary convulsion in that whole system; the effect of which on France, and even on all Europe, it is difficult to conjecture." ' (*Corr.* VI, eds. Cobban and Smith, p. 10, n.2.)

their former masters to coerce them. Men must have a certain fund of moderation to qualify them for Freedom else it becomes noxious to themselves and a perfect nuisance to every body else.

The same attitude, that of a concerned and generally disapproving spectator, is reflected in Burke's other comments during 1789. The disapproval deepens, however. On 10 October 1789, after the revolutionary removal of the king from Versailles to Paris, he writes to his son about

... the portentous state of France – where the Elements which compose Human Society seem all to be dissolved, and a world of Monsters to be produc'd in the place of it – where Mirabeau presides as the Grand Anarch; and the late Grand Monarch makes a figure as ridiculous as pitiable. I expect to hear of his dismissing the Regiment he has called to his aid, for drinking his health ... and that he has chosen a corps of Paris Amazons for his Body Guard. (*Corr.* VI, pp. 29–30.)

On 4 November Chames-Jean-François de Pont, the 'very young gentleman at Paris' of the prefatory page of the *Reflections*, wrote to Burke that letter to which the *Reflections* are, in form, a reply. 'Son Coeur', he said,

a battu pour la première fois au nom de Liberté en vous en entendant parler. ... Si vous Daignez l'assurer que les françois sont Dignes d'être libres, qu'ils sauront Distinguer la liberté de la licence et un Gouvernement légitime d'un pouvoir Despotique; si vous daignez enfin l'assurer que la Révolution Commencée Réussira, fier de votre témoignage il ne sera jamais abattu par le Découragement qui Suit Souvent l'Espérance. (*Corr.* VI, pp. 31–2.)

At no time from the beginning of the Revolution to his death could Burke have given the reassurance sought by his young correspondent, but his original reply* is far removed in tone and character from the fierce polemic of

---

*This is the letter of 'October 1789' referred to in Burke's prefatory page. Cobban and Smith, however, establish that it was written in November, and probably not forwarded before the end of that year. (*Corr.* VI, pp. 39–50.)

the *Reflections*. He emphasizes his ignorance of the actual situation and his distrust of his own judgement. 'If I should seem . . .' he says, 'to express myself in the language of disapprobation, be so good as to consider it as no more than the expression of doubt.' He defines that freedom which he loves: 'The Liberty I mean is *social* freedom. It is that state of things in which Liberty is secured by the equality of Restraint; a Constitution of things in which the liberty of no one Man and no body of Men and no Number of men can find Means to trespass on the liberty of any Person or any description of Persons in the Society.' Failing this, failing the establishment of

real *practical* Liberty with a Government powerful to Protect, impotent to invade it. . . . You may have subverted Monarchy, but not recover'd freedom. . . . You are now to live in a new order of things; under a plan of Government of which no Man can speak from experience. . . . The French may be yet to go through more transmigrations.

Burke offers advice not in the taste of this enlighten'd age and indeed . . . no better than the late ripe fruit of mere experience – Never wholly separate in your mind the merits of any Political Question from the Men who are concerned in it. . . . The power of bad men is no indifferent thing . . .' The letter concludes with praise of prudence and moderation:

Prudence (in all things a Virtue, in Politicks the first of Virtues). . . . Believe me, Sir, in all changes in the State, Moderation is a Virtue, not only amiable but powerful. It is a disposing, arranging, conciliating, cementing Virtue . . . to dare to be fearful when all about you are full of presumption and confidence. . . .

These sagacious and memorable admonitions are in no way inconsistent with the *Reflections* – which contain several passages in the same strain – but the fire of that great tract has not yet been kindled. Nor is there as yet any note of alarm. 'As to France,' he writes to Earl

Fitzwilliam about the time when he must have been composing the reply to de Pont,

if I were to give way to the speculations which arise in my
Mind from the present State of things and from the causes
which have given rise to it and which now begin to be unfolded,
I should think it a country undone ... I should certainly wish to
see France circumscribed within moderate bounds. The interest
of this Country requires, perhaps the Interests of mankind require, that she should not be in a position despotically to give
the Law to Europe: But I think I see many inconveniences only
not to Europe at large, but to this Country in particular from
the total political extinction of a great civilized Nation situated
in the heart of this our Western system.*

It was not very long before Burke, and after him many
others, were struck by 'inconveniences' of a quite different character. Up to the end of 1789, however, he remains detached, and little moved. 'The affairs both of
France and England', he writes to his friend Philip Francis
in December,

are rendered little more to us than a matter of Curiosity; with
the one our Duty gives us no concern; with the other we are
not sufferd to intermeddle with any Effect or any Credit: and
after all perhaps the follies of France, by which we are not yet
affected may employ ones curiosity more pleasantly, and as
usefully, as the depravity of England which is more calculated
to give us pain.†

It is in January 1790 that the mood of contemplation
begins to give place to one of action. A letter written to
an unknown, probably in the latter half of that month‡

* *Corr.* VI, 12 November 1789.

† *Corr.* VI, pp. 55–8, 17 December 1789.

‡ The editors of *Corr.* VI date (p. 78) this 'at some time around the
middle or the latter half of January 1790'. They also show that
Burke did not read Dr Price's sermon and the correspondence of the
Revolution Society until his arrival in London 'for the meeting of
Parliament on the 21st' *Corr.* VI, p. 81. The conclusion of the letter
seems to show the influence of this reading.

seems to register within itself the transition. In that letter
he is more philosophical, or teleological, about the situation
in France than he is ever to be again: 'Man is a gregarious
animal. He will by degrees provide some convenience suitable to this his natural disposition; and this strange thing
may some time or other, assume a more habitable form.
The fish will at length make a shell which will fit him.'
Then, after some scathing remarks about Voltaire and
Rousseau, he strikes a new note of concern: 'I see some
people here are willing that we should become their scholars
and reform our state on the French model. They have
begun; and it is high time for those who wish to preserve
morem majorum to look about them.'

The first phase of Burke's counter-revolutionary
activity – the phase of the *Reflections* – was that of
fighting the influence of these people in England. In this
phase he did not see the danger mainly in France itself,
but in the kind of thinking which had in his view produced the events in France, and in the men who favoured
the introduction of this kind of thinking into England.
The danger came home to him on his reading of Dr
Price's sermon and the Revolution Society's correspondence with the National Assembly.* Shortly afterwards, in
Parliament, Charles James Fox praised the French Revolution highly, saying that he 'exulted in it from feelings
and from principle'. Pitt also looked forward to a recon-
structed and free France 'as one of the most brilliant
powers in Europe'. It was then that Burke on 9 February
1790 for the first time took a public stand against the
principles of the Revolution. The published account of
his speech makes clear that his principal declared concern is the danger of infection spreading from France to
England:

That the house must perceive, from his coming forward to

* *Reflections* pp. 91–6 and notes 2–5, pp. 379–80.

mark an expression or two of his best friend, how anxious he was to keep the distemper of France from the least countenance in England, where he was sure some wicked persons had shewn a strong disposition to recommend an imitation of the French spirit of reform. He was so strongly opposed to any the least tendency towards the *means* of introducing a democracy like theirs, as well as to the *end* itself, that much as it would afflict him, if such a thing could be attempted, and that any friend of his could concur in such measures, (he was far, very far, from believing they could,) he would abandon his best friends, and join with his worst enemies to oppose either the means or the end; and to resist all violent exertions of the spirit of innovation, so distant from all principles of true and safe reformation; a spirit well calculated to overturn states, but perfectly unfit to amend them.*

The *Reflections on the Revolution in France* develop, defend and illustrate this argument.

3

The early, though not immediate success of the *Reflections* with the propertied classes – amid the growing alarm caused by the progress of the Revolution – and its effect in restoring Burke to royal favour† and in earning

---

* Speech on the Army Estimates, 1790. *Works* III, pp. 209–81.

†In March of the year following the appearance of the *Reflections* Mrs Burke proudly repeated to her brother-in-law a conversation with George III: 'You have been of *use to us all*, it is a general opinion, is it not so Lord Stair? ... It is, said Lord Stair; – Your Majesty's adopting it, Sir, will make the opinion general, said Ned – I know it is the general opinion, and I know that there is no Man who calls himself a Gentleman that must not think himself obliged to you, for you have supported the cause of the Gentlemen.' (*Corr.* VI, pp. 237–9. Jane Burke to W. Burke, 21 March 1791.) Some months before, Burke had noted that he had received 'from the Duke of Portland, Lord Fitzwilliam, the Duke of Devonshire, Lord John Cavendish Montagu, and a long et cetera of the old Stamina of

him a pension* in his retirement naturally led Burke's opponents to suggest that he had – as would now be said – 'sold out', abandoning his real principles for praise and money. Tom Paine in *Rights of Man* had charged bribery; contemporary cartoons made play with the congenial theme; Marx, years afterwards was content to account for Burke's counter-revolutionary writing in this way.† How else explain the defection from the cause of liberty of the man who had, as was claimed, championed the cause of the American Revolution? The charge was rendered plausible by Burke's complicated financial situation, his costly establishment at Beaconsfield – on which Dr Johnson had commented '*Non equidem invideo; miror magis*' – and the reputation attaching to 'the Burkes' because of certain past financial transactions.‡

---

the Whiggs a most full approbation of the principles of that work [the *Reflections*] and a kind indulgence to the execution'. (*Corr.* VI, pp. 176–80, to Sir G. Elliot, 29 November 1790.)

*A civil list pension of £1,200 a year, granted in 1795. In a letter to Fitzwilliam, after the breach with Fox, Burke complains that Fox condoned 'a base charge that I could have no other motive for the part, which during [sic] near two years I had taken against the propagation of French principles in this Kingdom, than a secret Bribe which I had received from the Ministers.' (*Corr.* VI, pp. 271–6; 5 June 1791.)

† See footnote 1, p. 1. Marx quoted Burke's *Thoughts and Details on Scarcity* (1795): 'The laws of commerce, which are the laws of nature and therefore the laws of God.' 'No wonder', added Marx, 'that obedient to the laws of God and of Nature he always sold himself in the best market.' (*Capital*, I, p. 760, n2.)

‡ See Dixon Wecter, *Edmund Burke and his Kinsmen: A Study of the Statesman's financial integrity and private relationship* (Boulder, 1939). 'Without too great an accusation of personal selfishness against the impressionable erratic Irishman,' writes Wecter, 'one may connect his early championship of the East India Company from about 1766 to 1772 with his kinsmen's interests and partiality to "the Funds" and his later assault upon the pride and arrogance of that Company in advancing Fox's East India Bill of 1783 and the

However plausible it may have seemed to contemporary and other opponents – and the debate round the *Reflections* has remained so live that opponents have always had a tendency to become contemporary – the charge that Burke turned against the Revolution for gain cannot be sustained. Long ago, at the outset of his career – as a condition indeed of having a career at all – Burke had cast in his lot with an important section of the men of rank and property. He was himself one of the most notable examples of the conjuncture which he thought most redoubtable to ordered society: ability without property. Had he been born in similar social circumstances in Arras in the 1750s, or in Dublin or Belfast in the 1760s, he might conceivably have been a revolutionary, and dangerous in proportion to his mighty powers. Mary Wollstonecraft thought so: 'Reading your *Reflections* warily over, it has continually struck me, that had you been a Frenchman, you would have been, in spite of your respect for rank and antiquity, a violent revolutionist. . . . Your imagination would have taken fire . . .'* As it was, born in Dublin in 1729, he placed his ability from

subsequent impeachment of Hastings with the fact that Will Burke [a kinsman and close friend of Edmund's] in the meantime had changed from a London speculator to "a Government servant in India".' Commenting on Mr Wecter's investigation of the Burke finances, Professor Copeland says: '. . . it is now quite clear that both Richard [Edmund's brother] and Will were on occasion dishonourable in their financial dealings. Edmund, though he has never been proved to have been consciously dishonourable, was so closely associated with the other two that he was inevitably and quite properly given part of the blame for their acts.' (*Edmund Burke; Six Essays*, London, 1960.)

A Vindication of the Rights of Man (1790). Burke's son Richard – though he warmly and even indiscreetly supported his father's politics – thought he would have stood to gain by a revolution: 'I see to myself personally great positive and Evident Interest from such changes as have happened in France . . . or anything like them.' (*Sheffield Papers*; R. Burke Jr. to Fitzwilliam, 20 July 1790.)

the beginning at the service of men of rank and property. He remained faithful, without servility, to the party he had chosen. His writings on American affairs were not revolutionary; they were, rather, an attempt to prevent the development and exacerbation of a revolutionary situation. It is true that he never condemned the American Revolution, as he did the French, but then the secession of a group of colonies is not an event similar to the overthrow of the settled order of a major state, even though the word 'Revolution' is used about both. Burke's letters of the second half of 1789 – quoted above – show that his attitude towards the French Revolution was disapproving from the very beginning, even before there was any question of his taking a public stand. Even allowing for Burke's unusual gifts of political foresight, an attack on the French Revolution cannot have looked, in the first half of 1790, like a promising pathway to a pension. In 1790 the French Revolution did not seem dangerous, to most Englishmen. France seemed even to be 'settling down'. Burke himself had been informed, towards the end of 1789, 'that heats are beginning to abate'.* The period from the transfer of the king to Paris (October 1789) to his attempted escape (June 1791) is one of the quietest in the Revolution: the 'initial tumults' are over; constitution-making is in progress, with much talk of the English example; the principal events that were to be thought of as the 'horrors of the Revolution', the September massacres, execution of the King and Queen, the Reign of Terror – all are in the future. In this context the vehemence of Burke's attack, while certain to alienate many of Burke's political friends, was not certain to attract new support and in

---

* *Corr.* VI, pp. 39–50; reply to de Pont, November 1789; see above, pp. 14–15. Burke had originally hesitated to send the letter because 'in Seasons of Jealousy suspicion is vigilant', but released it on learning of the abatement of heats.

fact its immediate effect seems to have been even to increase his unpopularity. A recent writer has summed up
the situation just after the publication of the *Reflections*:

Thus Burke had no immediate success either with Government or with Opposition. The general feeling in political
circles was that Burke, though eloquent and ingenious, went too
far in this opinions; too far in his total and systematic opposition to the French revolution; too far in his attack on the
dissenters and reformers; too far in his apprehensions of
danger to the English constitution; too far in making public
scenes, and breaking friendships, on an issue that need never
have been publicly debated at all.*

What saved his reputation was the progress of the Revolution in the direction he had foretold. In the debate in
which Burke committed himself – in February 1790 – Pitt
himself spoke about the Revolution in a conciliatory
spirit. Even in later years when events, seeming to confirm many of Burke's dire predictions, had drawn Burke
and the Government closer together, it is never a case of
his following a Government line, but rather of his re-
proaching the Government for its pragmatic attitude and
lack of counter-revolutionary zeal.

4

'What I most envy Burke for', said Dr Johnson, 'is, his
being constantly the same.'† Johnson seems to have had

* R. R. Fennessy, o.f.m.: *Burke, Paine and the Rights of Man*, The
Hague, 1963, (pp. 193–4).

† Boswell's *Journal of a Tour to the Hebrides*, 15 August 1773.
Coleridge thought the same: 'No man was ever more like himself'
than Edmund Burke (*Essay on the Grounds of Government*, 1809).
Tom Moore on the other hand found in him 'a want of moral
identity observable through his life and writings'. (*Memoirs of
Sheridan*, 1825.) Moore, unlike the more politically minded Mackintosh, saw Burke's attitude towards the French Revolution as a
complete break with his earlier position.

in his mind primarily the equable temperament which was Burke's in his middle years, but a reader of Burke is likely to find the comment applicable in a more general sense to his work, including the *Reflections*. The more one reads Burke the more one is impressed, I think, by a deep inner consistency, not always of language or opinion, but of feeling: a consistency of which the root principles are a strong capacity for affection, and a strong distrust of all reasoning not inspired by affection for what is near and dear. 'I have no great opinion of that sublime abstract, metaphysic reversionary, contingent humanity, which in *cold blood* can subject the *present time* and those whom we *daily see and converse with* to immediate calamities in favour of the *future and uncertain* benefit of persons who *only exist in idea*.'* The amount of added emphasis, unusual in Burke, is, I think, proportionate to the strength of his feelings on this theme. (See *Reflections* p. 315, the passage ending 'so many little images of the great country in which the heart found something which it could fill'). This consistency by no means excludes complexity and contradictions; rather, it is the consistency of a complex and powerful personality, successfully withstanding unusual stress.

Burke's family affections were – in the eyes of some English contemporaries – excessive, in that they went out not merely to his immediate family – his wife Jane, his idolized son, Richard, his brother Richard – but also to what a modern anthropologist would call his 'extended family'. 'He always marched', as Professor Copeland has said, 'at the head of a clan.'† Cousins from Ireland, relatives of all kinds down on their luck, were welcome at Beaconsfield. In society, Burke's 'train' was so full of brogue as to shock

---

* *Corr.* VI, pp. 104–9; to A. J. F. Dupont, post 29 March 1790.
† *Edmund Burke: Six Essays.*

even his admirers.* Had Burke been the purely self-seeking
adventurer whom some of his opponents depicted, he
would have acted differently towards his compromising
relatives. These affections of his extended beyond – but not
indefinitely beyond – his family. They took in the country
of his birth, and his mother's co-religionists; he never ceased
to struggle for concessions in Ireland, and relief for Catholics. Compromising connexions again: an ambitious Irish
adventurer in eighteenth-century England would, if guided
by pure calculation, have avoided these topics: it did not
help Burke to be caricatured in the garb of a Jesuit, or to
have it said – by Wilkes – that his oratory 'stank of whiskey
and potatoes'. Burke's affection also held, life-long, to his
old Quaker school-master Shackleton, and his son, to his
patron, the Marquess of Rockingham, and in general, in the
more attenuated form of 'loyalty' to that section of English
society – the Whig oligarchy – whose interests he had
served, and through whose patronage he and his clan had
established themselves. And in proportion as he loved or
respected these groups of people, and the settings in which
they lived, he hated all that seemed, to his powerful and
sensitive intelligence, to menace them.†

Yet the span is great: between the ruined Irish
Catholics and the owners of the wealth of England there

* 'Burke has now got such a train after him as would sink anybody but himself: his son, who is quite *nauseated* by all mankind;
his brother, who is liked rather better than his son, but is rather
oppressive with animal spirits and brogue; and his cousin Will
Burke ... a fresh charge on any prospects of power Burke may
ever have. Mrs Burke, has in her charge Miss French, the most
perfect *she Paddy* that ever was caught.' (Sir G. Elliot, 2 May 1793
– *Life and Letters of Sir G. Elliot*, ed. Countess of Minto, London
1874: II, 136.)

† 'The moral sentiments, so nearly connected with early prejudice
as to be almost one and the same thing, will assuredly not live
long under a discipline which has for its basis the destruction of all
prejudices.' *Works* III, p. 108.

is a chasm for Burke's affections to bridge. I believe, on grounds which will now be set out, that there is a connexion between the tensions of this spanning and the emotional charge, the pathos and fury, of the *Reflections*.

It is entirely natural that it should have been the words of the dissenting divine, Dr Price,* that set in motion the avalanche of Burke's eloquence against the Revolution. Burke's feelings towards the Dissenters were strong and mixed, and for some time past his hostile feelings towards them had been predominant. In the late spring of 1789, well before French affairs were occupying the minds of Englishmen, Richard Bright wrote asking for his support for a measure of relief for the Dissenters. Burke's reply is revealing:

There are no Men on Earth to whom I have been more attached, and with a more sincere Esteem and Affection, than to some amongst the Dissenters. From my earliest years my Connexions have been very much with them. I flatter myself that I have still friends of that denomination. They were once indulgent enough to Me to think that (according to my scanty Power of obliging) they had some sort of obligation to me. In the Year 1784, a great Change took place,† and all of them who seem'd to act in Corps, have held me out to publick Odium, as one of a gang of Rebels and Regicides, which had conspired at one blow to subvert the Monarchy, to annihilate, without cause, all the Corporate privileges in the Kingdom and totally to destroy this Constitution. It is not their fault that I am in a situation to be asked by them or by anybody else, for my poor Vote . . .‡

It was not to be long before Burke had a chance of turning against Dissenters of the school of Dr Price every one

---

* See n.5, pp. 379–80.

† The reference is to Pitt's electoral victory of that year, in which the dissenting influence contributed to the overwhelming defeat of the Whigs – and thereby to Burke's isolation in his last years.

‡ *Corr.* V, pp. 470–74; 8–9 May 1789.

of the charges which he regarded the Dissenting body as having used against the Whigs – partiality to rebellion, regicide, subversion and innovation, and enmity to the Constitution. On 13 February 1790 Bright again wrote to Burke looking for support for his measure.* By this time Burke had read Price and others, and had made his speech on the Army Estimates: the *Reflections* were brewing. Burke replies with a new grimness:

Since the last years applications many things have either happend, or come to my knowledge, which add not a little to my disposition to persevere in my former State of inactivity [i.e. on dissenting petitions]. Extraordinary things have happened in France; extraordinary things have been said and done here, and published with great ostentation, in order to draw us into a connexion and concurrence with that nation upon the principles of its proceedings, and to lead us to an imitation of them. I think such designs, as far as they go, highly dangerous to the constitution and the prosperity of this Country. I have had lately put into my hands, and but very lately, two extraordinary works,† so sanctiond as to leave no Doubt upon my Mind that a considerable party is formed, and is proceeding systematically, to the destruction of this Constitution in some of its essential parts. I was much surprised to find religious assemblies turned into a sort of places of exercise and discipline for politicks, and for the nourishment of a party which seems to have contention and power much more than Piety for its Object . . .‡

It is clear, I think, that had the Dissenting influence been used in favour of the Whigs, instead of against them, in 1784, his reaction to the language of Price, Palmer, Robinson and the others would have been likely to be more temperate.§ Burke was a passionate man, strong in

* *Sheffield Papers.*

† Palmer's *Protestant Dissenter's Catechism* and Robinson's *Principles of Nonconformity.*

‡ *Corr.* VI, pp. 82–5; to R. Bright, 18 February 1790.

§ The fierceness of his personal resentment breaks out at the end of the second letter to Bright. For Burke to support the Dissenters' his resentments as in his affections, and it is not to be supposed that he did not enjoy giving the Dissenters back something of what he considered them to have given him six years before. But Burke's specific political resentments against the Dissenters, joined to the frustration of his later years in Parliament, had the effect of setting free the deeper forces of his being. Had Rockingham lived, had he and his friends been in power, had they enjoyed Dissenting support, it is hardly possible that Burke could have written with untrammelled eloquence about the Revolution in France. Frustrated, he was free.*

The significance of Burke's quarrel with Dissenters in his writings on the Revolution† goes much deeper than the specific quarrel over party politics. It was natural that Dissenters – and ordinary English Protestants generally – should welcome the early stages of the French Revolution because they saw in them the overthrow of Popery. The

―――――――――――

petition would be, he says, 'a very bad example, and of a most immoral tendency, to the world; in teaching Men, that they may persecute and calumniate their true friend ... and yet that they may ... make use of his abilities for the service of their *party*. This My dear Sir, is a terrible example.'

*A hostile contemporary saw this frustration and wounded vanity as the actual *causes* of the *Reflections*: 'You were the Cicero of one side of the house for years,' wrote Mary Wollstonecraft 'and then to sink into oblivion, to see your *weary* honours fade before you, was enough to arouse all that was human in you and make you produce your impassioned *Reflections* ...' (*A Vindication of the Rights of Man*). Disraeli, in *Sybil*, adopted a similar interpretation. 'Burke poured forth the vials of his hoarded vengeance into the agitated heart of Christendom,' etc. Vengeance against Fox for taking the Whig leadership from Burke, Disraeli thought.

† The quarrel did not cease with the publication of the *Reflections*. Late in 1791, for example, he writes that 'What I look to with seriousness is the Phalanx of Party which exists in the body of the dissenters', and estimates that nine-tenths of these are devoted 'to the principles of the French Revolution'. (*Corr.* VI, pp. 418–22; to Dundas, 30 September 1791.)

very first achievement for which Dr Price was *thankful* was 'a diffusion of knowledge, which has undermined superstition and error'.* To most Englishmen of the day, whether Dissenters or not, these words must have sounded quite proper, used as they were in a context which necessarily implied that the 'superstition and error' were of the Romish kind. But Burke was not English, although he often wrote and spoke in the character of an Englishman. He was Irish and of old native, not recent settler stock; in the words of a modern biographer, 'Edmund Burke was pure Irish'.† This distinction was, in some ways, more basic than that of formal religious profession. The recent settlers were, in general, militant in their Protestantism, which they associated with their title to their lands and their dominant position in society. Those of the older stock who had become Protestant were always suspect of having done so to escape the operation of the Penal Laws – to keep their land, if they had any, and to have access to careers. Burke himself was exposed to such suspicion, as we have seen; early in his career he was denounced to Rockingham as a crypto-Catholic.‡ There is no need to doubt his denial; the whole tenor of his writing makes it clear that he was not a man likely to cherish one set of dogmas – or other abstractions – beneath a feigned belief

* *Reflections*, p. 157.

† The name Burke is of Norman origin but Norman and Gaelic blood had long been intermingled. Burke's father, says Sir Philip Magnus, 'came of a family which had long been merged with the Celtic population of the country.' (*Edmund Burke: A Life*, London, 1939; pp. 1, 5.)

‡ In 1765 enemies of Burke informed the Duke of Newcastle, who informed Rockingham, that Burke was a papist educated by the Jesuits. Burke, denying the story, offered to resign but Rockingham refused his resignation. (Carl B. Cone, *Burke and the Nature of Politics: The Age of the American Revolution*, Kentucky University Press, pp. 71–2.)

in another set. His feelings are another matter. To an unknown correspondent who – at the height of the Revolution controversy – inquired about his religious beliefs,
he replied that having been baptized and educated in the
Church of England he had 'seen no cause to abandon
that communion. When I do, I shall act upon my conviction or my mistake. I think that Church harmonizes
with our civil constitution . . . I am attached to Christianity at large; much from conviction: more from affection.'*

It will be seen that the references to the Church of
England are cool and politic, provisional and contingent.
It is not to the Church of England – still less to Protestantism – that he is attached, 'much from conviction; more
from affection'; it is to 'Christianity at large'. This is odd.
Nothing could be more foreign to Burke's habitual way of
thinking, writing and feeling than to be more attracted to
something 'at large' than to his own subdivision of it. If
for once he shows no enthusiasm for his 'little platoon'†
and is all for the Army 'at large', we are justified I think in
inferring that he does not feel himself to be quite in the
right platoon. This would not be surprising. Burke's
mother was a Catholic; so was his father-in-law and friend,
Dr Nugent; his father, Richard Burke 'seems' according to
Professor Thomas Copeland 'to have conformed to the
Established Church 13 March 1722 about the time he began
to practise law in Dublin.'‡ In order to practise law at this
time and place one was obliged to conform to the Established Church. Edmund's wife Jane was, like him, the child of
a 'mixed marriage'. It is not known where Edmund and she
were married, and there is a tradition that it was a Catholic

* *Corr.* VI, pp. 214–16; to an unknown 26 January 1791.

† *Reflections*, p. 135 'to love the little platoon we belong to in
society, is the first (the germ as it were) of public affections'.

‡ *Corr.* I, p. 274 n. See, however, Postscript on p. 81.

marriage solemnized in Paris.* The 'clan' at whose head
Edmund Burke marched was shot through with Catholicism; and this at a place and time in which Protestantism
might be feigned, but Catholicism, being socially and
economically disadvantageous to the verge of ruin, must
be presumed to be based on firm conviction. Burke might
'see no cause to abandon' the communion of the Church
of England but his family background was such – and his
family feeling so strong – that he could not possibly contemplate attacks on the Church of Rome with any of the
feelings of a proper Englishman – with detachment, com-
placency or downright approbation.† This emotional disposition in religious matters has surely much to do both
with the nature and with the promptness of his response to
the events in France.

5

Burke's Irish origin and connexions affect his response
to the Revolution in other ways besides the religious.
Englishmen of rank and wealth in the late eighteenth
century – before 1793 – could not easily imagine social
revolution as a reality. 'The Burkes', close to the rawness
and deep social and political resentments of Ireland, were
much more aware of the underside of society, and conscious of danger. Richard Burke, Jr – who often expressed
his father's thought with indiscreet vehemence – wrote,
at the time when the *Reflections* were being composed,
a vivid warning to Lord Fitzwilliam, whose agent he

* Basil O'Connell, 'The Rt. Hon. Edmund Burke ... a Basis for a
Pedigree', *Journal of the Cork Historical and Archaeological Society*,
Vol. LXI, pp. 257–74, January–June 1956.

† W. B. Yeats in his later years liked to think of Burke – with
Swift, Berkeley, Goldsmith, Grattan and Parnell – as among the
glories of a specific Anglo-Irish Protestant tradition. (See *The Senate
Speeches of W. B. Yeats*, ed. Donald R. Pierce, London 1961.) The
real Burke resists confinement in this category.

was: 'Think when you walk the streets of Peterborough
that they lie under the stones and that they will come out
of the rotten tenements you have purchased of Mr Parker
to lord it over the lord of those tenements. What will then
become of the persuasive eloquence, the moderating concessions and the temporizing expedients of Mr Fox?'* The
placid tone of Lord Fitzwilliam's reply† does not suggest
that young Burke succeeded in communicating his vision.
Here, as usual at this time, the Burke mind, haunted by
the phantom of revolution,‡ was baffled by 'those who
could not believe it was possible she could at all exist . . .'
An Irishman could not be so sceptical, or so placid; revolt

* *Sheffield Papers*; 29 July 1790.

† Richard was trying to get the great Whig lord to reprimand and
disavow Fox and Sheridan, the Whig leaders in the Commons who
had praised the Revolution. He said he wrote without his father's
knowledge, but that 'I know I speak his sentiments as well as my
own.' Fitzwilliam indicated that the timing and character of any
'*caveat*' were matters for him to determine (July and August 1790).

‡ The expression is not entirely rhetorical. It is surprising how
often Burke's references to the Revolution use supernatural or
fantastic terms. The revolutionary leaders are 'suddenly and as it
were by enchantment snatched from the humblest rank' (*Reflections*, p. 130); they are men who hack their father in pieces and
put him into the 'kettle of magicians' (ibid. p. 194). In private
letters he calls the Revolution 'this strange, nameless, wild, enthusiastic thing' (January 1791) and 'this vile chimera, and sick mans
dream of Government' (26 September 1791); the friends of the
Revolution in England are 'the infernal faction' (September 1792);
their Press 'the Newspapers of Hell' (October 1792). In his last years
as might be expected, this imagery became more obsessive – see
the passage beginning 'The Revolution harpies of France, sprung
from night and hell', in *A Letter to a Noble Lord* (1796); the 'spectre'
passage in the first *Letter on a Regicide Peace* (1796); the 'questionable shape' (second *Letter*, 1796). And in the last unfinished *Letter*,
he writes: 'In the time I have lived to, I always seem to walk on
enchanted ground. Everything is new and, according to the fashionable phrase, revolutionary.' Burke also uses ghostly imagery about
Ireland (see p. 36).

was in fact imminent in Ireland, and broke out in 1798, the year after Burke's death. No man in England had been more painfully conscious of its imminence than Burke. 'We regarded as the great Evil of the time,' he wrote to Dr Hussey in December 1796, 'the growth of Jacobinism, and we were very well assured that from a variety of causes no part of these Countries were more favourable to the growth of that Evil than our unfortunate country.'* He abhorred the movement of the United Irishmen, which sought to bring together dissenters and Catholics in one national, democratic, revolutionary movement under French inspiration and with French aid – 'those who, without any regard to religion, clubb all kinds of discontents together, in order to produce all kinds of disorders'.† Yet, where the Irish Catholics were concerned, he makes a unique allowance, if not for a legitimate kind of Jacobinism, at least for a kind rooted in human nature; the two categories are, in Burke's mind, very close together. 'That Jacobinism,' he wrote to Hussey,

which is Speculative in its Origin and which arises from Wantonness and fullness of bread may possibly be kept under by firmness and prudence. . . . But the Jacobinism which arises from Penury and irritation, from scorned loyalty and rejected Allegiance, has much deeper roots. They take their nourishment from the bottom of human Nature . . . and not from humour or caprice or the opinions of the Day about privileges or Liberties.‡

Burke's references to the danger of revolution in Ireland are naturally most frequent in the last years of his life, the period closest to the impending revolt. But Ireland was never far from his thoughts. As a modern Burke

* *Sheffield Papers; c.* 6 December 1796.

† *Sheffield Papers;* to Hussey, 18 May 1795.

‡ To Hussey, *c.* 6 December 1796. There is no doubt that Burke had the Irish Catholics in mind in this passage: the Irish Dissenters he regarded as quite a privileged body.

scholar has written: '... like every other responsible and intelligent Irishman with sufficient heart from that day to this, Burke carried Ireland round with him as his personal "old man of the sea".'* Burke had written in 1780 that when he first came into Parliament, fourteen years before, what had been 'first and uppermost in my Thoughts, was the hope without injury to this Country to be somewhat useful to the place of my Birth and education....'† We know from the draft tract against the Popery Laws, written shortly before his election to Parliament, how this hope then worked, and this tract is perfectly consistent with all that he afterwards wrote on the condition of Ireland.‡

It is reasonable therefore to assume that his vision of Ireland – an oppressed and dangerous Ireland – was a permanent part of Burke's imaginative landscape. His relation to Ireland made impossible for him two of the stock responses of Englishmen to the opening stages of the Revolution: that of approval for what seemed an anti-Papist reformation and that of 'It can't happen here'. 'Here', for Burke, was not only England but also Ireland, so that revolution for him was from the beginning a thing imaginable. This goes some way to explain the alertness and promptitude of Burke's response, the fact that he was

---

* T. H. D. Mahoney, *Edmund Burke and Ireland*, London, 1960, p. ix.

† *Sheffield Papers*; to Thomas Burgh, New Year's Day, 1780. He added that when he felt this hope to be dashed 'all the lustre of my imaginary rank was tarnished; and I felt degraded even by my elevation.'

‡ *Letter to the Rt. Hon. Edmund Perry* (1778); *Letter to Thomas Burgh* (1780); *Letter to John Merlott* (1780); *Letter to a Peer of Ireland* (1782); *Letter to Sir Hercules Langrishe* (1792); *Letter to William Smith* (January 1795); *Second Letter to Sir Hercules Langrishe* (1795); *Letter to Richard Burke* (1792). Works V, pp. 486, 491, 510, 282; III, p. 298; VI, pp. 49, 56, 61.

the first man of importance in England to descry and denounce a danger which within a few years agitated the mind of every man of property. This explains Burke's sensitivity, his nose for smoke; it does not, however, explain the intensity of his counter-revolutionary passion. He was not himself by the standards of the time a man of property, although he managed to maintain a certain state; the charges that he was working for a bribe or a pension cannot, as we have seen, be sustained;* his attachment to the Whig oligarchs was real, but hardly passionate; Burke at the time of the composition of the *Reflections* was ageing, disappointed and overworked, burdened with the enormous complexities of the management of the impeachment of Warren Hastings. From a man in such a situation, aware of the danger in France, one might expect a prudent word of warning, hardly more. Whence, then, comes the tremendous emotional force that animates not only the misleadingly named *Reflections* but all his writings on the Revolution, up to and including the fourth *Letter on a Regicide Peace*, left unfinished at his death?

A question of this type, whether it concerns the living or the dead, cannot be answered with certainty. I should like to offer here a conjectural answer which seems to me to be in full accord with what we know of Burke's life and writings. This is that Burke, in his counter-revolutionary writings, is partially liberating – in a permissible way – a suppressed revolutionary part of his own personality. These writings – which appear at first sight to be an integral defence of the established order – con-

---

* It is doubtful, in any case, whether eloquence of the order of the *Reflections* could be mercenary. An ambassador of a certain small but diplomatically significant country once argued his official case with the present writer. Finding his arguments unacceptable he sighed and said: 'They pay me to say these things, but why should I insist? They don't pay me all that much.'

stitute in one of their aspects – and this to Burke not the least important – a heavy blow against the established order in the country of Burke's birth, and against the dominant system of ideas in England itself.

6

The established order in Ireland was *the Protestant ascendancy*, the legalized supremacy of the Protestant minority over the Catholic majority. This supremacy rested on the revolutionary settlement of 1688, still commemorated in Belfast and environs as the glorious origin of permanent Roman Catholic subordination. Burke as a Whig necessarily adhered to the principles of the Glorious Revolution; whether or not self-interest originally guided the Irish adventurer in adhering to the Whig cause, it is clear that personal loyalties, habits and intellectual convictions – matters that Burke was not disposed to separate too sharply – soon bound him closely to the Whigs as a body. But if Burke as a Whig cherished, at least in theory, the Glorious Revolution, Burke as an Irishman, with close emotional bonds to the conquered, detested the Protestant ascendancy which that Revolution had riveted on the people of his country. This detestation seems in some of his earlier declarations to be covered by 'a politic, well-wrought veil'; it becomes open, and even violently so, in the unguarded writings of his last years. 'I think I can hardly exaggerate the malignity of the principles of Protestant ascendancy as it affects Ireland ...'* 'The word protestant is the charm, that locks up in the dungeon of servitude three millions of your people ...'†

Burke's view of Irish history, and his feelings about it,

* *Second Letter to Sir Hercules Langrishe* (1795). Works VI, p. 56.
† *Letter to Richard Burke esq.* (1792). Works VI, p. 61.

come to the surface in a remarkable unfinished letter to
his son, Richard, written in 1792. If members of the
ascendancy in Ireland were wiser, he says, they would
not lay stress upon the origin of their property in confiscation.

They would not set men upon calling from the quiet sleep of
death any Samuel, to ask him, by what act ' of arbitrary monarchs, by what inquisitions of corrupted tribunals, and tortured
jurors, by what fictitious tenures, invented to dispossess whole
unoffending tribes and their chieftains! [*sic*] They would not
conjure up the ghosts from the ruins of castles and churches, to
tell for what attempt to struggle for the independence of an
Irish legislature, and to raise armies of volunteers, without regular commissions from the Crown in support of that independence, the estates of the old Irish nobility and gentry had been
confiscated. They would not wantonly call on those phantoms,
to tell by what English acts of parliament, forced upon two reluctant kings, the lands of their country were put up to a mean
and scandalous auction in every goldsmith's shop in London;
or chopped in pieces, and cut into rations, to pay the mercenary
soldiery of a regicide usurper. They would not be so fond of
titles under Cromwell, who, if he avenged an Irish rebellion
against the sovereign authority of the parliament of England,
had himself rebelled against the very parliament whose sovereignty he asserted full as much as the Irish nation, which
he was sent to subdue and confiscate, could rebel against that
parliament, or could rebel against the king, against whom both
he and the parliament, which he served, and which he betrayed,
had both of them rebelled.*

As for the native Irish, if they had indeed committed
the crime of rebellion, 'they rued it in their persons and
in those of their children and grandchildren even to the
fifth and sixth generations.'
The contrast between this passionate outburst and the
references in earlier, public speeches to the untroubled har-

* *Works* VI pp. 61–80; dated by Dr J. A. Woods as before 19
February 1792.

mony of Ireland's connexion with Britain, is proof of the tension that long existed between Burke's public *persona* and so important a part of his feelings as that which concerned his people and the land of his birth.* This tension was released by the French Revolution, and specifically by the welcome given to that Revolution by Dr Price and his friends. For Price and his friends, by placing the French Revolution in the line of the English one, were reminding Burke of how revolutionary, how anti-Catholic, and to him how alien had been the English revolution.† This intruding vision had to be exorcized: much of the argument – and the most forced part of the argument – both of the *Reflections* and the *Appeal from the New to the Old Whigs* consists of an attempt to show that the English Revolution, unlike the French one, had not been really revolutionary at all – an attempt which we can judge successful only by choosing to forget about the contributions of the contemporaries of Henry VIII and of Oliver Cromwell. But the drama of Burke's writings about the Revolution, and much of their power, comes from the collaboration in them of two personalities. It is as if the words and actions of Price and his friends had awakened,

* Compare the highly idealized view of Irish history in the famous 'Speech on Conciliation with the Colonies' (1775); *Works* I, p. 450: 'It was not English arms, but the English constitution, that conquered Ireland.' In the same speech Burke uses the purity of Protestantism in some of the colonies as an argument in their favour. Both points are in sharp contrast with the tone of his last writings.

† The trouble of Burke's mind, in relation to the impact of the Glorious Revolution in Ireland, is clear from a tortuous passage in the letter, from which I have already quoted, to Richard Burke. Burke does not 'presume to defend' the Irish for their rebellion against the English parliament but thinks, first, that 'palliation' and 'extenuation' should be admitted; that the Irish resisted King William 'on the very same principle that the English and Scotch resisted King James'; finally, that the 'Irish Catholics must have been the very worst and the most truly unnatural of rebels – had they not supported King James.

within that reasonable elderly Whig, a slumbering Jacobite.*

In relation to England and Europe the 'Jacobite'
position is of course a counter-revolutionary one. But in
relation to Ireland, the Jacobite aspiration is objectively
revolutionary, since it is an expression of the will of the
conquered people to shake off its servitude. Thus, where
Burke is at his most extravagantly counter-revolutionary,
in relation to France and Europe, he is most subtly subversive in relation to the existing order in his own
country. His argument, addressed to the nobility and
gentry of England, seeks to persuade these classes that
their interests are bound up with Catholicism in Europe,
that Catholicism is a bastion of order while Protestantism
in its militantly anti-Catholic forms – the Protestantism
of the Dissenters and their sympathizers – is the natural
seed-bed of Jacobinism.† This argument, if accepted, was
ultimately ruinous to the prevailing caste-system in Ireland, to which the doctrine that loyalty required anti-
Popery was the breath of life. And the argument was
accepted, in its 'pro-Catholic' part, though later and
more hesitantly than Burke hoped. It is known that
Burke's words carried great weight with the classes to
which they were addressed, and that they played a part

* Obviously it is not suggested that Burke was politically a Jacobite: he was far too practical a man to be anything of the kind. The
point here is that he was emotionally in sympathy with the
Catholics of Ireland, whose Jacobite loyalty was at the root of the
penalties still being imposed on them in Burke's time.

† 'A man is certainly the most perfect Protestant who protests
against the whole Christian religion.' (*A letter to Sir Hercules Langrishe*, 1792; Works III, p. 313.) See also the sarcastic references in
A Letter on the Affairs of Ireland (1797) to 'the Protestant directory
of Paris ... and the Protestant hero, Buonaparte ...' (*Works* VI,
p. 87.) In an English context, however, Burke in the *Reflections*
writes in the character of a Protestant, but one who does not
violently condemn the Roman system of religion (pp. 257–70).

in the evolution of British policy in the direction he desired.* The Catholic Relief Act of 1793 – conferring the franchise – and in 1795 the foundation of Maynooth – a Catholic seminary with State support – were important steps in this direction.† Under the Union, the Protestant ascendancy was progressively dismantled, except in the one region, Eastern Ulster, where it had a wide popular base. From the point of view of an ordinary member of the ruling class in Ireland in Burke's day, these were revolutionary developments, initially fostered by the dissemination of an ostensibly counter-revolutionary tract. Still from the same point of view, the spectre of Jacobinism had been cunningly used to rehabilitate Popery and Papists.† There can be no doubt that the rehabilitation of Catholicism was part of Burke's intention; he explicitly argues in this sense, seeking to inculcate a preference for 'superstition' as against atheism. That it was only a part of his intention is obvious: his detestation of Jacobinism is real and even obsessive; there is no question of its being feigned for an ulterior motive. Yet his anti-Jacobinism cannot be separated from his sense of identification with Catholics, that is to say from his Irish origins.

In a letter of 1795 he says that his 'whole politics centre in anti-Jacobinism'; that 'the first, last and middle object of Jacobin hostility is religion'; that the practice of Catholicism by its professor 'forms as things stand, the

* Burke had tried – with less success – to make use of the American Revolution in the same sense. The persecution of 'a *nation*' – as he described the Irish Catholics – might once perhaps have been conducted with safety: 'But there is a revolution in our affairs which makes it prudent to be just.' (Speech at Bristol, 1780; *Works* II, p. 155.)

† See Carl B. Cone, *Burke and the Nature of Politics: The Age of the French Revolution*, pp. 487–8. Burke came to be regarded as 'the chief, if not the sole mover of all the measures with respect to Irish Catholics'.

most effectual barrier, if not the sole barrier against Jacobinism'; and 'that in Ireland particularly the Roman Catholic religion should be upheld in high respect and veneration.'* The Burke who was revolted by the Jacobin persecution of 'refractory' priests and nuns was the same Burke who had been revolted by the hanging and quartering of the 'rebel' Father Sheehy in 1766.† He could not then cry out in open protest; he had candidly explained to Irish friends why he could not attempt publicly to defend an accused Irish papist.‡ But it was possible for him to champion publicly the cause of the French Catholics, in 1790-97, and in championing them, indirectly to vindicate and so raise up his family and fellow-countrymen. Is it unreasonable to see in the extraordinary flow of controlled but passionate eloquence that begins with the *Reflections*, the release of an inner indignation long pent up by prudent policy?

The significance of Burke's Irishness in relation to his writings on the French Revolution has I think been generally underestimated or misunderstood. This tendency is encouraged by the requirements of classification: 'Burke on Ireland' is a separate matter from 'Burke on France' or 'Burke on America'. Yet – as Yeats so clearly saw – it is all the same Burke. Burke was never a man of tidy compartments, and we may be sure that the feelings and ideas – not separate compartments either – of the man who writes to Sir Hercules Langrishe about Ireland are identical with those of the man who writes to M. de Pont about France.

* To William Smith, Esq, 26 May 1795. *Works* VI, p. 53.

† See *Corr.* I, pp. 248–9.

‡ *ibid.*, pp. 215–16. He asks his uncle – whose son had abducted a Protestant heiress, which was a capital offence – to reflect 'how newly and almost as a stranger I am come about these people' – in England – and that 'many industrious endeavours' had been made to ruin him. (To Patrick Nagle: 14 October 1765.)

The tendency to miss the significance of Burke's Irishness is also encouraged by other factors. These include
the general impression that Burke is Anglo-Irish and
belongs in the Protestant tradition.* In fact there is nothing 'Anglo' at all about what we know of his family connexions and he himself – at least in the late writings with
which we are here concerned – eschews the designation
'Protestant'. Finally, some who have been impressed by
Burke's writings on the French Revolution have ignored
the Irish factor, probably because of a conviction that,
in comparison with the mighty issues treated in the
Reflections, the concerns of Ireland were trivial and
parochial. As a general proposition this is very defensible,
yet it is misleading in relation to Burke. The Irish situation is of little importance on the scale of the great
Revolution, yet it was the Irish situation that had formed
Edmund Burke, and Ireland and Jacobinism constituted
the alternating and overlapping preoccupations of his last,
haunted years. The author of the *Reflections on the
Revolution in France* wrote in the *persona* of an Englishman – which is in itself a cause of confusion – but was
in fact Irish to the marrow of his bones.

* Thus the late Joseph Hone in his excellent biography *W. B.
Yeats* (1865–1939) – London, 1942 – stated that Yeats was 'haunted
by the question : how to bring the aristocratic and Protestant tradition of Swift, Berkeley and Burke into line with the modern
"Gaelic" nationalism' (p. 379). In fact Burke was as 'Gaelic' as any
modern nationalist and more Gaelic than some. Burke seems more
aristocratic in a literary retrospect than he did to his contemporaries,
who were inclined to regard him as 'an Irish upstart from the Catholic underworld across the Bristol Channel' (Sir Philip Magnus,
Edmund Burke, p. 216). Burke's relation to Protestantism is discussed
in the text.

7

The interpretation here suggested has a bearing on a puzzling question: that of Burke's style or styles. Burke in his writings on the French Revolution has three basic manners, which he can also combine in varying proportions. There is what one might call the Whig manner: rational, perspicacious, business-like. This had been the prevailing manner of his speeches and writings on America and remains the prevailing tone of the greater part of the *Reflections*, though not of the passages that are most often quoted. It is a tone well adapted to its purpose, which is that of convincing people who have a great deal to lose that certain policies are, and other policies are not, in accordance with their interests. In this tone, he warns the Whig lords that the confiscation of Church property in France – a design to which many were favourably disposed by varying combinations of 'Reformation' and 'Enlightenment' principles – constitutes an actual threat to their own economic survival:

The great source of my solicitude is, lest it should ever be considered in England as the policy of a state to seek a resource in confiscations of any kind; or that any one description of citizens should be brought to regard any of the others as their proper prey.... Revolutions are favourable to confiscation; and it is impossible to know under what obnoxious names the next confiscations will be authorized. I am sure that the principles predominant in France extend to the very many persons, in all countries who think their innoxious indolence their security. This kind of innocence in proprietors may be argued into inutility and inutility into an unfitness for their estates. (*Reflections*, pp. 263–5.)

It can scarcely have been possible for any landed Whig to read that passage without his approbation for anti-Popery enlightenment becoming sensibly diminished.

Burke's second manner might be called 'Jacobite': both Gothic and pathetic. The most notable example of this in the *Reflections* is the famous passage about the Queen of France (pp. 169–70) which many have been taught to think of as typical Burke. It is typical, but of a manner that Burke employs very sparingly.* Indeed those who read this passage as an isolated excerpt miss much of its force, which comes from a change of tone, a catch in the voice, an emotional break through the rational crust. And once one is aware of this reserve of underlying emotion, even the more prosaic parts of the argument take on a more formidable sonority.

Burke's third manner is a peculiar kind of furious irony. Irony is a marked characteristic of Irish writing; I have argued elsewhere† that the Irish predicament, with its striking contrasts between pretences and realities, has been unusually favourable to the development of this mode of expression. In terms of our interpretation of Burke's particular predicament, it may be said that the friction between outer Whig and inner 'Jacobite' was both ironic itself, and productive of that oblique aggressiveness which is the driving force of irony. Burke's irony, in his writings on the French Revolution seems more aggressive than oblique; he is in an attacking position. Yet his irony is more oblique than it seems, since his savage sarcasm, openly directed at the apologists for the French Revolution, tells in a sidelong way against the dominant Protestant culture into which he was apparently assimilated.

In the *Reflections* itself, Burke's irony is subdued, flashing out only now and then in an aside: 'That argument

---

*As Hazlitt justly observed : 'Burke was so far from being a gaudy or flowery writer that he was one of the severest writers we have'. (*Essay on the Character of Burke*, 1807.)

† See the essay 'Our Wits About Us' in *Writers and Politics*.

will do very well, with a lamp-post for its second . . .' 'The king has been brought to declare the dauphin shall be educated in a conformity to his situation. If he is made to conform to his situation, he will have no education at all.' In his later writings on the Revolution – writings no longer partly guarded, but bitter, indignant, reckless and triumphant – his irony comes in sustained bursts. His famous *Letter to a Noble Lord* (1796) – against the Duke of Bedford, who had opposed the granting of a pension to Burke – is an exercise in irony which impressed Karl Marx, with good reason. Burke's irony is never subtle; it comes at times close to House of Commons humour, which in turn comes close to schoolboy humour,* but its roughness is often transfigured by a combination of gusto, fantasy and Hibernian hyperbole which is all Burke's own. Two passages about cats are worth quoting. The first is from the *Letter to a Noble Lord*, and concerns the way the real Parisian revolutionaries look on their English aristocratic sympathizers, like the Duke of Bedford:

'Whatever his Grace may think of himself, they look upon him, and everything that belongs to him, with no more regard than they do upon the whiskers of that little long-tailed animal, that has been long the game of the grave, demure, insidious, spring-nailed, velvet-pawed, green-eyed philosophers, whether going upon two legs or upon four.'†

The second passage from the first of the *Letters on a Regicide Peace*, concerns an argument, used by the advocates of peace with France (in 1796), that an agreement

---

* Hazlitt thought his speeches at times 'bordering too much on buffoonery'. Dr Johnson had a poor opinion of his wit: ' 'tis low, 'tis conceit. . . . Burke never once made a good joke.' See the useful collection of critical opinions about Burke in the volume *Edmund Burke: Selections*, edited by A. M. D. Hughes and published by the Clarendon Press in 1921.

† *Letter to a Noble Lord* (1796); *Works* V, p. 142.

had already been concluded with more disreputable authorities, the piratical rulers of Algiers.

Have the gentlemen, who borrowed this happy parallel, no idea of the different conduct to be held with regard to the very same evil at an immense distance, and when it is at your door? ... I can contemplate, without dread, a royal or a national tiger on the borders of PEGU. I can look at him, with an easy curiosity, as prisoner within bars in the menagerie of the tower. But if, by habeas corpus or otherwise, he was to come into the lobby of the House of Commons while your door was open, any of you would be more stout than wise, who would not gladly make your escape out of the back windows. I certainly should dread more from a wild cat in my bed-chamber, than from all the lions that roar in the deserts behind Algiers. But in this parallel it is the cat that is at a distance, and the lions and tigers that are in our ante-chambers and our lobbies. Algiers is not near; Algiers is not powerful; Algiers is not our neighbour; Algiers is not infectious. Algiers, whatever it may be, is an old creation; and we have good data to calculate all the mischief to be apprehended from it. When I find Algiers transferred to Calais, I will tell you what I think of that point.*

Of the three manners which we have distinguished —

---

*First *Letter on a Regicide Peace* (1796); *Works* V, p. 225. The white-hot invective of the *Letters* sometimes produces effects which are more like a caricaturist's irony than a writer's. This is his picture in the same *Letter* of diplomatic relations resumed between the Revolutionary Government in Paris and the Courts of Europe: 'At the opening of those doors, what a sight it must be to behold the plenipotentiaries of royal impotence, in the precedency which they will intrigue to obtain, and which will be granted to them according to the seniority of their degradation, sneaking into the regicide presence, and, with the relics of the smile, which they had dressed up for the levee of their masters, still flickering on their curled lips, presenting the faded remains of their courtly graces, to meet the scornful, ferocious, sardonic grin of a bloody ruffian, who, whilst he is receiving their homage, is measuring them with his eye, and fitting to their size the slider of his guillotine!' (ibid. p. 171.)

the 'Whig', the 'Jacobite' and the ironic – only the first is found in relative abundance in the pure state; it forms the staple of the *Reflections*. The 'Jacobite' manner, in its pure state, is very rare: the 'Queen' passage in the *Reflections* and, in the *Letters on a Regicide Peace*, the passage about 'the tomb of the murdered monarchy' – quoted at the beginning of this introduction – are the two great set-pieces in this manner. Once this mood has been established, however, Burke can evoke it again with the economy of an aside:

'Pity that Cloots had not had a reprieve from the guillotine till he had completed his work! But that engine fell before the curtain had fallen upon all the dignity of the earth.'*

In many of the most striking passages in the *Reflections* Burke uses a manner intermediate between the 'Whig' and the 'Jacobite' – more elevated than the first, and less theatrical than the second – a manner both earnest and stately, befitting a thoughtful Tory Churchman. This is the tone of the famous argument sanctifying the principle of inheritance by assimilating it to the natural order (pp. 119–20) of the defence of inequality in property (p. 140); of the theory of continuity and of partnership – 'a partnership not only between those who are living, but between those who are living, those who are dead and those who are to be born.' (pp. 194–5.) It is on this middle ground that Burke is at his most assured; this is the mode which harmonizes the Whig and the Jacobite within him; this is also the tone in which he can, with the greatest authority, reach that audience for which his words are intended – the landed proprietors of England, and after them men of property generally. These words lend grandeur, gravity and religious solemnity to the defence

* Fourth of the *Letters on a Regicide Peace*: published posthumously; *Works* V, p. 388.

of interests. They prepare the mood and the demeanour of English Conservatism and Liberal Conservatism for the nineteenth century. Once the essentials of the *status quo* were so magisterially defined and defended, the hint of the Jacobite in the background must have been pleasing rather than obnoxious. It shed something of the pathos and glamour of a lost cause on a cause which those to whom Burke appealed were determined should not be lost at all. At the same time, the acceptance of that pathos and glamour did something to rehabilitate the most ir-remediably lost of British causes. Roman Catholicism develops the appeal of the romantic, at a time when such an appeal was beginning to be socially relevant.

Burke has another manner situated between the ironic and the 'Whig', just as his earnest and stately manner lies between 'Whig' and 'Jacobite'. This second median is that of his aphorisms and epigrams. The master of the rolling period is also a master of the concise. The writings on the Revolution are rich in those pithy and memorable generalities with which the eighteenth century enriched our culture. Yet the Burkian epigram has a particular turn of its own: in his hands this notably cerebral form is directed against intellectual presumption: 'Wisdom is not the most severe corrector of folly'; 'No cold rela-tion is a zealous citizen'; '... Whilst you pique nature against you, you do unwisely to trust to duty.'* These are not isolated epiphanies; they have a social significance. Intellectual presumption – or self-confidence – is the morale of the revolutionary, whereby he is enabled to call established order into question, in society, in the State, in the Church, in the family. This is the way in which ability makes its inroads into property. In using his mag-nificent intelligence to depreciate the claims of intelligence, Burke as usual is discharging a double function. He

* These three are from the *Reflections*.

serves the interests of the property owners, thus earning their gratitude. And at the same time he rehabilitates
religion, and notably – though discreetly and by indirec-
tion – that form of religion which throughout the
eighteenth century had been most exposed to the remorse-
less onslaughts of Reason. And the form in which he does
this is in itself the demonstration that he possesses in
high measure the quality which he seeks to subordinate.
A radical rationalist seeking to lecture Edmund Burke on
the importance of intelligence already stands warned, by
the quality of Burke's language, that his lecture will be
given every opportunity to sound ridiculous.

It is convenient to distinguish, in Burke's prose, these
various manners and combinations of manner.* But his
grace and strength are best manifested in the lyrical buoy-
ancy with which he moves from one manner, and from
one level of intensity, to another. He can soar from invective and irony to the heights of romantic pathos – in
the 'Queen' passage – and from that height swoop again
into invective with renewed momentum. Or, turning in a
much smaller space, he can move in the course of a single
sentence from a pastoral tenderness in the opening, on
to a conclusion of Rhadamanthine irony: 'All the little
quiet rivulets, that watered an humble, a contracted, but
not an unfruitful field, are to be lost in the waste expanse,
and boundless, barren ocean of the homicide philan-
thopy of France.'†

Swift transitions of mood are of course among the
traditional resources of oratory and advocacy: Burke

* Several other combinations could be distinguished if space permitted. There is for example a manner median between the 'stately'
and the ironic which Burke likes to use against Dr Price and which
Mary Wollstonecraft hit off beautifully : 'Gothic affability is the
mode you think proper to adopt, the condescension of a Baron, not
the civility of a liberal man.' (*A Vindication of the Rights of Men*.)

† Third of the *Letters on a Regicide Peace* (1797). *Works* V, p. 268.

knew his Cicero.* Burke possesses to the full the resources
of traditional oratory – its repertoire of tricks – yet his
effects are unique and without precedent. No other
orator or political writer either before or after him has
his combination of qualities: his wide range of articu-
late emotion, his intuitive grasp of social forces, his
capacity for analytical argument, his pathos, fantasy and
wit and his power to marshal all these, through a superb
command over the resources of the language, towards
ends clearly discerned and passionately desired.

8

The very richness and variety of Burke's *Reflections*
have from the beginning charmed and dazzled some, but
puzzled and alienated others. The *Reflections* are difficult
to classify, and to some minds this is a scandal. The title
of the work does not harmonize with its tone, which is
often passionate and always contentious; the work starts
out as a letter, and ends up as a mixture of a treatise, a pam-
phlet and a speech. Even before the *Reflections* were
published at all, serious exception had been taken to their
form. Philip Francis, who worked with Burke on the
impeachment of Warren Hastings, found the first portion
of the *Reflections* which Burke sent him 'very loosely put

* Taine thought it was 'of no use for Burke to study Cicero'
because he remained 'half a barbarian'. 'The fine Greek or French
distinction has never found a place among the Germanic nations.'
He goes on to praise Burke, in extravagant and inappropriate
language. The quotations are from Vol. III of the 1965 New York
edition of H. Taine, *History of English Literature*. Hazlitt as usual
was more to the point: 'Burke had not the polished elegance, the
glossy neatness, the artful regularity, the exquisite modulation of
Cicero. He had a thousand times more richness and originality of
mind, more strength and pomp of diction.' (*Essay on the Character
of Burke*, 1807.)

together'.* Since Burke is undertaking 'to correct and instruct another Nation' and appealing in effect 'to all
Europe' he ought to write 'with special deliberation'.
'Away with all jest and sneer and sarcasm. Let every thing
you say be grave, direct and serious.' †

Burke was hurt – acknowledging Francis's letter he says
'I have not slept since' – but not shaken: 'The composition you say is loose; and I am quite sure it is. I never
intended it should be otherwise ...'‡ On receiving the
published *Reflections* Francis is still more severe, in a half-
playful manner which Burke must have found even more
offensive than a plain condemnation:

'I wish you would let me teach you to write English.
... Why will you not allow Yourself to be persuaded, that
polish is material to preservation? It has not yet been
in my power to read more than one third of your book. I
must taste it deliberately; the flavour is too high; the
Wine is too rich; I cannot take a draught of it.' §

Like many a stylistic critic, Francis disliked the substance as well as the form. Some others, who also disliked
the substance, were more percipient. An early critic, Sir
James Mackintosh saw immediately that this form, disorderly as it appeared, in fact infinitely multiplied the force
of Burke's argument:

He can cover the most ignominious retreat by a brilliant
allusion. He can parade his arguments with masterly general-

* *Corr.* VI, pp. 85–7; Francis to Burke, 19 February 1790.

† ibid. This was not the first or the last time that such advice
was offered by an English critic to an Irish writer. Francis also
condemns Burke's pathos in the 'Queen' passage: see pp. 169–70 and
note.

‡ *Corr.* VI, pp. 88–92; Burke to Francis, 20 February 1790.

§ *Corr.* VI, pp. 150–55; Francis to Burke, 3, 4 November 1790. Un-
derstandably Burke found Francis's reply more like 'the method of
controversy' than, 'the animadversions of a friend'. (Burke to
Francis, 9 November 1790.)

ship where they are strong. He can escape from an intolerable position into a splendid declamation. He can sap the most impregnable conviction by pathos and put to flight a host of syllogisms with a sneer. Absolved from all the laws of vulgar method, he can advance a groupe of magnificent horrors to make a breach in our hearts, through which the most undisciplined rabble of arguments may enter in triumph.*

Francis, with his 'deliberation' and 'polish' had missed the point which Mackintosh so sharply saw. And it was Mackintosh, the most acute of Burke's early critics, who first defined – as early as 1791 – the real character of the *Reflections*:

'It is the manifesto of a counter-revolution . . .'

Mackintosh's observations on Burke's method, and his definition of the character of his book, represent Burke as above all a propagandist. Whatever about the 'above all' – a matter to which we shall return – there can be no doubt that Burke was a conscious and deliberate propagandist. He has some claim indeed to be the first modern propagandist: the first to be conscious of a need for organized effort, adequately financed, and reinforced by 'State action',† to mould public opinion on questions of ideology and international policy. He was the first also to give a lead in such an effort.‡ His originality of course should not be exaggerated: since the Reformation and

* *Vindiciae Gallicae* (1791). Mackintosh lived to retract his attack on Burke and indeed to reverse completely the trend of his earlier judgement. Burke, according to the Mackintosh of 1799, 'is only not esteemed the most severe and sagacious of reasoners, because he was the most eloquent of men, the perpetual force and vigour of his arguments being hid from vulgar observation by the dazzling glories in which they were enshrined.' (R. J. Mackintosh, *Memoirs of . . . Sir James Mackintosh*, London, 1835, p. 91.)

† The principal role of the State in the matter was to be the suppression of the propaganda of the other side. See p. 61.

‡ A modern French writer on the counter-revolution states: 'Parmi tous les théoriciens de la contre-révolution, le premier, dont les

Counter-reformation all Western Europe had rung with propaganda; the eighteenth century was the heyday of the pamphleteer. Burke's originality was not in engaging in propaganda, but in thinking seriously about its nature and its power and on how best to use it. He was acutely conscious of the part which the anti-religious and other propaganda of Voltaire and his friends had played in undermining the *ancien régime*, and of the need for an organized counter-attack. His treatment of this subject in the *Reflections* – see the passage (p. 211) beginning 'Along with the monied interest, a new description of men had grown up ... I mean the political men of letters.' – receives further development in the second of the *Letters on a Regicide Peace*:

The correspondence of the monied and the mercantile world, the literary intercourse of academics, but, above, all, the press, of which they [the middle class] had in a manner entire possession, made a kind of electrick communication everywhere.* The press in reality has made every government, in its spirit, almost democratick. Without it the great, the first moments in this Revolution could not, perhaps, have been given.

Burke was disgusted at the lack of interest among the French aristocratic refugees in propaganda. In January 1791 he wrote to one of these seeking certain information – details about the French system of land tenure – which might be 'useful hereafter in any Systematick proceeding towards disposing the publick in this Country in your favour which I wish some French Gentlemen here would undertake under the direction of some judicious English.'† Burke continued to press this idea, but was dismayed by the

œuvres aient eu un retentissement international, a été l'Anglais Edmund Burke.' Jacques Godechot (*La Contre-Révolution*, 1789–1804, Paris, 1961.)

* *Works* V p. 259. Burke here seems to anticipate Marshall McLuhan.

† *Corr.* VI pp. 206–8; Burke to Vicomte de Cicé 24 January 1791.

apparent inertia of the French nobility in this domain, compared with the activity of their opponents. '... The Emissaries of the Usurpation here are exceedingly active in propagating Stories which tend to alienate the minds of people of this Country from the suffering Cause. Not one french Refugee has intelligence or spirit enough to contradict them.'* He urged that the French emigrés should raise money for this purpose: 'If their avarice or their dissipation will afford nothing to their honour or their safety – their Case is additionally deplorable.'†

In this, as in much else, Burke was in advance of the time which he was defending: it was left to him, single-handed, to conduct the effective propaganda of the counter-revolution. In his own writings he is – among other things – a conscious propagandist. He uses emotional language by deliberate policy. There was nothing new, for him, in this; as a practical politician he had long been aware of the value of verbal violence. Before the outbreak of the French Revolution, and when his mind was occupied with quite different matters, he had written to a colleague in Opposition, suggesting that if the Opposition did not intend to give up altogether, they ought 'to change that tone of calm reasoning which certainly does not belong to great and affecting interests ... [a] style of argument, so very different from that by which Lord North was run down ...'‡

Two years later, in connexion with the impeachment of

A detailed questionnaire is appended, essentially similar to what a modern counter-propagandist might put to, for example, a Tibetan refugee in order to gather material for a speech at the United Nations.

* *Corr.* VI pp. 241–3; Burke to Chevalier de la Bintinaye, March 1791.

† ibid.

‡ *Corr.* V pp. 436–45; Burke to Windham, *c.* 24 January 1789. He went on to recommend the publication of 'strong manifestoes'.

Warren Hastings, he developed his theory of verbal violence, in rebutting a suggestion from Lord Chancellor Thur-
low that 'the calm mode of Enquiry' would be the most
rewarding approach: 'The *calm mode of Enquiry* would be
a very temperate method of our losing our Object; and a
very certain mode of finding no calmness on the side of our
adversary. Our being mobbish is our only chance for his
being reasonable.'

He became increasingly 'mobbish' as the 'great and
affecting interest' of the reaction to the French Revolution
took hold: the *Reflections*, as compared with the later
Letters on a Regicide Peace almost seems a model of the
'calm mode of Enquiry'. In relation to *Appeal from the
New to the Old Whigs* (1791) he shows himself as consciously committed to that method of tactical over-state-
ment† which distinguishes the true propagandist from the
mere believer in a cause. Writing to his son Richard, and
having noted that only about 10 per cent even of the Whigs
favour French Revolutionary principles, he goes on: 'It
may be asked, why I represent the whole party as tolerat-
ing, and by a toleration countenancing, these proceedings.
It is to get the better of their inactivity and to stimulate
them to a publick declaration . . .'‡

The fact that Burke writes as a conscious propagandist

* *Corr.* VI, pp. 197–9; Burke to W. Adam, 4 January 1791.

†*Under*-statement also: 'Falsehood and delusion are allowed in no
case whatever: but, as in the exercise of all the virtues, there is an
economy of truth. It is a sort of temperance, by which a man speaks
truth with measure that he may speak it the longer.' (First of the
Letters on a Regicide Peace, 1796; *Works* V, p. 230.)

‡ *Corr.* VI, pp. 315–20; Edmund Burke to Richard Burke Jr, 5
August 1791, It was a shrewdly calculated blow. 'There is not a
single man in opposition who will not be understood to be in Burke's
opinion an Enemy to the present constitution of this country, for
who, will it be said, can know them so well as Mr Burke?' Portland
to Lawrence, 23 August 1791. (*Sheffield Papers.*)

and practical politician, with an eye to the probable immediate consequences of his words, is too often left out of account by undiscriminating admirers, who like to think of him as essentially a political philosopher. The importance of the propaganda element should not, however, be exaggerated either. There is no reason at all to doubt the sincerity of Burke's indignation, aroused by the discovery of the existence and character of English sympathy with the French Revolution. This indignation burns quite as brightly in his private correspondence as in his published tracts. The opinion, presented by Marx and others, that it was all feigned, that he was simply 'playing the Romantic'* as he had 'played the Liberal', cannot be seriously defended. Calculation comes in, not in pretending an emotion which is not there, but in deciding how much of a genuinely-felt emotion to release publicly; how far to let oneself go. In certain circumstances – had the Whigs been in office, for example, and he with them – Burke could hardly have 'let himself go' at all. But when he does decide to let go, he inevitably releases greater forces than any calculation could determine in advance. He enters the controversy as a Whig, and ends up the idol of the Tories. He 'runs down' his friend Charles James Fox, as he had once run down Lord North. It is extremely improbable that these results were calculated in advance. It is more probable that Burke had never fully realized – until the events in France provided the critical test – how profoundly he was at odds with much that was fundamental in the philosophy of Englishmen with whom he had allied himself: Englishmen who cherished the principles of the Glorious Revolution and of the Enlightment, and felt these principles to be essentially the same, or at least to have a common root – a rational rejection of superstition.

* p. 9; n.1.

Nor did the Tories – despite their praise of him – seem much better to him. They were lukewarm and pragmatic, prepared to sustain a limited war with France, but not dedicated to the counter-revolutionary principle. Towards the end the practical politician Burke seems to die away; the *Letters on a Regicide Peace* are certainly propaganda but it is a strange, passionately personal sort of propaganda, the prophetic outpouring – almost at times the raving – of a man isolated, inconsolably bereaved, dying, yet rejoicing in his incomparable power to express his fury in words whose sheer exuberance is still astounding. The *Letters* are the deathless propaganda of a dying man in favour of 'a long war'* – a war which did not in fact end until nearly twenty years after his death.

9

It is not surprising that in our own time the counter-revolutionary propaganda in Burke's late writings should have been used for the purposes of the cold war. The first to realize the possibilities of Burke for twentieth-century anti-communism seems to have been A. V. Dicey, who, in an article† published in 1918 hit upon the simple but effective expedient of substituting 'Russia' for 'France' in a number of Burke's most ardent counter-revolutionary invectives. It was not however until the setting in of the real cold war, in the late forties, that Burke's works began to be systematically quarried for anti-communist purposes and that Burke's stature as a systematic thinker began to be

---

*'I speak it emphatically and with a desire that it should be marked, in a *long* war; because without such a war, no experience has yet told us that a dangerous power has ever been reduced to measure or to reason.' First *Letter on a Regicide Peace*, 1796; *Works* V, p. 195.

† 'Burke on Bolshevism', in *Nineteenth Century and After*, July–December 1918. See also A. A. Baumann: *Burke the Founder of Conservatism*, London, 1929.

correspondingly exalted. The process began with the publication of *Burke's Politics*, an anthology with an introduction by Ross Hoffman and Paul Levack in 1949. A number of American scholars and writers, and including a strong Catholic element, set themselves to extol Burke as a great political philosopher and exponent of National Law, as well as of a stable order, foreshadowing the Atlantic Community.* Members of this school were disposed to overlook or minimize the practical, polemical and propagandist elements in Burke's writing and to magnify the importance and consistency of his 'philosophy'. They attached inordinate importance to two sentences of Hoffman's and Levack's:

'Burke's politics ... were grounded on recognition of the universal law of reason and justice ordained by God as the foundation of a good community. In this recognition the Machiavellian schism between politics and morality is closed ...'† Mr Peter J. Stanlis, one of the most productive writers in this group, sees 1949 – the year of the Hoffman epiphany – as the beginning of a 'counter-revolution on traditional grounds' in Burke scholarship. A reviewer of Mr Peter J. Stanlis in the *Burke Newsletter* – of which Mr Peter J. Stanlis was co-editor – averred that he could 'think of no sentence in the whole range of modern scholarship that has had greater effect than this apparently simple factual statement by Messrs Hoffman and Levack.'‡

To present Burke as a sort of semi-official spokesman for the law of nature has the effect of conferring on his writings

* 'He saw ... what we Americans are groping for today as we seek to organize a stable, international order ...' (*Burke's Politics*, New York, 1949, p. xxxvi.) This effort demanded a 'restoration', which is not further defined. Presumably the 'rolling back of the Iron Curtain' was included in it.

† *Burke's Politics*, 1949, p. xv.

‡ Warren Fleischauer in *Burke Newsletter*, Spring-Summer 1963.

a superhuman authority. To challenge Burke's argument is then to fly in the face of nature. And as Burke himself, in a very different connexion, sardonically observed: 'The nature of things is, I admit, a sturdy adversary.'* A sturdy ally also.

Both Burke and the sturdy ally were enlisted for specific political purposes. The *Burke Newsletter*, which recorded the progress of the 'counter-revolution in Burke scholarship', was originally published as part of *Modern Age*, an American right-wing periodical.† 'Burke studies', according to Burke's American biographer, Mr Carl B. Cone, 'are a very self-conscious part of our contemporary conservative revival.'‡ The specific utility of Burke for the conservative revivalists has been most clearly explained by one of their intellectual leaders, Mr Russell Kirk:

Burke's concept of the comity of nations and of the law of nations, and of the necessity for combining against revolutionary fanaticism apply almost unaltered to the present circumstances of this nation. . . . Burke is little 'dated' . . .

For America plays today the role which was Britain's at the end of the eighteenth century: like the English then we Americans have become, without willing it, the defenders of civilization against the enemies of order and justice and freedom and

* Third of the *Letters on a Regicide Peace* (1797); *Works* V, p. 281.

† This arrangement held good from 1959 to the beginning of 1961 when, as a result of changed editorial policy, *Modern Age* ceased to publish the *Burke Newsletter*. There were always some neo-conservatives who disliked the emphasis on Burke. As a student of the neo-conservative movement has pointed out, there are 'manifold problems in trying to package Burke for the American Market'. (E. Cain, *They'd Rather be Right*, New York, 1963.)

‡ *Burke Newsletter*, Spring 1962. Mr Cone is uneasy about elevating Burke's rhetoric into a philosophy: 'I think there are reasons for doubting some of his statements when we remember that Burke was invariably pleading a cause . . .' True, but then the 'contemporary conservative revival' is pleading a cause too.

the traditions of civility. Ours are imperial duties, requiring imperial intellects for their execution.*

Burke's writings, then, are to be a school for 'imperial intellects', preparing them for the 'imperial duties' imposed on them by the need to combat 'revolutionary fanaticism'. They are to furnish splendid language and respected antecedents – in the venerable penumbra of the Natural Law and of 'order, justice and freedom' – to validate the policy of American counter-revolutionary imperialism, and to train minds in the service of this policy.†

More astute conservative minds than Mr Kirk's have already perceived that Burke is not an entirely reliable ally. Some reasons for this are discussed in Section 11 of this introduction. It is clear, however, that appropriately expounded, Burke's later writings, beginning with the *Reflections*, can supply copious and precious material for counter-revolutionary indoctrination, adaptable to imperial purposes. Once we make the equation Jacobin = Communist – as we can without significantly departing from the principles of Burke's hostility to Jacobinism – we can derive from Burke's later writings a repertory of

---

* *Burke Newsletter*, Winter 1962–3. Mr Kirk was reviewing Mr Clinton J. Rossiter's *Conservatism in America*, which had 'reservations about Burke as a guide to conservative action in our time'. There is an edition of the *Reflections* with an introduction by Mr Russell Kirk in a series called 'Classics of Conservatism' (New Rochelle, N.Y., no date). In it he describes the *Reflections* as 'the work which is now the foundation of modern conservatism in Britain, America and Western countries generally'.

† 'Burke', writes Professor Alfred Cobban, 'has escaped from the more foolish jibes of the left in Britain only to fall a victim to the uncritical adulation of the right in America.... These attempts to condemn or applaud the ideas or annex the name and reputation of Burke, like any other attempt to exploit the past to the advantage of transient political interests, are not history.' *Edmund Burke and the Revolt Against the Eighteenth Century*. Preface to Second Edition, London, 1960.

maxims and incitements in support of – and even going beyond – the foreign policy, which is associated with the name of John Foster Dulles, and which still exerts a powerful influence over United States action today.

For Burke, as for Dulles, the revolutionary doctrine is the expression of incarnate evil: 'Those who have made the exhibition of the 14th day of July are capable of every evil. They do not commit crimes for their designs; but they form designs that they may commit crimes. It is not their necessity, but their nature that impels them.'* This evil has a central and strategic habitation from which it must be dislodged: 'This evil in the heart of Europe must be extirpated from that center, or no part of the circumference can be free from the mischief which radiates from it, and which will spread circle beyond circle, in spite of all the little defensive precautions which can be employed against them.'† It is a formidable enterprise – to be opposed by armed force – for the subversion of all values:

We now have our arms in our hands; we have the means of opposing the sense, the courage and the resources of England to the deepest, the most craftily devised, the best combined and the most extensive design that ever was carried on, since the beginning of the world against all property, all order, all religion, all law, and all real freedom.‡

The evil doctrine, the armed forces at the disposal of those professing the doctrine, and the sympathizers with the doctrine in other lands constitute one united threat which must be met by force:

* Letter to a member of the National Assembly (1791). *Works* II, p. 534.
† *Heads for Consideration on the Present State of Affairs* (written in November 1792). *Works* III, p. 409.
‡ *Preface to M. Brissot's Address to his Constituents* (1794). *Works,* III pp. 525–6.

We are at war with a system, which, by its essence, is inimical to all other governments, and which makes peace or war, as peace and war may best contribute to their subversion. It is with an *armed doctrine* that we are at war. It has, by its essence, a faction of opinion, and of interest, and of enthusiasm, in every country. To us it is a Colossus which bestrides our channel. It has one foot on a foreign shore, the other upon the British soil. Thus advantaged, if it can at all exist, it must finally prevail.*

The struggle against the *armed doctrine* is a '*religious war*',† a 'new crusade'.‡ It must be waged not merely by armed force abroad but by repression at home; the Judges 'should directly censure the circulation of treasonable Books, factious federations and any communication or communion with wicked and desperate people in other Countries'.§

The 'domino' theory of President Eisenhower – which still inspires American policy in the Far East – had an early exponent in Burke: 'If Spain falls, Naples will speedily follow. Prussia is quite certain.... Italy is broken and divided; Switzerland is jacobinized, I am afraid, completely.'‖

The war he preaches against the armed doctrine is total, ruthless and ideological. He foresees, very early, that such warfare will be more cruel than any past warfare and accepts the necessity for this:

The mode of civilized war will not be practised; nor are the French who act on the present system entitled to expect it. They,

* First *Letter on a Regicide Peace* (1796). *Works* V, pp. 164–5.

† *Remarks on the Policy of the Allies* (begun in October 1793); emphasis as in the text. *Works* III, p. 442.

‡ Second of the *Letters on a Regicide Peace* (1796). *Works* V, p. 234.

§ Edmund Burke to Richard Burke Sr, 24 July 1791; *Corr.* VI, p. 307.

‖ *Remarks on the Policy of the Allies* (begun in October 1793). *Works* III, p. 441.

whose known policy is to assassinate every citizen whom they suspect to be discontented by their tyranny, and to corrupt the soldiery of every open enemy, must look for no modified hostility. All war, which is not battle will be military execution. This will beget acts of retaliation from you; and every retaliation will beget a new revenge. The hell-hounds of war, on all sides, will be uncoupled and unmuzzled. The new school of murder and barbarism, set up in Paris, having destroyed (so far as in it lies) all the other manners and principles which have hitherto civilized Europe, will destroy also the mode of civilized war, which more than anything else, has distinguished the christian world.*

From the point of view of a Dulles or of a Dean Rusk, indeed, the disadvantage of Burke's counter-revolutionary writings is that they go further than prudent counter-revolutionists in our time have so far judged practicable. For Burke scornfully condemns the idea that what we now call 'containment' will suffice against the doctrine; it must be destroyed at its centre:

In France is the bank of deposit and the bank of circulation, of all the pernicious principles that are forming in every state. It will be a folly scarcely deserving of pity, and too mischievous for contempt to think of restraining it in any other country, whilst it is predominant there.†

If Burke's counter-revolutionary writings are literally transposed into modern terms they are appropriate not so much to the moderate Right as to the farthest reaches of American reaction. Their rhetoric contains the justification for a policy of preventive war. They could have been invoked in favour of war with the Soviet Union in the 'forties. They could now be used in favour of war with China.

* *Letter to a Member of the National Assembly* (1791). Works II, pp. 542–3.
† Second of the *Letters on a Regicide Peace* (1796). Works V, p. 232.

10

Such a conclusion should in itself be a warning against facile transposition. The fact that Burke advocated counter-revolutionary war against France does not permit his authority to be legitimately invoked in support of counter-revolutionary war against Russia, China or any other nation today. Communist principles are certainly fully as detestable, from a Burkian point of view, as Jacobin principles. But the circumstances are widely different, and Burke repeatedly refuses to recommend or endorse a course of action without knowing in detail the circumstances of the case:

Circumstances (which with some gentlemen pass for nothing) give in reality to every political principle its distinguishing colour and discriminating effect. The circumstances are what render every civil and political scheme beneficial or noxious to mankind.*

And again:

I must see with my own eyes, I must, in a manner touch with my own hands, not only the fixed but the momentary circumstances, before I could venture to suggest any political project whatsoever. I must know the power and disposition to accept, to execute, to persevere. I must see the means of correcting the plan, where correctives would be wanted. I must see the things; I must see the men.†

We cannot guess what Burke might advise could he see 'the things' and 'the men' of today. Certainly he would favour whatever course of action seemed to him, *in the circumstances*, most appropriate to prevent the spread of Communist principles and power. It is inconceivable that, in the circumstances of the thermo-nuclear balance of terror, he could support a policy of war with

* *Reflections*, p. 90.

† *Letter to a Member of the National Assembly* (1791). *Works* II, p. 549.

the Soviet Union. It is even improbable that, in the
circumstances of present relations between the main
branches of the human race, he would favour war with
China.* Nor do his writings really imply support for that
policy which those who most often quote him with approval are in fact pursuing: the 'containment' of Communism by multiple forms of intervention in the under-
developed world. It is not just that he explicitly rejects
a similar policy in the circumstances of his own day;†
changed circumstances could warrant changed policy.
There is something more fundamental in Burke to which
the realities of the 'containment' policy are necessarily
repugnant. Burke distinguished between revolutionary
movements arising from 'wantonness and fullness of
bread' and those which draw their sustenance from 'the
bottom of human nature'. Those Asian movements which
the 'containment' policy is pledged to crush – such as the
Front of National Liberation in Vietnam – can hardly be
said to arise from 'wantonness and fullness of bread'.
Burke understood very well the feelings of a conquered
people – feelings that were necessarily in his own bones –
and he even reluctantly condoned that form of revolutionary action which comes first to a desperate peasantry:
agrarian terrorism.‡ Burke also understood the force of

* ' . . . You ought not, in reason, to trifle with so large a mass of
the interests and feelings of the human race. You could at no time
do so without guilt; and be assured you will not be able to do it
long with impunity.' (Speech on Conciliation with the Colonies,
1775.) *Works* I, p. 457.

† Above, p. 62.

‡ 'Dreadful it is; but it is now plain enough that Catholick *defenderism* is the only restraint upon Protestant *Ascendancy*.' *Sheffield
Papers*; Burke to Hussey, 18 January 1796. 'Defenderism' was the
term in use for the form of agrarian terrorism then practised in
Ireland. About thirty years before some of Burke's own relatives
had been implicated in the similar movement of the White Boys.
Corr. I, pp. 147–8.

those national and even tribal loyalties which are at least as important as any ideological factors in the revolutionary movements of today. The implications of 'containment', that world-wide American *ascendancy*, could never be wholly attractive to him.* Inevitably there is in such a policy an element of hubris, of the overweening, which repelled Burke, and against which he expressly warned the England of his day:

Among precautions against ambition, it may not be amiss to take one precaution against our *own*. I must fairly say, I dread our *own* power, and our *own* ambition; I dread our being too much dreaded. It is ridiculous to say we are not men; and that as men, we shall never wish to aggrandize ourselves in some way or other. Can we say, that even at this very hour we are not invidiously aggrandized? We are already in possession of almost all the commerce of the world. Our empire in India is an awful thing. If we should come to be in a condition not only to have all this ascendant in commerce, but to be absolutely able, without the least control, to hold the commerce of all other nations totally dependent upon our good pleasure, we may say that we shall not abuse this astonishing, and hitherto unheard-of, power. But every other nation will think we shall abuse it. It is impossible but that, sooner or later, this state of things must produce a combination against us which may end in our ruin.†

This passage seems to have escaped the attention of Mr Russell Kirk when he invoked the authority of Burke, and the example of Burke's England, in support of America's

---

*Not that the techniques of containment would always be abhorrent to him. He repudiated what he called a '*strange notion*' – 'that one State has not a right to interfere according to its discretion, in the interior Affairs of another'. (*Sheffield Papers*; Burke to Grenville, August 1792.) What is in question now, however, is precisely the 'discretion' with which the 'right' is exercised.

† *Remarks on the Policy of the Allies* (begun in October 1793). *Works* III, pp. 448.

'imperial duties' today. Burke was a counter-revolutionary but he cannot easily be accounted an imperialist; he showed a deep distrust for contemporary forms of imperialist psychology, not merely in relation to America, in his earlier years – an America then an object, not a source, of imperialism – but in relation to India and Ireland in his later years, and also because of the implications of such psychology for the imperial power itself. One cannot legitimately invoke Burke's authority in support of *any* specific policy to be applied in circumstances unknown to him. But particularly one cannot invoke it in support of a policy which contains strong elements about which he is known to have had profound misgivings: the extension of imperial commitments, the crushing of spontaneous peasant movements, *ascendancy*, hubris.*

It may well be argued that in our day the practice of counter-revolution, which Burke favoured, required what he did not favour: the extension of imperialism. Modern conditions – on this argument – put the prime nuclei of revolutionary infection out of reach. All that can be done is to prevent the infection from spreading to other lands. Some countries – notably the advanced, industrialized countries, Western Europe and Japan – are in a position to resist the infection on their own. But in those lands

---

* The argument about *prestige*, on which the justification of America's Vietnam war has been made to hinge, is one of which he once disposed effectively : 'They tell you, Sir, that your dignity is tied to it. I know now how it happens, but this dignity of yours is a terrible incumbrance to you; for it has of late been ever at war with your interest, your equity, and every idea of your policy. Shew the thing you contend for to be reason; shew it to be common sense; shew it to be the means of attaining some useful end; and then I am content to allow it what dignity you please. But what dignity is derived from the perseverance in absurdity, is more than I could ever discern.' (Speech on American Taxation, 1774.) *Works* I, p. 393.

which are not in such a position — many of the poor countries — the thing must be done for them, and this necessarily involves the assertion of authority over them, directly or indirectly, by the counter-revolutionary power. This assertion of authority is likely to be called 'aid' rather than imperialism but it does contain the essence of imperial rule: the final say is not with a native authority but with a foreign one.

If counter-revolution required imperialism in the circumstances of today, then Burke's thought as it has come down to us from its formulation in different circumstances is inapplicable as a whole. We can, however, reasonably hold that a conservative who fears the overextension of his country's power — as Senator Fulbright does — can claim descent from Burke with just as much validity as the practioners of counter-revolutionary containment.

II

How a writer actually *is* read and applied is, however, a matter of more practical importance than how he ought to be read, or how far he can be legitimately applied. There can be little doubt that Burke is now read and praised mainly as a conservative and counter-revolutionary writer, available in support and validation of the containment of communism. It was not always the counter-revolutionary Burke that seemed most important. Throughout the nineteenth century, liberal as well as conservative minds in Britain were nourished on him.* Indeed

* Even conservative Victorian minds could not conceive that Burke could again be used for counter-revolutionary purposes: 'No-one at the present day,' declared Edward Dowden, 'can desire to convert Edmund Burke's skin into a drum on which to beat an anti-revolutionary tattoo. The time is past for that kind of polemical criticism ...' (*The French Revolution and English Literature*, London, 1897.)

that 'subversive' element in Burke, which we have noted
in relation to Ireland, frightened some nineteenth-century
conservatives. Morley tells us that when Gladstone was
pondering his Home Rule choice he read Burke and made
extracts from him.* 'We may easily imagine,' writes Morley, 'how the heat from that profound and glowing fur-
nace still further influenced strong purposes and exalted
resolution in Mr Gladstone. The Duke of Argyll wrote to
say he was sorry to hear of the study of Burke: "Your
perfervidum ingenium Scoti does not need being touched
with a live coal from that Irish altar." '†

But if, amid the relative political stability of nineteenth-
century Britain, Burke could appear radical and almost
revolutionary, conditions in which revolution is felt as
a real threat tend to provoke an interest in Burke in his
counter-revolutionary aspect. This was so in nineteenth-
century Europe. The German translator of the *Reflections*, Friedrich von Gentz (1768–1832) was Metternich's
confidential adviser and principal secretary to the Congress of Vienna, and Burke's counter-revolutionary
writings – together with those of Maistre and Bonald –
provided inspiration for the leaders and propagandists of
the Holy Alliance. It is not surprising that in our own
day the advocates of a new Holy Alliance – of international policings on a scale of which Metternich could not
have dreamt – should revive interest in this aspect of
Burke. This is the meaning of the famous 'counter-
revolution in Burke scholarship' which seeks to extri-
cate the counter-revolutionary champion from what Mr
Peter J. Stanlis has called 'the great Serbonian bog of
positivist scholarship on Burke'. That is to say that the

* Not of course from the *Reflections*. It was 'on Ireland and
America' – not France – that Gladstone found Burke 'a magazine
of wisdom'.

† Morley, *Gladstone*, III, p. 280.

complex Burke whom nineteenth-century Britain knew, the writer who could inspire Gladstone and frighten the Duke of Argyll, is repudiated in favour of the idea of a Burke without contradictions or paradoxes, a pure essence of conservative thought, for the inspiration and invigoration of the intellectual heirs of Metternich.*

That those who advocate or approve the contemporary counter-revolution should interest themselves in the *Reflections* requires no demonstration. But why should those who oppose the contemporary counter-revolution, and the neo-conservatism which is among its more overt intellectual expressions, be invited to read this first modern counter-revolutionary manifesto?

The fact that such a question is certain to be asked is in itself indicative of a peculiar, and apparently deep-rooted, weakness in left-wing thinking. The intelligent rightist does not ask to be given reasons why he should read Marx and the Marxists. He reads them because they are important, and because they are on the other side. He learns from them and sometimes is warned by them: for example a German bourgeois could learn from the writings of Marx and Engels in the nineteenth century that it would be unwise to proceed too hastily in the matter of the abolition of feudal vestiges. The intelligent rightist makes use of the Marxist insights – as generations of bourgeois historians have done – but for his own purposes, as Guderian made use of de Gaulle. He learns from his adversaries about the strengths and weaknesses of his own position – and of theirs.

* Not all of those who have exalted Burke as a conservative political philosopher have endorsed or accepted neo-conservative applications of his 'teachings'. Mr Peter J. Stanlis, indeed, has strongly repudiated the modern conservative claim to Burke as 'their spokesman in practical politics' (*Burke Newsletter*, Vol. III, Spring 1962).

The intellectual left on the other hand – though with some notable exceptions – has a strong tendency to neglect its adversaries and to dismiss even their most influential writings, unread, with a sneer. This is associated, I believe, with another pronounced tendency on the left: that which runs to misunderstanding and underestimating the forces opposed to it. In fact the left should devote to the *Reflections* not less thought than the right has long given to *The Communist Manifesto*. The fact that Burke's manifesto aroused and rallied the first modern counter-revolutionary movement, and that it is still invoked for the contemporary counter-revolution should be reason enough to study this manifesto with care.

Granted that one can learn from Burke, without agreeing with his main argument, what is it that one can learn? It is not, certainly, a system of political philosophy. Burke is deliberately unsystematic and the various systems called 'Burke's philosophy' which pedants have constructed, out of the hollower components of his rhetoric and the commonplaces of his education, are sad, boring objects, not worth consideration. Nor, obviously, do we look to Burke for an analysis of the French Revolution. As a result of the opening of archives, and the labour of generations of historians, we know – or can know – more about the French Revolution than even the most alert contemporary, studying the Revolution from a distance, could have known. But even if Burke had known much more than he actually did, the *Reflections* would still not be interesting as historical analysis because that is not what they are intended to be. Burke had deliberately rejected 'the mode of calm Enquiry'; he was prepared when necessary to practise an 'economy of truth'. His words are not those of analysis; they are those of purposeful persuasion.

But this is no ordinary effort at persuasion. It is, as

Burke says, 'the late, ripe fruit of mere experience'. Burke's explicit argument is of less importance than the experience which is behind it, the acquired range of feeling both for the great forces of politics and for its detail. The feeling for the great forces reaches the level of the prophetic. Reading Burke with classes, I have found that undergraduates readily assume that the *Reflections* occur at a much later stage in the Revolution than is actually the case: that the September Massacres, the execution of the King and Queen, the Terror, have already happened, whereas of course they all lie in the future.* It is true that this is an effect not only of Burke's prophetic sense but also of his rhetoric. He exaggerates what has already happened, but he does so in and with the sense of what is going to happen. The contrast is extraordinary between Burke's grim foreboding, in 1790, and the tone of his pro-Revolutionary correspondents, Paine and Cloots, who write at this same time to assure him that the troubles are over, the glorious and almost bloodless Revolution is complete.† The transmigrations and 'varieties of untried being' which Burke foresaw for the Revolution were to bring about the death-sentence for both Paine and Cloots, and for Cloots the guillotine itself.

Burke not only foresaw deepening violence, and war on a scale overshadowing all past wars (above, p. 61), but he specifically predicted the emergence of a military despot: the event occurred nine years after his prophecy, and two years after his own death, on the 18th Brumaire 1799. It is true – and the point is usually overlooked by

---

* No serious student, I agree, could make such a mistake; but then the serious student, by definition incapable of such things, is almost as rare as economic man.

† *Corr.* VI, pp. 67–75, 109–15; Paine to Burke 17 January 1790 ... Cloots to Burke, 12 May 1790 ... 'Leave your Island, my dear Burke, come to France.'

Burke's admirers – that these prophecies were in great measure self-fulfilling. The hostility against Revolutionary France, which Burke deliberately sought to arouse, and the war against Revolutionary France, which Burke so persistently advocated, caused the Revolution to assume more violent forms, and created the need for the military dictatorship. This, however, does not really diminish what must be allowed to Burke's clairvoyance. Foreign reaction against the Revolution, and the Revolutionary response to that reaction, were among the factors he allowed for; his statements on the nature of the counter-revolutionary war show him fully aware of the functioning of the dialectics of violence. He knows that against the invasion which he urges, Revolutionary France may muster reserves of strength then generally unsuspected:

'France is weak indeed, divided and deranged', he wrote in January 1791, 'but God knows when the things come to be tried, whether the Invaders would not find that this enterprize was not to support a party, – but to conquer a Kingdom.'*

He foresaw, as well as urged, 'a *long* war'. He knew, in 1796, that his world stood 'at the beginning of great troubles'.† With the full power of a penetrating intelligence and a far-ranging imagination he measured the dimensions of what had begun in 1789. His contemporaries thought he was exaggerating, and in a sense he was, but as reality expanded to meet his exaggeration, it became apparent that it was those 'who had kept their heads' who had failed to understand.

Burke's eye for significant detail, his feel for the actual texture of day-to-day politics, is not less remarkable than his sense of the great forces; the two are interrelated, and make up a political intuition of unequalled sensibility. A

---

* Burke to John Trevor; *Corr.* V, pp. 216–19.
† First of the *Letters on a Regicide Peace. Works* V, p. 157.

single aside of Burke's can be richer in political instruction than a whole treatise by certain abstract analysts. The *Reflections* are rich in such 'late, ripe fruit'. Sometimes these comments take the form of a shrewd insight into the adversary:

'You will smile here at the consistency of those democratists who, when they are not on their guard, treat the humbler part of the community with the greatest contempt, whilst, at the same time they pretend to make them the depositories of all power.'*

Sometimes an insight produces an aphorism like this one about literature and the Left:

'Men of letters, fond of distinguishing themselves, are rarely averse to innovation.'

Sometimes it is a generalization, derived from a firm grasp of political reality, like this first, classic definition of the essentially bourgeois character of the Revolution:

'The whole of the power obtained by this revolution will settle in the towns among the burghers and the monied directors who lead them.'

Examples could be multiplied at length. But it is nearly as wrong to anthologize the *Reflections*† as it would be to attempt to paraphrase or systematize them. They have to be read as a whole, a unique political work of art.

12

'There is no wise man in politics, with an important decision to make', said the late Harold Laski, 'who would not do well to refresh his mind by discussion with

* Dr Price had referred to 'the dregs of the people'; compare Marx's references to the 'scum' which makes up the *lumpenproletariat*.

† Hazlitt's saying applies: '... the only specimen of Burke is, *all that he wrote*'. (*Essay on the Character of Burke*, 1807.)

Burke's mind.' Burke's various 'liberal' positions, Laski went on,

> ought not to blind us to the inescapable fact that, at bottom, Burke was an extreme conservative, who has given deep comfort to men of liberal temper less by the mark of his understanding than by a temperament so generous and so compassionate that, on important occasions, it swept him beyond the normal harbour where he felt at ease with his mind.*

Coming from well outside the conservative and liberal-conservative circles in which Burke is most often praised, this is a notable tribute. Yet I cannot feel that Laski's effort to solve the problem of why this 'extreme conservative' should so appeal to 'men of liberal temper' is altogether successful.

Burke's generosity and compassion were not so super-abundant as Laski suggests. He was certainly generous and compassionate in his personal relations, and in civil matters – he earned unpopularity by opposing putting homosexuals in the stocks – but in the politics of his last years he could be hard and fierce; there is nothing notably compassionate about the deliberate advocacy of 'a *long* war' – whose atrocious character is acknowledged in advance – combined with severe internal repression.† Nor is it so clear that 'at bottom' Burke was an extreme conservative. He reached in his old age the position of an extreme conservative, but it would be hard to demonstrate that this was 'the normal harbour where he felt at

---

* An address delivered at Trinity College, Dublin, on the occasion of the bi-centenary of the foundation of Burke's Club (14 March 1947). Laski here passed a 'test' of Hazlitt's: 'It has always been with me a test of the sense and candour of any one belonging to the opposite party, whether he allowed Burke to be a great man.' (*On the Character of Burke*, 1807.)

† Burke's counter-revolutionary ferocity in his last years shocked some of his sympathizers. 'Burke', wrote Lady Elliot on 14 April 1795, 'has filled many people with horror by what he said in the

ease with his mind'. I am not sure that he felt at ease with his mind at all: his contemporaries do not seem to have thought of him in this way – indeed they often thought he was hysterical – and minds which feel at ease are not often as active as Burke's was. The cadences of Burke's prose, and the patina which now for us spreads over the eighteenth century, have produced an illusion: we tend to see a Burke more mellow than the Burke of reality. If the real Burke had been 'at bottom' an extreme conservative, this would be surprising. He was an outsider, from a land in which his people were oppressed; a land whose prevailing system of government he never ceased to seek to undermine. These are not conditions in which conservatism becomes 'the normal harbour' of the mind. Mary Wollstonecraft was surely more perceptive when she saw in Burke a man who might have been 'a violent revolutionist'.

He never became a revolutionist but there continued to smoulder in him, in relation to Irish matters, a badly suppressed rebel. It is not a peculiarity of temperament, but the peculiarity of his situation – what I have called the Jacobite/Whig situation – that shapes his form of conservatism. One may reasonably conjecture also that the contradictions in Burke's position enrich his eloquence, extend its range, deepen its pathos, heighten its fantasy and make possible its strange appeal to 'men of liberal temper'. On this interpretation, part of the secret

House three nights ago. On Sheridan saying that embodying the emigrants was an act of cruelty, as if they were taken prisoners they would meet with no mercy, and desiring to know whether, if this was the case and they were all butchered, whether we were to retaliate and give no quarter to any prisoners we took, Burke exclaimed, "Certainly we should revenge ourselves on those in our hands." This seems to me and to most people too horrid to have come from the mouth of a man of humanity and feeling ...' (*Life of Sir G. Elliot*, II, pp. 288–9). See also *Works* III, p. 414.

of his power to penetrate the processes of the revolution derives from a suppressed sympathy with revolution, combined with an intuitive grasp of the subversive possibilities of *counter*-revolutionary propaganda, as affecting the established order in the land of his birth. This gives his 'extreme conservatism' its peculiar character, radically different from that of European reactionaries, like Maistre and Bonald. Unlike them he has reason to know how a revolutionary might feel; for him the forces of revolution and counter-revolution exist not only in the world at large but also within himself.

EDMUND BURKE:
A BIOGRAPHICAL NOTE

EDMUND BURKE was born in Dublin in January 1729. His father was an attorney, who belonged to the Established Church, but may have been brought up as a Catholic (see Introduction, p. 29; also Postscript to this Note). His mother, born Mary Nagle, was a Catholic. Edmund Burke was brought up as a member of the Established Church, although his early schooling was at a 'hedge school' conducted by a (presumably) Catholic teacher named O'Halloran in the ruined castle of Monanimy at Ballyduff, Co. Cork.

In 1741 he was sent to a school at Ballitore, Co. Kildare, kept by Abraham Shackleton, a member of the Society of Friends. In 1744 he entered Trinity College, Dublin, where he took his B.A. degree in 1748. In 1750 he went to London to read for the bar. Little is known of his life from this time to about 1757, but he was not called to the Bar. In 1756 he published his first literary works, *A Vindication of Natural Society* and *A Philosophical Inquiry into the Origin of Our Ideas of the Sublime and the Beautiful.* The latter work interested Lessing and Herder, and had a certain influence on the development of aesthetic theory on the Continent. About a century later, in *What is Art?*, the old and anti-aesthetic Tolstoy was to use it, to show that the sublime meant war, and the beautiful meant sex.*

---

* Tolstoy would have strongly approved of Burke's schoolmate, Shackleton, who advertised his refusal to teach 'those authors who recommend in seducing language the illusions of love and the abominable trade of war'. (Quoted in A. P. Samuels, *The Early Life, Correspondence and Writings of the Rt Hon. Edmund Burke LL.D.,* Cambridge, 1923, p. 130.)

At some time in the winter of 1756–7 Edmund Burke married Jane Nugent: where and how is not known.

The Burkes had two sons: Richard (1758–94), and Christopher, who died in childhood.

In 1758–9 Edmund Burke undertook the production of the *Annual Register*, with which he continued to be associated for more than thirty years. During 1759 he became secretary to William Gerard Hamilton (1729–96) who in 1761 became chief secretary under Lord Halifax, Lord-Lieutenant of Ireland. Having broken with Hamilton in 1765, Burke became, in that year, private secretary to the second Marquess of Rockingham (1730–82) who had just been appointed First Lord of the Treasury. Rockingham befriended Burke (and was helped by him) as long as he lived, and advanced him money. Burke was by this time a member of the Club in Gerrard Street, and became a life-long friend of Garrick, Reynolds and Johnson.

By the influence of Lord Verney (1712?–91) Burke was elected to parliament for the borough of Wendover, and took his seat 14 January 1766. He supported the Rockingham Whigs, who were in office from July 1766 to July 1767, and he followed Rockingham into opposition. In 1768 he bought the estate of Gregories, at Beaconsfield in Buckinghamshire; a purchase considerably beyond his means, as a result of which he was in financial difficulties for the rest of his life. In 1769 he published his *Observations on a late Publication Intituled 'The Present State of the Nation'*, and in 1770 *Thoughts on the Cause of the Present Discontents*, two weighty political pamphlets. In 1770 he was elected agent in London to the state of New York, for which he earned a salary of £500 a year. In 1773 he visited Paris and saw the 'delightful vision' to which he refers in the *Reflections*. It is probable that he was shocked by French levity and rationalism at this time.

By the elections of 1774 he became a member for Bristol and laid down the principle that a parliamentary representative betrays his constituents if he sacrifices his judgement to their opinion.

From 1774 on he became a friend and ally of Charles James Fox, with whom he conducted a strong opposition to Lord North's administration. His speeches 'On American Taxation' (1774) and 'On Moving his Resolutions for Conciliation with the Colonies' (1775) constituted a powerful exposure of the folly of the Government's American policy. In 1777 he and his 'Rockingham' friends withdrew from Parliament on all questions relating to America; he justified this policy in the 'Letter to the Sheriffs of Bristol'.

In 1780 he lost his Bristol seat, having offended the Bristol merchants by his advocacy of the commercial rights of Ireland, and also having aroused 'religious prejudices'. Lord Rockingham however provided him with a seat for his borough of Malton.*

When Rockingham took office in 1782 Burke was not offered a seat in the Cabinet but became paymaster of the forces. Lord Rockingham's death in 1782 was a severe blow to Burke personally, and to his prospects. He became paymaster again under the Portland coalition government (1783) but his conduct in this office attracted controversy and censure. After the fall of the Portland Government, and the triumph of Pitt by the elections of 1784, Burke was in opposition again, and unpopular in the new House, where he was frequently interrupted and treated with contempt. At this time he immersed himself in the preparations for his impeachment of Warren Hastings (1732–1818) for his conduct of the administration of India.

---

* Burke had also been returned for Malton in 1774, but chose to sit for Bristol. He continued to represent Malton from 1780 until his retirement in 1794.

This impeachment, which continued in the Commons in 1786, began by attracting great public interest but did nothing to increase his popularity, as Hastings had many friends in the House. In the regency crisis of 1788 Fox, who was expected to form a government, did not send for Burke, with whom he had worked so long, but planned instead to appoint him paymaster again and provide him with a pension.

By the time of the French Revolution, then, Burke – whose party in any case remained in opposition – was a rather isolated figure, unpopular, frustrated, hard-pressed by exhausting labours, and to some extent already estranged from his old parliamentary friends and colleagues.

For Burke's reaction to the news of the French Revolution, and its impact on England, and his writings about the Revolution, see the Introduction.

The *Reflections on the Revolution in France* were written during the first half of 1790 and published in November 1790. They enjoyed an immense, though not an immediate success in Britain and among the enemies of the French Revolution on the European continent, where they were translated into French in 1790 and into German in 1793. They provoked many replies, of which the best known is Tom Paine's *The Rights of Man* (1791). Two other notable replies are Mary Wollstonecraft's *A Vindication of the Rights of Men* (1790) and James Mackintosh's *Vindiciae Gallicae* (1791).

Burke's speeches and writings on the Revolution brought about worsened relations with Fox, leading to a final breach, in the House, on 6 May 1791. Burke was now a man without a party but the actual course of the Revolution, on the lines he had foreseen, enormously raised his reputation in the eyes of people of property (see the Introduction). In the remaining years of his life his mind was preoccupied principally by the affairs of France and of Ireland: the inter-relation of these preoccupations is discussed in the Intro-duction.

In June 1794, having finished his labours on the Hast-ings case, Burke retired from Parliament, and Lord Fitz-william gave his seat at Malton to his son Richard. Rich-ard died in August 1794. Burke was overwhelmed with grief, but his activity was undiminished. His last writings, notably the *Letter to a Noble Lord* (1796), and the *Letters on a Regicide Peace* (1796–7) contain some of the most splendid examples of his rhetoric. Following the recall of his friend Lord Fitzwilliam from his Viceroyalty in Ire-land, where in accordance with Burke's advice he had been bent on conciliation and the completion of Catholic eman-cipation, Burke was greatly troubled in his mind, not only by the victories of revolutionary France but by the menac-ing situation in Ireland, where rebellion was to break out in the year after his death, 1798.

Burke died at Beaconsfield on 9 July 1797. 'Here is but one event,' wrote George Canning 'but that is an event for the world – Burke is dead.'

POSTSCRIPT

In a letter received while this edition was in proof, Prof. Thomas Copeland wrote, about Burke's father: 'Almost nothing is certain about him. Even his conforming in 1722. Some Richard Burke conformed then and it may have been he. But Richard Burke's not an uncommon name and the Conformity Rolls are our only evidence.' (Copeland to Editor, 25 April 1968.)

Mr Basil O'Connell has stated: 'That Richard Burke, father of Edmund Burke, did conform has been the univer-sal tradition of the statesman's Nagle collaterals of whom the present writer is one.' (*Journal of the Cork Historical and Archaeological Society*, LX, 192, July–December 1955.)

*Facsimile of the title page of the first edition
of* Reflections on the Revolution in France.

REFLECTIONS

ON THE

REVOLUTION IN FRANCE,

AND ON THE

PROCEEDINGS IN CERTAIN SOCIETIES IN LONDON

RELATIVE TO THAT EVENT.

IN A

LETTER

INTENDED TO HAVE BEEN SENT TO A GENTLEMAN IN PARIS.

BY THE RIGHT HONOURABLE

EDMUND BURKE.

———

LONDON:

PRINTED FOR J. DODSLEY, IN PALL-MALL.

M.DCC.XC.

It may not be unnecessary to inform the Reader, that the following Reflections had their origin in a correspondence between the Author and a very young gentleman at Paris, who did him the honour of desiring his opinion upon the important transactions, which then, and ever since, have so much occupied the attention of all men. An answer was written some time in the month of October 1789; 'but it was kept back upon prudential considerations. That letter is alluded to in the beginning of the following sheets. It has been since forwarded to the person to whom it was addressed. The reasons for the delay in sending it were assigned in a short letter to the same gentleman. This produced on his part a new and pressing application for the Author's sentiments.

The Author began a second and more full discussion on the subject. This he had some thoughts of publishing early in the last spring; but the matter gaining upon him, he found that what he had undertaken not only far exceeded the measure of a letter, but that its importance required rather a more detailed consideration than at that time he had any leisure to bestow upon it. However, having thrown down his first thoughts in the form of a letter, and indeed when he sat down to write, having intended it for a private letter, he found it difficult to change the form of address, when his sentiments had grown into a greater extent, and had received another direction. A different plan, he is sensible, might be more favourable to a commodious division and distribution of his matter.

DEAR SIR,

You are pleased to call again, and with some earnestness, for my thoughts on the late proceedings in France. I will not give you reason to imagine, that I think my sentiments of such value as to wish myself to be solicited about them. They are of too little consequence to be very anxiously either communicated or withheld. It was from attention to you, and to you only, that I hesitated at the time, when you first desired to receive them. In the first letter I had the honour to write to you, and which at length I send, I wrote neither for nor from any description of men; nor shall I in this. My errors, if any, are my own. My reputation alone is to answer for them.

You see, Sir, by the long letter I have transmitted to you, that, though I do most heartily wish that France may be animated by a spirit of rational liberty, and that I think you bound, in all honest policy, to provide a permanent body, in which that spirit may reside, and an effectual organ, by which it may act, it is my misfortune to entertain great doubts concerning several material points in your late transactions.

You imagined, when you wrote last, that I might possibly be reckoned among the approvers of certain proceedings in France, from the solemn public seal of sanction they have received from two clubs of gentlemen in London, called the Constitutional Society, and the Revolution Society.[2]

I certainly have the honour to belong to more clubs than one, in which the constitution of this kingdom and the principles of the glorious Revolution, are held in high reverence: and I reckon myself among the most forward in my zeal for maintaining that constitution and those principles in their utmost purity and vigour. It is because I do so, that I think it necessary for me, that there should be no mistake. Those who cultivate the memory of our revolution, and those who are attached to the constitution of this kingdom, will take good care how they are involved with persons who, under the pretext of zeal towards the Revolution and Constitution, too frequently wander from their true principles; and are ready on every occasion to depart from the firm but cautious and deliberate spirit which produced the one, and which presides in the other. Before I proceed to answer the more material particulars in your letter, I shall beg leave to give you such information as I have been able to obtain of the two clubs which have thought proper, as bodies, to interfere in the concerns of France; first assuring you, that I am not, and that I have never been, a member of either of those societies.

The first, calling itself the Constitutional Society, or Society for Constitutional Information, or by some such title, is, I believe, of seven or eight years standing. The institution of this society appears to be of a charitable, and so far of a laudable, nature: it was intended for the circulation, at the expence of the members, of many books, which few others would be at the expence of buying; and which might lie on the hands of the booksellers, to the great loss of an useful body of men. Whether the books so charitably circulated, were ever as charitably read, is more than I know. Possibly several of them have been exported to France; and, like goods not in request here, may with you have found a market. I have heard much talk of the lights to be drawn from books that are sent from hence. What improvements they have had in their passage (as it is said some liquors are meliorated by crossing the sea) I cannot tell: But I never heard a man of common judgment, or the least degree of information, speak a word in praise of the greater part of the publications circulated by that society; nor have their proceedings been accounted, except by some of themselves, as of any serious consequence.

Your National Assembly seems to entertain much the same opinion that I do of this poor charitable club. As a nation, you reserved the whole stock of your eloquent acknowledgments for the Revolution Society; when their fellows in the Constitutional were, in equity, entitled to some share. Since you have selected the Revolution Society as the great object of your national thanks and praises, you will think me excuseable in making its late conduct the subject of my observations. The National Assembly of France has given importance to these gentlemen by adopting them; and they return the favour, by acting as a committee in England for extending the principles of the National Assembly. Henceforward we must consider them as a kind of privileged persons; as no inconsiderable members in the diplomatic body. This is one among the revolutions which have given splendour to obscurity, and distinction to undiscerned merit. Until very lately I do not recollect to have heard of this club. I am quite sure that it never occupied a moment of my thoughts; nor, I believe, those of any person out of their own set. I find, upon enquiry, that on the anniversary of the Revolution in 1688, a club of dissenters, but of what denomination I know not, have long had the custom of hearing a sermon in one of their churches; and that afterwards they spent the day cheerfully, as other clubs do, at the tavern. But I never heard that any public measure, or political system, much less that the merits of the constitution of any foreign nation, had been the subject of a formal proceeding at their festivals; until, to my inexpressible surprize, I found them in a

sort of public capacity, by a congratulatory address, giving
an authoritative sanction to the proceedings of the National Assembly in France.

In the antient principles and conduct of the club, so far
at least as they were declared, I see nothing to which I
could take exception. I think it very probable, that for
some purpose, new members may have entered among
them; and that some truly christian politicians, who love
to dispense benefits, but are careful to conceal the hand
which distributes the dole, may have made them the instruments of their pious designs. Whatever I may have
reason to suspect concerning private management, I shall
speak of nothing as of a certainty, but what is public.

For one, I should be sorry to be thought, directly or indirectly, concerned in their proceedings. I certainly take
my full share, along with the rest of the world, in my individual and private capacity, in speculating on what has
been done, or is doing, on the public stage; in any place
antient or modern; in the republic of Rome, or the republic
of Paris: but having no general apostolical mission, being
a citizen of a particular state, and being bound up in a
considerable degree, by its public will, I should think it, at
least improper and irregular, for me to open a formal public correspondence with the actual government of a foreign
nation, without the express authority of the government
under which I live.

I should be still more unwilling to enter into that correspondence, under any thing like an equivocal description,
which to many, unacquainted with our usages, might
make the address, in which I joined, appear as the act of
persons in some sort of corporate capacity, acknowledged
by the laws of this kingdom, and authorized to speak the
sense of some part of it. On account of the ambiguity and
uncertainty of unauthorized general descriptions, and of
the deceit which may be practised under them, and not

from mere formality, the house of Commons would reject the most sneaking petition for the most trifling object, under that mode of signature to which you have thrown open the folding-doors of your presence chamber, and have ushered into your National Assembly, with as much ceremony and parade, and with as great a bustle of applause, as if you had been visited by the whole representative majesty of the whole English nation. If what this society has thought proper to send forth had been a piece of argument, it would have signified little whose argument it was. It would be neither the more nor the less convincing on account of the party it came from. But this is only a vote and resolution. It stands solely on authority; and in this case it is the mere authority of individuals, few of whom appear. Their signatures ought, in my opinion, to have been annexed to their instrument. The world would then have the means of knowing how many they are; who they are; and of what value their opinions may be, from their personal abilities, from their knowledge, their experience, or their lead and authority in this state.[3] To me, who am but a plain man, the proceeding looks a little too refined, and too ingenious; it has too much the air of a political stratagem, adopted for the sake of giving, under an high-sounding name, an importance to the public declarations of this club, which, when the matter came to be closely inspected, they did not altogether so well deserve. It is a policy that has very much the complexion of a fraud.

I flatter myself that I love a manly, moral, regulated liberty as well as any gentleman of that society, be he who he will; and perhaps I have given as good proofs of my attachment to that cause, in the whole course of my public conduct. I think I envy liberty as little as they do, to any other nation. But I cannot stand forward, and give praise or blame to any thing which relates to human actions, and human concerns, on a simple view of the object, as it stands stripped of every relation, in all the nakedness and solitude of metaphysical abstraction. Circumstances (which with some gentlemen pass for nothing) give in reality to every political principle its distinguishing colour, and discriminating effect. The circumstances are what render every civil and political scheme beneficial or noxious to mankind. Abstractedly speaking, government, as well as liberty, is good; yet could I, in common sense, ten years ago, have felicitated France on her enjoyment of a government (for she then had a government) without enquiry what the nature of that government was, or how it was administered? Can I now congratulate the same nation upon its freedom? Is it because liberty in the abstract may be classed amongst the blessings of mankind, that I am seriously to felicitate a madman, who has escaped from the protecting restraint and wholesome darkness of his cell, on his restoration to the enjoyment of light and liberty? Am I to congratulate an highwayman and murderer, who has broke prison, upon the recovery of his natural rights? This would be to act over again the scene of the criminals condemned to the gallies, and their heroic deliverer, the metaphysic Knight of the Sorrowful Countenance.[4]

When I see the spirit of liberty in action, I see a strong principle at work; and this, for a while, is all I can possibly know of it. The wild *gas*, the fixed air is plainly broke loose: but we ought to suspend our judgment until the first effervescence is a little subsided, till the liquor is cleared, and until we see something deeper than the agitation of a troubled and frothy surface. I must be tolerably sure, before I venture publicly to congratulate men upon a blessing, that they have really received one. Flattery corrupts both the receiver and the giver; and adulation is not of more service to the people than to kings. I should therefore suspend my congratulations on the new liberty of France, until I was informed how it had been combined with government; with public force; with the discipline and obedience of armies; with the collection of an effective and well-distributed revenue; with morality and religion; with the solidity of property; with peace and order: with civil and social manners. All these (in their way) are good things too; and, without them, liberty is not a benefit whilst it lasts, and is not likely to continue long. The effect of liberty to individuals is, that they may do what they please: We ought to see what it will please them to do, before we risque congratulations, which may be soon turned into complaints. Prudence would dictate this in the case of separate insulated private men; but liberty, when men act in bodies, is *power*. Considerate people, before they declare themselves, will observe the use which is made of *power*; and particularly of so trying a thing as *new* power in *new* persons, of whose principles, tempers, and dispositions, they have little or no experience, and in situations where those who appear the most stirring in the scene may possibly not be the real movers.

All these considerations however were below the transcendental dignity of the Revolution Society. Whilst I continued in the country, from whence I had the honour of writing to you, I had but an imperfect idea of their transactions. On my coming to town, I sent for an account of their proceedings, which had been published by their authority, containing a sermon of Dr Price, with the Duke de Rochefaucault's and the Archbishop of Aix's letter, and several other documents annexed.[5] The whole of that publication, with the manifest design of connecting the affairs of France with those of England, by drawing us into an imitation of the conduct of the National Assembly, gave me a considerable degree of uneasiness. The effect of that conduct upon the power, credit, prosperity, and tranquility of France, became every day more evident. The form of constitution to be settled, for its future polity, became more clear. We are now in a condition to discern, with tolerable exactness, the true nature of the object held up to our imitation. If the prudence of reserve and decorum dictates silence in some circumstances, in others prudence of an higher order may justify us in speaking our thoughts. The beginnings of confusion with us in England are at present feeble enough; but with you, we have seen an infancy still more feeble, growing by moments into a strength to heap mountains upon mountains, and to wage war with Heaven itself. Whenever our neighbour's house is on fire, it cannot be amiss for the engines to play a little on our own. Better to be despised for too anxious apprehensions, than ruined by too confident a security.

Sollicitous chiefly for the peace of my own country, but by no means unconcerned for your's, I wish to communicate more largely, what was at first intended only for your private satisfaction. I shall still keep your affairs in my eye, and continue to address myself to you. Indulging myself in the freedom of epistolary intercourse, I beg leave to throw out my thoughts, and express my feelings, just as they arise in my mind, with very little attention to formal method. I set out with the proceedings of the Revolution Society; but I shall not confine myself to them. Is it possible I should? It looks to me as if I were in a great crisis, not of the affairs of France alone, but of all Europe, perhaps of more than Europe. All circumstances taken together, the French revolution is the most astonishing that has hitherto happened in the world. The most wonderful things are brought about in many instances by means the most absurd and ridiculous; in the most ridiculous modes; and apparently, by the most contemptible instruments. Every thing seems out of nature in this strange chaos of levity and ferocity, and of all sorts of crimes jumbled together with all sorts of follies. In viewing this monstrous tragi-comic scene, the most opposite passions necessarily succeed, and sometimes mix with each other in the mind; alternate contempt and indignation; alternate laughter and tears; alternate scorn and horror.

It cannot however be denied, that to some this strange scene appeared in quite another point of view. Into them it inspired no other sentiments than those of exultation and rapture. They saw nothing in what has been done in France, but a firm and temperate exertion of freedom; so consistent, on the whole, with morals and with piety, as to make it deserving not only of the secular applause of dashing Machiavelian politicians, but to render it a fit theme for all the devout effusions of sacred eloquence.

On the forenoon of the 4th of November last, Doctor Richard Price, a non-conforming minister of eminence, preached at the dissenting meeting-house of the Old Jewry, to his club or society, a very extraordinary miscellaneous sermon, in which there are some good moral and religious sentiments, and not ill expressed, mixed up in a sort of porridge of various political opinions and reflections: but the revolution in France is the grand ingredient in the cauldron. I consider the address transmitted by the Revolution Society to the National Assembly, through Earl Stanhope,[6] as originating in the principles of the sermon, and as a corollary from them. It was moved by the preacher of that discourse. It was passed by those who came reeking from the effect of the sermon, without any censure or qualification, expressed or implied. If, however, any of the gentlemen concerned shall wish to separate the sermon from the resolution, they know how to acknowledge the one, and to disavow the other. They may do it: I cannot.

For my part, I looked on that sermon as the public declaration of a man much connected with literary caballers, and intriguing philosophers; with political theologians, and theological politicians, both at home and abroad. I know they set him up as a sort of oracle; because, with the best intentions in the world, he naturally *philippizes*, and chaunts his prophetic song in exact unison with their designs.[7]

That sermon is in a strain which I believe has not been heard in this kingdom, in any of the pulpits which are tolerated or encouraged in it, since the year 1648, when a predecessor of Dr Price, the Reverend Hugh Peters,[8] made the vault of the king's own chapel at St James's ring with the honour and privilege of the Saints, who, with the 'high praises of God in their mouths, and a *two*-edged sword in their hands, were to execute judgment on the heathen, and punishments upon the *people*; to bind their *kings* with chains, and their *nobles* with fetters of iron.'* Few harangues from the pulpit, except in the days of your league in France, or in the days of our solemn league and convenant in England, have ever breathed less of the spirit of moderation than this lecture in the Old Jewry. Supposing, however, that something like moderation were visible in this political sermon; yet politics and the pulpit are terms that have little agreement. No sound ought to be heard in the church but the healing voice of Christian charity. The cause of civil liberty and civil government gains as little as that of religion by this confusion of duties. Those who quit their proper character, to assume what does not belong to them, are, for the greater part, ignorant both of the character they leave, and of the character they assume. Wholly unacquainted with the world in which they are so fond of meddling, and inexperienced in all its affairs, on which they pronounce with so much confidence, they have nothing of politics but the passions they excite. Surely the church is a place where one day's truce ought to be allowed to the dissensions and animosities of mankind.

This pulpit style, revived after so long a discontinuance,

* Psalm cxlix.

had to me the air of novelty, and of a novelty not wholly
without danger. I do not charge this danger equally to
every part of the discourse. The hint given to a noble and
reverend lay-divine, who is supposed high in office in one
of our universities,* and to other lay-divines 'of *rank* and
literature,'[9] may be proper and seasonable, though somewhat new. If the noble *Seekers*[10] should find nothing to
satisfy their pious fancies in the old staple of the national
church, or in all the rich variety to be found in the well-
assorted warehouses of the dissenting congregations, Dr
Price advises them to improve upon non-conformity; and
to set up, each of them, a separate meeting-house upon his
own particular principles.† It is somewhat remarkable that
this reverend divine should be so earnest for setting up
new churches, and so perfectly indifferent concerning the
doctrine which may be taught in them. His zeal is of a
curious character. It is not for the propagation of his own
opinions, but of any opinions. It is not for the diffusion of
truth, but for the spreading of contradiction. Let the noble
teachers but dissent, it is no matter from whom or from
what. This great point once secured, it is taken for granted
their religion will be rational and manly. I doubt whether
religion would reap all the benefits which the calculating
divine computes from this 'great company of great
preachers.' It would certainly be a valuable addition of
nondescripts to the ample collection of known classes,
genera and species, which at present beautify the *hortus*

* Discourse on the Love of our Country, Nov. 4, 1789, by Dr
Richard Price, 3d edition, p. 17 and 18.

† 'Those who dislike that mode of worship which is prescribed
by public authority ought, if they can find *no* worship *out* of the
church which they approve, *to set up a separate worship for themselves*; and by doing this, and giving an example of a rational and
manly worship, men of *weight* from their *rank* and literature may
do the greatest service to society and the world.' P. 18. Dr Price's
Sermon.

siccus[11] of dissent. A sermon from a noble duke, or a noble
marquis, or a noble earl, or baron bold, would certainly
increase and diversify the amusements of this town, which
begins to grow satiated with the uniform round of its
vapid dissipations. I should only stipulate that these new
Mess-Johns[12] in robes and coronets should keep some sort
of bounds in the democratic and levelling principles which
are expected from their titled pulpits. The new evangelists
will, I dare say, disappoint the hopes that are conceived of
them. They will not become, literally as well as figuratively,
polemic divines, nor be disposed so to drill their congregations that they may, as in former blessed times, preach their
doctrines to regiments of dragoons, and corps of infantry
and artillery. Such arrangements, however favourable to
the cause of compulsory freedom, civil and religious, may
not be equally conducive to the national tranquillity. These
few restrictions I hope are no great stretches of intolerance, no very violent exertions of despotism.

But I may say of our preacher, '*utinam nugis tota illa
dedisset tempora saevitiae.*'[13] – All things in this his fulmin-
ating bull are not so innoxious a tendency. His doctrines
affect our constitution in its vital parts. He tells the Revolution Society, in this political sermon, that his majesty 'is
almost the *only* lawful king in the world, because the *only*
one who owes his crown to the *choice of his people*.' As to
the kings of *the world*, all of whom (except one) this arch-
pontiff of the *rights of men*, with all the plenitude, and
with more than the boldness of the papal deposing power
in its meridian fervour of the twelfth century, puts into
one sweeping clause of ban and anathema, and proclaims
usurpers by circles of longitude and latitude, over the
whole globe, it behoves them to consider how they admit
into their territories these apostolic missionaries, who are
to tell their subjects they are not lawful kings. That is their
concern. It is ours, as a domestic interest of some moment,

seriously to consider the solidity of the *only* principle upon which these gentlemen acknowledge a king of Great Britain to be entitled to their allegiance.

This doctrine, as applied to the prince now on the British throne, either is nonsense, and therefore neither true nor false, or it affirms a most unfounded, dangerous, illegal, and unconstitutional position. According to this spiritual doctor of politics, if his majesty does not owe his crown to the choice of his people, he is no *lawful* king. Now nothing can be more untrue than that the crown of this kingdom is so held by his majesty. Therefore if you follow their rule, the king of Great Britain, who most certainly does not owe his high office to any form of popular election, is in no respect better than the rest of the gang of usurpers, who reign, or rather rob, all over the face of this our miserable world, without any sort of right or title to the allegiance of their people. The policy of this general doctrine, so qualified, is evident enough. The propagators of this political gospel are in hopes their abstract principle (their principle that a popular choice is necessary to the legal existence of the sovereign magistracy) would be overlooked whilst the king of Great Britain was not affected by it. In the mean time the ears of their congregations would be gradually habituated to it, as if it were a first principle admitted without dispute. For the present it would only operate as a theory, pickled in the preserving juices of pulpit eloquence, and laid by for future use. *Condo et compono quae mox depromere possim.*[14] By this policy, whilst our government is soothed with a reservation in its favour, to which it has no claim, the security, which it has in common with all governments, so far as opinion is security, is taken away.

Thus these politicians proceed, whilst little notice is taken of their doctrines; but when they come to be examined upon the plain meaning of their words and the direct tendency of their doctrines, then equivocations and slippery constructions come into play. When they say the king owes his crown to the choice of his people, and is therefore the only lawful sovereign in the world, they will perhaps tell us they mean to say no more than that some of the king's predecessors have been called to the throne by some sort of choice; and therefore he owes his crown to the choice of his people. Thus, by a miserable subterfuge, they hope to render their proposition safe, by rendering it nugatory. They are welcome to the asylum they seek for their offence, since they take refuge in their folly. For, if you admit this interpretation, how does their idea of election differ from our idea of inheritance? And how does the settlement of the crown in the Brunswick line derived from James the first, come to legalize our monarchy, rather than that of any of the neighbouring countries? At some time or other, to be sure, all the beginners of dynasties were chosen by those who called them to govern. There is ground enough for the opinion that all the kingdoms of Europe were, at a remote period, elective, with more or fewer limitations in the objects of choice; but whatever kings might have been here or elsewhere, a thousand years ago, or in whatever manner the ruling dynasties of England or France may have begun, the King of Great Britain is at this day king by a fixed rule of succession, according to the laws of his country; and whilst the legal conditions of the compact of sovereignty are performed by him (as they are performed) he holds his crown in contempt of the choice of the Revolution Society, who have not a single vote for a king amongst them, either individually or collectively; though I make no doubt they would soon erect themselves into an electoral college, if things were ripe to give effect to their claim. His majesty's heirs and successors, each in his time and order, will come to the crown with the same contempt of their choice with which his majesty has succeeded to that he wears.

Whatever may be the success of evasion in explaining away the gross error of *fact*, which supposes that his majesty (though he holds it in concurrence with the wishes) owes his crown to the choice of his people, yet nothing can evade their full explicit declaration, concerning the principle of a right in the people to choose, which right is directly maintained, and tenaciously adhered to. All the oblique insinuations concerning election bottom in this proposition, and are referable to it. Lest the foundation of the king's exclusive legal title should pass for a mere rant of adulatory freedom, the political Divine proceeds dogmatically to assert,* that by the principles of the Revolution the people of England have acquired three fundamental rights, all which, with him, compose one system and lie together in one short sentence; namely, that we have acquired a right

1. 'To choose our own governors.'
2. 'To cashier them for misconduct.'
3. 'To frame a government for ourselves.'

This new, and hitherto unheard-of bill of rights, though made in the name of the whole people, belongs to those gentlemen and their faction only. The body of the people of England have no share in it. They utterly disclaim it. They will resist the practical assertion of it with their lives and fortunes. They are bound to do so by the laws of their country, made at the time of that very Revolution, which is appealed to in favour of the fictitious rights claimed by the society which abuses its name.

These gentlemen of the Old Jewry, in all their reasonings on the Revolution of 1688, have a revolution which happened in England about forty years before, and the late French revolution, so much before their eyes, and in their

* P. 34, Discourse on the Love of our Country, by Dr Price.

hearts, that they are constantly confounding all the three together. It is necessary that we should separate what they confound. We must recall their erring fancies to the *acts* of the Revolution which we revere, for the discovery of its true *principles*. If the *principles* of the Revolution of 1688 are any where to be found, it is in the statute called the *Declaration of Right*.[15] In that most wise, sober, and considerate declaration, drawn up by great lawyers and great statesmen, and not by warm and inexperienced enthusiasts, not one word is said, nor one suggestion made, of a general right 'to choose our own *governors*; to cashier them for misconduct; and to *form* a government for *ourselves*.'

This Declaration of Right (the act of the 1st of William and Mary, sess. 2. ch. 2.) is the cornerstone of our constitution, as reinforced, explained, improved, and in its fundamental principles for ever settled. It is called 'An act for declaring the rights and liberties of the subject, and for *settling* the *succession* of the crown.' You will observe, that these rights and this succession are declared in one body, and bound indissolubly together.

A few years after this period, a second opportunity offered for asserting a right of election to the crown. On the prospect of a total failure of issue from King William, and from the Princess, afterwards Queen Anne, the consideration of the settlement of the crown, and of a further security for the liberties of the people, again came before the legislature. Did they this second time make any provision for legalizing the crown on the spurious Revolution principles of the Old Jewry? No. They followed the principles which prevailed in the Declaration of Right; indicating with more precision the persons who were to inherit in the Protestant line. This act also incorporated, by the same policy, our liberties, and an hereditary succession in the same act. Instead of a right to choose our own governors, they declared that the *succession* in that line (the protestant line drawn from James the First) was absolutely necessary 'for the peace, quiet, and security of the realm,' and that it was equally urgent on them 'to maintain a *certainty in the succession* thereof, to which the subjects may safely have recourse for their protection.' Both these acts, in which are heard the unerring, unambiguous oracles of Revolution policy, instead of countenancing the delusive, gypsey predictions of a 'right to choose our governors,' prove to a demonstration how totally adverse the wisdom of the nation was from turning a case of necessity into a rule of law.

Unquestionably there was at the Revolution, in the person of King William, a small and a temporary deviation from the strict order of a regular hereditary succession; but it is against all genuine principles of jurisprudence to draw a principle from a law made in a special case, and regarding an individual person. *Privilegium non transit in exemplum.*[16] If ever there was a time favourable for establishing the principle, that a king of popular choice was the only legal king, without all doubt it was at the Revolution. Its not being done at that time is a proof that the nation was of opinion it ought not to be done at any time. There is no person so completely ignorant of our history, as not to know, that the majority in parliament of both parties were so little disposed to any thing resembling that principle, that at first they were determind to place the vacant crown, not on the head of the prince of Orange, but on that of his wife Mary, daughter of King James, the eldest born of the issue of that king, which they acknowledged as undoubtedly his.[17] It would be to repeat a very trite story, to recall to your memory all those circumstances which demonstrated that their accepting King William was not properly a *choice*; but, to all those who did not wish, in effect to recall King James, or to deluge their country in blood, and again to bring their religion, laws, and liberties into the peril they had just escaped, it was an act of *necessity*, in the strictest moral sense in which necessity can be taken.

In the very act, in which for a time, and in a single case, parliament departed from the strict order of inheritance, in favour of a prince, who, though not next, was however very near in the line of succession, it is curious to observe how Lord Somers,[18] who drew the bill called the Declaration of Right, has comported himself on that delicate occasion. It is curious to observe with what address this temporary solution of continuity is kept from the eye; whilst all that could be found in this act of necessity to countenance the idea of an hereditary succession is brought forward, and fostered, and made the most of, by this great man, and by the legislature who followed him. Quitting the dry, imperative style of an act of parliament, he makes the lords and commons fall to a pious, legislative ejaculation, and declare, that they consider it 'as a marvellous providence, and merciful goodness of God to this nation, to preserve their said majesties *royal* persons, most happily to reign over us *on the throne of their ancestors*, for which, from the bottom of their hearts, they return their humblest thanks and praises.' – The legislature plainly had in view the act of recognition of the first of Queen Elizabeth, Chap. 3d, and of that of James the First, Chap. 1st, both acts strongly declaratory of the inheritable nature of the crown; and in many parts they follow, with a nearly literal precision, the words and even the form of thanksgiving, which is found in these old declaratory statutes.

The two houses, in the act of king William, did not thank God that they had found a fair opportunity to assert a right to choose their own governors, much less to make an election the *only lawful* title to the crown. Their having been in a condition to avoid the very appearance of it, as

much as possible, was by them considered as a providential
escape. They threw a politic, well-wrought veil over every
circumstance tending to weaken the rights, which in the
meliorated order of succession they meant to perpetuate;
or which might furnish a precedent for any future departure from what they had then settled for ever. Accordingly,
that they might not relax the nerves of their monarchy,
and that they might preserve a close conformity to the
practice of their ancestors, as it appeared in the declaratory
statutes of queen Mary* and queen Elizabeth, in the next
clause they vest, by recognition, in their majesties, *all* the
legal prerogatives of the crown, declaring, 'that in them
they are most *fully*, rightfully, and *intirely* invested, incorporated, united, and annexed.' In the clause which follows, for preventing questions, by reason of any pretended
titles to the crown, they declare (observing also in this the
traditionary language, along with the traditionary policy
of the nation, and repeating as from a rubric the language
of the preceding acts of Elizabeth and James) that on the
preserving 'a *certainty* in the SUCCESSION thereof, the
unity, peace, and tranquillity of this nation doth, under
God, wholly depend.'

   They knew that a doubtful title of succession would but
too much resemble an election; and that an election would
be utterly destructive of the 'unity, peace, and tranquillity
of this nation,' which they thought to be considerations
of some moment. To provide for these objects, and therefore to exclude for ever the Old Jewry doctrine of 'a right
to choose our own governors,' they follow with a clause,
containing a most solemn pledge, taken from the preceding
act of Queen Elizabeth, as solemn a pledge as ever was or
can be given in favour of an hereditary succession, and as
solemn a renunciation as could be made of the principles
by this society imputed to them. 'The lords spiritual and

* 1st Mary, Sess. 3. ch. I.

temporal, and commons, do, in the name of all the people aforesaid, most humbly and faithfully submit *themselves, their heirs and posterities for ever;* and do faithfully promise, that they will stand to, maintain, and defend their said majesties, and also the *limitation of the crown*, herein specified and contained, to the utmost of their powers,' &c.&c.

So far is it from being true, that we acquired a right by the Revolution to elect our kings, that if we had possessed it before, the English nation did at that time most solemnly renounce and abdicate it, for themselves and for all their posterity for ever. These gentlemen may value themselves as much as they please on their whig principles; but I never desire to be thought a better whig than Lord Somers; or to understand the principles of the Revolution better than those by whom it was brought about; or to read in the declaration of right any mysteries unknown to those whose penetrating style has engraved in our ordinances, and in our hearts, the words and spirit of that immortal law.

It is true that, aided with the powers derived from force and opportunity, the nation was at that time, in some sense, free to take what course it pleased for filling the throne; but only free to do so upon the same grounds on which they might have wholly abolished their monarchy, and every other part of their constitution. However they did not think such bold changes within their commission. It is indeed difficult, perhaps impossible, to give limits to the mere *abstract* competence of the supreme power, such as was exercised by parliament at that time; but the limits of a *moral* competence, subjecting, even in powers more indisputably sovereign, occasional will to permanent reason, and to the steady maxims of faith, justice, and fixed fundamental policy, are perfectly intelligible, and perfectly binding upon those who exercise any authority, under any name, or under any title, in the state. The house of lords, for instance, is not morally competent to dissolve the house of commons; no, nor even to dissolve itself, nor to abdicate, if it would, its portion in the legislature of the kingdom. Though a king may abdicate for his own person, he cannot abdicate for the monarchy. By as strong, or by a stronger reason, the house of commons cannot renounce its share of authority. The engagement and pact of society, which generally goes by the name of the constitution, forbids such invasion and such surrender. The constituent parts of a state are obliged to hold their public faith with each other, and with all those who derive any serious interest under their engagements, as much as the whole state is bound to keep its faith with separate communities. Otherwise competence and power would soon be confounded, and no law be left but the will of a prevailing force. On this principle the succession of the crown has always been what it now is, an hereditary succession by law: in the old line it was a succession by the common law; in the new by the statute law, operating on the principles of the common law, not changing the substance, but regulating the mode, and describing the persons. Both these descriptions of law are of the same force, and are derived from an equal authority, emanating from the common agreement and original compact of the state, *communi sponsione reipublicae,*[19] and as such are equally binding on king, and people too, as long as the terms are observed, and they continue the same body politic.

It is far from impossible to reconcile, if we do not suffer ourselves to be entangled in the mazes of metaphysic sophistry, the use both of a fixed rule and an occasional deviation; the sacredness of an hereditary principle of succession in our government, with a power of change in its application in cases of extreme emergency. Even in that extremity (if we take the measure of our rights by our exercise of them at the Revolution) the change is to be confined to the peccant part only; to the part which produced the necessary deviation; and even then it is to be effected without a decomposition of the whole civil and political mass, for the purpose of originating a new civil order out of the first elements of society.

A state without the means of some change is without the means of its conservation. Without such means it might even risque the loss of that part of the constitution which it wished the most religiously to preserve. The two principles of conservation and correction operated strongly at the two critical periods of the Restoration and Revolution, when England found itself without a king. At both those periods the nation had lost the bond of union in their antient edifice; they did not however, dissolve the whole fabric. On the contrary, in both cases they regenerated the deficient part of the old constitution through the parts which were not impaired. They kept these old parts exactly as they were, that the part recovered might be suited to them. They acted by the ancient organized states in the shape of their old organization, and not by the organic *moleculae* of a disbanded people. At no time, perhaps, did the sovereign legislature manifest a more tender regard to that fundamental principle of British constitutional policy, than at the time of the Revolution, when it deviated from the direct line of hereditary succession. The crown was carried somewhat out of the line in which it had before moved; but the new line was derived from the same stock. It was still a line of hereditary descent; still an hereditary descent in the same blood, though an hereditary descent qualified with protestantism. When the legislature altered the direction, but kept the principle, they shewed that they held it inviolable.

On this principle, the law of inheritance had admitted some amendment in the old time, and long before the aera of the Revolution. Some time after the conquest great questions arose upon the legal principles of hereditary descent. It became a matter of doubt, whether the heir *per capita* or the heir *per stirpes* was to succeed;[20] but whether the heir *per capita* gave way when the heirdom *per stirpes* took place, or the Catholic heir when the Protestant was preferred, the inheritable principle survived with a sort of immortality through all transmigrations – *multosque per annos stat fortuna domus et avi numerantur avorum*.[21] This is the spirit of our constitution, not only in its settled course, but in all its revolutions. Whoever came in, or however he came in, whether he obtained the crown by law, or by force, the hereditary succession was either continued or adopted.

The gentlemen of the Society for Revolutions see nothing in that of 1688 but the deviation from the constitution; and they take the deviation from the principle for the principle. They have little regard to the obvious consequences of their doctrine, though they must see, that it leaves positive authority in very few of the positive institutions of this country. When such an unwarrantable maxim is once established, that no throne is lawful but the elective, no one act of the princes who preceded their aera of fictitious election can be valid. Do these theorists mean to imitate some of their predecessors, who dragged the bodies of our antient sovereigns out of the quiet of their tombs? Do they mean to attaint and disable backwards all the kings that have reigned before the Revolution, and consequently to stain the throne of England with the blot of a continual usurpation? Do they mean to invalidate, annul, or to call into question, together with the titles of the whole line of our kings, that great body of our statute law which passed under those whom they treat as usurpers? to annul laws of inestimable value to our liberties – of as great value at least as any which have passed at or since the period of the Revolution? If kings, who did not

owe their crown to the choice of their people, had no title
to make laws, what will become of the statute *de tallagio
non concedendo?* – of the *petition of right?* – of the act of
habeas corpus?[22] Do these new doctors of the rights of
men presume to assert, that King James the Second, who
came to the crown as next of blood, according to the rules
of a then unqualified succession, was not to all intents and
purposes a lawful king of England, before he had done any
of those acts which were justly construed into an abdication of his crown? If he was not, much trouble in parliament might have been saved at the period these gentlemen
commemorate. But King James was a bad king with a good
title, and not an usurper. The princes who succeeded according to the act of parliament which settled the crown
on the electress Sophia and on her descendants, being Protestants, came in as much by a title of inheritance as King
James did. He came in according to the law, as it stood at
his accession to the crown; and the princes of the House of
Brunswick came to the inheritance of the crown, not by
election, but by the law, as it stood at their several accessions of Protestant descent and inheritance, as I hope I
have shewn sufficiently.

The law by which this royal family is specifically destined to the succession, is the act of the 12th and 13th of
King William. The terms of this act bind 'us and our
heirs, and our *posterity*, to them, their *heirs*, and their
posterity,' being Protestants, to the end of time, in the
same words as the declaration of right had bound us to the
heirs of King William and Queen Mary. It therefore secures both an hereditary crown and an hereditary allegiance. On what ground, except the constitutional policy
of forming an establishment to secure that kind of succession which is to preclude a choice of the people for ever,
could the legislature have fastidiously rejected the fair and
abundant choice which our own country presented to

them, and searched in strange lands for a foreign princess, from whose womb the line of our future rulers were to derive their title to govern millions of men through a series of ages?

The Princess Sophia was named in the act of settlement of the 12th and 13th of King William, for a *stock* and root of *inheritance* to our kings, and not for her merits as a temporary administratrix of a power, which she might not, and in fact did not, herself ever exercise. She was adopted for one reason, and for one only, because, says the act, 'the most excellent Princess Sophia, Electress and Dutchess Dowager of Hanover, is *daughter* of the most excellent Princess Elizabeth, late Queen of Bohemia, *daughter* of our late *Sovereign lord* King James the First, of happy memory, and is hereby declared to be the next in *succession* in the Protestant line,' &c. &c.; 'and the crown shall continue to the *heirs* of her body, being Protestants.' This limitation was made by parliament, that through the Princess Sophia an inheritable line, not only was to be continued in future but (what they thought very material) that through her it was to be connected with the old stock of inheritance in King James the First; in order that the monarchy might preserve an unbroken unity through all ages, and might be preserved (with safety to our religion) in the old approved mode by descent, in which, if our liberties had been once endangered, they had often, through all storms and struggles of prerogative and privilege, been preserved. They did well. No experience has taught us, that in any other course or method than that of an *hereditary crown*, our liberties can be regularly perpetuated and preserved sacred as our *hereditary right*. An irregular, convulsive movement may be necessary to throw off an irregular, convulsive disease. But the course of succession is the healthy habit of the British constitution. Was it that the legislature wanted, at the act for the limitation of the crown in the Hanoverian line, drawn through the female descendants of James the First, a due sense of the inconveniencies of having two or three, or possibly more, foreigners in succession to the British throne? No! – they had a due sense of the evils which might happen from such foreign rule and more than a due sense of them. But a more decisive proof cannot be given of the full conviction of the British nation, that the principles of the Revolution did not authorize them to elect kings at their pleasure, and without any attention to the antient fundamental principles of our government, than their continuing to adopt a plan of hereditary Protestant succession in the old line, with all the dangers and all the inconveniencies of its being a foreign line full before their eyes, and operating with the utmost force upon their minds.

A few years ago I should be ashamed to overload a matter, so capable of supporting itself, by the then unnecessary support of any argument; but this seditious, unconstitutional doctrine is now publicly taught, avowed, and printed. The dislike I feel to revolutions, the signals for which have so often been given from pulpits; the spirit of change that is gone abroad; the total contempt which prevails with you, and may come to prevail with us, of all antient institutions, when set in opposition to a present sense of convenience, or to the bent of a present inclination: all these considerations make it not unadviseable, in my opinion, to call back our attention to the true principles of our own domestic laws; that you, my French friend, should begin to know, and that we should continue to cherish them. We ought not, on either side of the water, to suffer ourselves to be imposed upon by the counterfeit wares which some persons, by a double fraud, export to you in illicit bottoms, as raw commodities of British growth though wholly alien to our soil, in order afterwards to smuggle them back again into this country, manufactured after the newest Paris fashion of an improved liberty.

The people of England will not ape the fashions they have never tried; nor go back to those which they have found mischievous on trial. They look upon the legal hereditary succession of their crown as among their rights, not as among their wrongs; as a benefit, not as a grievance; as a security for their liberty, not as a badge of servitude. They look on the frame of their commonwealth, *such as it stands*, to be of inestimable value; and they conceive the undisturbed succession of the crown to be a pledge of the stability and perpetuity of all the other members of our constitution.

I shall beg leave, before I go any further, to take notice of some paltry artifices, which the abettors of election as the only lawful title to the crown, are ready to employ, in order to render the support of the just principles of our constitution a task somewhat invidious. These sophisters substitute a fictitious cause, and feigned personages, in whose favour they suppose you engaged, whenever you defend the inheritable nature of the crown. It is common with them to dispute as if they were in a conflict with some of those exploded fanatics of slavery, who formerly maintained, what I believe no creature now maintains, 'that the crown is held by divine hereditary, and indefeasible right.' – These old fanatics of single arbitrary power dogmatized as if hereditary royalty was the only lawful government in the world, just as our new fanatics of popular arbitrary power, maintain that a popular election is the sole lawful source of authority. The old prerogative enthusiasts, it is true, did speculate foolishly, and perhaps impiously too, as if monarchy had more of a divine sanction than any other mode of government; and as if a right to govern by inheritance were in strictness *indefeasible* in every person, who should be found in the succession to a throne, and under every circumstance, which no civil or political right can be. But an absurd opinion concerning the king's hereditary right to the crown does not prejudice one that is rational, and bottomed upon solid principles of law and policy. If all the absurd theories of lawyers and divines were to vitiate the objects in which they are conversant, we should have no law, and no religion, left in the world. But an absurd theory on one side of a question forms no justification for alledging a false fact, or promulgating mischievous maxims on the other.

The second claim of the Revolution Society is 'a right of cashiering their governors for *misconduct.*' Perhaps the apprehensions our ancestors entertained of forming such a precedent as that 'of cashiering for misconduct,' was the cause that the declaration of the act which implied the abdication of king James, was, if it had any fault, rather too guarded, and too circumstantial.* But all this guard, and all this accumulation of circumstances, serves to shew the spirit of caution which predominated in the national councils, in a situation in which men irritated by oppression, and elevated by a triumph over it, are apt to abandon themselves to violent and extreme courses: it shews the anxiety of the great men who influenced the conduct of affairs at that great event, to make the Revolution a parent of settlement, and not a nursery of future revolutions.

No government could stand a moment, if it could be blown down with any thing so loose and indefinite as an opinion of '*misconduct.*' They who led at the Revolution, grounded the virtual abdication of King James upon no such light and uncertain principle. They charged him

* 'That King James the second, having endeavoured to *subvert the constitution* of the kingdom, by breaking the *original contract* between king and people, and by the advice of jesuits, and other wicked persons, having violated the *fundamental laws*, and *having withdrawn himself out of the kingdom*, hath *abdicated* the government, and the throne is thereby *vacant.*'

with nothing less than a design, confirmed by a multitude of illegal overt acts, to *subvert the Protestant church and state*, and their *fundamental*, unquestionable laws and liberties: they charged him with having broken the *original contract* between king and people. This was more than *misconduct*. A grave and overruling necessity obliged them to take the step they took, and took with infinite reluctance, as under that most rigorous of all laws. Their trust for the future preservation of the constitution was not in future revolutions. The grand policy of all their regulations was to render it almost impracticable for any future sovereign to compel the states of the kingdom to have again recourse to those violent remedies. They left the crown what, in the eye and estimation of law, it had ever been, perfectly irresponsible. In order to lighten the crown still further, they aggravated responsibility on ministers of state. By the statute of the 1st of king William, sess. 2d, called '*the act for declaring the rights and liberties of the subject, and for settling the succession of the crown*,' they enacted, that the ministers should serve the crown on the terms of that declaration. They secured soon after the *frequent meetings of parliament*, by which the whole government would be under the constant inspection and active controul of the popular representative and of the magnates of the kingdom. In the next great constitutional act, that of the 12th and 13th of King William, for the further limitation of the crown, and *better* securing the rights and liberties of the subject, they provided, 'that no pardon under the great seal of England should be pleadable to an impeachment by the commons in parliament.' The rule laid down for government in the Declaration of Right, the constant inspection of parliament, the practical claim of impeachment, they thought infinitely a better security not only for their constitutional liberty, but against the vices of administration, than the reservation of a right so difficult in the practice, so uncertain in the issue, and often so mischievous in the consequences, as that of 'cashiering their governors.'

Dr Price, in this sermon,* condemns very properly the practice of gross, adulatory addresses to kings. Instead of this fulsome style, he proposes that his majesty should be told, on occasions of congratulation, that 'he is to consider himself as more properly the servant than the sovereign of his people.' For a compliment, this new form of address does not seem to be very soothing. Those who are servants, in name, as well as in effect, do not like to be told of their situation, their duty, and their obligations. The slave, in the old play, tells his master, '*Haec commemoratio est quasi exprobratio.*'[23] It is not pleasant as compliment; it is not wholesome as instruction. After all, if the king were to bring himself to echo this new kind of address, to adopt it in terms, and even to take the appellation of Servant of the People as his royal style, how either he or we should be much mended by it, I cannot imagine. I have seen very assuming letters, signed, Your most obedient humble servant. The proudest domination that ever was endured on earth took a title of still greater humility than that which is now proposed for sovereigns by the Apostle of Liberty. Kings and nations were trampled upon by the foot of one calling himself 'the Servant of Servants;' and mandates for deposing sovereigns were sealed with the signet of 'the Fisherman.'[24]

I should have considered all this as no more than a sort of flippant vain discourse, in which, as in an unsavoury fume, several persons suffer the spirit of liberty to evaporate, if it were not plainly in support of the idea, and a part of the scheme of 'cashiering kings for misconduct.' In that light it is worth some observation.

Kings, in one sense, are undoubtedly the servants of the

* P. 22, 23, 24.

people, because their power has no other rational end than
that of the general advantage; but it is not true that they
are, in the ordinary sense (by our constitution, at least)
any thing like servants; the essence of whose situation is
to obey the commands of some other, and to be remove-
able at pleasure. But the king of Great Britain obeys no
other person; all other persons are individually, and collectively too, under him, and owe to him a legal obedience.
The law, which knows neither to flatter nor to insult, calls
this high magistrate, not our servant, as this humble Divine
calls him, but 'our sovereign Lord the King;' and we, on
our parts, have learned to speak only the primitive language of the law, and not the confused jargon of their
Babylonian pulpits.

As he is not to obey us, but as we are to obey the law in
him, our constitution has made no sort of provision towards rendering him, as a servant, in any degree responsible. Our constitution knows nothing of a magistrate like
the *Justicia* of Arragon;[ac] nor of any court legally appointed, nor of any process legally settled for submitting
the king to the responsibility belonging to all servants. In
this he is not distinguished from the commons and the
lords; who, in their several public capacities, can never be
called to an account for their conduct; although the Revolution Society chooses to assert, in direct opposition to one
of the wisest and most beautiful parts of our constitution,
that 'a king is no more than the first servant of the public,
created by it, *and responsible to it.*'

Ill would our ancestors at the Revolution have deserved
their fame for wisdom, if they had found no security for
their freedom, but in rendering their government feeble in
its operations, and precarious in its tenure; if they had
been able to contrive no better remedy against arbitrary
power than civil confusion. Let these gentlemen state who
that *representative* public is to whom they will affirm the

king, as a servant, to be responsible. It will be then time enough for me to produce to them the positive statute law which affirms that he is not.

The ceremony of cashiering kings, of which these gentlemen talk so much at their ease, can rarely, if ever, be performed without force. It then becomes a case of war, and not of constitution. Laws are commanded to hold their tongues amongst arms; and tribunals fall to the ground with the peace they are no longer able to uphold. The Revolution of 1688 was obtained by a just war, in the only case in which any war, and much more a civil war, can be just. 'Justa bella quibus *necessaria*.'[26] The question of dethroning, or, if these gentlemen like the phrase better, 'cashiering kings,' will always be, as it has always been, an extraordinary question of state, and wholly out of the law; a question (like all other questions of state) of dispositions, and of means, and of probable consequences, rather than of positive rights. As it was not made for common abuses, so it is not to be agitated by common minds. The speculative line of demarcation, where obedience ought to end, and resistance must begin, is faint, obscure, and not easily definable. It is not a single act, or a single event, which determines it. Governments must be abused and deranged indeed, before it can be thought of; and the prospect of the future must be as bad as the experience of the past. When things are in that lamentable condition, the nature of the disease is to indicate the remedy to those whom nature has qualified to administer in extremities this critical, ambiguous, bitter portion to a distempered state. Times and occasions, and provocations, will teach their own lessons. The wise will determine from the gravity of the case; the irritable from sensibility to oppression; the high-minded from disdain and indignation at abusive power in unworthy hands; the brave and bold from the love of honourable danger in a generous cause: but, with or without right, a revolution will be the very last resource of the thinking and the good.

The third head of right, asserted by the pulpit of the Old Jewry, namely, the 'right to form a government for ourselves,' has, at least, as little countenance from any thing done at the Revolution, either in precedent or principle, as the two first of their claims. The Revolution was made to preserve our *antient* indisputable laws and liberties, and that *antient* constitution of government which is our only security for law and liberty. If you are desirous of knowing the spirit of our constitution, and the policy which predominated in that great period which has secured it to this hour, pray look for both in our histories, in our records, in our acts of parliament, and journals of parliament, and not in the sermons of the Old Jewry, and the after-dinner toasts of the Revolution Society. – In the former you will find other ideas and another language. Such a claim is as ill-suited to our temper and wishes as it is unsupported by any appearance of authority. The very idea of the fabrication of a new government, is enough to fill us with disgust and horror. We wished at the period of the Revolution, and do now wish, to derive all we possess as *an inheritance from our forefathers*. Upon that body and stock of inheritance we have taken care not to inoculate any cyon alien to the nature of the original plant. All the reformations we have hitherto made, have proceeded upon the principle of reference to antiquity; and I hope, nay I am persuaded, that all those which possibly may be made hereafter, will be carefully formed upon analogical precedent, authority, and example.

Our oldest reformation is that of Magna Charta. You will see that Sir Edward Coke, that great oracle of our law, and indeed all the great men who follow him, to Blackstone,* are industrious to prove the pedigree of our liber-

* See Blackstone's Magna Charta, printed at Oxford, 1759.

ties.[27] They endeavour to prove, that the antient charter, the Magna Charta of King John, was connected with another positive charter from Henry I. and that both the one and the other were nothing more than a re-affirmance of the still more antient standing law of the kingdom. In the matter of fact, for the greater part, these authors appear to be in the right; perhaps not always: but if the lawyers mistake in some particulars, it proves my position still the more strongly; because it demonstrates the powerful pre-possession towards antiquity, with which the minds of all our lawyers and legislators, and of all the people whom they wish to influence, have been always filled; and the stationary policy of this kingdom in considering their most sacred rights and franchises as an *inheritance*.

In the famous law of the 3d of Charles I. called the *Petition of Right*, the parliament says to the king, 'your subjects have *inherited* this freedom,' claiming their franchises not on abstract principles 'as the rights of men,' but as the rights of Englishmen, and as a patrimony derived from their forefathers. Selden,[28] and the other profoundly learned men, who drew this petition of right, were as well acquainted, at least, with all the general theories concerning the 'rights of men,' as any of the discoursers in our pulpits, or on your tribune; full as well as Dr Price, or as the Abbé Seyes.[29] But, for reasons worthy of that practical wisdom which superseded their theoretic science, they preferred this positive, recorded, *hereditary* title to all which can be dear to the man and the citizen, to that vague speculative right, which exposed their sure inheritance to be scrambled for and torn to pieces by every wild litigious spirit.

The same policy pervades all the laws which have since been made for the preservation of our liberties. In the 1st of William and Mary, in the famous statute, called the Declaration of Right, the two houses utter not a syllable of

'a right to frame a government for themselves.' You will
see, that their whole care was to secure the religion, laws,
and liberties, that had been long possessed, and had been
lately endangered. 'Taking* into their most serious consideration the *best* means for making such an establishment, that their religion, laws, and liberties, might not be
in danger of being again subverted,' they auspicate all their
proceedings, by stating as some of those *best* means, 'in the
first place' to do '*as their ancestors in like cases have usually* done for vindicating their *antient* rights and liberties,
to *declare*;' – and then they pray the king and queen, 'that
it may be *declared* and enacted, that *all and singular* the
rights and liberties *asserted and declared* are the true *antient* and indubitable rights and liberties of the people of
this kingdom.'

You will observe, that from Magna Charta to the Declaration of Right, it has been the uniform policy of our
constitution to claim and assert our liberties, as an *en-
tailed inheritance* derived to us from our forefathers, and
to be transmitted to our posterity; as an estate specially belonging to the people of this kingdom without any reference whatever to any other more general or prior right. By
this means our constitution preserves an unity in so great
a diversity of its parts. We have an inheritable crown; an
inheritable peerage; and an house of commons and a people
inheriting privileges, franchises, and liberties, from a long
line of ancestors.

This policy appears to me to be the result of profound
reflection; or rather the happy effect of following nature,
which is wisdom without reflection, and above it. A spirit
of innovation is generally the result of a selfish temper and
confined views.[30] People will not look forward to posterity,
who never look backward to their ancestors. Besides, the
people of England well know, that the idea of inheritance

*1 W. and M.

furnishes a sure principle of conservation, and a sure principle of transmission; without at all excluding a principle
of improvement. It leaves acquisition free; but it secures
what it acquires. Whatever advantages are obtained by a
state proceeding on these maxims, are locked fast as in a
sort of family settlement; grasped as in a kind of mortmain for ever. By a constitutional policy, working after
the pattern of nature, we receive, we hold, we transmit our
government and our privileges, in the same manner in
which we enjoy and transmit our property and our lives.
The institutions of policy, the goods of fortune, the gifts
of Providence, are handed down, to us and from us, in the
same course and order. Our political system is placed in a
just correspondence and symmetry with the order of the
world, and with the mode of existence decreed to a permanent body composed of transitory parts; wherein, by
the disposition of a stupendous wisdom, moulding together
the great mysterious incorporation of the human race, the
whole, at one time, is never old, or middle-aged, or young,
but in a condition of unchangeable constancy, moves on
through the varied tenour of perpetual decay, fall, renovation, and progression. Thus, by preserving the method of
nature in the conduct of the state, in what we improve we
are never wholly new; in what we retain we are never
wholly obsolete. By adhering in this manner and on those
principles to our forefathers, we are guided not by the
superstition of antiquarians, but by the spirit of philosophic analogy. In this choice of inheritance we have given
to our frame of polity the image of a relation in blood;
binding up the constitution of our country with our dearest domestic ties; adopting our fundamental laws into the
bosom of our family affections; keeping inseparable, and
cherishing with the warmth of all their combined and mutually reflected charities, our state, our hearths, our sepul-
chres, and our altars.

Through the same plan of a conformity to nature in our artificial institutions, and by calling in the aid of her unerring and powerful instincts, to fortify the fallible and feeble contrivances of our reason, we have derived several other, and those no small benefits, from considering our liberties in the light of an inheritance. Always acting as if in the presence of canonized forefathers, the spirit of freedom, leading in itself to misrule and excess, is tempered with an awful gravity. This idea of a liberal descent inspires us with a sense of habitual native dignity, which prevents that upstart insolence almost inevitably adhering to and disgracing those who are the first acquirers of any distinction. By this means our liberty becomes a noble freedom. It carries an imposing and majestic aspect. It has a pedigree and illustrating ancestors. It has its bearings and its ensigns armorial. It has its gallery of portraits; its monumental inscriptions; its records, evidences, and titles. We procure reverence to our civil institutions on the principle upon which nature teaches us to revere individual men; on account of their age; and on account of those from whom they are descended. All your sophisters cannot produce any thing better adapted to preserve a rational and manly freedom than the course that we have pursued, who have chosen our nature rather than our speculations, our breasts rather than our inventions, for the great conservatories and magazines of our rights and privileges.

You might, if you pleased, have profited of our example, and have given to your recovered freedom a correspondent dignity. Your privileges, though discontinued, were not lost to memory. Your constitution, it is true, whilst you were out of possession, suffered waste and dilapidation; but you possessed in some parts the walls, and in all the foundations of a noble and venerable castle. You might have repaired those walls; you might have built on those old foundations. Your constitution was suspended before it was perfected; but you had the elements of a constitution very nearly as good as could be wished.[31] In your old states you possessed that variety of parts corresponding with the various descriptions of which your community was happily composed; you had all that combination, and all that opposition of interests, you had that action and counteraction which, in the natural and in the political world, from the reciprocal struggle of discordant powers, draws out the harmony of the universe. These opposed and conflicting interests, which you considered as so great a blemish in your old and in our present constitution, interpose a salutary check to all precipitate resolutions; They render deliberation a matter not of choice, but of necessity; they make all change a subject of *compromise*, which naturally begets moderation; they produce *temperaments*, preventing the sore evil of harsh, crude, unqualified reformations; and rendering all the headlong exertions of arbitrary power, in the few or in the many, for ever impracticable. Through that diversity of members and interests, general liberty had as many securities as there were separate views in the several orders; whilst by pressing down the whole by the weight of a real monarchy, the separate parts would have been prevented from warping and starting from their allotted places.

You had all these advantages in your antient states; but you chose to act as if you had never been moulded into civil society, and had every thing to begin anew. You began ill, because you began by despising every thing that belonged to you. You set up your trade without a capital. If the last generations of your country appeared without much lustre in your eyes, you might have passed them by, and derived your claims from a more early race of ancestors. Under a pious predilection for those ancestors, your imaginations would have realized in them a standard of virtue and wisdom, beyond the vulgar practice of the hour: and you would have risen with the example to whose imitation you aspired. Respecting your forefathers, you would have been taught to respect yourselves. You would not have chosen to consider the French as a people of yesterday, as a nation of low-born servile wretches until the emancipating year of 1789. In order to furnish, at the expence of your honour, an excuse to your apologists here for several enormities of yours, you would not have been content to be represented as a gang of Maroon slaves,[32] suddenly broke loose from the house of bondage, and therefore to be pardoned for your abuse of the liberty to which you were not accustomed and ill fitted. Would it not, my worthy friend, have been wiser to have you thought, what I, for one, always thought you, a generous and gallant nation, long misled to your disadvantage by your high and romantic sentiments of fidelity, honour, and loyalty; that events had been unfavourable to you, but that you were not enslaved through any illiberal or servile disposition; that in your most devoted submission, you were actuated by a principle of public spirit, and that it was your country you worshipped, in the person of your king? Had you made it to be understood, that in the delusion of this amiable error you had gone further than your wise ancestors; that you were resolved to resume your ancient privileges, whilst you preserved the spirit of your ancient and your recent loyalty and honour; or, if diffident of yourselves, and not clearly discerning the almost obliterated constitution of your ancestors, you had looked to your neighbours in this land, who had kept alive the ancient principles and models of the old common law of Europe meliorated and adapted to its present state – by following wise examples you would have given new examples of wisdom to the world. You would have rendered the cause of liberty venerable in the eyes of every worthy mind in every nation. You would have shamed despotism

from the earth, by shewing that freedom was not only
reconcileable, but as, when well disciplined it is, auxiliary
to law. You would have had an unoppressive but a productive revenue. You would have had a flourishing commerce to feed it. You would have had a free constitution;
a potent monarchy; a disciplined army; a reformed and
venerated clergy; a mitigated but spirited nobility, to lead
your virtue, not to overlay it; you would have had a
liberal order of commons, to emulate and to recruit that
nobility; you would have had a protected, satisfied, laborious, and obedient people, taught to seek and to recognize
the happiness that is to be found by virtue in all conditions; in which consists the true moral equality of mankind, and not in that monstrous fiction, which, by
inspiring false ideas and vain expectations into men destined to travel in the obscure walk of laborious life, serves
only to aggravate and imbitter that real inequality, which
it never can remove; and which the order of civil life
establishes as much for the benefit of those whom it must
leave in an humble state, as those whom it is able to exalt
to a condition more splendid, but not more happy. You
had a smooth and easy career of felicity and glory laid open
to you, beyond any thing recorded in the history of the
world; but you have shewn that difficulty is good for man.

Compute your gains: see what is got by those extravagant and presumptuous speculations which have taught
your leaders to despise all their predecessors, and all their
contemporaries, and even to despise themselves, until the
moment in which they became truly despicable. By following those false lights, France has bought undignified
calamities at a higher price than any nation has purchased
the most unequivocal blessings! France has bought poverty by crime! France has not sacrificed her virtue to her
interest; but she has abandoned her interest, that she might
prostitute her virtue. All other nations have begun the

fabric of a new government, or the reformation of an old, by establishing originally, or by enforcing with greater exactness some rites or other of religion. All other people have laid the foundations of civil freedom in severer manners, and a system of a more austere and masculine morality. France, when she let loose the reins of regal authority, doubled the licence, of a ferocious dissoluteness in manners, and of an insolent irreligion in opinions and practices; and has extended through all ranks of life, as if she were communicating some privilege, or laying open some secluded benefit, all the unhappy corruptions that usually were the disease of wealth and power. This is one of the new principles of equality in France.

France, by the perfidy of her leaders, has utterly disgraced the tone of lenient council in the cabinets of princes, and disarmed it of its most potent topics. She has sanctified the dark suspicious maxims of tyrannous distrust; and taught kings to tremble at (what will hereafter be called) the delusive plausibilities, of moral politicians. Sovereigns will consider those who advise them to place an unlimited confidence in their people, as subverters of their thrones; as traitors who aim at their destruction, by leading their easy good-nature, under specious pretences, to admit combinations of bold and faithless men into a participation of their power. This alone (if there were nothing else) is an irreparable calamity to you and to mankind. Remember that your parliament of Paris told your king, that in calling the states together, he had nothing to fear but the prodigal excess of their zeal in providing for the support of the throne. It is right that these men should hide their heads. It is right that they should bear their part in the ruin which their counsel has brought on their sovereign and their country. Such sanguine declarations tend to lull authority asleep; to encourage it rashly to engage in perilous adventures of untried policy; to neglect those provisions, preparations, and precautions, which distinguish benevolence from imbecillity; and without which no man can answer for the salutary effect of any abstract plan of government or of freedom. For want of these, they have seen the medicine of the state corrupted into its poison. They have seen the French rebel against a mild and lawful monarch, with more fury, outrage, and insult, than ever any people has been known to rise against the most illegal usurper, or the most sanguinary tyrant. Their resistance was made to concession; their revolt was from protection; their blow was aimed at an hand holding out graces, favours, and immunities.

This was unnatural. The rest is in order. They have found their punishment in their success. Laws overturned; tribunals subverted; industry without vigour; commerce expiring; the revenue unpaid, yet the people impoverished; a church pillaged, and a state not relieved; civil and military anarchy made the constitution of the kingdom; every thing human and divine sacrificed to the idol of public credit, and national bankruptcy the consequence; and to crown all, the paper securities of new, precarious, tottering power, the discredited paper securities of impoverished fraud, and beggared rapine, held out as a currency for the support of an empire, in lieu of the two great recognized species that represent the lasting conventional credit of mankind, which disappeared and hid themselves in the earth from whence they came, when the principle of property, whose creatures and representatives they are, was systematically subverted.

Were all these dreadful things necessary? were they the inevitable results of the desperate struggle of determined patriots, compelled to wade through blood and tumult, to the quiet shore of a tranquil and prosperous liberty? No! nothing like it. The fresh ruins of France, which shock our feelings wherever we can turn our eyes, are not the devastation of civil war; they are the sad but instructive monuments of rash and ignorant counsel in time of profound peace. They are the display of inconsiderate and presumptuous, because unresisted and irresistible authority. The persons who have thus squandered away the precious treasure of their crimes, the persons who have made this prodigal and wild waste of public evils (the last stake reserved for the ultimate ransom of the state) have met in their progress with little, or rather with no opposition at all. Their whole march was more like a triumphal procession than the progress of a war. Their pioneers have gone before them, and demolished and laid every thing level at their feet. Not one drop of *their* blood have they shed in the cause of the country they have ruined. They have made no sacrifices to their projects of greater consequence than their shoe-buckles, whilst they were imprisoning their king, murdering their fellow citizens, and bathing in tears, and plunging in poverty and distress, thousands of worthy men and worthy families. Their cruelty has not even been the base result of fear. It has been the effect of their sense of perfect safety, in authorizing treasons, robberies, rapes, assassinations, slaughters, and burnings throughout their harrassed land. But the cause of all was plain from the beginning.

This unforced choice, this fond election of evil, would appear perfectly unaccountable, if we did not consider the composition of the National Assembly; I do not mean its formal constitution, which, as it now stands, is exceptionable enough, but the materials of which in a great measure it is composed, which is of ten thousand times greater consequence than all the formalities in the world. If we were to know nothing of this Assembly but by its title and function, no colours could paint to the imagination any thing more venerable. In that light the mind of an enquirer, subdued by such an awful image as that of the virtue and wisdom of a whole people collected into a focus, would pause and hesitate in condemning things even of the very worst aspect. Instead of blameable, they would appear only mysterious. But no name, no power, no function, no artificial institution whatsoever, can make the men of whom any system of authority is composed, any other than God, and nature, and education, and their habits of life have made them. Capacities beyond these the people have not to give. Virtue and wisdom may be the objects of their choice; but their choice confers neither the one nor the other on those upon whom they lay their ordaining hands. They have not the engagement of nature, they have not the promise of revelation for any such powers.

After I had read over the list of the persons and descriptions elected into the *Tiers Etat*, nothing which they afterwards did could appear astonishing. Among them, indeed, I saw some of known rank; some of shining talents; but of any practical experience in the state, not one man was to be found. The best were only men of theory. But whatever the distinguished few may have been, it is the substance and mass of the body which constitutes its character, and must finally determine its direction. In all bodies, those who will lead, must also, in a considerable degree, follow. They must conform their propositions to the taste, talent, and disposition of those whom they wish to conduct: therefore, if an Assembly is viciously or feebly composed in a very great part of it, nothing but such a supreme degree of virtue as very rarely appears in the world, and for that reason cannot enter into calculation, will prevent the men of talents disseminated through it from becoming only the expert instruments of absurd projects! If what is the more likely event, instead of that unusual degree of virtue, they should be actuated by sinister ambition and a lust of meretricious glory, then the feeble part of the Assembly, to whom at first they conform, becomes in its turn the dupe and instrument of their designs. In this political traffick the leaders will be obliged to bow to the ignorance of their followers, and the followers to become subservient to the worst designs of their leaders.

To secure any degree of sobriety in the propositions made by the leaders in any public assembly, they ought to respect, in some degree perhaps to fear, those whom they conduct. To be led any otherwise than blindly, the followers must be qualified, if not for actors, at least for judges; they must also be judges of natural weight and authority. Nothing can secure a steady and moderate conduct in such assemblies, but that the body of them should be respectably composed, in point of condition in life, of permanent property, of education, and of such habits as enlarge and liberalize the understanding.

In the calling of the states general of France, the first thing which struck me, was a great departure from the antient course. I found the representation for the Third Estate composed of six hundred persons. They were equal in number to the representatives of both the other orders. If the orders were to act separately, the number would not, beyond the consideration of the expence, be of much moment. But when it became apparent that the three orders were to be melted down into one, the policy and necessary effect of this numerous representation became obvious. A very small desertion from either of the other two orders must throw the power of both into the hands of the third. In fact, the whole power of the state was soon resolved into that body. Its due composition became therefore of infinitely the greater importance.

Judge, Sir, of my surprize, when I found that a very great proportion of the Assembly (a majority, I believe, of the members who attended) was composed of practitioners in the law. It was composed not of distinguished magistrates, who had given pledges to their country of their science, prudence, and integrity; not of leading advocates, the glory of the bar; not of renowned professors in universities; – but for the far greater part, as it must in such a number, of the inferior, unlearned, mechanical, merely instrumental members of the profession. There were distinguished exceptions; but the general composition was of obscure provincial advocates, of stewards of petty local jurisdictions, country attornies, notaries, and the whole train of the ministers of municipal litigation, the fomentors and conductors of the petty war of village vexation. From the moment I read the list I saw distinctly, and very nearly as it has happened, all that was to follow.

The degree of estimation in which any profession is held becomes the standard of the estimation in which the professors hold themselves. Whatever the personal merits of many individual lawyers might have been, and in many it was undoubtedly very considerable, in that military kingdom, no part of the profession had been much regarded, except the highest of all, who often united to their professional offices great family splendour, and were invested with great power and authority. These certainly were highly respected, and even with no small degree of awe. The next rank was not much esteemed; the mechanical part was in a very low degree of repute.

Whenever the supreme authority is invested in a body so composed, it must evidently produce the consequences of supreme authority placed in the hands of men not taught habitually to respect themselves; who had no previous fortune in character at stake; who could not be expected to bear with moderation, or to conduct with discretion, a power which they themselves, more than any others, must be surprized to find in their hands. Who could flatter himself that these men, suddenly, and, as it were, by enchantment, snatched from the humblest rank of subordination, would not be intoxicated with their unprepared greatness? Who could conceive, that men who are habitually meddling, daring, subtle, active, of litigious dispositions and unquiet minds, would easily fall back into their old condition of obscure contention, and laborious, low, unprofitable chicane? Who could doubt but that, at any expence to the state, of which they understood nothing, they must pursue their private interests, which they understood but too well? It was not an event depending on chance or contingency. It was inevitable; it was necessary; it was planted in the nature of things. They must *join* (if their capacity did not permit them to *lead*) in any project which could procure to them a *litigious constitution*; which could lay open to them those innumerable lucrative jobs which follow in the train of all great convulsions and revolutions in the state, and particularly in all great and violent permutations of property. Was it to be expected that they would attend to the stability of property, whose existence had always depended upon whatever rendered property questionable, ambiguous, and insecure? Their objects would be enlarged with their elevation, but their disposition and habits, and mode of accomplishing their designs, must remain the same.

Well! but these men were to be tempered and restrained by other descriptions, of more sober minds, and more enlarged understandings. Were they then to be awed by the super-eminent authority and awful dignity of an handful of country clowns who have seats in that Assembly, some of whom are said not to be able to read and write? and by not a greater number of traders, who, though somewhat more instructed, and more conspicuous in the order of society, had never known any thing beyond their counting-house? No! both these descriptions were more formed to be overborne and swayed by the intrigues and artifices of lawyers, than to become their counterpoise. With such a dangerous disproportion, the whole must needs be governed by them. To the faculty of law was joined a pretty considerable proportion of the faculty of medicine. This faculty had not, any more than that of the law, possessed in France its just estimation. Its professors therefore must have the qualities of men not habituated to sentiments of dignity. But supposing they had ranked as they ought to do, and as with us they do actually, the sides of sick beds are not the academies for forming statesmen and legislators. Then came the dealers in stocks and funds, who must be eager, at any expence, to change their ideal paper wealth for the more solid substance of land. To these were joined men of other descriptions, from whom as little knowledge of or attention to the interests of a great state was to be expected, and as little regard to the stability of any institution; men formed to be instruments, not controls. Such in general was the composition of the *Tiers Etat* in the National Assembly; in which was scarcely to be perceived the slightest traces of what we call the natural landed interest of the country.

We know that the British house of commons, without shutting its doors to any merit in any class, is, by the sure operation of adequate causes, filled with every thing illustrious in rank, in descent, in hereditary and in acquired opulence, in cultivated talents, in military, civil, naval, and politic distinction, that the country can afford. But supposing, what hardly can be supposed as a case, that the house of commons should be composed in the same manner with the Tiers Etat in France, would this dominion of chicane be borne with patience, or even conceived without horror? God forbid I should insinuate any thing derogatory to that profession, which is another priesthood, administering the rites of sacred justice. But whilst I revere men in the functions which belong to them, and would do, as much as one man can do, to prevent their exclusion from any, I cannot, to flatter them, give the lye to nature. They are good and useful in the composition;

they must be mischievous if they preponderate so as virtually to become the whole. Their very excellence in their peculiar functions may be far from a qualification for others. It cannot escape observation, that when men are too much confined to professional and faculty habits, and, as it were, inveterate in the recurrent employment of that narrow circle, they are rather disabled than qualified for whatever depends on the knowledge of mankind, on experience in mixed affairs, on a comprehensive connected view of the various complicated external and internal interests which go to the formation of that multifarious thing called a state.

After all, if the house of commons were to have an wholly professional and faculty composition, what is the power of the house of commons, circumscribed and shut in by the immovable barriers of laws, usages, positive rules of doctrine and practice, counterpoized by the house of lords, and every moment of its existence at the discretion of the crown to continue, prorogue, or dissolve us? The power of the house of commons, direct or indirect, is indeed great; and long may it be able to preserve its greatness, and the spirit belonging to true greatness, at the full; and it will do so, as long as it can keep the breakers of law in India from becoming the makers of law for England.[33] The power, however, of the house of commons, when least diminished, is as a drop of water in the ocean, compared to that residing in a settled majority of your National Assembly. That Assembly, since the destruction of the orders, has no fundamental law, no strict convention, no respected usage to restrain it. Instead of finding themselves obliged to conform to a fixed constitution, they have a power to make a constitution which shall conform to their designs. Nothing in heaven or upon earth can serve as a control on them. What ought to be the heads, the hearts, the dispositions, that are qualified, or that dare, not only to make laws under a fixed constitution, but at one heat to strike out a totally new constitution for a great kingdom, and in every part of it, from the monarch on the throne to the vestry of a parish? But – '*fools rush in where angels fear to tread.*' In such a state of unbounded power, for undefined and undefinable purposes, the evil of a moral and almost physical inaptitude of the man to the function must be the greatest we can conceive to happen in the management of human affairs.

Having considered the composition of the third estate as it stood in its original frame, I took a view of the representatives of the clergy. There too it appeared, that full as little regard was had to the general security of property, or to the aptitude of the deputies for their public purposes, in the principles of their election. That election was so contrived as to send a very large proportion of mere country curates to the great and arduous work of new-modelling a state; men who never had seen the state so much as in a picture; men who knew nothing of the world beyond the bounds of an obscure village; who, immersed in hopeless poverty, could regard all property, whether secular or ecclesiastical, with no other eye than that of envy; among whom must be many, who, for the smallest hope of the meanest dividend in plunder, would readily join in any attempts upon a body of wealth, in which they could hardly look to have any share, except in a general scramble. Instead of balancing the power of the active chicaners in the other assembly, these curates must necessarily become the active coadjutors, or at best the passive instruments of those by whom they had been habitually guided in their petty village concerns. They too could hardly be the most conscientious of their kind, who, presuming upon their incompetent understanding, could intrigue for a trust which led them from their natural relation to their flocks, and their natural spheres of action, to undertake the regeneration of kingdoms. This preponderating weight being added to the force of the body of chicane in the Tiers Etat, compleated that momentum of ignorance, rashness, presumption, and lust of plunder, which nothing has been able to resist.

To observing men it must have appeared from the beginning, that the majority of the Third Estate, in conjunction with such a deputation from the clergy as I have described, whilst it pursued the destruction of the nobility, would inevitably become subservient to the worst designs of individuals in that class. In the spoil and humiliation of their own order these individuals would possess a sure fund for the pay of their new followers. To squander away the objects which made the happiness of their fellows, would be to them no sacrifice at all. Turbulent, discontented men of quality, in proportion as they are puffed up with personal pride and arrogance, generally despise their own order. One of the first symptoms they discover of a selfish and mischievous ambition, is a profligate disregard of a dignity which they partake with others. To be attached to the subdivision, to love the little platoon we belong to in society, is the first principle (the germ as it were) of public affections. It is the first link in the series by which we proceed towards a love to our country and to mankind. The interests of that portion of social arrangement is a trust in the hands of all those who compose it; and as none but bad men would justify it in abuse, none but traitors would barter it away for their own personal advantage.

There were, in the time of our civil troubles in England (I do not know whether you have any such in your Assembly in France) several persons, like the then Earl of Holland,[34] who by themselves or their families had brought an odium on the throne, by the prodigal dispensation of its bounties towards them, who afterwards joined in the rebellions arising from the discontents of which they were themselves the cause; men who helped to subvert that throne to which they owed, some of them, their existence, others all that power which they employed to ruin their benefactor. If any bounds are set to the rapacious demands of that sort of people, or that others are permitted to partake in the objects they would engross, revenge and envy soon fill up the craving void that is left in their avarice. Confounded by the complication of distempered passions, their reason is disturbed; their views become vast and perplexed; to others inexplicable; to themselves uncertain. They find, on all sides, bounds to their unprincipled ambition in any fixed order of things. But in the fog and haze of confusion all is enlarged, and appears without any limit.

When men of rank sacrifice all ideas of dignity to an ambition without a distinct object, and work with low instruments and for low ends, the whole composition becomes low and base. Does not something like this now appear in France? Does it not produce something ignoble and inglorious? a kind of meanness in all the prevalent policy? a tendency in all that is done to lower along with individuals all the dignity and importance of the state? Other revolutions have been conducted by persons, who whilst they attempted or effected changes in the commonwealth, sanctified their ambition by advancing the dignity of the people whose peace they troubled. They had long views. They aimed at the rule, not at the destruction of their country. They were men of great civil, and great military talents, and if the terror, the ornament of their age. They were not like Jew brokers contending with each other who could best remedy with fraudulent circulation and depreciated paper the wretchedness and ruin brought on their country by their degenerate councils. The compliment made to one of the great bad men of the old stamp (Cromwell) by his kinsman, a favourite poet of that time, shews what it was he proposed, and what indeed to a great degree he accomplished in the success of his ambition:

> Still as *you* rise, the *state*, exalted too,
> Finds no distemper whilst 'tis chang'd by *you*;
> Chang'd like the world's great scene, when without noise
> The rising sun night's vulgar lights destroys.[35]

These disturbers were not so much like men usurping power, as asserting their natural place in society. Their rising was to illuminate and beautify the world. Their conquest over their competitors was by outshining them. The hand that, like a destroying angel, smote the country, communicated to it the force and energy under which it suffered. I do not say (God forbid) I do not say, that the virtues of such men were to be taken as a balance to their crimes; but they were some corrective to their effects. Such was, as I said, our Cromwell.[36] Such were your whole race of Guises, Condés, and Colignis.[37] Such the Richlieus, who in more quiet times acted in the spirit of a civil war. Such, as better men, and in a less dubious cause, were your Henry the 4th and your Sully,[38] though nursed in civil confusions, and not wholly without some of their taint. It is a thing to be wondered at, to see how very soon France, when she had a moment to respire, recovered and emerged from the longest and most dreadful civil war that ever was known in any nation. Why? Because, among all their massacres, they had not slain the *mind* in their country. A conscious dignity, a noble pride, a generous sense of glory and emulation, was not extinguished. On the contrary, it was kindled and inflamed. The organs also of the state, however shattered, existed. All the prizes of honour and virtue, all the rewards, all the distinctions, remained. But your present confusion, like a palsy, has attacked the fountain of life itself. Every person in your country, in a situation to be actuated by a principle of honour, is disgraced and degraded, and can entertain no sensation of life, except in a mortified and humiliated indignation. But

this generation will quickly pass away. The next generation of the nobility will resemble the artificers and clowns,
and money-jobbers, usurers, and Jews,[39] who will be always
their fellows, sometimes their masters. Believe me, Sir,
those who attempt to level, never equalize. In all societies,
consisting of various descriptions of citizens, some description must be uppermost. The levellers therefore only
change and pervert the natural order of things; they load
the edifice of society, by setting up in the air what the
solidity of the structure requires to be on the ground. The
associations of taylors and carpenters, of which the republic (of Paris, for instance) is composed, cannot be equal to
the situation, into which, by the worst of usurpations, an
usurpation on the prerogatives of nature, you attempt to
force them.

The chancellor of France[40] at the opening of the states,
said, in a tone of oratorial flourish, that all occupations
were honourable. If he meant only, that no honest employment was disgraceful, he would not have gone beyond the
truth. But in asserting, that any thing is honourable, we
imply some distinction in its favour. The occupation of an
hair-dresser, or of a working tallow-chandler, cannot be
a matter of honour to any person – to say nothing of a
number of other more servile employments. Such descriptions of men ought not to suffer oppression from the state;
but the state suffers oppression, if such as they, either individually or collectively, are permitted to rule. In this
you think you are combating prejudice, but you are at war
with nature.*

* Ecclesiasticus, chap. xxxviii, verse 24, 25. 'The wisdom of a
learned man cometh by opportunity of leisure : and he that hath
little business shall become wise.' – 'How can he get wisdom that
holdeth the plough, and that glorieth in the goad ; that driveth oxen ;
and is occupied in their labours ; and whose talk is of bullocks?'
Ver. 27. 'So every carpenter and work-master that laboureth night
and day.' &c.

I do not, my dear Sir, conceive you to be of that sophistical captious spirit, or of that uncandid dulness, as to require, for every general observation or sentiment, an explicit detail of the correctives and exceptions, which reason will presume to be included in all the general propositions which come from reasonable men. You do not imagine, that I wish to confine power, authority, and distinction to blood, and names, and titles. No, Sir. There is no qualification for government, but virtue and wisdom, actual or presumptive. Wherever they are actually found, they have, in whatever state, condition, profession or trade, the passport of Heaven to human place and honour. Woe to the country which would madly and impiously reject the service of the talents and virtues, civil, military, or religious, that are given to grace and to serve it; and would condemn to obscurity every thing formed to diffuse lustre and glory around a state. Woe to that country too, that passing into the opposite extreme, considers a low education, a mean contracted view of things, a sordid mercenary occupation, as a preferable title to command. Every thing ought to be open; but not indifferently to every man. No rotation; no appointment by lot; no mode of election operating in the spirit of sortition or rotation, can be generally good in a government conversant in extensive objects. Because they have no tendency, direct or indirect, to select the man with a view to the duty, or to accommodate the one to the other, I do not hesitate to say, that the road to eminence

---

Ver. 33. 'They shall not be sought for in public counsel, nor sit high in the congregation: They shall not sit on the judges seat, nor understand the sentence of judgement: they cannot declare justice and judgement, and they shall not be found where parables are spoken.'

Ver. 34. 'But they will maintain the state of the world.'

I do not determine whether this book be canonical, as the Gallican church (till lately) has considered it, or apocryphal, as here it is taken. I am sure it contains a great deal of sense, and truth.[41]

and power, from obscure condition, ought not to be made too easy, nor a thing too much of course. If rare merit be the rarest of all rare things, it ought to pass through some sort of probation. The temple of honour ought to be seated on an eminence. If it be open through virtue, let it be remembered too, that virtue is never tried but by some difficulty, and some struggle.

Nothing is a due and adequate representation of a state, that does not represent its ability, as well as its property. But as ability is a vigorous and active principle, and as property is sluggish, inert, and timid,[42] it never can be safe from the invasions of ability, unless it be, out of all proportion, predominant in the representation. It must be represented too in great masses of accumulation, or it is not rightly protected. The characteristic essence of property, formed out of the combined principles of its acquisition and conservation, is to be *unequal*. The great masses therefore which excite envy, and tempt rapacity, must be put out of the possibility of danger. Then they form a natural rampart about the lesser properties in all their gradations. The same quantity of property, which is by the natural course of things divided among many, has not the same operation. Its defensive power is weakened as it is diffused. In this diffusion each man's portion is less than what, in the eagerness of his desires, he may flatter himself to obtain by dissipating the accumulations of others. The plunder of the few would indeed give but a share inconceivably small in the distribution to the many. But the many are not capable of making this calculation; and those who lead them to rapine, never intend this distribution.

The power of perpetuating our property in our families is one of the most valuable and interesting circumstances belonging to it, and that which tends the most to the perpetuation of society itself. It makes our weakness subservient to our virtue; it grafts benevolence even upon avarice.

The possessors of family wealth, and of the distinction which attends hereditary possession (as most concerned in it) are the natural securities for this transmission. With us, the house of peers is formed upon this principle. It is wholly composed of hereditary property and hereditary distinction; and made therefore the third of the legislature; and in the last event, the sole judge of all property in all its subdivisions. The house of commons too, though not necessarily, yet in fact, is always so composed in the far greater part. Let those large proprietors be what they will, and they have their chance of being amongst the best, they are at the very worst, the ballast in the vessel of the commonwealth. For though hereditary wealth, and the rank which goes with it, are too much idolized by creeping sycophants, and the blind abject admirers of power, they are too rashly slighted in shallow speculations of the petulant, assuming, short-sighted coxcombs of philosophy. Some decent regulated pre-eminence, some preference (not exclusive appropriation) given to birth, is neither unnatural, nor unjust, nor impolitic.

It is said, that twenty-four millions ought to prevail over two hundred thousand. True; if the constitution of a kingdom be a problem of arithmetic. This sort of discourse does well enough with the lamp-post for its second: to men who *may* reason calmly, it is ridiculous. The will of the many, and their interest, must very often differ; and great will be the difference when they make an evil choice. A government of five hundred country attornies and obscure curates is not good for twenty-four millions of men, though it were chosen by eight and forty millions; nor is it the better for being guided by a dozen of persons of quality, who have betrayed their trust in order to obtain that power. At present, you seem in every thing to have strayed out of the high road of nature. The property of France does not govern it. Of course property is destroyed, and rational liberty has no existence. All you have got for the present is a paper circulation, and a stock-jobbing constitution: and as to the future, do you seriously think that the territory of France, upon the republican system of eighty-three independent municipalities (to say nothing of the parts that compose them) can ever be governed as one body, or can ever be set in motion by the impulse of one mind? When the National Assembly has completed its work, it will have accomplished its ruin. These commonwealths will not long bear a state of subjection to the republic of Paris. They will not bear that this one body should monopolize the captivity of the king, and the dominion over the assembly calling itself National. Each will keep its own portion of the spoil of the church to itself; and it will not suffer either that spoil, or the more just fruits of their industry, or the natural produce of their soil, to be sent to swell the insolence, or pamper the luxury of the mechanics of Paris. In this they will see none of the equality, under the pretence of which they have been tempted to throw off their allegiance to their sovereign, as well as the antient constitution of their country. There can be no capital city in such a constitution as they have lately made. They have forgot, that when they framed democratic governments, they had virtually dismembered their country. The person whom they persevere in calling king, has not power left to him by the hundredth part sufficient to hold together this collection of republics. The republic of Paris will endeavour indeed to compleat the debauchery of the army, and illegally to perpetuate the assembly, without resort to its constituents, as the means of continuing its despotism. It will make efforts, by becoming the heart of a boundless paper circulation, to draw every thing to itself; but in vain. All this policy in the end will appear as feeble as it is now violent.

If this be your actual situation, compared to the situation to which you were called, as it were by the voice of God and man, I cannot find it in my heart to congratulate you on the choice you have made, or the success which has attended your endeavours. I can as little recommend to any other nation a conduct grounded on such principles, and productive of such effects. That I must leave to those who can see further into your affairs than I am able to do, and who best know how far your actions are favourable to their designs. The gentlemen of the Revolution Society, who were so early in their congratulations, appear to be strongly of opinion that there is some scheme of politics relative to this country, in which your proceedings may, in some way, be useful. For your Dr Price, who seems to have speculated himself into no small degree of fervour upon this subject, addresses his auditory in the following very remarkable words: 'I cannot conclude without re-calling *particularly* to your recollection a consideration which I have *more than once alluded to*, and which prob-ably your thoughts have *been all along anticipating*; a con-sideration with which my *mind is impressed more than I can express*. I mean the consideration of the *favourable-ness of the present times to all exertions in the cause of liberty*.'

It is plain that the mind of this *political* Preacher was at the time big with some extraordinary design; and it is very probable, that the thoughts of his audience, who under-stood him better than I do, did all along run before him in his reflection, and in the whole train of consequences to which it led.

Before I read that sermon, I really thought I had lived in a free country; and it was an error I cherished, because it gave me a greater liking to the country I lived in. I was in-deed aware, that a jealous, ever-waking vigilance, to guard the treasure of our liberty, not only from invasion, but from decay and corruption, was our best wisdom and our first duty. However, I considered that treasure rather as a possession to be secured than as a prize to be contended for. I did not discern how the present time came to be so very favourable to all *exertions* in the cause of freedom. The present time differs from any other only by the circumstance of what is doing in France. If the example of that nation is to have an influence on this, I can easily conceive why some of their proceedings which have an unpleasant aspect, and are not quite reconcileable to humanity, generosity, good faith, and justice, are palliated with so much milky good-nature towards the actors, and borne with so much heroic fortitude towards the sufferers. It is certainly not prudent to discredit the authority of an example we mean to follow. But allowing this, we are led to a very natural question; – What is that cause of liberty, and what are those exertions in its favour, to which the example of France is so singularly auspicious? Is our monarchy to be annihilated, with all the laws, all the tribunals, and all the antient corporations of the kingdom? Is every land-mark of the country to be done away in favour of a geometrical and arithmetical constitution? Is the house of lords to be voted useless? Is episcopacy to be abolished? Are the church lands to be sold to Jews and jobbers; or given to bribe new-invented municipal republics into a participation in sacrilege? Are all the taxes to be voted grievances, and the revenue reduced to a patriotic contribution, or patriotic presents? Are silver shoe-buckles to be substituted in the place of the land tax and the malt tax, for the support of the naval strength of this kingdom? Are all orders, ranks, and distinctions to be confounded, that out of universal anarchy, joined to national bankruptcy, three or four thousand democracies should be formed into eighty-three, and that they may all, by some sort of unknown attractive power, be organized into one? For this great end, is the army to be seduced from its discipline and its fidelity, first, by every kind of debauchery, and then by the terrible precedent of a donative in the encrease of pay? Are the curates to be seduced from their bishops, by holding out to them the delusive hope of a dole out of the spoils of their own order? Are the citizens of London to be drawn from their allegiance, by feeding them at the expence of their fellow-subjects? Is a compulsory paper currency to be substituted in the place of the legal coin of this kingdom? Is what remains of the plundered stock of public revenue to be employed in the wild project of maintaining two armies to watch over and to fight with each other? – If these are the ends and means of the Revolution Society, I admit they are well assorted; and France may furnish them for both with precedents in point.

I see that your example is held out to shame us. I know that we are supposed a dull sluggish race, rendered passive by finding our situation tolerable; and prevented by a mediocrity of freedom from ever attaining to its full perfection. Your leaders in France began by affecting to admire, almost to adore, the British constitution; but as they advanced they came to look upon it with a sovereign contempt. The friends of your National Assembly amongst us have full as mean an opinion of what was formerly thought the glory of their country. The Revolution Society has discovered that the English nation is not free. They are convinced that the inequality in our representation is a 'defect in our constitution so *gross and palpable*, as to make it excellent chiefly in *form* and *theory*.'* That a representation in the legislature of a kingdom is not only the basis of all constitutional liberty in it, but of '*all legitimate government*; that without it a *government* is nothing but an *usurpation*;' – that 'when the representation is *partial*, the kingdom possesses liberty only *partially*; and if extremely partial it gives only a *semblance*; and if not only

* Discourse on the Love of our Country, 3d edit. p. 39.

extremely partial, but corruptly chosen, it becomes a *nuisance.*' Dr Price considers this inadequacy of representation
as our *fundamental grievance*; and though, as to the corruption of this semblance of representation, he hopes it is
not yet arrived to its full perfection of depravity; he fears
that 'nothing will be done towards gaining for us this *essential blessing,* until some *great abuse of power* again provokes our resentment, or some *great calamity* again alarms
our fears, or perhaps till the acquisition of a *pure and equal
representation by other countries,* whilst we are *mocked*
with the *shadow,* kindles our shame.' To this he subjoins a
note in these words. 'A representation, chosen chiefly by
the Treasury, and a *few* thousands of the *dregs* of the
people, who are generally paid for their votes.'

You will smile here at the consistency of those democratists, who, when they are not on their guard, treat the
humbler part of the community with the greatest contempt, whilst, at the same time, they pretend to make them
the depositories of all power. It would require a long discourse to point out to you the many fallacies that lurk in
the generality and equivocal nature of the terms 'inade-
quate representation.' I shall only say here, in justice to
that old-fashioned constitution, under which we have long
prospered, that our representation has been found perfectly adequate to all the purposes for which a representation of the people can be desired or devised. I defy the
enemies of our constitution to shew the contrary. To detail the particulars in which it is found so well to promote
its ends, would demand a treatise on our practical constitution. I state here the doctrine of the Revolutionists, only
that you and others may see, what an opinion these gentlemen entertain of the constitution of their country, and
why they seem to think that some great abuse of power,
or some great calamity, as giving a chance for the blessing of a constitution according to their ideas, would be

much palleated to their feelings; you see *why they* are so much enamoured of your fair and equal representation, which being once obtained, the same effects might follow. You see they consider our house of commons as only 'a semblance,' 'a form,' 'a theory,' 'a shadow,' 'a mockery,' perhaps 'a nuisance.'

These gentlemen value themselves on being systematic; and not without reason. They must therefore look on this gross and palpable defect of representation, this fundamental grievance (so they call it) as a thing not only vicious in itself, but as rendering our whole government absolutely *illegitimate*, and not at all better than a downright *usurpation*. Another revolution, to get rid of this illegitimate and usurped government, would of course be perfectly justifiable, if not absolutely necessary. Indeed their principle, if you observe it with any attention, goes much further than to an alteration in the election of the house of commons; for, if popular representation, or choice, is necessary to the *legitimacy* of all government, the house of lords is, at one stroke, bastardized and corrupted in blood. That house is no representative of the people at all, even in 'semblance or in form.' The case of the crown is altogether as bad. In vain the crown may endeavour to screen itself against these gentlemen by the authority of the establishment made on the Revolution. The Revolution which is resorted to for a title, on their system, wants a title itself. The Revolution is built, according to their theory, upon a basis not more solid than our present formalities, as it was made by an house of lords not representing any one but themselves; and by an house of commons exactly such as the present, that is, as they term it, by a mere 'shadow and mockery' of representation.

Something they must destroy, or they seem to themselves to exist for no purpose. One set is for destroying the civil power through the ecclesiastical; another for demolishing the ecclesiastick through the civil. They are aware that the worst consequences might happen to the public in accomplishing this double ruin of church and state; but they are so heated with their theories, that they give more than hints, that this ruin, with all the mischiefs that must lead to it and attend it, and which to themselves appear quite certain, would not be unacceptable to them, or very remote from their wishes. A man amongst them of great authority, and certainly of great talents,[43] speaking of a supposed alliance between church and state, says, 'perhaps *we must wait for the fall of the civil powers* before this most unnatural alliance be broken. Calamitous no doubt will that time be. But what convulsion in the political world ought to be a subject of lamentation, if it be attended with so desirable an effect?' You see with what a steady eye these gentlemen are prepared to view the greatest calamities which can befall their country!

It is no wonder therefore, that with these ideas of every thing in their constitution and government at home, either in church or state, as illegitimate and usurped, or, at best as a vain mockery, they look abroad with an eager and passionate enthusiasm. Whilst they are possessed by these ancestors, the fundamental laws of their country, the fixed notions, it is vain to talk to them of the practice of their form of a constitution, whose merits are confirmed by the solid test of long experience, and an increasing public strength and national prosperity. They despise experience as the wisdom of unlettered men; and as for the rest, they have wrought under-ground a mine that will blow up at one grand explosion all examples of antiquity, all precedents, charters, and acts of parliament. They have 'the rights of men.' Against these there can be no prescription; against these no agreement is binding: these admit no temperament, and no compromise: any thing withheld from their full demand is so much of fraud and injustice.

Against these their rights of men let no government look
for security in the length of its continuance, or in the
justice and lenity of its administration. The objections of
these speculatists, if its forms do not quadrate with their
theories, are as valid against such an old and beneficent
government as against the most violent tyranny, or the
greenest usurpation. They are always at issue with governments, not on a question of abuse, but a question of competency, and a question of title. I have nothing to say to
the clumsy subtilty of their political metaphysics. Let
them be their amusement in the schools. – '*Illa se jactet in
aula – Aeolus, et clauso ventorum carcere regnet.*'[44] But
let them not break prison to burst like a *Levanter*,[45] to
sweep the earth with their hurricane, and to break up the
fountains of the great deep to overwhelm us.

Far am I from denying in theory; full as far is my heart
from withholding in practice (if I were of power to give
or to withhold) the *real* rights of men. In denying their
false claims of right, I do not mean to injure those which
are real, and are such as their pretended rights would totally destroy. If civil society be made for the advantage of
man, all the advantages for which it is made become his
right. It is an institution of beneficence; and law itself is
only beneficence acting by a rule. Men have a right to live
by that rule; they have a right to justice; as between their
fellows, whether their fellows are in politic function or in
ordinary occupation. They have a right to the fruits of
their industry; and to the means of making their industry
fruitful. They have a right to the acquisitions of their
parents; to the nourishment and improvement of their offspring; to instruction in life, and to consolation in death.
Whatever each man can separately do, without trespassing
upon others, he has a right to do for himself; and he has
a right to a fair portion of all which society, with all its
combinations of skill and force, can do in his favour. In

this partnership all men have equal rights; but not to equal things. He that has but five shillings in the partnership, has as good a right to it, as he that has five hundred pounds has to his larger proportion. But he has not a right to an equal dividend in the product of the joint stock; and as to the share of power, authority, and direction which each individual ought to have in the management of the state, that I must deny to be amongst the direct original rights of man in civil society; for I have in my contemplation the civil social man, and no other. It is a thing to be settled by convention.

If civil society be the offspring of convention, that convention must be its law. That convention must limit and modify all the descriptions of constitution which are formed under it. Every sort of legislative judicial, or executory power are its creatures. They can have no being in any other state of things; and how can any man claim, under the conventions of civil society, rights which do not so much as suppose its existence? Rights which are absolutely repugnant to it? One of the first motives to civil society, and which becomes one of its fundamental rules, is, *that no man should be judge in his own cause*. By this each person has at once divested himself of the first fundamental right of uncovenanted man, that is, to judge for himself, and to assert his own cause. He abdicates all right to be his own governor. He inclusively, in a great measure, abandons the right of self-defence, the first law of nature. Men cannot enjoy the rights of an uncivil and of a civil state together. That he may obtain justice he gives up his right of determining what it is in points the most essential to him. That he may secure some liberty, he makes a surrender in trust of the whole of it.

Government is not made in virtue of natural rights, which may and do exist in total independence of it; and exist in much greater clearness, and in a much greater degree of abstract perfection: but their abstract perfection is their practical defect. By having a right to every thing they want every thing. Government is a contrivance of human wisdom to provide for human *wants*. Men have a right that these wants should be provided for by this wisdom. Among these wants is to be reckoned the want, out of civil society, of a sufficient restraint upon their passions. Society requires not only that the passions of individuals should be subjected, but that even in the mass and body as well as in the individuals, the inclinations of men should frequently be thwarted, their will controlled, and their passions brought into subjection. This can only be done *by a power out of themselves*; and not, in the exercise of its function, subject to that will and to those passions which it is its office to bridle and subdue. In this sense the restraints on men, as well as their liberties, are to be reckoned among their rights. But as the liberties and the restrictions vary with times and circumstances, and admit of infinite modifications, they cannot be settled upon any abstract rule; and nothing is so foolish as to discuss them upon that principle.

The moment you abate any thing from the full rights of men, each to govern himself, and suffer any artificial positive limitation upon those rights, from that moment the whole organization of government becomes a consideration of convenience. This it is which makes the constitution of a state, and the due distribution of its powers, a matter of the most delicate and complicated skill. It requires a deep knowledge of human nature and human necessities, and of the things which facilitate or obstruct the various ends which are to be pursued by the mechanism of civil institutions. The state is to have recruits to its strength, and remedies to its distempers. What is the use of discussing a man's abstract right to food or to medicine? The question is upon the method of procuring and administering them. In that deliberation I shall always advise to call in the aid of the farmer and the physician, rather than the professor of metaphysics.

The science of constructing a commonwealth, or renovating it, or reforming it, is, like every other experimental science, not to be taught *à priori*. Nor is it a short experience that can instruct us in that practical science; because the real effects of moral causes are not always immediate; but that which in the first instance is prejudicial may be excellent in its remoter operation; and its excellence may arise even from the ill effects it produces in the beginning. The reverse also happens; and very plausible schemes, with very pleasing commencements, have often shameful and lamentable conclusions. In states there are often some obscure and almost latent causes, things which appear at first view of little moment, on which a very great part of its prosperity or adversity may most essentially depend. The science of government being therefore so practical in itself, and intended for such practical purposes, a matter which requires experience, and even more experience than any person can gain in his whole life, however sagacious and observing he may be, it is with infinite caution that any man ought to venture upon pulling down an edifice which has answered in any tolerable degree for ages the common purposes of society, or on building it up again, without having models and patterns of approved utility before his eyes.

These metaphysic rights entering into common life, like rays of light which pierce into a dense medium, are, by the laws of nature, refracted from their straight line. Indeed in the gross and complicated mass of human passions and concerns, the primitive rights of men undergo such a variety of refractions and reflections, that it becomes absurd to talk of them as if they continued in the simplicity of their original direction. The nature of man is intricate;

the objects of society are of the greatest possible complexity; and therefore no simple disposition or direction of power can be suitable either to man's nature, or to the quality of his affairs. When I hear the simplicity of contrivance aimed at and boasted of in any new political constitutions, I am at no loss to decide that the artificers are grossly ignorant of their trade, or totally negligent of their duty. The simple governments are fundamentally defective, to say no worse of them. If you were to contemplate society in but one point of view, all these simple modes of polity are infinitely captivating. In effect each would answer its single end much more perfectly than the more complex is able to attain all its complex purposes. But it is better that the whole should be imperfectly and anomalously answered, than that, while some parts are provided for with great exactness, others might be totally neglected, or perhaps materially injured, by the over-care of a favourite member.

The pretended rights of these theorists are all extremes; and in proportion as they are metaphysically true, they are morally and politically false. The rights of men are in a sort of *middle*, incapable of definition, but not impossible to be discerned. The rights of men in governments are their advantages; and these are often in balances between differences of good; in compromises sometimes between good and evil, and sometimes, between evil and evil. Political reason is a computing principle; adding, subtracting, multiplying, and dividing, morally and not metaphysically or mathematically, true moral denominations.

By these theorists the right of the people is almost always sophistically confounded with their power. The body of the community, whenever it can come to act, can meet with no effectual resistance; but till power and right are the same, the whole body of them has no right inconsistent with virtue, and the first of all virtues, prudence.

Men have no right to what is not reasonable, and to what is not for their benefit; for though a pleasant writer said, *Liceat perire poetis*. When one of them, in cold blood, is said to have leaped into the flames of a volcanic revolution, *Ardentem frigidus Ætnam insiluit*,[46] I consider such a frolic rather as an unjustifiable poetic licence, than as one of the franchises of Parnassus; and whether he were poet or divine, or politician that chose to exercise this kind of right, I think that more wise, because more charitable thoughts would urge me rather to save the man, than to preserve his brazen slippers as the monuments of his folly.

The kind of anniversary sermons, to which a great part of what I write refers, if men are not shamed out of their present course, in commemorating the fact, will cheat many out of the principles, and deprive them of the benefits of the Revolution they commemorate. I confess to you, Sir, I never liked this continual talk of resistance and revolution, or the practice of making the extreme medicine of the constitution its daily bread. It renders the habit of society dangerously valetudinary: it is taking periodical doses of mercury sublimate, and swallowing down repeated provocatives of cantharides to our love of liberty.[47]

This distemper of remedy, grown habitual, relaxes and wears out, by a vulgar and prostituted use, the spring of that spirit which is to be exerted on great occasions. It was in the most patient period of Roman servitude that themes of tyrannicide made the ordinary exercise of boys at school – *cum perimit sævos classis numerosa tyrannos*.[48] In the ordinary state of things, it produces in a country like ours the worst effects, even on the cause of that liberty which it abuses with the dissoluteness of an extravagant speculation. Almost all the high-bred republicans of my time have, after a short space, become the most decided, thorough-paced courtiers; they soon left the business of a tedious, moderate, but practical resistance to those of us whom, in the pride and intoxication of their theories, they have slighted, as not much better than tories. Hypocrisy, of course, delights in the most sublime speculations; for, never intending to go beyond speculation, it costs nothing to have it magnificent. But even in cases where rather levity than fraud was to be suspected in these ranting speculations, the issue has been much the same. These professors, finding their extreme principles not applicable to cases which call only for a qualified, or, as I may say, civil and legal resistance, in such cases employ no resistance at all. It is with them a war or a revolution, or it is nothing. Finding their schemes of politics not adapted to the state of the world in which they live, they often come to think lightly of all public principle; and are ready, on their part, to abandon for a very trivial interest what they find of very trivial value. Some indeed are of more steady and persevering natures; but these are eager politicians out of parliament, who have little to tempt them to abandon their favourite projects. They have some change in the church or state, or both, constantly in their view. When that is the case, they are always bad citizens, and perfectly unsure connexions. For, considering their speculative designs as of infinite value, and the actual arrangement of the state as of no estimation, they are at best indifferent about it. They see no merit in the good, and no fault in the vicious management of public affairs; they rather rejoice in the latter, as more propitious to revolution. They see no merit or demerit in any man, or any action, or any political principle, any further than as they may forward or retard their design of change: they therefore take up, one day, the most violent and stretched prerogative, and another time the wildest democratic ideas of freedom, and pass from the one to the other without any sort of regard to cause, to person, or to party.

In France you are now in the crisis of a revolution, and

in the transit from one form of government to another – you cannot see that character of men exactly in the same situation in which we see it in this country. With us it is militant; with you it is triumphant; and you know how it can act when its power is commensurate to its will. I would not be supposed to confine those observations to any description of men, or to comprehend all men of any description within them – No! far from it. I am as incapable of that injustice, as I am of keeping terms with those who profess principles of extremes; and who under the name of religion teach little else than wild and dangerous politics. The worst of these politics of revolution is this; they temper and harden the breast, in order to prepare it for the desperate strokes which are sometimes used in extreme occasions. But as these occasions may never arrive, the mind receives a gratuitous taint; and the moral sentiments suffer not a little, when no political purpose is served by the depravation. This sort of people are so taken up with their theories about the rights of man, that they have totally forgot his nature. Without opening one new avenue to the understanding, they have succeeded in stopping up those that lead to the heart. They have perverted in themselves, and in those that attend to them, all the well-placed sympathies of the human breast.

This famous sermon of the Old Jewry breathes nothing but this spirit through all the political part. Plots, massacres, assassinations, seem to some people a trivial price for obtaining a revolution. A cheap, bloodless reformation, a guiltless liberty, appear flat and vapid to their taste. There must be a great change of scene; there must be a magnificent stage effect; there must be a grand spectacle to rouze the imagination, grown torpid with the lazy enjoyment of sixty years security, and the still unanimating repose of public prosperity. The Preacher found them all in the French revolution. This inspires a juvenile warmth through his whole frame. His enthusiasm kindles as he advances; and when he arrives at his peroration, it is in a full blaze. Then viewing, from the Pisgah of his pulpit, the free, moral, happy, flourishing, and glorious state of France, as in a bird-eye landscape of a promised land, he breaks out into the following rapture:

'What an eventful period is this! I am *thankful* that I have lived to it; I could almost say, *Lord, now lettest thou thy servant depart in peace, for mine eyes have seen thy salvation.* – I have lived to see a *diffusion* of knowledge which has undermined superstition and error. – I have lived to see the *rights of men* better understood than ever; and nations panting for liberty which seemed to have lost the idea of it. – I have lived to see *Thirty Millions of People*, indignant and resolute, spurning at slavery, and demanding liberty with an irresistible voice. *Their King led in triumph, and an arbitrary monarch surrendering himself to his subjects.*'*

Before I proceed further, I have to remark, that Dr Price seems rather to over-value the great acquisitions of light which he has obtained and diffused in this age. The last century appears to me to have been quite as much enlightened. It had, though in a different place, a triumph as memorable as that of Dr Price; and some of the great preachers of that period partook of it as eagerly as he has done in the triumph of France. On the trial of the Rev. Hugh Peters for high treason, it was deposed, that when King Charles was brought to London for his trial, the Apostle of Liberty in that day conducted the *triumph*.

*Another of these reverend gentlemen,[49] who was witness to some of the spectacles which Paris has lately exhibited – expresses himself thus, 'A King dragged in submissive triumph by his conquering subjects is one of those appearances of grandeur which seldom rise in the prospect of human affairs, and which, during the remainder of my life, I shall think of with wonder and gratification.' These gentlemen agree marvellously in their feelings.

'I saw,' says the witness, 'his majesty in the coach with six horses, and Peters riding before the king *triumphing*.' Dr Price, when he talks as if he had made a discovery, only follows a precedent; for, after the commencement of the king's trial, this precursor, the same Dr Peters, concluding a long prayer at the royal chapel at Whitehall, (he had very triumphantly chosen his place) said, 'I have prayed and preached these twenty years; and now I may say with old Simeon, *Lord, now lettest thou thy servant depart in peace, for mine eyes have seen thy salvation*.'*[50] Peters had not the fruits of his prayer; for he neither departed so soon as he wished, nor in peace. He became (what I heartily hope none of his followers may be in this country) himself a sacrifice to the triumph which he led as Pontiff. They dealt at the Restoration, perhaps, too hardly with this poor good man. But we owe it to his memory and his sufferings, that he had as much illumination, and as much zeal, and had as effectually undermined all *the superstition and error* which might impede the great business he was engaged in, as any who follow and repeat after him, in this age, which would assume to itself an exclusive title to the knowledge of the rights of men, and all the glorious consequences of that knowledge.

After this sally of the preacher of the Old Jewry, which differs only in place and time, but agrees perfectly with the spirit and letter of the rapture of 1648, the Revolution Society, the fabricators of governments, the heroic band of *cashierers* of *monarchs*, electors of sovereigns, and leaders of kings in triumph, strutting with a proud consciousness of the diffusion of knowledge, of which every member had obtained so large a share in the donative, were in haste to make a generous diffusion of the knowlege they had thus gratuitously received. To make this bountiful communication, they adjourned from the

* State Trials, vol. ii. p. 360, p. 363.

church in the Old Jewry, to the London Tavern; where the same Dr Price, in whom the fumes of his oracular tripod were not entirely evaporated, moved and carried the resolution, or address of congratulation, transmitted by Lord Stanhope to the National Assembly of France.

I find a preacher of the gospel prophaning the beautiful and prophetic ejaculation, commonly called '*nunc dimittis*,' made on the first presentation of our Saviour in the Temple, and applying it, with an inhuman and unnatural rapture, to the most horrid, atrocious, and afflicting spectacle, that perhaps ever was exhibited to the pity and indignation of mankind. This '*leading in triumph*,' a thing in its best form unmanly and irreligious, which fills our Preacher with such unhallowed transports, must shock, I believe, the moral taste of every well-born mind. Several English were the stupified and indignant spectators of that triumph. It was (unless we have been strangely deceived) a spectacle more resembling a procession of American savages, entering into Onondaga,[51] after some of their murders called victories, and leading into hovels hung round with scalps, their captives, overpowered with the scoffs and buffets of women as ferocious as themselves, much more than it resembled the triumphal pomp of a civilized martial nation; – if a civilized nation, or any men who had a sense of generosity, were capable of a personal triumph over the fallen and afflicted.

This, my dear Sir, was not the triumph of France. I must believe that, as a nation, it overwhelmed you with shame and horror. I must believe that the National Assembly find themselves in a state of the greatest humiliation, in not being able to punish the authors of this triumph, or the actors in it; and that they are in a situation in which any enquiry they may make upon the subject, must be destitute even of the appearance of liberty or impartiality. The apology of that Assembly is found in their situation; but when we approve what they *must* bear, it is in us the degenerate choice of a vitiated mind.

With a compelled appearance of deliberation, they vote under the dominion of a stern necessity. They sit in the heart, as it were, of a foreign republic: they have their residence in a city whose constitution has emanated neither from the charter of their king, nor from their legislative power. There they are surrounded by an army not raised either by the authority of their crown, or by their command; and which, if they should order to dissolve itself, would instantly dissolve them. There they sit, after a gang of assassins had driven away some hundreds of the members;[52] whilst those who held the same moderate principles, with more patience or better hope, continued every day exposed to outrageous insults and murderous threats. There a majority, sometimes real, sometimes pretended, captive itself, compels a captive king to issue as royal edicts, at third hand, the polluted nonsense of their most licentious and giddy coffee-houses. It is notorious, that all their measures are decided before they are debated. It is beyond doubt, that under the terror of the bayonet, and the lamp-post, and the torch to their houses, they are obliged to adopt all the crude and desperate measures suggested by clubs composed of a monstrous medley of all conditions, tongues, and nations. Among these are found persons, in comparison of whom Catiline would be thought scrupulous, and Cethegus[53] a man of sobriety and moderation. Nor is it in these clubs alone that the publick measures are deformed into monsters. They undergo a previous distortion in academies, intended as so many seminaries for these clubs, which are set up in all the places of publick resort. In these meetings of all sorts, every counsel, in proportion as it is daring, and violent, and perfidious, is taken for the mark of superior genius. Humanity and compassion are ridiculed as the fruits of superstition and ig-

norance. Tenderness to individuals is considered as treason
to the public. Liberty is always to be estimated perfect as
property is rendered insecure. Amidst assassination, massacre, and confiscation, perpetrated or meditated, they are
forming plans for the good order of future society. Em-
bracing in their arms the carcases of base criminals, and
promoting their relations on the title of their offences, they
drive hundreds of virtuous persons to the same end, by
forcing them to subsist by beggary or by crime.

The Assembly, their organ, acts before them the farce
of deliberation with as little decency as liberty. They act
like the comedians of a fair before a riotous audience;
they act amidst the tumultuous cries of a mixed mob of
ferocious men, and of women lost to shame, who, according to their insolent fancies, direct, control, applaud,
explode them;[54] and sometimes mix and take their seats
amongst them; domineering over them with a strange
mixture of servile petulance and proud presumptuous
authority. As they have inverted order in all things, the
gallery is in the place of the house. This Assembly, which
overthrows kings and kingdoms, has not even the physiognomy and aspect of a grave legislative body – *nec color
imperii, nec frons erat ulla senatus.*[55] They have a power
given to them, like that of the evil principle, to subvert
and destroy; but none to construct, except such machines
as may be fitted for further subversion and further destruction.

Who is it that admires, and from the heart is attached
to national representative assemblies, but must turn with
horror and disgust from such a profane burlesque, and
abominable perversion of that sacred institute? Lovers of
monarchy, lovers of republicks, must alike abhor it. The
members of your Assembly must themselves groan under
the tyranny of which they have all the shame, none of
the direction, and little of the profit. I am sure many of

the members who compose even the majority of that body, must feel as I do, notwithstanding the applauses of the Revolution Society. – Miserable king! miserable Assembly! How must that assembly be silently scandalized with those of their members, who could call a day which seemed to blot the sun out of Heaven, 'un beau jour!'* How must they be inwardly indignant at hearing others, who thought fit to declare to them, 'that the vessel of the state would fly forward in her course towards regeneration with more speed than ever,' from the stiff gale of treason and murder, which preceded our Preacher's triumph! What must they have felt, whilst with outward patience and inward indignation they heard of the slaughter of innocent gentlemen in their houses, that 'the blood spilled was not the most pure?'[57] What must they have felt, when they were besieged by complaints of disorders which shook their country to its foundations, at being compelled coolly to tell the complainants, that they were under the protection of the law, and that they would address the king (the captive king) to cause the laws to be enforced for their protection; when the enslaved ministers of that captive king had formally notified to them, that there were neither law, nor authority, nor power left to protect? What must they have felt at being obliged, as a felicitation on the present new year, to request their captive king to forget the stormy period of the last, on account of the great good which *he* was likely to produce to his people; to the complete attainment of which good they adjourned the practical demonstrations of their loyalty, assuring him of their obedience, when he should no longer possess any authority to command?

This address was made with much good-nature and affection, to be sure. But among the revolutions in France, must be reckoned a considerable revolution in their ideas

* 6th of October, 1789.[56]

of politeness. In England we are said to learn manners at second-hand from your side of the water, and that we dress our behaviour in the frippery of France. If so, we are still in the old cut; and have not so far conformed to the new Parisian mode of good-breeding, as to think it quite in the most refined strain of delicate compliment (whether in condolence or congratulation) to say, to the most humiliated creature that crawls upon the earth, that great public benefits are derived from the murder of his servants, the attempted assassination of himself and of his wife, and the mortification, disgrace, and degradation, that he has personally suffered. It is a topic of consolation which our ordinary of Newgate would be too humane to use to a criminal at the foot of the gallows. I should have thought that the hangman of Paris, now that he is liberalized by the vote of the National Assembly, and is allowed his rank and arms in the Herald's College of the rights of men, would be too generous, too gallant a man, too full of the sense of his new dignity, to employ that cutting consolation to any of the persons whom the *leze nation* might bring under the administration of his *executive powers*.

A man is fallen indeed, when he is thus flattered. The anodyne draught of oblivion, thus drugged, is well calculated to preserve a galling wakefulness, and to feed the living ulcer of a corroding memory. Thus to administer the opiate potion of amnesty, powdered with all the ingredients of scorn and contempt, is to hold to his lips, instead of 'the balm of hurt minds,' the cup of human misery full to the brim, and to force him to drink it to the dregs.

Yielding to reasons, at least as forcible as those which were so delicately urged in the compliment on the new year, the king of France will probably endeavour to forget these events, and that compliment. But history, who keeps a durable record of all our acts, and exercises her awful censure over the proceedings of all sorts of sovereigns, will not forget, either those events, or the aera of this liberal refinement in the intercourse of mankind. History will record, that on the morning of the 6th of October 1789, the king and queen of France, after a day of confusion, alarm, dismay, and slaughter, lay down, under the pledged security of public faith, to indulge nature in a few hours of respite, and troubled melancholy repose. From this sleep the queen was first startled by the voice of the centinel at her door, who cried out to her, to save herself by flight – that this was the last proof of fidelity he could give – that they were upon him, and he was dead. Instantly he was cut down. A band of cruel ruffians and assassins, reeking with his blood, rushed into the chamber of the queen, and pierced with an hundred strokes of bayonets and poniards the bed, from whence this persecuted woman had but just time to fly almost naked, and through ways unknown to the murderers had escaped to seek refuge at the feet of a king and husband, not secure of his own life for a moment.

This king, to say no more of him, and this queen, and their infant children (who once would have been the pride and hope of a great and generous people) were then forced to abandon the sanctuary of the most splendid palace in the world, which they left swimming in blood, polluted by massacre, and strewed with scattered limbs and mutilated carcases. Thence they were conducted into the capital of their kingdom. Two had been selected from the unprovoked, unresisted, promiscuous slaughter, which was made of the gentlemen of birth and family who composed the king's body guard. These two gentlemen, with all the parade of an execution of justice, were cruelly and publickly dragged to the block, and beheaded in the great court of the palace. Their heads were stuck upon spears, and led the procession; whilst the royal captives who followed in the train were slowly moved along, amidst the horrid yells, and shrilling screams, and frantic dances, and infamous contumelies, and all the unutterable abominations of the furies of hell, in the abused shape of the vilest of women. After they had been made to taste, drop by drop, more than the bitterness of death, in the slow torture of a journey of twelve miles, protracted to six hours, they were, under a guard, composed of those very soldiers who had thus conducted them through this famous triumph, lodged in one of the old palaces of Paris, now converted into a Bastile for kings.

Is this a triumph to be consecrated at altars? to be commemorated with grateful thanksgiving? to be offered to the divine humanity with fervent prayer and enthusiastick ejaculation? – The Theban and Thracian Orgies, acted in France, and applauded only in the Old Jewry, I assure you, kindle prophetic enthusiasm in the minds but of very few people in this kingdom; although a saint and apostle, who may have revelations of his own, and who has so completely vanquished all the mean superstitions of the heart, may incline to think it pious and decorous to compare it with the entrance into the world of the Prince of Peace, proclaimed in an holy temple by a venerable sage, and not long before not worse announced by the voice of angels to the quiet innocence of shepherds.[58]

At first I was at a loss to account for this fit of unguarded transport. I knew, indeed, that the sufferings of monarchs make a delicious repast to some sort of palates. There were reflexions which might serve to keep this appetite within some bounds of temperance. But when I took one circumstance into my consideration, I was obliged to confess, that much allowance ought to be made for the Society, and that the temptation was too strong for common discretion; I mean, the circumstance of the Io Paean[59] of the triumph, the animating cry which called 'for all the BISHOPS to be hanged on the lampposts,'* might well have brought forth a burst of enthusiasm on the foreseen consequences of this happy day. I allow to so much enthusiasm some little deviation from prudence. I allow this prophet to break forth into hymns of joy and thanksgiving on an event which appears like the precursor of the Millenium, and the projected fifth monarchy,[61] in the destruction of all church establishments. There was, however (as in all human affairs there is) in the midst of this joy something to exercise the patience of these worthy gentlemen, and to try the long-suffering of their faith. The actual murder of the king and queen, and their child, was wanting to the other auspicious circumstances of this '*beautiful day.*' The actual murder of the bishops, though called for by so many holy ejaculations, was also wanting. A groupe of regicide and sacriligious slaughter, was indeed boldly sketched, but it was only sketched. It unhappily was left unfinished, in this great history-piece of the massacre of innocents. What hardy pencil of a great master, from the school of the rights of men, will finish it, is to be seen hereafter. The age has not yet the compleat benefit of that diffusion of knowledge that has undermined superstition and error; and the king of France wants another object or two, to consign to oblivion, in consideration of all the good which is to arise from his own sufferings, and the patriotic crimes of an enlightened age.†

* Tous les Eveques à la lanterns.[60]

† It is proper here to refer to a letter written upon this subject by an eye-witness. That eye-witness was one of the most honest, intelligent, and eloquent members of the National Assembly, one of the most active and zealous reformers of the state. He was obliged to secede from the assembly; and he afterwards became a voluntary exile, on account of the horrors of this pious triumph, and the dis-

Although this work of our new light and knowledge, did not go to the length, that in all probability it was intended it should be carried; yet I must think, that such treatment of any human creatures must be shocking to

positions of men, who, profiting of crimes, if not causing them, have taken the lead in public affairs.

EXTRACT of M. de Lally Tollendal's Second Letter to a Friend.

'Parlons du parti que j'ai pris; il est bien justifié dans ma conscience. – Ni cette ville coupable, ni cette assemblée plus coupable encore, ne meritoient que je me justifie; mais j'ai à cœur que vous, et les personnes qui pensent comme vous, ne me condamnent pas. – Ma santé, je vous jure, me rendoit mes fonctions impossibles; mais meme en les mettant de coté il a eté au-dessus de mes forces de supporter plus long-tems l'horreur que me causoit ce sang, – ces têtes, – cette reine *presque egorgée*, – ce roi, – amené *esclave*, – entrant à Paris, au milieu de ses assassins, et precedé des tetes de ses mal heureux gardes. – Ces perfides janissaires, ces assassins, ces femmes cannibales, ce cri de, TOUS LES EVEQUES A LA LANTERNE, dans le moment ou le roi entre sa capitale avec deux eveques de son conseil dans sa voiture. Un *coup de fusil*, que j'ai vu tirer dans un *des carosses de la reine*. M. Bailey appellant cela *un beau jour*. L'assemblée ayant declaré froidement le matin, qu'il n'étoit pas de sa dignité d'aller toute entiere environner le roi. M. Mirabeau disant impunement dans cette assemblée, que le vaisseau de l'état, loins d'etre arrêté dans sa course, s'élanceroit avec plus de rapidité que jamais vers sa régénération. M. Barnave, riant avec lui, quand des flots de sang couloient autour de nous. Le vertueux Mounier* echappant par miracle à vingt assassins, qui avoient voulu faire de sa tete un trophée de plus.

'Voila ce qui me fit jurer de ne plus mettre le pied *dans cette caverne d'Antropophages* [the National Assembly] où je n'avois plus de force d'élever la voix, ou depuis six semaines je l'avois elevée en vain. Moi, Mounier, et tous les honnêtes gens, ont le dernier effort à faire pour le bien étoit d'en sortir. Aucune idée de crainte ne s'est approchée de moi. Je rougirois de m'en defendre. J'avois encore reçû sur la route de la part de ce peuple,

*N.B. Mr. Mounier was then speaker of the National Assembly. He has since been obliged to live in exile, though one of the firmest asserters of liberty.[62]

any but those who are made for accomplishing Revolutions. But I cannot stop here. Influenced by the inborn feelings of my nature, and not being illuminated by a single ray of this new-sprung modern light, I confess to you, Sir, that the exalted rank of the persons suffering, and particularly the sex, the beauty, and the amiable qualities of the descendant of so many kings and emperors, with the tender age of royal infants, insensible only through infancy and innocence of the cruel outrages to which their parents were exposed, instead of being a subject of exultation, adds not a little to my sensibility on that most melancholy occasion.

I hear that the august person, who was the principle object of our preacher's triumph, though he supported himself, felt much on that shameful occasion. As a man, it became him to feel for his wife and his children, and the faithful guards of his person, that were massacred in cold blood about him; as a prince, it became him to feel for the strange and frightful transformation of his civil-

---

moins coupable que ceux qui l'ont enivré de fureur, des acclamations, et des applaudissements, dont d'autres auroient été flattés, et qui m'ont fait fremir. C'est à l'indignation, c'est à l' horreur, c'est aux convulsions, physiques, que se seul aspect du sang me fait eprouver que j'ai cedé. On brave une seule mort; on la brave plusieurs fois, quand elle peut être utile. Mais aucune puissance sous le Ciel, mais aucune opinion publique ou privée n'ont le droit de me condamner à souffrir inutilement mille supplices par minute, et à perir de désespoir, de rage, au milieu des *triomphes*, du crime que je n'ai pu arrêter. Ils me proscriront, ils confisqueront mes biens. Je labourerai la terre, et je ne les verrai plus. – Voila ma justification. Vous pourez la lire, la montrer, la laisser copier; tant pis pour ceux qui ne la comprendront pas; ce ne sera alors moi qui auroit eu tort de la leur donner.'
This military man had not so good nerves as the peaceable gentleman of the Old Jewry. – See Mons. Mounier's narrative of these transactions; a man also of honour and virtue, and talents, and therefore a fugitive.

ized subjects, and to be more grieved for them, than solicitous for himself. It derogates little from his fortitude, while it adds infinitely to the honour of his humanity. I am very sorry to say it, very sorry indeed, that such personages are in a situation in which it is not unbecoming in us to praise the virtues of the great.

I hear, and I rejoice to hear, that the great lady, the other object of the triumph, has borne that day (one is interested that beings made for suffering should suffer well) and that she bears all the succeeding days, that she bears the imprisonment of her husband, and her own captivity, and the exile of her friends, and the insulting adulation of addresses, and the whole weight of her accumulated wrongs, with a serene patience, in a manner suited to her rank and race, and becoming the offspring of a sovereign distinguished for her piety and her courage; that like her she has lofty sentiments; that she feels with the dignity of a Roman matron; that in the last extremity she will save herself from the last disgrace, and that if she must fall, she will fall by no ignoble hand.

It is now sixteen or seventeen years since I saw the queen of France, then the dauphiness, at Versailles; and surely never lighted on this orb, which she hardly seemed to touch, a more delightful vision.[63] I saw her just above the horizon, decorating and cheering the elevated sphere she just began to move in, – glittering like the morning-star, full of life, and splendor, and joy. Oh! What a revolution! and what an heart must I have, to contemplate without emotion that elevation and that fall! Little did I dream when she added titles of veneration to those of enthusiastic, distant, respectful love, that she should ever be obliged to carry the sharp antidote against disgrace concealed in that bosom; little did I dream that I should have lived to see such disasters fallen upon her in a nation of gallant men, in a nation of men of honour and of cavaliers. I thought ten thousand swords must have leaped from their scabbards to avenge even a look that threatened her with insult. – But the age of chivalry is gone. – That of sophisters, oeconomists, and calculators, has succeeded; and the glory of Europe is extinguished for ever. Never, never more, shall we behold that generous loyalty to rank and sex, that proud submission, that dignified obedience, that subordination of the heart, which kept alive, even in servitude itself, the spirit of an exalted freedom. The un-bought grace of life, the cheap defence of nations, the nurse of manly sentiment and heroic enterprize is gone! It is gone, that sensibility of principle, that chastity of honour, which felt a stain like a wound, which inspired courage whilst it mitigated ferocity, which ennobled whatever it touched, and under which vice itself lost half its evil, by losing all its grossness.

This mixed system of opinion and sentiment had its origin in the antient chivalry; and the principle, though varied in its appearance by the varying state of human affairs, subsisted and influenced through a long succession of generations, even to the time we live in. If it should ever be totally extinguished, the loss I fear will be great. It is this which has given its character to modern Europe. It is this which has distinguished it under all its forms of government, and distinguished it to its advantage, from the states of Asia, and possibly from those states which flourished in the most brilliant periods of the antique world. It was this, which, without confounding ranks, had produced a noble equality, and handed it down through all the gradations of social life. It was this opinion which mitigated kings into companions, and raised private men to be fellows with kings. Without force, or opposition, it subdued the fierceness of pride and power; it obliged sovereigns to submit to the soft collar of social esteem, compelled stern authority to submit to elegance, and gave a domination vanquisher of laws, to be subdued by manners.

But now all is to be changed. All the pleasing illusions, which made power gentle, and obedience liberal, which harmonized the different shades of life, and which, by a bland assimilation, incorporated into politics the sentiments which beautify and soften private society, are to be dissolved by this new conquering empire of light and reason. All the decent drapery of life is to be rudely torn off. All the super-added ideas, furnished from the wardrobe of a moral imagination, which the heart owns, and the understanding ratifies, as necessary to cover the defects of our naked shivering nature, and to raise it to dignity in our own estimation, are to be exploded as a ridiculous, absurd, and antiquated fashion.

On this scheme of things, a king is but a man; a queen is but a woman; a woman is but an animal; and an animal not of the highest order. All homage paid to the sex in general as such, and without distinct views, is to be regarded as romance and folly. Regicide, and parricide, and sacrilege, are but fictions of superstition, corrupting jurisprudence by destroying its simplicity. The murder of a king, or a queen, or a bishop, or a father, are only common homicide; and if the people are by any chance, or in any way gainers by it, a sort of homicide much the most pardonable, and into which we ought not to make too severe a scrutiny.

On the scheme of this barbarous philosophy, which is the offspring of cold hearts and muddy understandings, and which is as void of solid wisdom, as it is destitute of all taste and elegance, laws are to be supported only by their own terrors, and by the concern, which each individual may find in them, from his own private speculations, or can spare to them from his own private interests. In the groves of *their* academy, at the end of every visto, you see nothing but the gallows. Nothing is left which engages the affections on the part of the commonwealth. On the principles of this mechanic philosophy, our institutions can never be embodied, if I may use the expression, in persons; so as to create in us love, veneration, admiration, or attachment. But that sort of reason which banishes the affections is incapable of filling their place. These public affections, combined with manners, are required sometimes as supplements, sometimes as correctives, always as aids to law. The precept given by a wise man, as well as a great critic, for the construction of poems, is equally true as to states. *Non satis est pulchra esse poemata, dulcia sunto.*[64] There ought to be a system of manners in every nation which a well-formed mind would be disposed to relish. To make us love our country, our country ought to be lovely.

But power, of some kind or other, will survive the shock in which manners and opinions perish; and it will find other and worse means for its support. The usurpation which, in order to subvert antient institutions, has destroyed antient principles, will hold power by arts similar to those by which it has acquired it.[65] When the old feudal and chivalrous spirit of *Fealty*, which, by freeing kings from fear, freed both kings and subjects from the precautions of tyranny, shall be extinct in the minds of men, plots and assassinations will be anticipated by preventive murder and preventive confiscation, and that long roll of grim and bloody maxims, which form the political code of all power, not standing on its own honour, and the honour of those who are to obey it. Kings will be tyrants from policy when subjects are rebels from principle.

When antient opinions and rules of life are taken away, the loss cannot possibly be estimated. From that moment we have no compass to govern us; nor can we know distinctly to what port we steer. Europe undoubtedly, taken in a mass, was in a flourishing condition the day on which your Revolution was compleated. How much of that prosperous state was owing to the spirit of our old manners and opinions is not easy to say; but as such causes cannot be indifferent in their operation, we must presume, that, on the whole, their operation was beneficial.

We are but too apt to consider things in the state in which we find them, without sufficiently adverting to the causes by which they have been produced, and possibly may be upheld. Nothing is more certain, than that our manners, our civilization, and all the good things which are connected with manners, and with civilization, have, in this European world of ours, depended for ages upon two principles; and were indeed the result of both combined; I mean the spirit of a gentleman, and the spirit of religion. The nobility and the clergy, the one by profession, the other by patronage, kept learning in existence, even in the midst of arms and confusions, and whilst governments were rather in their causes than formed. Learning paid back what it received to nobility and to priesthood; and paid it with usury, by enlarging their ideas, and by furnishing their minds. Happy if they had all continued to know their indissoluble union, and their proper place! Happy if learning, not debauched by ambition, had been satisfied to continue the instructor, and not aspired to be the master! Along with its natural protectors and guardians, learning will be cast into the mire, and trodden down under the hoofs of a swinish multitude.*[66]

If, as I suspect, modern letters owe more than they are always willing to own to antient manners, so do other

* See the fate of Bailly and Condorcet, supposed to be here particularly alluded to. Compare the circumstances of the trial, and execution of the former with this prediction. [1803][67]

interests which we value full as much as they are worth. Even commerce, and trade, and manufacture, the gods of our oeconomical politicians, are themselves perhaps but creatures; are themselves but effects, which, as first causes, we choose to worship. They certainly grew under the same shade in which learning flourished. They too may decay with their natural protecting principles. With you, for the present at least, they all threaten to disappear together. Where trade and manufacturers are wanting to a people, and the spirit of nobility and religion remains, sentiment supplies, and not always ill supplies their place; but if commerce and the arts should be lost in an experiment to try how well a state may stand without these old fundamental principles, what sort of a thing must be a nation of gross, stupid, ferocious, and at the same time, poor and sordid barbarians, destitute of religion, honour, or manly pride, possessing nothing at present, and hoping for nothing hereafter?

I wish you may not be going fast, and by the shortest cut, to that horrible and disgustful situation. Already there appears a poverty of conception, a coarseness and vulgarity in all the proceedings of the assembly and of all their instructors. Their liberty is not liberal. Their science is presumptuous ignorance. Their humanity is savage and brutal.

It is not clear, whether in England we learned those grand and decorous principles, and manners, of which considerable traces yet remain, from you, or whether you took them from us. But to you, I think, we trace them best. You seem to me to be – *gentis incunabula nostræ.*[68] France has always more or less influenced manners in England; and when your fountain is choaked up and polluted, the stream will not run long, or not run clear with us, or perhaps with any nation. This gives all Europe, in my opinion, but too close and connected a concern in what is done in France. Excuse me, therefore, if I have dwelt too long on the atrocious spectacle of the sixth of October 1789, or have given too much scope to the reflections which have arisen in my mind on occasion of the most important of all revolutions, which may be dated from that day, I mean a revolution in sentiments, manners, and moral opinions. As things now stand, with every thing respectable destroyed without us, and an attempt to destroy within us every principle of respect, one is almost forced to apologize for harbouring the common feelings of men.

Why do I feel so differently from the Reverend Dr Price, and those of his lay flock, who will choose to adopt the sentiments of his discourse? – For this plain reason – because it is *natural* I should; because we are so made as to be affected at such spectacles with melancholy sentiments upon the unstable condition of mortal prosperity, and the tremendous uncertainty of human greatness; because in those natural feelings we learn great lessons; because in events like these our passions instruct our reason; because when kings are hurl'd from their thrones by the Supreme Director of this great drama, and become the objects of insult to the base, and of pity to the good, we behold such disasters in the moral, as we should behold a miracle in the physical order of things. We are alarmed into reflexion; our minds (as it has long since been observed) are purified by terror and pity; our weak unthinking pride is humbled, under the dispensations of a mysterious wisdom. – Some tears might be drawn from me, if such a spectacle were exhibited on the stage. I should be truly ashamed of finding in myself that superficial, theatric sense of painted distress, whilst I could exult over it in real life. With such a perverted mind, I could never venture to shew my face at a tragedy. People would think the tears that Garrick[69] formerly, or that Siddons not long since, have extorted from me, were the tears of hypocrisy; I should know them to be the tears of folly.

Indeed the theatre is a better school of moral sentiments than churches, where the feelings of humanity are thus outraged. Poets, who have to deal with an audience not yet graduated in the school of the rights of men, and who must apply themselves to the moral constitution of the heart, would not dare to produce such a triumph as a matter of exultation. There, where men follow their natural impulses, they would not bear the odious maxims of a Machiavelian policy, whether applied to the attainment of monarchical or democratic tyranny. They would reject them on the modern, as they once did on the antient stage, where they could not bear even the hypothetical proposition of such wickedness in the mouth of a personated tyrant, though suitable to the character he sustained. No theatric audience in Athens would bear what has been borne, in the midst of the real tragedy of this triumphal day; a principal actor weighing, as it were in scales hung in a shop of horrors, – so much actual crime against so much contingent advantage, – and after putting in and out weights, declaring that the balance was on the side of the advantages. They would not bear to see the crimes of new democracy posted as in a ledger against the crimes of old despotism, and the book-keepers of politics finding democracy still in debt, but by no means unable or unwilling to pay the balance. In the theatre, the first intuitive glance, without any elaborate process of reasoning, would shew, that this method of political computation, would justify every extent of crime. They would see, that on these principles, even where the very worst acts were not perpetrated, it was owing rather to the fortune of the conspirators than to their parsimony in the expenditure of treachery and blood. They would soon see, that criminal means once tolerated are soon preferred. They present a shorter cut to the object than through the highway of the moral virtues. Justifying perfidy and murder for public benefit, public benefit would soon become the pretext, and perfidy and murder the end; until rapacity, malice, revenge, and fear more dreadful than revenge, could satiate their insatiable appetites. Such must be the consequences of losing in the splendour of these triumphs of the rights of men, all natural sense of wrong and right.

But the Reverend Pastor exults in this 'leading in triumph,' because truly Louis XVIth was 'an arbitrary monarch;' that is, in other words, neither more nor less, than because he was Louis the XVIth, and because he had the misfortune to be born king of France, with the prerogatives of which, a long line of ancestors, and a long acquiescence of the people, without any act of his, had put him in possession. A misfortune it has indeed turned out to him, that he was born king of France. But misfortune is not crime, nor is indiscretion always the greatest guilt. I shall never think that a prince, the acts of whose whole reign were a series of concessions to his subjects, who was willing to relax his authority, to remit his prerogatives, to call his people to a share of freedom, not known, perhaps not desired by their ancestors; such a prince, though he should be subject to the common frailties attached to men and to princes, though he should have once thought it necessary to provide force against the desperate designs manifestly carrying on against his person, and the remnants of his authority; though all this should be taken into consideration, I shall be led with great difficulty to think he deserves the cruel and insulting triumph of Paris, and of Dr Price. I tremble for the cause of liberty, from such an example to kings. I tremble for the cause of humanity, in the unpunished outrages of the most wicked of mankind. But there are some people of that low and degenerate fashion of mind, that they look up with a sort of complacent awe and admiration to kings, who know to keep firm in their seat, to hold a strict hand over their subjects, to assert their prerogative, and by the awakened vigilance of a severe despotism, to guard against the very first approaches of freedom. Against such as these they never elevate their voice. Deserters from principle, listed with fortune, they never see any good in suffering virtue, nor any crime in prosperous usurpation.

If it could have been made clear to me, that the king and queen of France (those I mean who were such before the triumph) were inexorable and cruel tyrants, that they had formed a deliberate scheme for massacring the National Assembly (I think I have seen something like the latter insinuated in certain publications) I should think their captivity just. If this be true, much more ought to have been done, but done, in my opinion, in another manner. The punishment of real tyrants is a noble and awful act of justice; and it has with truth been said to be consolatory to the human mind. But if I were to punish a wicked king, I should regard the dignity in avenging the crime. Justice is grave and decorous, and in its punishments rather seems to submit to a necessity, than to make a choice. Had Nero, or Agrippina, or Louis the Eleventh, or Charles the Ninth, been the subject; if Charles the Twelfth of Sweden, after the murder of Patkul,[70] or his predecessor Christina, after the murder of Monaldeschi,[71] had fallen into your hands, Sir, or into mine, I am sure our conduct would have been different.

If the French king, or King of the French, (or by whatever name he is known in the new vocabulary of your constitution) has in his own person, and that of his Queen, really deserved these unavowed but unavenged murderous attempts, and those subsequent indignities more cruel than murder, such a person would ill deserve even that subordinate executory trust, which I understand is to be placed in him; nor is he fit to be called chief in a nation which he has outraged and oppressed. A worse choice for such an office in a new commonwealth, than that of a deposed tyrant, could not possibly be made. But to degrade and insult a man as the worst of criminals, and afterwards to trust him in your highest concerns, as a faithful, honest, and zealous servant, is not consistent in reasoning, nor prudent in policy, nor safe in practice. Those who could make such an appointment must be guilty of a more flagrant breach of trust than any they have yet committed against the people. As this is the only crime in which your leading politicians could have acted inconsistently, I conclude that there is no sort of ground for these horrid insinuations. I think no better of all the other calumnies.

In England, we give no credit to them. We are generous enemies: We are faithful allies. We spurn from us with disgust and indignation the slanders of those who bring us their anecdotes with the attestation of the flower-de-luce on their shoulder. We have Lord George Gordon[72] fast in Newgate; and neither his being a public proselyte to Judaism, nor his having, in his zeal against Catholick priests and all sorts of ecclesiastics, raised a mob (excuse the term, it is still in use here) which pulled down all our prisons, have preserved to him a liberty, of which he did not render himself worthy by a virtuous use of it. We have rebuilt Newgate, and tenanted the mansion. We have prisons almost as strong as the Bastile, for those who dare to libel the queens of France. In this spiritual retreat, let the noble libeller remain. Let him there meditate on his Thalmud, until he learns a conduct more becoming his birth and parts, and not so disgraceful to the antient religion to which he has become a proselyte; or until some persons from your side of the water, to please your new Hebrew brethren, shall ransom him. He may then be enabled to purchase, with the old hoards of the synagogue, and a very small poundage, on the long compound interest of the thirty pieces of silver (Dr Price has shewn us what miracles compound interest will perform in 1790 years) the lands which are lately discovered to have been unsurped by the Gallican church. Send us your popish Archbishop of Paris, and we will send you our protestant Rabbin. We shall treat the person you send us in exchange like a gentleman and an honest man, as he is; but pray let him bring with him the fund of his hospitality, bounty, and charity; and, depend upon it, we shall never confiscate a shilling of that honourable and pious fund, nor think of enriching the treasury with the spoils of the poor-box.

To tell you the truth, my dear Sir, I think the honour of our nation to be somewhat concerned in the disclaimer of the proceedings of this society of the Old Jewry and the London Tavern. I have no man's proxy. I speak only from myself; when I disclaim, as I do with all possible earnestness, all communion with the actors in that triumph, or with the admirers of it. When I assert any thing else, as concerning the people of England, I speak from observation not from authority; but I speak from the experience I have had in a pretty extensive and mixed communication with the inhabitants of this kingdom, of all descriptions and ranks, and after a course of attentive observation, began early in life, and continued for near forty years. I have often been astonished, considering that we are divided from you but by a slender dyke of about twenty-four miles, and that the mutual intercourse between the two countries has lately been very great, to find how little you seem to know of us. I suspect that this is owing to your forming a judgment of this nation from certain publications, which do, very erroneously, if they do at all, represent the opinions and dispositions generally prevalent in England. The vanity, restlessness, petulance, and spirit of intrigue of several petty cabals, who attempt to hide their total want of consequence in bustle and noise, and puffing, and mutual quotation of each other, makes you imagine that our contemptuous neglect of their abilities is a mark of general acquiescence in their opinions. No such thing, I assure you. Because half a dozen grasshoppers under a fern make the field ring with their importunate chink, whilst thousands of great cattle, reposed beneath the shadow of the British oak, chew the cud and are silent, pray do not imagine, that those who make the noise are the only inhabitants of the field; that of course, they are many in number; or that, after all, they are other than the little shrivelled, meagre, hopping, though loud and troublesome insects of the hour.

I almost venture to affirm, that not one in a hundred amongst us participates in the 'triumph' of the Revolution Society. If the king and queen of France, and their children, were to fall into our hands by the chance of war, in the most acrimonious of all hostilities (I deprecate such an event, I deprecate such hostility) they would be treated with another sort of triumphal entry into London. We formerly have had a king of France in that situation; you have read how he was treated by the victor in the field; and in what manner he was afterwards received in England. Four hundred years have gone over us; but I believe we are not materially changed since that period. Thanks to our sullen resistance to innovation, thanks to the cold sluggishness of our national character, we still bear the stamp of our forefathers. We have not (as I conceive) lost the generosity and dignity of thinking of the fourteenth century; nor as yet have we subtilized ourselves into savages. We are not the converts of Rousseau; we are not the disciples of Voltaire;[73] Helvetius[74] has made no progress amongst us. Atheists are not our preachers; madmen are not our lawgivers. We know that *we* have made no discoveries; and we think that no discoveries are to be made, in morality; nor many in the great principles of government, nor in the ideas of liberty, which were understood long before we were born, altogether as well as they will be after the grave has heaped its mould upon our presumption, and the silent tomb shall have imposed its law on our pert loquacity. In England we have not yet been completely embowelled of our natural entrails; we still feel within us, and we cherish and cultivate, those inbred sentiments which are the faithful guardians, the active monitors of our duty, the true supporters of all liberal and manly morals. We have not been drawn and trussed, in order that we may be filled, like stuffed birds in a museum, with chaff and rags, and paltry, blurred shreds of paper about the rights of man. We preserve the whole of our feelings still native and entire, unsophisticated by pedantry and infidelity. We have real hearts of flesh and blood beating in our bosoms. We fear God; we look up with awe to kings; with affection to parliaments; with duty to magistrates; with reverence to priests; and with respect to nobility.* Why? Because when such ideas are brought before our minds, it is *natural* to be affected; because all other feelings are false and spurious, and tend to corrupt our minds, to vitiate our primary morals, to

---

* The English are, I conceive, misrepresented in a Letter published in one of the papers, by a gentleman thought to be a dissenting minister. – When writing to Dr Price, of the spirit which prevails at Paris, he says, 'The spirit of the people in this place has abolished all the proud *distinctions* which the *king* and *nobles* had usurped in their minds; whether they talk of *the king*, *the noble*, *or the priest*, their whole language is that of the most *enlightened and liberal amongst the English.*' If this gentleman means to confine the terms *enlightened and liberal* to one set of men in England, it may be true. It is not generally so.

render us unfit for rational liberty; and by teaching us a servile, licentious, and abandoned insolence, to be our low sport for a few holidays, to make us perfectly fit for, and justly deserving of slavery, through the whole course of our lives.

You see, Sir, that in this enlightened age I am bold enough to confess, that we are generally men of untaught feelings; that instead of casting away all our old prejudices, we cherish them to a very considerable degree, and, to take more shame to ourselves, we cherish them because they are prejudices; and the longer they have lasted, and the more generally they have prevailed, the more we cherish them. We are afraid to put men to live and trade each on his own private stock of reason; because we suspect that this stock in each man is small, and that the individuals would do better to avail themselves of the general bank and capital of nations, and of ages. Many of our men of speculation, instead of exploding general prejudices, employ their sagacity to discover the latent wisdom which prevails in them. If they find what they seek, and they seldom fail, they think it more wise to continue the prejudice, with the reason involved, than to cast away the coat of prejudice, and to leave nothing but the naked reason; because prejudice, with its reason, has a motive to give action to that reason, and an affection which will give it permanence. Prejudice is of ready application in the emergency; it previously engages the mind in a steady course of wisdom and virtue, and does not leave the man hesitating in the moment of decision, sceptical, puzzled, and unresolved. Prejudice renders a man's virtue his habit; and not a series of unconnected acts. Through just prejudice, his duty becomes a part of his nature.

Your literary men, and your politicians, and so do the whole clan of the enlightened among us, essentially differ in these points. They have no respect for the wisdom of others; but they pay it off by a very full measure of confidence in their own. With them it is a sufficient motive to destroy an old scheme of things, because it is an old one. As to the new, they are in no sort of fear with regard to the duration of a building run up in haste; because duration is no object to those who think little or nothing has been done before their time, and who place all their hopes in discovery. They conceive, very systematically, that all things which give perpetuity are mischievous, and therefore they are at inexpiable war with all establishments. They think that government may vary like modes of dress, and with as little ill effect. That there needs no principle of attachment, except a sense of present conveniency, to any constitution of the state. They always speak as if they were of opinion that there is a singular species of compact between them and their magistrates, which binds the magistrate, but which has nothing reciprocal in it, but that the majesty of the people has a right to dissolve it without any reason, but its will. Their attachment to their country itself, is only so far as it agrees with some of their fleeting projects; it begins and ends with that scheme of polity which falls in with their momentary opinion.

These doctrines, or rather sentiments, seem prevalent with your new statesmen. But they are wholly different from those on which we have always acted in this country.

I hear it is sometimes given out in France, that what is doing among you is after the example of England. I beg leave to affirm, that scarcely any thing done with you has originated from the practice or the prevalent opinions of this people, either in the act or in the spirit of the proceeding. Let me add, that we are as unwilling to learn these lessons from France, as we are sure that we never taught them to that nation. The cabals here who take a sort of share in your transactions as yet consist but of an handful of people. If unfortunately by their intrigues, their sermons, their publications, and by a confidence derived from an expected union with the counsels and forces of the French nation, they should draw considerable numbers into their faction, and in consequence should seriously attempt any thing here in imitation of what has been done with you, the event, I dare venture to prophesy, will be, that, with some trouble to their country, they will soon accomplish their own destruction. This people refused to change their law in remote ages, from respect to the infallibility of popes; and they will not now alter it from a pious implicit faith in the dogmatism of philosophers; though the former was armed with the anathema and crusade, and though the latter should act with the libel and the lamp-iron.

Formerly your affairs were your own concern only. We felt for them as men; but we kept aloof from them, because we were not citizens of France. But when we see the model held up to ourselves, we must feel as Englishmen, and feeling, we must provide as Englishmen. Your affairs, in spite of us, are made a part of our interest; so far at least as to keep at a distance your panacea, or your plague. If it be a panacea, we do not want it. We know the consequences of unnecessary physic. If it be a plague; it is such a plague, that the precautions of the most severe quarantine ought to be established against it.

I hear on all hands that a cabal, calling itself philosophic, receives the glory of many of the late proceedings; and that their opinions and systems are the true actuating spirit of the whole of them. I have heard of no party in England, literary or political, at any time, known by such a description. It is not with you composed of those men, is it? whom the vulgar, in their blunt, homely style, commonly call Atheists and Infidels? If it be, I admit that we too have had writers of that description, who made some noise in their day. At present they repose in lasting oblivion. Who, born within the last forty years, has read one word of Colins, and Toland, and Tindal, and Chubb, and Morgan, and that whole race who called themselves Freethinkers? Who now reads Bolingbroke?[75] Who ever read him through? Ask the booksellers of London what is become of all these lights of the world. In as few years their few successors will go to the family vault of 'all the Capulets.' But whatever they were, or are, with us, they were and are wholly unconnected individuals. With us they kept the common nature of their kind, and were not gregarious. They never acted in corps, nor were known as a faction in the state, nor presumed to influence, in that name or character, or for the purposes of such a faction, on any of our public concerns. Whether they ought so to exist, and so be permitted to act, is another question. As such cabals have not existed in England, so neither has the spirit of them had any influence in establishing the original frame of our constitution, or in any one of the several reparations and improvements it has undergone. The whole has been done under the auspices, and is confirmed by the sanctions of religion and piety. The whole has emanated from the simplicity of our national character, and from a sort of native plainness and directness of understanding, which for a long time characterized those men who have successively obtained authority amongst us. This disposition still remains, at least in the great body of the people.

We know, and what is better we feel inwardly, that religion is the basis of civil society, and the source of all good and of all comfort.*[76] In England we are so convinced

---

* Sit igitur hoc ab initio persuasum civibus, dominos esse omnium rerum ac moderatores, deos; eaque, quae gerantur, eorum geri vi,

of this, that there is no rust of superstition, with which the accumulated absurdity of the human mind might have crusted it over in the course of ages, that ninety-nine in a hundred of the people of England would not prefer to impiety. We shall never be such fools as to call in an enemy to the substance of any system to remove its corruptions, to supply its defects, or to perfect its construction. If our religious tenets should ever want a further elucidation, we shall not call on atheism to explain them. We shall not light up our temple from that unhallowed fire. It will be illuminated with other lights. It will be perfumed with other incense, than the infectious stuff which is imported by the smugglers of adulterated metaphysics. If our ecclesiastical establishment should want a revision, it is not avarice or rapacity, public or private, that we shall employ for the audit, or receipt, or application of its consecrated revenue. – Violently condemning neither the Greek nor the Armenian, nor, since heats are subsided, the Roman system of religion, we prefer the Protestant; not because we think it has less of the Christian religion in it, but because, in our judgment, it has more. We are protestants, not from indifference but from zeal.[77]

We know, and it is our pride to know, that man is by his constitution a religious animal; that atheism is against, not only our reason but our instincts; and that it cannot prevail long. But if, in the moment of riot, and in a drunken delirium from the hot spirit drawn out of the alembick of hell, which in France is now so furiously boiling, we should uncover our nakedness by throwing off that

---

ditione, ac numine; eosdemque optime de genere hominum mereri; et qualis quisque sit, quid agat, quid in se admittat, qua mente, qua pietate colat religiones intueri: piorum et impiorum habere rationem. His enim rebus imbutae mentes haud sane abhorrebunt ab utili et a vera sententia. Cic. de Legibus, 1. 2.[78]

Christian religion which has hitherto been our boast and comfort, and one great source of civilization amongst us, and among many other nations, we are apprehensive (being well aware that the mind will not endure a void) that some uncouth, pernicious, and degrading supersition, might take place of it.

For that reason, before we take from our establishment the natural human means of estimation, and give it up to contempt, as you have done, and in doing it have incurred the penalties you well deserve to suffer, we desire that some other may be presented to us in the place of it. We shall then form our judgment.

On these ideas, instead of quarrelling with establishments, as some do, who have made a philosophy and a religion of their hostility to such institutions, we cleave closely to them. We are resolved to keep an established church, an established monarchy, an established aristocracy, and an established democracy, each in the degree it exists, and in no greater. I shall shew you presently how much of each of these we possess.

It has been the misfortune (not as these gentlemen think it, the glory) of this age, that every thing is to be discussed, as if the constitution of our country were to be always a subject rather of altercation than enjoyment. For this reason, as well as for the satisfaction of those among you (if any such you have among you) who may wish to profit of examples, I venture to trouble you with a few thoughts upon each of these establishments. I do not think they were unwise in antient Rome, who, when they wished to new-model their laws, sent commissioners to examine the best constituted republics within their reach.

First, I beg leave to speak of our church establishment, which is the first of our prejudices, not a prejudice destitute of reason, but involving in it profound and extensive wisdom. I speak of it first. It is first, and last, and midst in our minds. For, taking ground on that religious system, of which we are now in possession, we continue to act on the early received, and uniformly continued sense of mankind. That sense not only, like a wise architect, hath built up the august fabric of states, but like a provident proprietor, to preserve the structure from prophanation and ruin, as a sacred temple, purged from all the impurities of fraud, and violence, and injustice, and tyranny, hath solemnly and for ever consecrated the commonwealth, and all that officiate in it. This consecration is made, that all who administer in the government of men, in which they stand in the person of God himself, should have high and worthy notions of their function and destination; that their hope should be full of immortality; that they should not look to the paltry pelf of the moment, nor to the temporary and transient praise of the vulgar, but to a solid, permanent existence, in the permanent part of their nature, and to a permanent fame and glory, in the example they leave as a rich inheritance to the world.

Such sublime principles ought to be infused into persons of exalted situations; and religious establishments provided, that may continually revive and enforce them. Every sort of moral, every sort of civil, every sort of politic institution, aiding the rational and natural ties that connect the human understanding and affections to the divine, are not more than necessary, in order to build up that wonderful structure, Man; whose prerogative it is, to be in a great degree a creature of his own making;[79] and who when made as he ought to be made, is destined to hold no trivial place in the creation. But whenever man is put over men, as the better nature ought ever to preside, in that case more particularly, he should as nearly as possible be approximated to his perfection.

The consecration of the state, by a state religious establishment, is necessary also to operate with an wholesome awe upon free citizens; because, in order to secure their freedom, they must enjoy some determinate portion of power. To them therefore a religion connected with the state, and with their duty towards it, becomes even more necessary than in such societies, where the people by the terms of their subjection are confined to private sentiments, and the management of their own family concerns. All persons possessing any portion of power ought to be strongly and awefully impressed with an idea that they act in trust; and that they are to account for their conduct in that trust to the one great master, author and founder of society.

This principle ought even to be more strongly impressed upon the minds of those who compose the collective sovereignty than upon those of single princes. Without instruments, these princes can do nothing. Whoever uses instruments, in finding helps, finds also impediments. Their power is therefore by no means compleat; nor are they safe in extreme abuse. Such persons, however elevated by flattery, arrogance, and self-opinion, must be sensible that, whether covered or not by positive law, in some way or other they are accountable even here for the abuse of their trust. If they are not cut off by a rebellion of their people, they may be strangled by the very Janissaries kept for their security against all other rebellion. Thus we have seen the king of France sold by his soldiers for an encrease of pay. But where popular authority is absolute and unrestrained, the people have an infinitely greater, because a far better founded confidence in their own power. They are themselves, in a great measure, their own instruments. They are nearer to their objects. Besides, they are less under responsibility to one of the greatest controlling powers on earth, the sense of fame and estimation. The share of infamy that is likely to fall to the lot of each individual in public acts, is small indeed; the operation of opinion being in the inverse ratio to the number of those who abuse power. Their own approbation of their own acts has to them the appearance of a public judgment in their favour. A perfect democracy is therefore the most shameless thing in the world. As it is the most shameless, it is also the most fearless. No man apprehends in his person he can be made subject to punishment. Certainly the people at large never ought: for as all punishments are for example towards the conservation of the people at large, the people at large can never become the subject of punishment by any human hand.* It is therefore of infinite importance that they should not be suffered to imagine that their will, any more than that of kings, is the standard of right and wrong.

They ought to be persuaded that they are full as little entitled, and far less qualified, with safety to themselves, to use any arbitrary power whatsoever; that therefore they are not, under a false shew of liberty, but, in truth, to exercise an unnatural inverted domination, tyrannically to exact, from those who officiate in the state, not an entire devotion to their interest, which is their right, but an abject submission to their occasional will; extinguishing thereby, in all those who serve them, all moral principle, all sense of dignity, all use of judgment, and all consistency of character, whilst by the very same process they give themselves up a proper, a suitable, but a most contemptible prey to the servile ambition of popular sycophants or courtly flatterers.

When the people have emptied themselves of all the lust of selfish will, which without religion it is utterly impossible they ever should, when they are conscious that they exercise, and exercise perhaps in an higher link of

* Quicquid multis peccatur inultum.[80]

the order of delegation, the power, which to be legitimate must be according to that eternal immutable law, in which will and reason are the same, they will be more careful how they place power in base and incapable hands. In their nomination to office, they will not appoint to the exercise of authority, as to a pitiful job, but as to an holy function; not according to their sordid selfish interest, nor to their wanton caprice, nor to their arbitrary will; but they will confer that power (which any man may well tremble to give or to receive) on those only, in whom they may discern that predominant proportion of active virtue and wisdom, taken together and fitted to the charge, such, as in the great and inevitable mixed mass of human imperfections and infirmities, is to be found.[81]

When they are habitually convinced that no evil can be acceptable, either in the act or the permission, to him whose essence is good, they will be better able to extirpate out of the minds of all magistrates, civil, ecclesiastical, or military, any thing that bears the least resemblance to a proud and lawless domination.

But one of the first and most leading principles on which the commonwealth and the laws are consecrated, is lest the temporary possessors and life-renters in it, unmindful of what they have received from their ancestors, or of what is due to their posterity, should act as if they were the entire masters; that they should not think it amongst their rights to cut off the entail, or commit waste on the inheritance, by destroying at their pleasure the whole original fabric of their society; hazarding to leave to those who come after them, a ruin instead of an habitation – and teaching these successors as little to respect their contrivances, as they had themselves respected the institutions of their forefathers. By this unprincipled facility of changing the state as often, and as much, and in as many ways as there are floating fancies or fashions, the whole chain and continuity of the commonwealth would be broken. No one generation could link with the other. Men would become little better than the flies of a summer.

And first of all the science of jurisprudence, the pride of the human intellect, which, with all its defects, redundancies, and errors, is the collected reason of ages, combining the principles of original justice with the infinite variety of human concerns, as a heap of old exploded errors, would be no longer studied. Personal self-sufficiency and arrogance (the certain attendants upon all those who have never experienced a wisdom greater than their own) would usurp the tribunal. Of course, no certain laws, establishing invariably grounds of hope and fear, would keep the actions of men in a certain course, or direct them to a certain end. Nothing stable in the modes of holding property, or exercising function, could form a solid ground on which any parent could speculate in the education of his offspring, or in a choice for their future establishment in the world. No principles would be early worked into the habits. As soon as the most able instructor had completed his laborious course of institution, instead of sending forth his pupil, accomplished in a virtuous discipline, fitted to procure him attention and respect, in his place in society, he would find every thing altered; and that he had turned out a poor creature to the contempt and derision of the world, ignorant of the true grounds of estimation. Who would insure a tender and delicate sense of honour to beat almost with the first pulses of the heart, when no man could know what would be the test of honour in a nation, continually varying the standard of its coin? No part of life would retain its acquisitions. Barbarism with regard to science and literature, unskilfulness with regard to arts and manufactures, would infallibly succeed to the want of a steady education and settled principle; and thus the commonwealth itself would, in a few generations, crumble away, be disconnected into the dust and powder of individuality, and at length dispersed to all the winds of heaven.

To avoid therefore the evils of inconstancy and versatility, ten thousand times worse than those of obstinacy and the blindest prejudice, we have consecrated the state, that no man should approach to look into its defects or corruptions but with due caution; that he should never dream of beginning its reformation by its subversion; that he should approach to the faults of the state as to the wounds of a father, with pious awe and trembling sollicitude. By this wise prejudice we are taught to look with horror on those children of their country who are prompt rashly to hack that aged parent in pieces, and put him into the kettle of magicians, in hopes that by their poisonous weeds, and wild incantations, they may regenerate the paternal constitution, and renovate their father's life.

Society is indeed a contract. Subordinate contracts for objects of mere occasional interest may be dissolved at pleasure – but the state ought not to be considered as nothing better than a partnership agreement in a trade of pepper and coffee, callico or tobacco, or some other such low concern, to be taken up for a little temporary interest, and to be dissolved by the fancy of the parties. It is to be looked on with other reverence; because it is not a partnership in things subservient only to the gross animal existence of a temporary and perishable nature. It is a partnership in all science; a partnership in all art; a partnership in every virtue, and in all perfection. As the ends of such a partnership cannot be obtained in many generations, it becomes a partnership not only between those who are living, but between those who are living, those who are dead, and those who are to be born. Each contract of each particular state is but a clause in the great primaeval contract of eternal society, linking the lower with the higher natures, connecting the visible and invisible world, according to a fixed compact sanctioned by the inviolable oath which holds all physical and all moral natures, each in their appointed place. This law is not subject to the will of those, who by an obligation above them, and infinitely superior, are bound to submit their will to that law. The municipal corporations of that universal kingdom are not morally at liberty at their pleasure, and on their speculations of a contingent improvement, wholly to separate and tear asunder the bands of their subordinate community, and to dissolve it into an unsocial, uncivil, unconnected chaos of elementary principles. It is the first and supreme necessity only, a necessity that is not chosen but chooses, a necessity paramount to deliberation, that admits no discussion, and demands no evidence, which alone can justify a resort to anarchy. This necessity is no exception to the rule; because this necessity itself is a part too of that moral and physical disposition of things to which man must be obedient by consent or force; but if that which is only submission to necessity should be made the object of choice, the law is broken, nature is disobeyed, and the rebellious are outlawed, cast forth, and exiled, from this world of reason, and order, and peace, and virtue, and fruitful penitence, into the antagonist world of madness, discord, vice, confusion, and unavailing sorrow.

These, my dear Sir, are, were, and I think long will be the sentiments of not the least learned and reflecting part of this kingdom. They who are included in this description, form their opinions on such grounds as such persons ought to form them. The less enquiring receive them from an authority which those whom Providence dooms to

live on trust need not be ashamed to rely on. These two
sorts of men move in the same direction, tho' in a different place. They both move with the order of the universe. They all know or feel this great antient truth:
'Quod illi principi et praepotenti deo qui omnem hunc
mundum regit, nihil eorum quae quidem fiant in terris
acceptius quam concilia et caetus hominum jure sociati
quae civitates appellantur.'[82] They take this tenet of the
head and heart, not from the great name which it immediately bears, nor from the greater from whence it is
derived; but from that which alone can give true
weight and sanction to any learned opinion, the common
nature and common relation of men. Persuaded that all
things ought to be done with reference, and referring all
to the point of reference to which all should be directed,
they think themselves bound, not only as individuals in
the sanctuary of the heart, or as congregated in that personal capacity, to renew the memory of their high origin
and cast; but also in their corporate character to perform
their national homage to the institutor, and author and
protector of civil society; without which civil society
man could not by any possibility arrive at the perfection
of which his nature is capable, nor even make a remote
and faint approach to it. They conceive that He who gave
our nature to be perfected by our virtue, willed also the
necessary means of its perfection – He willed therefore
the state – He willed its connexion with the source and
original archetype of all perfection. They who are convinced of this his will, which is the law of laws and the
sovereign or sovereigns, cannot think it reprehensible, that
this our corporate fealty and homage, that this our recognition of a signiory paramount, I had almost said this
oblation of the state itself, as a worthy offering on the high
altar of universal praise, should be performed as all publick solemn acts are performed, in buildings, in musick,

in decoration, in speech, in the dignity of persons, according to the customs of mankind, taught by their nature; that is, with modest splendour, with unassuming state, with mild majesty and sober pomp. For those purposes they think some part of the wealth of the country is as usefully employed as it can be, in fomenting the luxury of individuals. It is the publick ornament. It is the publick consolation. It nourishes the publick hope. The poorest man finds his own importance and dignity in it, whilst the wealth and pride of individuals at every moment makes the man of humble rank and fortune sensible of his inferiority, and degrades and vilifies his condition. It is for the man in humble life, and to raise his nature, and to put him in mind of a state in which the privileges of opulence will cease, when he will be equal by nature, and may be more than equal by virtue, that this portion of the general wealth of his country is employed and sanctified.

I assure you I do not aim at singularity. I give you opinions which have been accepted amongst us, from very early times to this moment, with a continued and general approbation, and which indeed are so worked into my mind, that I am unable to distinguish what I have learned from others from the results of my own meditation.

It is on some such principles that the majority of the people of England, far from thinking a religious, national establishment unlawful, hardly think it lawful to be without one. In France you are wholly mistaken if you do not believe us above all other things attached to it, and beyond all other nations; and when this people has acted unwisely and unjustifiably in its favour (as in some instances they have done most certainly) in their very errors you will at least discover their zeal.

This principle runs through the whole system of their polity. They do not consider their church establishment as convenient, but as essential to their state; not as a thing heterogeneous and separable; something added for accommodation; what they may either keep up or lay aside, according to their temporary ideas of convenience. They consider it as the foundation of their whole constitution, with which, and with every part of which, it holds an indissoluble union. Church and state are ideas inseparable in their minds, and scarcely is the one ever mentioned without mentioning the other.

Our education is so formed as to confirm and fix this impression. Our education is in a manner wholly in the hands of ecclesiastics, and in all stages from infancy to manhood. Even when our youth, leaving schools and universities, enter that most important period of life which begins to link experience and study together, and when with that view they visit other countries, instead of old domestics whom we have seen as governors to principal men from other parts, three-fourths of those who go abroad with our young nobility and gentlemen are ecclesiastics; not as austere masters, nor as mere followers; but as friends and companions of a graver character, and not seldom persons as well born as themselves. With them, as relations, they most commonly keep up a close connexion through life. By this connexion we conceive that we attach our gentlemen to the church; and we liberalize the church by an intercourse with the leading characters of the country.[83]

So tenacious are we of the old ecclesiastical modes and fashions of institution,[84] that very little alteration has been made in them since the fourteenth or fifteenth century; adhering in this particular, as in all things else, to our old settled maxim, never entirely nor at once to depart from antiquity. We found these old institutions, on the whole, favourable to morality and discipline; and we thought they were susceptible of amendment, without altering the ground. We thought that they were capable of receiving and meliorating, and above all of preserving the accessions of science and literature, as the order of Providence should successively produce them. And after all, with this Gothic and monkish education (for such it is in the ground-work) we may put in our claim to as ample and as early a share in all the improvements in science, in arts, and in literature, which have illuminated and adorned the modern world, as any other nation in Europe; we think one main cause of this improvement was our not despising the patrimony of knowledge which was left us by our forefathers.

It is from our attachment to a church establishment that the English nation did not think it wise to entrust that great fundamental interest of the whole to what they trust no part of their civil or military public service, that is to the unsteady and precarious contribution of individuals. They go further. They certainly never have suffered and never will suffer the fixed estate of the church to be converted into a pension, to depend on the treasury, and to be delayed, withheld, or perhaps to be extinguished by fiscal difficulties; which difficulties may sometimes be pretended for political purposes, and are in fact often brought on by the extravagance, negligence, and rapacity of politicians. The people of England think that they have constitutional motives, as well as religious, against any project of turning their independent clergy into ecclesiastical pensioners of state. They tremble for their liberty, from the influence of a clergy dependent on the crown; they tremble for the public tranquillity from the disorders of a factious clergy, if it were made to depend upon any other than the crown. They therefore made their church, like their king and their nobility, independent.

From the united considerations of religion and constitutional policy, from their opinion of a duty to make a sure provision for the consolation of the feeble and the instruction of the ignorant, they have incorporated and identified the estate of the church with the mass of *private property*, of which the state is not the proprietor, either for use or dominion, but the guardian only and the regulator. They have ordained that the provision of this establishment might be as stable as the earth on which it stands, and should not fluctuate with the Euripus[85] of funds and actions.

The men of England, the men, I mean, of light and leading in England, whose wisdom (if they have any) is open and direct, would be ashamed, as of a silly deceitful trick, to profess any religion in name, which by their proceedings they appeared to contemn. If by their conduct (the only language that rarely lies) they seemed to regard the great ruling principle of the moral and the natural world, as a mere invention to keep the vulgar in obedience, they apprehend that by such a conduct they would defeat the politic purpose they have in view. They would find it difficult to make others to believe in a system to which they manifestly gave no credit themselves. The Christian statesmen of this land would indeed first provide for the *multitude*; because it is the *multitude*; and is therefore, as such, the first object in the ecclesiastical institution, and in all institutions. They have been taught, that the circumstance of the gospels being preached to the poor, was one of the great tests of its true mission. They think, therefore, that those do not believe it, who do not take care it should be preached to the poor. But as they know that charity is not confined to any one description, but ought to apply itself to all men who have wants, they are not deprived of a due and anxious sensation of pity to the distresses of the miserable great. They are not repelled through a fastidious delicacy, at the stench of their arrogance and presumption, from a medicinal attention to their mental blotches and running sores. They are sensible, that religious instruction is of more consequence to them than to any others; from the greatness of the temptation to which they are exposed; from the important consequences that attend their faults; from the contagion of their ill example; from the necessity of bowing down the stubborn neck of their pride and ambition to the yoke of moderation and virtue; from a consideration of the fat stupidity and gross ignorance concerning what imports men most to know, which prevails at courts, and at the head of armies, and in senates, as much as at the loom and in the field.

The English people are satisfied that to the great the consolations of religion are as necessary as its instructions. They too are among the unhappy. They feel personal pain and domestic sorrow. In these they have no privilege, but are subject to pay their full contingent to the contributions levied on mortality. They want this sovereign balm under their gnawing cares and anxieties, which being less conversant about the limited wants of animal life, range without limit, and are diversified by infinite combinations in the wild and unbounded regions of imagination. Some charitable dole is wanting to these, our often very unhappy brethren, to fill the gloomy void that reigns in minds which have nothing on earth to hope or fear; something to relieve in the killing languor and over-laboured lassitude of those who have nothing to do; something to excite an appetite to existence in the palled satiety which attends on all pleasures which may be bought, where nature is not left to her own process, where even desire is anticipated, and therefore fruition defeated by meditated schemes and contrivances of delight; and no interval, no obstacle, is interposed between the wish and the accomplishment.

The people of England know how little influence the

teachers of religion are likely to have with the wealthy and powerful of long standing, and how much less with the newly fortunate, if they appear in a manner no way assorted to those with whom they must associate, and over whom they must even exercise, in some cases, something like an authority. What must they think of that body of teachers, if they see it in no part above the establishment of their domestic servants? If the poverty were voluntary, there might be some difference. Strong instances of self-denial operate powerfully in our minds; and a man who has no wants has obtained great freedom and firmness, and even dignity. But as the mass of any description of men are but men, and their poverty cannot be voluntary, that disrespect which attends upon all Lay poverty, will not depart from the Ecclesiastical. Our provident constitution has therefore taken care that those who are to instruct presumptuous ignorance, those who are to be censors over insolent vice, should neither incur their contempt, nor live upon their alms; nor will it tempt the rich to a neglect of the true medicine of their minds. For these reasons, whilst we provide first for the poor, and with a parental solicitude, we have not relegated religion (like something we were ashamed to shew) to obscure municipalities or rustic villages. No! We will have her to exalt her mitred front in courts and parliaments. We will have her mixed throughout the whole mass of life, and blended with all the classes of society. The people of England will shew to the haughty potentates of the world, and to their talking sophisters, that a free, a generous, an informed nation, honours the high magistrates of its church; that it will not suffer the insolence of wealth and titles, or any other species of proud pretension, to look down with scorn upon what they look up to with reverence; nor presume to trample on that acquired personal nobility, which they intend always to be, and which often is the fruit, not the reward, (for what can be the reward?) of learning, piety, and virtue. They can see, without pain or grudging, an Archbishop precede a Duke. They can see a Bishop of Durham, or a Bishop of Winchester, in possession of ten thousand pounds a year; and cannot conceive why it is in worse hands than estates to the like amount in the hands of this Earl, or that Squire; although it may be true, that so many dogs and horses are not kept by the former, and fed with the victuals which ought to nourish the children of the people. It is true, the whole church revenue is not always employed, and to every shilling, in charity; nor perhaps ought it; but something is generally so employed. It is better to cherish virtue and humanity, by leaving much to free will, even with some loss to the object, than to attempt to make men mere machines and instruments of a political benevolence. The world on the whole will gain by liberty, without which virtue cannot exist.

When once the commonwealth has established the estates of the church as property, it can, consistently, hear nothing of the more or the less. Too much and too little are treason against property. What evil can arise from the quantity in any hand, whilst the supreme authority has the full, sovereign superintendance over this, as over all property, to prevent every species of abuse; and, whenever it notably deviates, to give to it a direction agreeable to the purposes of its institution.

In England most of us conceive that it is envy and malignity towards those who are often the beginners of their own fortune, and not a love of the self-denial and mortification of the antient church, that makes some look askance at the distinctions, and honours, and revenues, which, taken from no person, are set apart for virtue. The ears of the people in England are distinguishing. They hear these men speak broad. Their tongue betrays them. Their language is in the *patois* of fraud; in the cant and gibberish of hypocrisy. The people of England must think so, when these praters affect to carry back the clergy to that primitive evangelic poverty which, in the spirit, ought always to exist in them, (and in us too, however we may like it) but in the thing must be varied, when the relation of that body to the state is altered; when manners, when modes of life, when indeed the whole order of human affairs has undergone a total revolution. We shall believe those reformers to be then honest enthusiasts, not as now we think them, cheats and deceivers, when we see them throwing their own goods into common, and submitting their own persons to the austere discipline of the early church.

With these ideas rooted in their minds, the commons of Great Britain, in the national emergencies, will never seek their resource from the confiscation of the estates of the church and poor. Sacrilege and proscription are not among the ways and means in our committee of supply. The Jews in Change Alley have not yet dared to hint their hopes of a mortgage on the revenues belonging to the see of Canterbury. I am not afraid that I shall be disavowed, when I assure you that there is not *one* public man in this kingdom, whom you would wish to quote; no not one of any party or description, who does not reprobate the dishonest, perfidious, and cruel confiscation which the national assembly has been compelled to make of that property which it was their first duty to protect.

It is with the exultation of a little natural pride I tell you, that those amongst us who have wished to pledge the societies of Paris in the cup of their abominations, have been disappointed. The robbery of your church has proved a security to the possessions of ours. It has roused the people. They see with horror and alarm that enormous and shameless act of proscription. It has opened, and will more and more open their eyes upon the selfish enlargement of mind, and the narrow liberality of sentiment of insidious men, which commencing in close hypocrisy and fraud have ended in open violence and rapine. At home we behold similar beginnings. We are on our guard against similar conclusions.

I hope we shall never be so totally lost to all sense of the duties imposed upon us by the law of social union, as, upon any pretext of public service, to confiscate the goods of a single unoffending citizen. Who but a tyrant (a name expressive of every thing which can vitiate and degrade human nature) could think of seizing on the property of men, unaccused, unheard, untried, by whole descriptions, by hundreds and thousands together? who that had not lost every trace of humanity could think of casting down men of exalted rank and sacred function, some of them of an age to call at once for reverence and compassion, of casting them down from the highest situation in the commonwealth, wherein they were maintained by their own landed property, to a state of indigence, depression and contempt?

The confiscators truly have made some allowance to their victims from the scraps and fragments of their own tables from which they have been so harshly driven, and which have been so bountifully spread for a feast to the harpies of usury. But to drive men from independence to live on alms is itself great cruelty. That which might be a tolerable condition to men in one state of life, and not habituated to other things, may, when all these circumstances are altered, be a dreadful revolution; and one to which a virtuous mind would feel pain in condemning any guilt except that which would demand the life of the offender. But to many minds this punishment of *degradation* and *infamy* is worse than death. Undoubtedly it is an infinite aggravation of this cruel suffering, that the persons who were taught a double prejudice in favour of religion, by education and by the place they held in the administration of its functions, are to receive the remnants of their property as alms from the profane and impious hands of those who had plundered them of all the rest; to receive (if they are at all to receive) not from the charitable contributions of the faithful, but from the insolent tenderness of known and avowed Atheism, the maintenance of religion, measured out to them on the standard of the contempt in which it is held; and for the purpose of rendering those who receive the allowance vile and of no estimation in the eyes of mankind.

But this act of seizure of property, it seems, is a judgment in law, and not a confiscation. They have, it seems, found out in the academies of the *Palais Royale*, and the *Jacobins*,[86] that certain men had no right to the possessions which they held under law, usage, the decisions of courts, and the accumulated prescription of a thousand years. They say that ecclesiastics are fictitious persons, creatures of the state; whom at pleasure they may destroy, and of course limit and modify in every particular; that the goods they possess are not properly theirs, but belong to the state which created the fiction; and we are therefore not to trouble ourselves with what they may suffer in their natural feelings and natural persons, on account of what is done towards them in this their constructive character. Of what import is it, under what names you injure men, and deprive them of the just emoluments of a profession, in which they were not only permitted but encouraged by the state to engage; and upon the supposed certainty of which emoluments they had formed the plan of their lives, contracted debts, and led multitudes to an entire dependence upon them?

You do not imagine, Sir, that I am going to compliment this miserable distinction of persons with any long discussion. The arguments of tyranny are as contemptible as its force is dreadful. Had not your confiscators by their early crimes obtained a power which secures indemnity to all the crimes of which they have since been guilty, or that they can commit, it is not the syllogism of the logician but the lash of the executioner that would have refuted a sophistry which becomes an accomplice of theft and murder. The sophistick tyrants of Paris are loud in their declamations against the departed regal tyrants who in former ages have vexed the world. They are thus bold, because they are safe from the dungeons and iron cages of their old masters. Shall we be more tender of the tyrants of our own time, when we see them acting worse tragedies under our eyes? shall we not use the same liberty that they do, when we can use it with the same safety? when to speak honest truth only requires a contempt of the opinions of those whose actions we abhor?

This outrage on all the rights of property was at first covered with what, on the system of their conduct, was the most astonishing of all pretexts – a regard to national faith. The enemies to property at first pretended a most tender, delicate, and scrupulous anxiety for keeping the king's engagements with the public creditor. These professors of the rights of men are so busy in teaching others, that they have not leisure to learn any thing themselves; otherwise they would have known that it is to the property of the citizen, and not to the demands of the creditor of the state, that the first and original faith of civil society is pledged. The claim of the citizen is prior in time, paramount in title, superior in equity. The fortunes of individuals, whether possessed by acquisition, or by descent, or in virtue of a participation in the goods of some community, were no part of the creditor's security, expressed or implied. They never so much as entered into his head when he made his bargain. He well knew that the public, whether represented by a monarch, or by a senate, can pledge nothing but the public estate; and it can have no public estate, except in what it derives from a just and proportioned imposition upon the citizens at large. This was engage, and nothing else could be engaged to the public creditor. No man can mortgage his injustice as a pawn for his fidelity.

It is impossible to avoid some observation on the contradictions caused by the extreme rigour and the extreme laxity of the new public faith, which influenced in this transaction, and which influenced not according to the nature of the obligation, but to the description of the persons to whom it was engaged. No acts of the old government of the kings of France are held valid in the National Assembly, except its pecuniary engagements; acts of all others of the most ambiguous legality. The rest of the acts of that royal government are considered in so odious a light, that to have a claim under its authority is looked on as a sort of crime. A pension, given as a reward for service to the state, is surely as good a ground of property as any security for money advanced to the state. It is a better; for money is paid, and well paid, to obtain that service. We have however seen multitudes of people under this description in France, who never had been deprived of their allowances by the most arbitrary ministers, in the most arbitrary times, by this assembly of the rights of men, robbed without mercy. They were told, in answer to their claim to the bread earned with their blood, that their services had not been rendered to the country that now exists.

This laxity of public faith is not confined to those unfortunate persons. The assembly, with perfect consistency it must be owned, is engaged in a respectable deliberation how far it is bound by the treaties made with other nations under the former government and their Committee is to report which of them they ought to ratify, and which not. By this means they have put the external fidelity of this virgin state on a par with its internal.

It is not easy to conceive upon what rational principle the royal government should not, of the two, rather have possessed the power of rewarding service, and making treaties, in virtue of its prerogative, than that of pledging to creditors the revenue of the state actual and possible. The treasure of the nation, of all things, has been the least allowed to the prerogative of the king of France, or to the prerogative of any king in Europe. To mortgage the public revenue implies the sovereign dominion, in the fullest sense, over the public purse. It goes far beyond the trust even of a temporary and occasional taxation. The acts however of that dangerous power (the distinctive mark of a boundless despotism) have been alone held sacred. Whence arose this preference given by a democratic assembly to a body of property deriving its title from the most critical and obnoxious of all the exertions of monarchical authority? Reason can furnish nothing to reconcile inconsistency; nor can partial favour be accounted for upon equitable principles. But the contradiction and partiality which admit no justification, are not the less without an adequate cause; and that cause I do not think it difficult to discover.

By the vast debt of France a great monied interest had insensibly grown up, and with it a great power. By the ancient usages which prevailed in that kingdom, the general circulation of property, and in particular the mutual convertibility of land into money, and of money into land, had always been a matter of difficulty. Family settlements, rather more general and more strict than they are in England, the *jus retractus*,[87] the great mass of landed property held by the crown, and by a maxim of the French law held unalienably, the vast estates of the ec-clesiastic corporations, – all these had kept the landed and monied interests more separated in France, less miscible, and the owners of the two distinct species of property not so well disposed to each other as they are in this country.

The monied property was long looked on with rather an evil eye by the people. They saw it connected with their distresses, and aggravating them. It was no less envied by the old landed interests, partly for the same reasons that rendered it obnoxious to the people, but much more so as it eclipsed, by the splendour of an ostentatious luxury, the unendowed pedigrees and naked titles of several among the nobility. Even when the nobility, which repre-sented the more permanent landed interest, united them-selves by marriage (which sometimes was the case) with the other description, the wealth which saved the family from ruin, was supposed to contaminate and degrade it. Thus the enmities and heart-burnings of these parties were encreased even by the usual means by which discord is made to cease, and quarrels are turned into friendship. In the mean time, the pride of the wealthy men, not noble or newly noble, encreased with its cause. They felt with resentment an inferiority, the grounds of which they did not acknowledge. There was no measure to which they were not willing to lend themselves, in order to be revenged of the outrages of this rival pride, and to exalt their wealth to what they considered as its natural rank and estimation. They struck at the nobility through the crown and the church. They attacked them particularly on the side on which they thought them the most vulner-able, that is, the possessions of the church, which, through the patronage of the crown, generally devolved upon the nobility. The bishopricks, and the great commendatory abbies, were, with few exceptions, held by that order.

In this state of real, though not always perceived warfare between the noble ancient landed interest, and the new monied interest, the greatest because the most applicable strength was in the hands of the latter. The monied interest is in its nature more ready for any adventure; and its possessors more disposed to new enterprizes of any kind. Being of a recent acquisition, it falls in more naturally with any novelties. It is therefore the kind of wealth which will be resorted to by all who wish for change.

Along with the monied interest, a new description of men had grown up, with whom that interest soon formed a close and marked union; I mean the political Men of Letters. Men of Letters, fond of distinguishing themselves, are rarely averse to innovation. Since the decline of the life and greatness of Lewis the XIVth, they were not so much cultivated either by him, or by the regent, or the successors to the crown; nor were they engaged to the court by favours and emoluments so systematically as during the splendid period of that ostentatious and not impolitic reign. What they lost in the old court protection, they endeavoured to make up by joining in a sort of incorporation of their own; to which the two academies of France,[84] and afterwards the vast undertaking of the Encyclopædia,[88] carried on by a society of these gentlemen, did not a little contribute.

The literary cabal had some years ago formed something like a regular plan for the destruction of the Christian religion. This object they pursued with a degree of zeal which hitherto had been discovered only in the propagators of some system of piety. They were possessed with a spirit of proselytism in the most fanatical degree; and from thence, by an easy progress, with the spirit of persecution according to their means.* What was not to be done towards their great end by any direct or immediate act, might be wrought by a longer process through the medium of opinion. To command that opinion, the first step is to establish a dominion over those who direct it. They contrived to possess themselves, with great method and perseverance, of all the avenues to literary fame. Many of them indeed stood high in the ranks of literature and science. The world had done them justice; and in favour of general talents forgave the evil tendency of their peculiar principles. This was true liberality; which they returned by endeavouring to confine the reputation of sense, learning, and taste to themselves or their followers. I will venture to say that this narrow, exclusive spirit has not been less prejudicial to literature and to taste, than to morals and true philosophy. These Atheistical fathers have a bigotry of their own; and they have learnt to talk against monks with the spirit of a monk. But in some things they are men of the world. The resources of intrigue are called in to supply the defects of argument and wit. To this system of literary monopoly was joined an unremitting industry to blacken and discredit in every way, and by every means, all those who did not hold to their faction. To those who have observed the spirit of their conduct, it has long been clear that nothing was wanted but the power of carrying the intolerance of the tongue and of the pen into a persecution which would strike at property, liberty, and life.

The desultory and faint persecution carried on against them, more from compliance with form and decency than with serious resentment, neither weakened their strength, nor relaxed their efforts. The issue of the

* This (down to the end of the first sentence in the next paragraph) and some other parts here and there, were inserted, on his reading the manuscript, by my lost son. [1803]

whole was, that what with opposition, and what with success, a violent and malignant zeal, of a kind hitherto unknown in the world, had taken an entire possession of
their minds, and rendered their whole conversation,
which otherwise would have been pleasing and instructive, perfectly disgusting.[89] A spirit of cabal, intrigue, and
proselytism, pervaded all their thoughts, words, and
actions. And, as controversial zeal soon turns its thoughts
on force, they began to insinuate themselves into a correspondence with foreign princes; in hopes, through their
authority, which at first they flattered, they might bring
about the changes they had in view. To them it was indifferent whether these changes were to be accomplished
by the thunderbolt of despotism, or by the earthquake
of popular commotion. The correspondence between this
cabal, and the late king of Prussia,[90] will throw no small
light upon the spirit of all their proceedings.* For the same
purpose for which they intrigued with princes, they cultivated, in a distinguished manner, the monied interest
of France; and partly through the means furnished by
those whose peculiar offices gave them the most extensive
and certain means of communication, they carefully occupied all the avenues to opinion.

Writers, especially when they act in a body, and with
one direction, have great influence on the publick mind;
the allegiance therefore of these writers with the monied
interest† had no small effect in removing the popular
odium and envy which attended that species of wealth.
These writers, like the propagators of all novelties, pretended to a great zeal for the poor, and the lower orders,
whilst in their satires they rendered hateful, by every

* I do not chuse to shock the feeling of the moral reader with any
quotation of their vulgar, base, and profane language.

† Their connexion with Turgot[91] and almost all the people of the
finance. [1803]

exaggeration, the faults of courts, of nobility, and of priesthood. They became a sort of demagogues. They served as a link to unite, in favour of one object, obnoxious wealth to restless and desperate poverty.

As these two kinds of men appear principal leaders in all the late transactions, their junction and politics will serve to account, not upon any principles of law or of policy, but as a *cause*, for the general fury with which all the landed property of ecclesiastical corporations has been attacked; and the great care which, contrary to their pretended principles, has been taken, of a monied interest originating from the authority of the crown. All the envy against wealth and power, was artificially directed against other descriptions of riches. On what other principle than that which I have stated can we account for an appearance so extraordinary and unnatural as that of the ecclesiastical possessions, which had stood so many successions of ages and shocks of civil violences, and were guarded at once by justice, and by prejudice, being applied to the payment of debts, comparatively recent, invidious, and contracted by a decried and subverted government?

Was the public estate a sufficient stake for the public debts? Assume that it was not, and that a loss *must* be incurred somewhere – When the only estate lawfully possessed, and which the contracting parties had in contemplation at the time in which their bargain was made, happens to fail, who, according to the principles of natural and legal equity, ought to be the sufferer? Certainly it ought to be either the party who trusted; or the party who persuaded him to trust; or both; and not third parties who had no concern with the transaction. Upon any insolvency they ought to suffer who were weak enough to lend upon bad security, or they who fraudulently held out a security that was not valid. Laws are acquainted with no other rules of decision. But by the new institute of the rights of men, the only persons, who in equity ought to suffer, are the only persons who are to be saved harmless: those are to answer the debt who neither were lenders or borrowers, mortgagers or mortgagees.

What had the clergy to do with these transactions? What had they to do with any publick engagement further than the extent of their own debt? To that, to be sure, their estates were bound to the last acre. Nothing can lead more to the true spirit of the assembly, which sits for public confiscation, with its new equity and its new morality, than an attention to their proceeding with regard to this debt of the clergy. The body of confiscators, true to that monied interest for which they were false to every other, have found the clergy competent to incur a legal debt. Of course they declared them legally entitled to the property which their power of incurring the debt and mortgaging the estate implied; recognizing the rights of those persecuted citizens, in the very act in which they were thus grossly violated.

If, as I said, any persons are to make good deficiencies to the public creditor, besides the public at large, they must be those who managed the agreement. Why therefore are not the estates of all the comptrollers general confiscated?* Why not those of the long succession of ministers, financiers, and bankers who have been enriched whilst the nation was impoverished by their dealings and their counsels? Why is not the estate of Mr Laborde[92] declared forfeited rather than of the archbishop of Paris,[93] who has had nothing to do in the creation or in the jobbing of the public funds? Or, if you must confiscate old landed estates in favour of the money-jobbers, why is the penalty confined to one description? I do not know whether the expences of the duke de Choiseul[94] have left any thing of the infinite sums which he had derived from

*All have been confiscated in their turn. [1803]

the bounty of his master, during the transactions of a reign which contributed largely, by every species of prodigality in war and peace, to the present debt of France. If any such remains, why is not this confiscated? I remember to have been in Paris during the time of the old government. I was there just after the duke of d'Aiguillon[95] had been snatched (as it was generally thought) from the block by the hand of a protecting despotism. He was a minister, and had some concern in the affairs of that prodigal period. Why do I not see his estate delivered up to the municipalities in which it is situated? The noble family of Noailles[96] have long been servants, (meritorious servants I admit) to the crown of France, and have had of course some share in its bounties. Why do I hear nothing of the application of their estates to the public debt? Why is the estate of the duke de Rochefoucault[97] more sacred than that of the cardinal de Rochefoucault?[98] The former is, I doubt not, a worthy person; and (if it were not a sort of profaneness to talk of the use, of his affecting the title to the property) he makes a good use of his revenues; but it is no disrespect to him to say, what authentic information well warrants me in saying, that the use made of a property equally valid, by his brother* the cardinal archbishop of Rouen, was far more laudable and far more public-spirited. Can one hear of the proscription of such persons, and the confiscation of their effects, without indignation and horror? He is not a man who does not feel such emotions on such occasions. He does not deserve the name of a free man who will not express them.

Few barbarous conquerors have ever made so terrible a revolution in property. None of the heads of the Roman factions, when they established 'crudelem illam

---

* Not his brother, nor any near relation; but this mistake does not affect the argument. [1803]

Hastam'[99] in all their auctions of rapine, have ever set up to sale the goods of the conquered citizen to such an enormous amount. It must be allowed in favour of those tyrants of antiquity, that what was done by them could hardly be said to be done in cold blood. Their passions were inflamed, their tempers soured, their understandings confused, with the spirit of revenge, with the innumerable reciprocated and recent inflictions and retaliations of blood and rapine. They were driven beyond all bounds of moderation by the apprehension of the return of power with the return of property to the families of those they had injured beyond all hope of forgiveness.

These Roman confiscators, who were yet only in the elements of tyranny, and were not instructed in the rights of men to exercise all sorts of cruelties on each other without provocation, thought it necessary to spread a sort of colour over their injustice. They considered the vanquished party as composed of traitors who had borne arms, or otherwise had acted with hostility against the commonwealth. They regarded them as persons who had forfeited their property by their crimes. With you, in your improved state of the human mind, there was no such formality. You seized upon five millions sterling of annual rent, and turned forty or fifty thousand human creatures out of their houses, because 'such was your pleasure.' The tyrant, Harry the Eighth of England, as he was not better enlightened than the Roman Marius's and Sylla's, and had not studied in your new schools, did not know what an effectual instrument of despotism was to be found in that grand magazine of offensive weapons, the rights of men. When he resolved to rob the abbies, as the club of the Jacobins have robbed all the ecclesiastics, he began by setting on foot a commission to examine into the crimes and abuses which prevailed in those communities. As it might be expected, his commission reported truths, exaggerations, and falsehoods. But truly or falsely it reported abuses and offences. However, as abuses might be corrected, as every crime of persons does not infer a forfeiture with regard to communities, and as property, in that dark age, was not discovered to be a creature of prejudice, all those abuses (and there were enough of them) were hardly thought sufficient ground for such a confiscation as it was for his purposes to make. He therefore procured the formal surrender of these estates. All these operose proceedings were adopted by one of the most decided tyrants in the rolls of history, as necessary preliminaries, before he could venture, by bribing the members of his two servile houses with a share of the spoil, and holding out to them an eternal immunity from taxation, to demand a confirmation of his iniquitous proceedings by an act of parliament. Had fate reserved him to our times, four technical terms would have done his business, and saved him all this trouble; he needed nothing more than one short form of incantation – '*Philosophy, Light, Liberality, the Rights of Men.*'

I can say nothing in praise of those acts of tyranny, which no voice has hitherto ever commended under any of their false colours; yet in these false colours an homage was paid by despotism to justice. The power which was above all fear and all remorse was not set above all shame. Whilst Shame keeps its watch, Virtue is not wholly extinguished in the heart; nor will Moderation be utterly exiled from the minds of tyrants.

I believe every honest man sympathizes in his reflections with our political poet on that occasion, and will pray to avert the omen whenever these acts of rapacious despotism present themselves to his view or his imagination:

                    – May no such storm
Fall on our times, where ruin must reform.
Tell me (my muse) what monstrous, dire offence,
What crimes could any Christian king incense
To such a rage? Was't luxury, or lust?
Was *he* so temperate, so chaste, so just?
Were these their crimes? they were his own much more;
But wealth is crime enough to him that's poor.*

* The rest of the passage is this –

        Who having spent the treasures of his crown,
        Condemns their luxury to feed his own.
        And yet this act, to varnish o'er the shame
        Of sacrilege, must bear Devotion's name.
        No crime so bold, but would be understood
        A real, or at least a seeming good,
        Who fears not to do ill, yet fears the name;
        And, free from conscience, is a slave to fame.
        Thus he the church at once protects, and spoils:
        But princes' swords are sharper than their styles.
        And thus to th' ages past he makes amends,
        Their charity destroys, their faith defends.
        Then did Religion in a lazy cell,
        In empty aëry contemplations dwell;
        And, like the block, unmoved lay: but ours,
        As much too active, like the stork devours.
        Is there no temp'rate region can be known,
        Betwixt their frigid, and our torrid zone?
        Could we not wake from that lethargic dream,
        But to be restless in a worse extreme?
        And for that lethargy was there no cure,
        But to be cast into a calenture?
        Can knowledge have no bound, but must advance
        So far, to make us wish for ignorance?
        And rather in the dark to grope our way,
        Than, led by a false guide, to err by day?
        Who sees these dismal heaps, but would demand,
        What barbarous invader sack'd the land?
        But when he hears, no Goth, no Turk did bring
        This desolation, but a Christian king;

This same wealth, which is at all times treason and *lese nation* to indigent and rapacious despotism, under all modes of polity, was your temptation to violate property, law, and religion, united in one object. But was the state of France so wretched and undone, that no other resource but rapine remained to preserve its existence? On this point I wish to receive some information. When the states met, was the condition of the finances of France such, that, after œconomising on principles of justice and mercy through all departments, no fair repartition of burthens upon all the orders could possibly restore them? If such an equal imposition would have been sufficient, you well know it might easily have been made. Mr Necker,[101] in the budget which he laid before the Orders assembled at Versailles, made a detailed exposition of the state of the French nation.*

If we give credit to him, it was not necessary to have recourse to any new impositions whatsoever, to put the receipts of France on a balance with its expences. He stated the permanent charges of all descriptions, including the interest of a new loan of four hundred millions, at 531,444,000 livres; the fixed revenue at 475,294,000, making the deficiency 56,150,000, or short of 2,200,000 sterling. But to balance it, he brought forward savings and improvements of revenue (considered as entirely certain) to rather more than the amount of that deficiency; and he concludes with these emphatical words (p.39) 'Quel pays, Messieurs, que celui, ou, *sans impots* et *avec* de

---

When nothing, but the name of zeal, appears
'Twixt our best actions, and the worst of theirs,
What does he think our sacrilege would spare,
When such th' effects of our Devotion are?
    COOPER'S HILL, by Sir JOHN DENHAM.[100]

* Rapport de Mons. le Directeur général des finances, fait par ordre du Roi à Versailles. Mai 5, 1789.

simples objets *inappercus*, on peut faire disparoitre un de-
ficit qui a fait tant de bruit en Europe.' As to the re-
imbursement, the sinking of debt, and the other great
objects of public credit and political arrangement indicated in Mons. Necker's speech, no doubt could be entertained, but that a very moderate and proportioned
assessment on the citizens without distinction would have
provided for all of them to the fullest extent of their
demand.

If this representation of Mons. Necker was false, then
the assembly are in the highest degree culpable for having
forced the king to accept as his minister, and since the
king's deposition, for having employed as *their* minister,
a man who had been capable of abusing so notoriously
the confidence of his master and their own; in a matter
too of the highest moment, and directly appertaining to
his particular office. But if the representation was exact
(as, having always along with you, conceived a high
degree of respect for Mr Necker, I make no doubt it was)
then what can be said in favour of those, who, instead of
moderate, reasonable, and general contribution, have in
cold blood, and impelled by no necessity, had recourse
to a partial and cruel confiscation?

Was that contribution refused on a pretext of privilege, either on the part of the clergy or on that of the
nobility? No certainly. As to the clergy, they even ran
before the wishes of the third order. Previous to the meeting of the states, they had in all their instructions expressly directed their deputies to renounce every immunity, which put them upon a footing distinct from the
condition of their fellow-subjects. In this renunciation
the clergy were even more explicit than the nobility.

But let us suppose that the deficiency had remained at
the 56 millions, (or £. 2,200,000 sterling) as at first stated by
Mr. Necker. Let us allow that all the resources he opposed

to that deficiency were impudent and groundless fictions; and that the assembly (or their lords of articles* at the Jacobins) were from thence justified in laying the whole burthen of that deficiency on the clergy, – yet allowing all this, a necessity of £. 2,200,000 sterling will not support a confiscation to the amount of five millions. The imposition of £. 2,200,000 on the clergy, as partial, would have been oppressive and unjust, but it would not have been altogether ruinous to those on whom it was imposed; and therefore it would not have answered the real purpose of the managers.

Perhaps persons, unacquainted with the state of France, on hearing the clergy and the noblesse were privileged in point of taxation, may be led to imagine, that previous to the revolution these bodies had contributed nothing to the state. This is a great mistake. They certainly did not contribute equally with each other, nor either of them equally with the commons. They both however contributed largely. Neither nobility nor clergy enjoyed any exemption from the excise on consumable commodities, from duties of custom, or from any of the other numerous *indirect* impositions, which in France as well as here, make so very large a proportion of all payments to the public. The noblesse paid the capitation. They paid also a land-tax, called the twentieth penny, to the height sometimes of three, sometimes of four shillings in the pound; both of them *direct* impositions of no light nature, and no trivial produce. The clergy of the provinces annexed by conquest to France (which in extent make about an eighth part of the whole but in wealth a much larger proportion) paid likewise to the capitation and the twentieth penny, at the rate paid by the nobility. The clergy in the old provinces

---

* In the constitution of Scotland during the Stuart reigns, a committee sat for preparing bills; and none could pass, but those previously approved by them. This committee was called lords of articles.

did not pay the capitation; but they had redeemed themselves at the expence of about 24 millions, or a little more than a million sterling. They were exempted from the twentieths; but then they made free gifts; they contracted debts for the state; and they were subject to some other charges, the whole computed at about a thirteenth part of their clear income. They ought to have paid annually about forty thousand pounds more, to put them on a par with the contribution of the nobility.

When the terrors of this tremendous proscription hung over the clergy, they made an offer of a contribution, through the archbishop of Aix,[102] which for its extravagance, ought not to have been accepted. But it was evidently and obviously more advantageous to the public creditor, than any thing which could rationally be promised by the confiscation. Why was it not accepted? The reason is plain – There was no desire that the church should be brought to serve the state. The service of the state was made a pretext to destroy the church. In their way to the destruction of the church they would not scruple to destroy their country: and they have destroyed it. One great end in the project would have been defeated, if the plan of extortion had been adopted in lieu of the scheme of confiscation. The new landed interest connected with the new republic, and connected with it for its very being, could not have been created. This was among the reasons why that extravagant ransom was not accepted.

The madness of the project of confiscation, on the plan that was first pretended, soon became apparent. To bring this unwieldy mass of landed property, enlarged by the confiscation of all the vast landed domain of the crown, at once into market, was obviously to defeat the profits proposed by the confiscation, by depreciating the value of those lands, and indeed of all the landed estates throughout France. Such a sudden diversion of all its circulating money from trade to land, must be an additional mischief. What step was taken? Did the assembly, on becoming sensible of the inevitable ill effects of their projected sale, revert to the offers of the clergy? No distress could oblige them to travel in a course which was disgraced by any appearance of justice. Giving over all hopes from a general immediate sale, another project seems to have succeeded. They proposed to take stock in exchange for the church lands. In that project great difficulties arose in equalizing the objects to be exchanged. Other obstacles also presented themselves, which threw them back again upon some project of sale. The municipalities had taken an alarm. They would not hear of transferring the whole plunder of the kingdom to the stock-holders in Paris. Many of those municipalities had been (upon system) reduced to the most deplorable indigence. Money was no where to be seen. They were therefore led to the point that was so ardently desired. They panted for a currency of any kind which might revive their perishing industry. The municipalities were then to be admitted to a share in the spoil, which evidently rendered the first scheme (if ever it had been seriously entertained) altogether impracticable. Public exigencies pressed upon all sides. The minister of finance reiterated his call for supply with a most urgent, anxious, and boding voice. Thus pressed on all sides, instead of the first plan of converting their bankers into bishops and abbots, instead of paying the old debt, they contracted a new debt, at 3 per cent. creating a new paper currency, founded on an eventual sale of the church lands.[103] They issued this paper currency to satisfy in the first instance chiefly the demands made upon them by the *Bank of discount*,[104] the great machine, or paper-mill, of their fictitious wealth.

The spoil of the church was now become the only resource of all their operations in finance; the vital principle of all their politics; the sole security for the existence of their power. It was necessary by all, even the most violent means, to put every individual on the same bottom, and to bind the nation in one guilty interest to uphold this act, and the authority of those by whom it was done. In order to force the most reluctant into a participation of their pillage, they rendered their paper circulation compulsory in all payments. Those who consider the general tendency of their schemes to this one object as a centre; and a centre from which afterwards all their measures radiate, will not think that I dwell too long upon this part of the proceedings of the national assembly.

To cut off all appearance of connection between the crown and public justice, and to bring the whole under implicit obedience to the dictators in Paris, the old independent judicature of the parliaments,[105] with all its merits, and all its faults, was wholly abolished. Whilst the parliaments existed, it was evident that the people might some time or other come to resort to them, and rally under the standard of their antient laws. It became however a matter of consideration that the magistrates and officers, in the courts now abolished, *had purchased their places* at a very high rate, for which, as well as for the duty they performed, they received but a very low return of interest. Simple confiscation is a boon only for the clergy; – to the lawyers some appearances of equity are to be observed; and they are to receive compensation to an immense amount. Their compensation becomes part of the national debt, for the liquidation of which there is the one exhaustless fund. The lawyers are to obtain their compensation in the new church paper, which is to march with the new principles of judicature and legislature. The dismissed magistrates are to take their share of martyrdom with the ecclesiastics, or to receive their own property from such a fund and in such a manner, as all those, who have been seasoned with the antient principles of juris-prudence, and had been the sworn guardians of property, must look upon with horror. Even the clergy are to receive their miserable allowance out of the depreciated paper which is stamped with the indelible character of sacrilege, and with the symbols of their own ruin, or they must starve. So violent an outrage upon credit, property, and liberty, as this compulsory paper currency, has seldom been exhibited by the alliance of bankruptcy and tyranny, at any time, or in any nation.

In the course of all these operations, at length comes out the grand *arcanum*; – that in reality, and in a fair sense, the lands of the church (so far as any thing certain can be gathered from their proceedings) are not to be sold at all. By the late resolutions of the national assembly, they are indeed to be delivered to the highest bidder. But it is to be observed, that *a certain portion only of the purchase money is to be laid down*. A period of twelve years is to be given for the payment of the rest. The philosophic pur-chasers are therefore, on payment of a sort of fine, to be put instantly into possession of the estate. It becomes in some respects a sort of gift to them; to be held on the feudal tenure of zeal to the new establishment. This project is evidently to let in a body of purchasers without money. The consequence will be, that these purchasers, or rather grantees, will pay, not only from the rents as they accrue, which might as well be received by the state, but from the spoil of the materials of buildings, from waste in woods, and from whatever money, by hands habituated to the gripings of usury, they can wring from the miserable peas-ant. He is to be delivered over to the mercenary and arbi-trary discretion of men, who will be stimulated to every species of extortion by the growing demands on the grow-ing profits of an estate held under the precarious settle-ment of a new political system.

When all the frauds, impostures, violences, rapines, burnings, murders, confiscations, compulsory paper currencies, and every description of tyranny and cruelty employed to bring about and to uphold this revolution, have their natural effect, that is, to shock the moral sentiments of all virtuous and sober minds, the abettors of this philosophic system immediately strain their throats in a declamation against the old monarchical government of France. When they have rendered that deposed power sufficiently black, they then proceed in argument, as if all those who disapprove of their new abuses, must of course be partizans of the old; that those who reprobate their crude and violent schemes of liberty ought to be treated as advocates for servitude. I admit that their necessities do compel them to this base and contemptible fraud. Nothing can reconcile men to their proceedings and projects but the supposition that there is no third option between them and some tyranny as odious as can be furnished by the records of history, or by the invention of poets. This prattling of theirs hardly deserves the name of sophistry. It is nothing but plain impudence. Have these gentlemen never heard, in the whole circle of the worlds of theory and practice, of any thing between the despotism of the monarch and the despotism of the multitude? Have they never heard of a monarchy directed by laws, controlled and balanced by the great hereditary wealth and hereditary dignity of a nation; and both again controlled by a judicious check from the reason and feeling of the people at large acting by a suitable and permanent organ? Is it then impossible that a man may be found who, without criminal ill intention, or pitiable absurdity, shall prefer such a mixed and tempered government to either of the extremes; and who may repute that nation to be destitute of all wisdom and of all virtue, which, having in its choice to obtain such a government with ease, *or rather to confirm it when actually possessed*, thought proper to commit a thousand crimes, and to subject their country to a thousand evils, in order to avoid it? Is it then a truth so universally acknowledged, that a pure democracy is the only tolerable form into which human society can be thrown, that a man is not permitted to hesitate about its merits, without the suspicion of being a friend to tyranny, that is, of being a foe to mankind?

I do not know under what description to class the present ruling authority in France. It affects to be a pure democracy, though I think it in a direct train of becoming shortly a mischievous and ignoble oligarchy. But for the present I admit it to be a contrivance of the nature and effect of what it pretends to. I reprobate no form of government merely upon abstract principles. There may be situations in which the purely democratic form will become necessary. There may be some (very few, and very particularly circumstanced) where it would be clearly desireable. This I do not take to be the case of France, or of any other great country. Until now, we have seen no examples of considerable democracies. The antients were better acquainted with them. Not being wholly unread in the authors, who had seen the most of those constitutions, and who best understood them, I cannot help concurring with their opinion, that an absolute democracy, no more than absolute monarchy, is to be reckoned among the legitimate forms of government. They think it rather the corruption and degeneracy, than the sound constitution of a republic. If I recollect rightly, Aristotle observes, that a democracy has many striking points of resemblance with a tyranny.*

* When I wrote this I quoted from memory, after many years had elapsed from my reading the passage. A learned friend has found it, and it is as follows:

Τὸ ἦθος τὸ αὐτό, καὶ ἄμφω δεσποτικὰ τῶν βελτιόνων, καὶ τὰ ψηφίσματα. ὥσπερ ἐκεῖ τὰ ἐπιτάγματα. καὶ ὁ δημαγωγὸς καὶ ὁ

Of this I am certain, that in a democracy, the majority of the citizens is capable of exercising the most cruel oppressions upon the minority, whenever strong divisions prevail in that kind of polity, as they often must; and that oppression of the minority will extend to far greater numbers, and will be carried on with much greater fury, than can almost ever be apprehended from the dominion of a single sceptre. In such a popular persecution, individual sufferers are in a much more deplorable condition than in any other. Under a cruel prince they have the balmy compassion of mankind to assuage the smart of their wounds; they have the plaudits of the people to animate their generous constancy under their sufferings: but those who are subjected to wrong under multitudes, are deprived of all external consolation. They seem deserted by mankind; overpowered by a conspiracy of their whole species.

But admitting democracy not to have that inevitable tendency to party tyranny, which I suppose it to have, and admitting it to possess as much good in it when unmixed, as I am sure it possesses when compounded with other forms; does monarchy, on its part, contain nothing at all to recommend it? I do not often quote Bolingbroke, nor have his works in general, left any permanent impression on my mind.[106] He is a presumptuous and a superficial writer. But he has one observation, which, in my opinion, is

κόλαξ, οἱ αὐτοὶ καὶ νάλογσν. ἀκαὶ μάλισταδ ἑκάτεροιπαρ᾽ ἑκατέροις ἰσχύουσιν, ἰ ὀμὲν κόλακες παρὰ τυράννοις. οἱ δὲ δημαγωγοὶ παρὰ τοῖς δήμοις τοῖς τοιούτοις. –

'The ethical character is the same; both exercise despotism over the better class of citizens; and decrees are in the one, what ordinance and arrêts are in the other: the demagogue too, and the court favourite, are not unfrequently the same identical men, and always bear a close analogy; and these have the principal power, each in their respective forms of government, favourites with the absolute monarch, and demagogues with a people such as I have described.' Arist. Politic. lib. iv. cap. 4.

not without depth and solidity. He says, that he prefers a monarchy to other governments; because you can better in-graft any description of republic on a monarchy than any thing of monarchy upon the republican forms. I think him perfectly in the right. The fact is so historically; and it agrees well with the speculation.

I know how easy a topic it is to dwell on the faults of departed greatness. By a revolution in the state, the fawn-ing sycophant of yesterday, is converted into the austere critic of the present hour. But steady independent minds, when they have an object of so serious a concern to man-kind as government, under their contemplation, will dis-dain to assume the part of satirists and declaimers. They will judge of human institutions as they do of human characters. They will sort out the good from the evil, which is mixed in mortal institutions as it is in mortal men.

Your government in France, though usually, and I think justly, reputed the best of the unqualified or ill-qualified monarchies, was still full of abuses. These abuses accumu-lated in a length of time, as they must accumulate in every monarchy not under the constant inspection of a popular representative. I am no stranger to the faults and defects of the subverted government of France; and I think I am not inclined by nature or policy to make a panegyric upon any thing which is a just and natural object of censure. But the question is not now of the vices of that monarchy, but of its existence. Is it then true, that the French govern-ment was such as to be incapable or undeserving of re-form; so that it was of absolute necessity the whole fabric should be at once pulled down, and the area cleared for the erection of a theoretic experimental edifice in its place? All France was of a different opinion in the begin-ning of the year 1789. The instructions to the representa-tives to the states-general, from every district in that kingdom, were filled with projects for the reformation of that government, without the remotest suggestion of a design to destroy it. Had such a design been then even insinuated, I believe there would have been but one voice, and that voice for rejecting it with scorn and horror. Men have been sometimes led by degrees, sometimes hurried into things, of which, if they could have seen the whole together, they never would have permitted the most remote approach. When those instructions were given, there was no question but that abuses existed, and that they demanded a reform; nor is there now. In the interval between the instructions and the revolution, things changed their shape; and in consequence of that change, the true question at present is, Whether those who would have reformed, or those who have destroyed, are in the right?

To hear some men speak of the late monarchy of France, you would imagine that they were talking of Persia bleeding under the ferocious sword of Tæhmas Kouli Khân;[107] or at least describing the barbarous anarchic despotism of Turkey, where the finest countries in the most genial climates in the world are wasted by peace more than any countries have been worried by war; where arts are unknown, where manufactures languish, where science is extinguished, where agriculture decays, where the human race itself melts away and perishes under the eye of the observer. Was this the case of France? I have no way of determining the question but by a reference to facts. Facts do not support this resemblance. Along with much evil, there is some good in monarchy itself; and some corrective to its evil, from religion, from laws, from manners, from opinions, the French monarchy must have received; which rendered it (though by no means a free, and therefore by no means a good constitution) a despotism rather in appearance than in reality.

Among the standards upon which the effects of government on any country are to be estimated, I must consider the state of its population as not the least certain. No country in which population flourishes, and is in progressive improvement, can be under a *very* mischievous government. About sixty years ago, the Intendants of the generalities[108] of France made, with other matters, a report of the population of their several districts. I have not the books, which are very voluminous, by me, nor do I know where to procure them (I am obliged to speak by memory, and therefore the less positively) but I think the population of France was by them, even at that period, estimated at twenty-two millions of souls. At the end of the last century it had been generally calculated at eighteen. On either of these estimations France was not ill-peopled. Mr Necker, who is an authority for his own time at least equal to the Intendants for theirs, reckons, and upon apparently sure principles, the people of France, in the year 1780, at twenty-four millions six hundred and seventy thousand. But was this the probable ultimate term under the old establishment? Dr Price is of opinion, that the growth of population in France was by no means at its *acmé* in that year. I certainly defer to Dr Price's authority a good deal more in these speculations, than I do in his general politics. This gentleman, taking ground on Mr Necker's data, is very confident, that since the period of that minister's calculation, the French population has encreased rapidly; so rapidly that in the year 1789 he will not consent to rate the people of that kingdom at a lower number than thirty millions. After abating much (and much I think ought to be abated) from the sanguine calculation of Dr Price, I have no doubt that the population of France did encrease considerably during this later period: but supposing that it encreased to nothing more than will be sufficient to compleat the 24,670,000 to 25 millions, still a population of 25 millions, and that in an encreasing progress, on a space of about twenty-seven thousand square leagues, is immense. It is, for instance, a good deal more than the proportionable population of this island, or even than that of England, the best-peopled part of the united kingdom.

It is not universally true, that France is a fertile country. Considerable tracts of it are barren, and labour under other natural disadvantages. In the portions of that territory, where things are more favourable, as far as I am able to discover, the numbers of the people correspond to the indulgence of nature.* The Generality of Lisle (this I admit is the strongest example) upon an extent of 404½ leagues, about ten years ago, contained 734,600 souls, which is 1772 inhabitants to each square league. The middle term for the rest of France is about 900 inhabitants to the same admeasurement.

I do not attribute this population to the deposed government; because I do not like to compliment the contrivances of men, with what is due in a great degree to the bounty of Providence. But that decried government could not have obstructed, most probably it favoured, the operation of those causes (whatever they were) whether of nature in the soil, or in habits of industry among the people, which has produced so large a number of the species throughout that whole kingdom, and exhibited in some particular places such prodigies of population. I never will suppose that fabrick of a state to be the worst of all political institutions, which, by experience, is found to contain a principle favourable (however latent it may be) to the encrease of mankind.

The wealth of a country is another, and no contemptible standard, by which we may judge whether, on the whole, a government be protecting or destructive. France far ex-

* De l'Administration des Finances de la France, par Mons. Necker, vol. i. p. 288.

ceeds England in the multitude of her people; but I apprehend that her comparative wealth is much inferior to ours;
that it is not so equal in the distribution, nor so ready in
the circulation. I believe the difference in the form of the
two governments to be amongst the causes of this advantage on the side of England. I speak of England, not of the
whole British dominions; which, if compared with those
of France, will, in some degree, weaken the comparative
rate of wealth upon our side. But that wealth, which will
not endure a comparison with the riches of England, may
constitute a very respectable degree of opulence. Mr
Necker's book published in 1785,* contains an accurate
and interesting collection of facts relative to public economy and to political arithmetic; and his speculations on
the subject are in general wise and liberal. In that work
he gives an idea of the state of France, very remote from
the portrait of a country whose government was a perfect
grievance, an absolute evil, admitting no cure but through
the violent and uncertain remedy of a total revolution. He
affirms, that from the year 1726 to the year 1784, there
was coined at the mint of France, in the species of gold
and silver, to the amount of about one hundred millions
of pounds sterling.†

It is impossible that Mr Necker should be mistaken in
the amount of the bullion which has been coined in the
mint. It is a matter of official record. The reasonings of
this able financier, concerning the quantity of gold and
silver which remained for circulation, when he wrote in
1785, that is about four years before the deposition and
imprisonment of the French King, are not of equal certainty; but they are laid on grounds so apparently solid,
that it is not easy to refuse a considerable degree of assent
to his calculation. He calculates the *numeraire*, or what

* De l'Administration des Finances de la France, par M. Necker.
† Vol. iii. chap. 8. and chap. 9.

we call *specie*, then actually existing in France, at about eighty-eight millions of the same English money. A great accumulation of wealth for one country, large as that country is! Mr Necker was so far from considering this influx of wealth as likely to cease, when he wrote in 1785, that he presumes upon a future annual increase of two per cent. upon the money brought into France during the periods from which he computed.

Some adequate cause must have originally introduced all the money coined at its mint into that kingdom; and some cause as operative must have kept at home, or returned into its bosom, such a vast flood of treasure as Mr Necker calculates to remain for domestic circulation. Suppose any reasonable deductions from M. Necker's computation; the remainder must still amount to an immense sum. Causes thus powerful to acquire and to retain, cannot be found in discouraged industry, insecure property, and a positively destructive government. Indeed, when I consider the face of the kingdom of France; the multitude and opulence of her cities; the useful magnificence of her spacious high roads and bridges; the opportunity of her artificial canals and navigations opening the conveniences of maritime communication through a solid continent of so immense an extent; when I turn my eyes to the stupendous works of her ports and harbours, and to her whole naval apparatus, whether for war or trade; when I bring before my view the number of her fortifications, constructed with so bold and masterly a skill, and made and maintained at so prodigious a charge, presenting an armed front and impenetrable barrier to her enemies upon every side; when I recollect how very small a part of that extensive region is without cultivation, and to what complete perfection the culture of many of the best productions of the earth have been brought in France; when I reflect on the excellence of her manufactures and fabrics, second to none but ours, and in some particulars not second; when I contemplate the grand foundations of charity, public and private; when I survey the state of all the arts that beautify and polish life; when I reckon the men she has bred for extending her fame in war, her able statesmen, the multitude of her profound lawyers and theologians, her philosophers, her critics, her historians and antiquaries, her poets, and her orators sacred and profane, I behold in all this something which awes and commands the imagination, which checks the mind on the brink of precipitate and indiscriminate censure, and which demands, that we should very seriously examine, what and how great are the latent vices that could authorise us at once to level so spacious a fabric with the ground. I do not recognize, in this view of things, the despotism of Turkey. Nor do I discern the character of a government, that has been, on the whole, so oppressive, or so corrupt, or so negligent, as to be utterly unfit *for all reformation*. I must think such a government well deserved to have its excellencies heightened; its faults corrected; and its capacities improved into a British constitution.

Whoever has examined into the proceedings of that deposed government for several years back, cannot fail to have observed, amidst the inconstancy and fluctuation natural to courts, an earnest endeavour towards the prosperity and improvement of the country; he must admit, that it had long been employed, in some instances, wholly to remove, in many considerably to correct, the abusive practices and usages that had prevailed in the state; and that even the unlimited power of the sovereign over the persons of his subjects, inconsistent, as undoubtedly it was, with law and liberty, had yet been every day growing more mitigated in the exercise. So far from refusing itself to reformation, that government was open, with a censurable degree of facility, to all sorts of projects and projectors on the subject. Rather too much countenance was given to the spirit of innovation, which soon was turned against those who fostered it, and ended in their ruin. It is but cold, and no very flattering justice to that fallen monarchy, to say, that, for many years, it trespassed more by levity and want of judgment in several of its schemes, than from any defect in diligence or in public spirit. To compare the government of France for the last fifteen or sixteen years with wise and well-constituted establishments, during that, or during any period, is not to act with fairness. But if in point of prodigality in the expenditure of money, or in point of rigour in the exercise of power, it be compared with any of the former reigns, I believe candid judges will give little credit to the good intentions of those who dwell perpetually on the donations to favourites, or on the expences of the court, or on the horrors of the Bastile in the reign of Louis the XVIth.*

Whether the system, if it deserves such a name, now built on the ruins of that antient monarchy, will be able to give a better account of the population and wealth of the country, which it has taken under its care, is a matter very doubtful. Instead of improving by the change, I apprehend that a long series of years must be told before it can recover in any degree the effects of this philosophic revolution, and before the nation can be replaced on its former footing. If Dr Price should think fit, a few years hence, to favour us with an estimate of the population of France, he will hardly be able to make up his tale of thirty millions of souls, as computed in 1789, or the assembly's computation of twenty-six millions of that year; or even

---

* The world is obliged to Mr de Calonne for the pains he has taken to refute the scandalous exaggerations relative to some of the royal expences, and to detect the fallacious account given of pensions, for the wicked purpose of provoking the populace to all sorts of crimes.[109]

Mr Necker's twenty-five millions in 1780. I hear that there are considerable emigrations from France; and that many quitting that voluptuous climate, and that seductive *Circean* liberty, have taken refuge in the frozen regions, and under the British despotism, of Canada.

In the present disappearance of coin, no person could think it the same country, in which the present minister of the finances has been able to discover fourscore millions sterling in specie. From its general aspect one would conclude that it had been for some time past under the special direction of the learned academicians of Laputa and Balnibarbi.* Already the population of Paris has so declined, that Mr Necker stated to the national assembly the provision to be made for its subsistence at a fifth less than what had formerly been found requisite.† It is said (and I have never heard it contradicted) that an hundred thousand people are out of employment in that city, though it is become the seat of the imprisoned court and national assembly. Nothing, I am credibly informed, can exceed the shocking and disgusting spectacle of mendicancy displayed in that capital. Indeed, the votes of the national assembly leave no doubt of the fact. They have lately appointed a standing committee of mendicancy. They are contriving at once a vigorous police on this subject, and, for the first time, the imposition of a tax to maintain the poor, for whose present relief great sums appear on the face of the public accounts of the year.‡ In the mean time, the leaders of the legislative clubs and coffee-houses are in-

---

* See Gulliver's Travels for the idea of countries governed by philosophers.

† Mr de Calonne states the falling off of the population of Paris as far more considerable; and it may be so, since the period of Mr Necker's calculation.

‡Travaux de charité pour sub-	Liv.		£.	s.	d.
venir au manque de travail à					
Paris et dan les provinces	3,866,920	Stg	161,121	13	4

toxicated with admiration at their own wisdom and
ability. They speak with the most sovereign contempt of
the rest of the world. They tell the people, to comfort
them in the rags with which they have cloathed them,
that they are a nation of philosophers; and, sometimes, by
all the arts of quackish parade, by shew, tumult, and bustle,
sometimes by the alarms of plots and invasions, they attempt to drown the cries of indigence, and to divert the
eyes of the observer from the ruin and wretchedness of
the state. A brave people will certainly prefer liberty, ac-
companied with a virtuous poverty, to a depraved and
wealthy servitude. But before the price of comfort and
opulence is paid, one ought to be pretty sure it is real
liberty which is purchased, and that she is to be purchased
at no other price. I shall always, however, consider that

Destruction de vagbondage et de la mendicité	1,671,417	69,642	7	6
Primes pour l'importation de grains	5,671,907	236,329	9	2
Dépenses relatives aux subsis-tances, deduction fait des ré-couvremens qui ont eu lieu	39,871,790	1,661,324	11	8
Total – Liv.	51,082,034	Stg 2,128,418	1	8

When I sent this book to the press I entertained some doubt concerning the nature and extent of the last article in the above accounts, which is only under a general head, without any detail.
Since then I have seen M. de Calonne's work. I must think it a great
loss to me that I had not that advantage earlier. M. de Calonne
thinks this article to be on account of general subsistence: but as he
is not able to comprehend how so great a loss as upwards of
£1,661,000 sterling could be sustained on the difference between the
price and the sale of grain, he seems to attribute this enormous head
of charge to secret expences of the revolution. I cannot say any
thing positively on that subject. The reader is capable of judging, by
the aggregate of these immense charges, on the state and condition
of France; and the system of publick œconomy adopted in that
nation. These articles of account produced no enquiry or discussion
in the National Assembly.

liberty as very equivocal in her appearance, which has not wisdom and justice for her companions; and does not lead prosperity and plenty in her train.

The advocates for this revolution, not satisfied with exaggerating the vices of their antient government, strike at the fame of their country itself, by painting almost all that could have attracted the attention of strangers, I mean their nobility and their clergy, as objects of horror. If this were only a libel, there had not been much in it. But it has practical consequences. Had your nobility and gentry, who formed the great body of your landed men, and the whole of your military officers, resembled those of Germany, at the period when the Hanse-towns were necessitated to confederate against the nobles in defence of their property – had they been like the *Orsini* and *Vitelli* in Italy, who used to sally from their fortified dens to rob the trader and traveller – had they been such as the *Mamalukes* in Egypt, or the *Nayrs* on the coast of Malabar, I do admit, that too critical an enquiry might not be adviseable into the means of freeing the world from such a nuisance.[110] The statues of Equity and Mercy might be veiled for a moment. The tenderest minds, confounded with the dreadful exigence in which morality submits to the suspension of its own rules in favour of its own principles, might turn aside whilst fraud and violence were accomplishing the destruction of a pretended nobility which disgraced whilst it persecuted human nature. The persons most abhorrent from blood, and treason, and arbitrary confiscation, might remain silent spectators of this civil war between the vices.

But did the privileged nobility who met under the king's precept at Versailles, in 1789, or their constituents, deserve to be looked on as the *Nayres* or *Mamalukes* of this age, or as the *Orsini* and *Vitelli* of ancient times? If I had then asked the question, I should have passed for a madman. What have they since done that they were to be driven into exile, that their persons should be hunted about, mangled, and tortured, their families dispersed, their houses laid in ashes, that their order should be abolished, and the memory of it, if possible, extinguished, by ordaining them to change the very names by which they were usually known? Read their instructions to their representatives. They breathe the spirit of liberty as warmly, and they recommend reformation as strongly, as any other order. Their privileges relative to contribution were voluntarily surrendered; as the king, from the beginning, surrendered all pretence to a right of taxation. Upon a free constitution there was but one opinion in France. The absolute monarchy was at an end. It breathed its last, without a groan, without struggle, without convulsion. All the struggle, all the dissension arose afterwards upon the preference of a despotic democracy to a government of reciprocal controul. The triumph of the victorious party was over the principles of a British constitution.

I have observed the affectation, which, for many years past, has prevailed in Paris even to a degree perfectly childish, of idolizing the memory of your Henry the Fourth. If any thing could put one out of humour with that ornament to the kingly character, it would be this overdone style of insidious panegyric. The persons who have worked this engine the most busily, are those who have ended their panegyrics in dethroning his successor and descendant; a man, as good-natured at the least, as Henry the Fourth; altogether as fond of his people; and who has done infinitely more to correct the antient vices of the state than that great monarch did, or we are sure he ever meant to do. Well it is for his panegyrists that they have not him to deal with. For Henry of Navarre was a resolute, active, and politic prince. He possessed indeed great humanity and mildness; but an humanity and mildness that never stood in the way of his interests. He never sought to be loved without putting himself first in a condition to be feared. He used soft language with determined conduct. He asserted and maintained his authority in the gross, and distributed his acts of concession only in the detail. He spent the income of his prerogatives nobly; but he took care not to break in upon the capital; never abandoning for a moment any of the claims, which he made under the fundamental laws, nor sparing to shed the blood of those who opposed him, often in the field, sometimes upon the scaffold. Because he knew how to make his virtues respected by the ungrateful, he has merited the praises of those whom, if they had lived in his time, he would have shut up in the Bastile, and brought to punishment along with the regicides whom he hanged after he had famished Paris into a surrender.

If these panegyrists are in earnest in their admiration of Henry the Fourth, they must remember, that they cannot think more highly of him, than he did of the noblesse of France; whose virtue, honour, courage, patriotism, and loyalty were his constant theme.

But the nobility of France are degenerated since the days of Henry the Fourth. – This is possible. But it is more than I can believe to be true in any great degree. I do not pretend to know France as correctly as some others; but I have endeavoured through my whole life to make myself acquainted with human nature: otherwise I should be unfit to take even my humble part in the service of mankind. In that study I could not pass by a vast portion of our nature, as it appeared modified in a country but twenty-four miles from the shore of this island. On my best observation, compared with my best enquiries, I found your nobility for the greater part composed of men of an high spirit, and of a delicate sense of honour, both with regard to themselves individually, and with regard to their whole corps, over whom they kept, beyond what is common in other countries, a censorial eye. They were tolerably well-bred; very officious,[111] humane, and hospitable; in their conversation frank and open; with a good military tone; and reasonably tinctured with literature, particularly of the authors in their own language. Many had pretensions far above this description. I speak of those who were generally met with.

As to their behaviour to the inferior classes, they appeared to me to comport themselves towards them with good-nature, and with something more nearly approaching to familiarity, than is generally practised with us in the intercourse between the higher and lower ranks of life. To strike any person, even in the most abject condition, was a thing in a manner unknown, and would be highly disgraceful.[112] Instances of other ill-treatment of the humble part of the community were rare; and as to attacks made upon the property or the personal liberty of the commons, I never heard of any whatsoever from *them*; nor, whilst the laws were in vigour under the ancient government, would such tyranny in subjects have been permitted. As men of landed estates, I had no fault to find with their conduct, though much to reprehend, and much to wish changed, in many of the old tenures. Where the letting of their land was by rent, I could not discover that their agreements with their farmers were oppressive; nor when they were in partnership with the farmer, as often was the case, have I heard that they had taken the lion's share. The proportions seemed not inequitable. There might be exceptions; but certainly they were exceptions only. I have no reason to believe that in these respects the landed noblesse of France were worse than the landed gentry of this country; certainly in no respect more vexatious than the landholders, not noble, of their own nation. In cities the nobility had no manner of power; in the country very little. You know, Sir, that much of the civil government, and the police in the most essential parts, was not in the hands of that nobility which presents itself first to our consideration. The revenue, the system and collection of which were the most grievous parts of the French government, was not administered by the men of the sword; nor were they answerable for the vices of its principle, or the vexations, where any such existed, in its management.

Denying, as I am well warranted to do, that the nobility had any considerable share in the oppression of the people, in cases in which real oppression existed, I am ready to admit that they were not without considerable faults and errors. A foolish imitation of the worst part of the manners of England, which impaired their natural character without substituting in its place what perhaps they meant to copy, has certainly rendered them worse than formerly they were. Habitual dissoluteness of manners continued beyond the pardonable period of life, was more common amongst them than it is with us; and it reigned with the less hope of remedy, though possibly with something of less mischief, by being covered with more exterior decorum. They countenanced too much that licentious philosophy which has helped to bring on their ruin. There was another error amongst them more fatal. Those of the commons, who approached to or exceeded many of the nobility in point of wealth, were not fully admitted to the rank and estimation which wealth, in reason and good policy, ought to bestow in every country; though I think not equally with that of other nobility. The two kinds of aristocracy were too punctiliously kept asunder; less so, however, than in Germany and some other nations.

This separation, as I have already taken the liberty of suggesting to you, I conceive to be one principal cause of the destruction of the old nobility. The military, particularly, was too exclusively reserved for men of family. But after all, this was an error of opinion, which a conflicting opinion would have rectified. A permanent assembly, in which the commons had their share of power, would soon abolish whatever was too invidious and insulting in these distinctions; and even the faults in the morals of the nobility would have been probably corrected by the greater varieties of occupation and pursuit to which a constitution by orders would have given rise.

All this violent cry against the nobility I take to be a mere work of art. To be honoured and even privileged by the laws, opinions, and inveterate usages of our country, growing out of the prejudice of ages, has nothing to provoke horror and indignation in any man. Even to be too tenacious of those privileges, is not absolutely a crime. The strong struggle in every individual to preserve possession of what he has found to belong to him and to distinguish him, is one of the securities against injustice and despotism implanted in our nature. It operates as an instinct to secure property, and to preserve communities in a settled state. What is there to shock in this? Nobility is a graceful ornament to the civil order. It is the Corinthian capital of polished society. *Omnes boni nobilitati semper favemus,*[113] was the saying of a wise and good man. It is indeed one sign of a liberal and benevolent mind to incline to it with some sort of partial propensity. He feels no ennobling principle in his own heart who wishes to level all the artificial institutions which have been adopted for giving a body to opinion, and permanence to fugitive esteem. It is a sour, malignant, envious disposition, without taste for the reality, or for any image or representation of virtue, that sees with joy the unmerited fall of what had long flourished in splendour and in honour. I do not like to see any thing destroyed; any void produced in society; any ruin on the face of the land. It was therefore with no disappointment or dissatisfaction that my enquiries and observation did not present to me any incorrigible vices in the noblesse of France, or any abuse which could not be removed by a reform very short of abolition. Your noblesse did not deserve punishment; but to degrade is to punish.

It was with the same satisfaction I found that the result of my enquiry concerning your clergy was not dissimilar. It is not soothing news to my ears, that great bodies of men are incurably corrupt. It is not with much credulity I listen to any, when they speak evil of those whom they are going to plunder. I rather suspect that vices are feigned or exaggerated, when profit is looked for in their punishment. An enemy is a bad witness: a robber is a worse. Vices and abuses there were undoubtedly in that order, and must be. It was an old establishment, and not frequently revised. But I saw no crimes in the individuals that merited confiscation of their substance, nor those cruel insults and degradations, and that unnatural persecution which have been substituted in the place of meliorating regulation.[114]

If there had been any just cause for this new religious persecution, the atheistic libellers, who act as trumpeters to animate the populace to plunder, do not love any body so much as not to dwell with complacence on the vices of the existing clergy. This they have not done. They find themselves obliged to rake into the histories of former ages (which they have ransacked with a malignant and profligate industry) for every instance of oppression and persecution which has been made by that body or in its favour, in order to justify, upon very iniquitous, because very illogical principles of retaliation, their own persecutions, and their own cruelties. After destroying all other genealogies and family distinctions, they invent a sort of pedigree of crimes. It is not very just to chastise men for the offences of their natural ancestors; but to take the fiction of ancestry in a corporate succession, as a ground for punishing men who have no relation to guilty acts, except in names and general descriptions, is a sort of refinement in injustice belonging to the philosophy of this enlightened age. The assembly punishes men, many, if not most, of whom abhor the violent conduct of ecclesiastics in former times as much as their present persecutors can do, and who would be as loud and as strong in the expression of that sense, if they were not well aware of the purposes for which all this declamation is employed.

Corporate bodies are immortal for the good of the members, but not for their punishment. Nations themselves are such corporations. As well might we in England think of waging inexpiable war upon all Frenchmen for the evils which they have brought upon us in the several periods of our mutual hostilities. You might, on your part, think yourselves justified in falling upon all Englishmen on account of the unparalleled calamities brought upon the people of France by the unjust invasions of our Henries and our Edwards. Indeed we should be mutually justified in this exterminatory war upon each other, full as much as you are in the unprovoked persecution of your present countrymen, on account of the conduct of men of the same name in other times.

We do not draw the moral lessons we might from history. On the contrary, without care it may be used to vitiate our minds and to destroy our happiness. In history a great volume is unrolled for our instruction, drawing the materials of future wisdom from the past errors and infirmities of mankind. It may, in the perversion, serve for a magazine, furnishing offensive and defensive weapons for parties in church and state, and supplying the means of keeping alive, or reviving dissensions and animosities, and adding fuel to civil fury. History consists, for the greater part, of the miseries brought upon the world by pride, ambition, avarice, revenge, lust, sedition, hypocrisy, ungoverned zeal, and all the train of disorderly appetites, which shake the public with the same

> – troublous storms that toss
> The private state, and render life unsweet.[115]

These vices are the *causes* of those storms. Religion, morals, laws, prerogatives, privileges, liberties, rights of men, are the *pretexts*. The pretexts are always found in some specious appearance of a real good. You would not secure men from tyranny and sedition, by rooting out of the mind the principles to which these fraudulent pretexts apply? If you did, you would root out every thing that is valuable in the human breast. As these are the pretexts, so the ordinary actors and instruments in great public evils are kings, priests, magistrates, senates, parliaments, national assemblies, judges, and captains. You would not cure the evil by resolving, that there should be no more monarchs, nor ministers of state, nor of the gospel; no interpreters of law; no general officers; no public councils. You might change the names. The things in some shape must remain. A certain *quantum* of power must always exist in the community, in some hands, and under some appellation. Wise men will apply their remedies to vices, not to names; to the causes of evil which are permanent, not to the occasional organs by which they act, and the transitory modes in which they appear. Otherwise you will be wise historically, a fool in practice. Seldom have two ages the same fashion in their pretexts and the same modes of mischief. Wickedness is a little more inventive. Whilst you are discussing fashion, the fashion is gone by. The very same vice assumes a new body. The spirit transmigrates; and, far from losing its principle of life by the change of its appearance, it is renovated in its new organs with the fresh vigour of a juvenile activity. It walks abroad; it continues its ravages; whilst you are gibbeting the carcass, or demolishing the tomb. You are terrifying yourself with ghosts and apparitions, whilst your house is the haunt of robbers. It is thus with all those, who attending only to the shell and husk of history, think they are waging war with intolerance, pride, and cruelty, whilst, under colour of abhorring the ill principles of antiquated parties, they are authorizing and feeding the same odious vices in different factions, and perhaps in worse.

Your citizens of Paris formerly had lent themselves as the ready instruments to slaughter the followers of Calvin, at the infamous massacre of St. Bartholomew. What should we say to those who could think of retaliating on the Parisians of this day the abominations and horrors of that time? They are indeed brought to abhor *that* massacre. Ferocious as they are, it is not difficult to make them dislike it; because the politicians and fashionable teachers have no interest in giving their passions exactly the same direction. Still however they find it their interest to keep the same savage dispositions alive. It was but the other day that they caused this very massacre to be acted on the stage for the diversion of the descendants of those who committed it.[116] In this tragic farce they produced the cardinal of Lorraine in his robes of function, ordering general slaughter. Was this spectacle intended to make the Parisians abhor persecution, and loath the effusion of blood? — No, it was to teach them to persecute their own pastors; it was to excite them, by raising a disgust and horror of their clergy, to an alacrity in hunting down to destruction an order, which, if it ought to exist at all, ought to exist not only in safety, but in reverence. It was to stimulate their cannibal appetites (which one would think had been gorged sufficiently) by variety and seasoning; and to quicken them to an alertness in new murders and massacres, if it should suit the purpose of the Guises[117] of the day. An assembly, in which sat a multitude of priests and prelates, was obliged to suffer this indignity at its door. The author was not sent to the gallies, nor the players to the house of correction. Not long after this exhibition, those players came forward to the assembly to claim the rites of that very religion which they had dared to expose, and to shew their prostituted faces in the senate, whilst the archbishop of Paris,[118] whose function was known to his people only by his prayers and benedictions, and his wealth only by his alms, is forced to abandon his house, and to fly from his flock (as from ravenous wolves) because, truly, in the sixteenth century, the Cardinal of Lorraine was a rebel and a murderer.*

Such is the effect of the perversion of history, by those, who, for the same nefarious purposes, have perverted every other part of learning. But those who will stand upon that elevation of reason, which places centuries under our eye, and brings things to the true point of comparison, which obscures little names, and effaces the colours of little parties, and to which nothing can ascend but the spirit and moral quality of human actions, will say to the teachers of the Palais Royal, – the Cardinal of Lorraine was the murderer of the sixteenth century, you have the glory of being the murderers in the eighteenth; and this is the only difference between you. But history, in the nineteenth century, better understood, and better employed, will, I trust, teach a civilized posterity to abhor the misdeeds of both these barbarous ages. It will teach future priests and magistrates not to retaliate upon the speculative and inactive atheists of future times, the enormities committed by the present practical zealots and furious fanatics of that wretched error, which, in its quiescent state, is more than punished, whenever it is embraced. It will teach posterity not to make war upon either religion or philosophy, for the abuse which the hypocrites of both have made of the two most valuable blessings conferred upon us by the bounty of the universal Patron, who in all

* This is on a supposition of the truth of this story; but he was not in France at the time. One name serves as well as another. [1803]

things eminently favours and protects the race of man.

If your clergy, or any clergy, should shew themselves vicious beyond the fair bounds allowed to human infirmity, and to those professional faults which can hardly be separated from professional virtues, though their vices never can countenance the exercise of oppression, I do admit, that they would naturally have the effect of abating very much of our indignation against the tyrants who exceed measure and justice in their punishment. I can allow in clergymen, through all their divisions, some tenaciousness of their own opinion; some overflowings of zeal for its propagation; some predilection to their own state and office; some attachment to the interest of their own corps; some preference to those who listen with docility to their doctrines, beyond those who scorn and deride them. I allow all this, because I am a man who have to deal with men, and who would not, through a violence of toleration, run into the greatest of all intolerance. I must bear with infirmities until they fester into crimes.

Undoubtedly, the natural progress of the passions, from frailty to vice, ought to be prevented by a watchful eye and a firm hand. But is it true that the body of your clergy had past those limits of a just allowance? From the general style of your late publications of all sorts, one would be led to believe that your clergy in France were a sort of monsters; an horrible composition of superstition, ignorance, sloth, fraud, avarice, and tyranny. But is this true? Is it true, that the lapse of time, the cessation of conflicting interests, the woful experience of the evils resulting from party rage, have had no sort of influence gradually to meliorate their minds? Is it true, that they were daily renewing invasions on the civil power, troubling the domestic quiet of their country, and rendering the operations of its government feeble and precarious? Is it true, that the clergy of our times have pressed down the laity

with an iron hand, and were, in all places, lighting up the
fires of a savage persecution? Did they by every fraud endeavour to encrease their estates? Did they use to exceed
the due demands on estates that were their own? Or,
rigidly screwing up right into wrong, did they convert a
legal claim into a vexatious extortion? When not possessed of power, were they filled with the vices of those who
envy it? Were they enflamed with a violent litigious spirit
of controversy? Goaded on with the ambition of intellectual sovereignty, were they ready to fly in the face of all
magistracy, to fire churches, to massacre the priests of
other descriptions, to pull down altars, and to make their
way over the ruins of subverted governments to an empire
of doctrine, sometimes flattering, sometimes forcing the
consciences of men from the jurisdiction of public institutions into a submission to their personal authority, beginning with a claim of liberty and ending with an abuse
of power?

These, or some of these, were the vices objected, and not
wholly without foundation, to several of the churchmen
of former times, who belonged to the two great parties
which then divided and distracted Europe.

If there was in France, as in other countries there visibly
is, a great abatement, rather than any increase of these
vices, instead of loading the present clergy with the crimes
of other men, and the odious character of other times, in
common equity they ought to be praised, encouraged, and
supported, in their departure from a spirit which disgraced
their predecessors, and for having assumed a temper of
mind and manners more suitable to their sacred function.

When my occasions took me into France, towards the
close of the late reign, the clergy, under all their forms,
engaged a considerable part of my curiosity. So far from
finding (except from one set of men, not then very numerous though very active) the complaints and discontents

against that body, which some publications had given me reason to expect, I perceived little or no public or private uneasiness on their account. On further examination, I found the clergy in general, persons of moderate minds and decorous manners; I include the seculars, and the regulars of both sexes. I had not the good fortune to know a great many of the parochial clergy; but in general I received a perfectly good account of their morals, and of their attention to their duties. With some of the higher clergy I had a personal acquaintance; and of the rest in that class, very good means of information. They were, almost all of them, persons of noble birth. They resembled others of their own rank; and where there was any difference, it was in their favour. They were more fully educated than the military noblesse; so as by no means to disgrace their profession by ignorance, or by want of fitness for the exercise of their authority. They seemed to me, beyond the clerical character, liberal and open; with the hearts of gentlemen, and men of honour; neither insolent nor servile in their manners and conduct. They seemed to me rather a superior class; a set of men, amongst whom you would not be surprised to find a *Fenelon*.[119] I saw among the clergy in Paris (many of the description are not to be met with any where) men of great learning and candour; and I had reason to believe, that this description was not confined to Paris. What I found in other places, I know was accidental; and therefore to be presumed a fair sample. I spent a few days in a provincial town,[120] where, in the absence of the bishop, I passed my evenings with three clergymen, his vicars general, persons who would have done honour to any church. They were all well informed; two of them of deep, general, and extensive erudition, antient and modern, oriental and western; particularly in their own profession. They had a more extensive knowledge of our English divines than I expected; and they entered into the genius of those writers with a critical accuracy. One of these gentlemen is since dead, the Abbé *Morangis*.[121] I pay this tribute, without reluctance, to the memory of that noble, reverend, learned, and excellent person; and I should do the same, with equal cheerfulness, to the merits of the others, who I believe are still living, if I did not fear to hurt those whom I am unable to serve.

Some of these ecclesiastics of rank, are, by all titles, persons deserving of general respect. They are deserving of gratitude from me, and from many English. If this letter should ever come into their hands, I hope they will believe there are those of our nation who feel for their unmerited fall, and for the cruel confiscation of their fortunes, with no common sensibility. What I say of them is a testimony, as far as one feeble voice can go, which I owe to truth. Whenever the question of this unnatural persecution is concerned, I will pay it. No one shall prevent me from being just and grateful. The time is fitted for the duty; and it is particularly becoming to shew our justice and gratitude, when those who have deserved well of us and of mankind are labouring under popular obloquy and the persecutions of oppressive power.

You had before your revolution about an hundred and twenty bishops. A few of them were men of eminent sanctity, and charity without limit. When we talk of the heroic, of course we talk of rare, virtue. I believe the instances of eminent depravity may be as rare amongst them as those of transcendent goodness. Examples of avarice and of licentiousness may be picked out, I do not question it, by those who delight in the investigation which leads to such discoveries. A man, as old as I am, will not be astonished that several, in every description, do not lead that perfect life of self-denial, with regard to wealth or to pleasure, which is wished for by all, by some expected, but by none exacted with more rigour, than by those who are the most attentive to their own interests, or the most indulgent to their own passions. When I was in France, I am certain that the number of vicious prelates was not great. Certain individuals among them not distinguishable for the regularity of their lives, made some amends for their want of the severe virtues, in their possession of the liberal; and were endowed with qualities which made them useful in the church and state. I am told, that with few exceptions, Louis the Sixteenth had been more attentive to character, in his promotions to that rank, than his immediate predecessor; and I believe, (as some spirit of reform has prevailed through the whole reign) that it may be true. But the present ruling power has shewn a disposition only to plunder the church. It has punished *all* prelates; which is to favour the vicious, at least in point of reputation. It has made a degrading pensionary establishment, to which no man of liberal ideas or liberal condition will destine his children. It must settle into the lowest classes of the people. As with you the inferior clergy are not numerous enough for their duties; as these duties are, beyond measure, minute and toilsome; as you have left no middle classes of clergy at their ease, in future nothing of science or erudition can exist in the Gallican[122] church. To complete the project, without the least attention to the rights of patrons, the assembly has provided in future an elective clergy; an arrangement which will drive out of the clerical profession all men of sobriety; all who can pretend to independence in their function or their conduct; and which will throw the whole direction of the public mind into the hands of a set of licentious, bold, crafty, factious, flattering wretches, of such condition and such habits of life as will make their contemptible pensions (in comparison of which the stipend of an exciseman is lucrative and honourable) an object of low and illiberal intrigue. Those officers, whom they still call bishops, are to be elected to a provision comparatively mean, through the same arts, (that is, electioneering arts) by men of all religious tenets that are known or can be invented. The new lawgivers have not ascertained any thing whatsoever concerning their qualifications, relative either to doctrine or to morals; no more than they have done with regard to the subordinate clergy; nor does it appear but that both the higher and the lower may, at their discretion, practise or preach any mode of religion or irreligion that they please. I do not yet see what the jurisdiction of bishops over their subordinates is to be; or whether they are to have any jurisdiction at all.

In short, Sir, it seems to me, that this new ecclesiastical establishment is intended only to be temporary, and preparatory to the utter abolition, under any of its forms, of the Christian religion, whenever the minds of men are prepared for this last stroke against it, by the accomplishment of the plan for bringing its ministers into universal contempt. They who will not believe, that the philosophical fanatics who guide in these matters, have long entertained such a design, are utterly ignorant of their character and proceedings. These enthusiasts do not scruple to avow their opinion, that a state can subsist without any religion better than with one; and that they are able to supply the place of any good which may be in it, by a project of their own – namely, by a sort of education they have imagined, founded in a knowledge of the physical wants of men; progressively carried to an enlightened self-interest, which, when well understood, they tell us will identify with an interest more enlarged and public. The scheme of this education has been long known. Of late they distinguish it (as they have got an entire new nomenclature of technical terms) by the name of a *Civic Education.*

I hope their partizans in England, (to whom I rather attribute very inconsiderate conduct than the ultimate object in this detestable design) will succeed neither in the pillage of the ecclesiastics, nor in the introduction of a principle of popular election to our bishoprics and parochial cures. This, in the present condition of the world, would be the last corruption of the church; the utter ruin of the clerical character; the most dangerous shock that the state ever received through a misunderstood arrangement of religion. I know well enough that the bishoprics and cures, under kingly and seignoral patronage, as now they are in England, and as they have been lately in France, are sometimes acquired by unworthy methods; but the other mode of ecclesiastical canvas subjects them infinitely more surely and more generally to all the evil arts of low ambition, which, operating on and through greater numbers, will produce mischief in proportion.

Those of you who have robbed the clergy, think that they shall easily reconcile their conduct to all protestant nations; because the clergy, whom they have thus plundered, degraded, and given over to mockery and scorn, are of the Roman Catholic, that is, of *their own* pretended persuasion. I have no doubt that some miserable bigots will be found here as well as elsewhere, who hate sects and parties different from their own, more than they love the substance of religion; and who are more angry with those who differ from them in their particular plans and systems, than displeased with those who attack the foundation of our common hope. These men will write and speak on the subject in the manner that is to be expected from their temper and character. Burnet[123] says, that when he was in France, in the year 1683, 'the method which carried over the men of the finest parts to popery was this – they brought themselves to doubt of the whole Christian religion. When that was once done, it seemed a more

indifferent thing of what side or form they continued out-
wardly.' If this was then the ecclesiastic policy of France,
it is what they have since but too much reason to repent
of. They preferred atheism to a form of religion not agreeable to their ideas. They succeeded in destroying that form;
and atheism has succeeded in destroying them. I can
readily give credit to Burnet's story; because I have observed too much of a similar spirit (for a little of it is
'much too much') amongst ourselves. The humour, however, is not general.

The teachers who reformed our religion in England bore
no sort of resemblance to your present reforming doctors
in Paris. Perhaps they were (like those whom they opposed) rather more than could be wished under the influence of a party spirit; but they were most sincere be-
lievers; men of the most fervent and exalted piety; ready
to die (as some of them did die) like true heroes in defence
of their particular ideas of Christianity; as they would
with equal fortitude, and more chearfully, for that stock
of general truth, for the branches of which they contended
with their blood. These men would have disavowed with
horror those wretches who claimed a fellowship with
them upon no other titles than those of their having pillaged the persons with whom they maintained controversies, and their having despised the common religion, for
the purity of which they exerted themselves with a zeal,
which unequivocally bespoke their highest reverence for
the substance of that system which they wished to reform.
Many of their descendants have retained the same zeal;
but, (as less engaged in conflict) with more moderation.
They do not forget that justice and mercy are substantial
parts of religion. Impious men do not recommend themselves to their communion by iniquity and cruelty towards
any description of their fellow creatures.

We hear these new teachers continually boasting of

their spirit of toleration. That those persons should tolerate all opinions, who think none to be of estimation, is a matter of small merit. Equal neglect is not impartial kindness. The species of benevolence, which arises from contempt, is no true charity. There are in England abundance of men who tolerate in the true spirit of toleration. They think the dogmas of religion, though in different degrees, are all of moment; and that amongst them there is, as amongst all things of value, a just ground of preference. They favour, therefore, and they tolerate. They tolerate, not because they despise opinions, but because they respect justice. They would reverently and affectionately protect all religions, because they love and venerate the great principle upon which they all agree, and the great object to which they are all directed. They begin more and more plainly to discern, that we have all a common cause, as against a common enemy. They will not be so misled by the spirit of faction, as not to distinguish what is done in favour of their subdivision, from those acts of hostility, which, through some particular description, are aimed at the whole corps, in which they themselves, under another denomination, are included. It is impossible for me to say what may be the character of every description of men amongst us. But I speak for the greater part; and for them, I must tell you, that sacrilege is no part of their doctrine of good works; that, so far from calling you into their fellowship on such title, if your professors are admitted to their communion, they must carefully conceal their doctrine of the lawfulness of the proscription of innocent men; and that they must make restitution of all stolen goods whatsoever. Till then they are none of ours.

You may suppose that we do not approve your confiscation of the revenues of bishops, and deans, and chapters, and parochial clergy possessing independent estates arising from land, because we have the same sort of establishment in England. That objection, you will say, cannot hold as to the confiscation of the goods of monks and nuns, and the abolition of their order. It is true, that this particular part of your general confiscation does not affect England, as a precedent in point: but the reason applies; and it goes a great way. The long parliament confiscated the lands of deans and chapters in England on the same ideas upon which your assembly set to sale the lands of the monastic orders. But it is in the principle of injustice that the danger lies, and not in the description of persons on whom it is first exercised. I see, in a country very near us, a course of policy pursued, which sets justice, the common concern of mankind, at defiance. With the national assembly of France, possession is nothing; law and usage are nothing. I see the national assembly openly reprobate the doctrine of prescription, which* one of the greatest of their own lawyers tells us, with great truth, is a part of the law of nature. He tells us, that the positive ascertainment of its limits, and its security from invasion, were among the causes for which civil society itself has been instituted. If prescription be once shaken, no species of property is secure, when it once becomes an object large enough to tempt the cupidity of indigent power. I see a practice perfectly correspondent to their contempt of this great fundamental part of natural law. I see the confiscators begin with bishops, and chapters, and monasteries; but I do not see them end there. I see the princes of the blood, who, by the oldest usages of that kingdom, held large landed estates, (hardly with the compliment of a debate) deprived of their possessions, and in lieu of their stable independent property, reduced to the hope of some precarious, charitable pension, at the pleasure of an assembly, which of course will pay little regard to the rights of pensioners at pleasure, when it despises those of legal proprietors. Flushed

* Domat.[124]

with the insolence of their first inglorious victories, and pressed by the distresses caused by their lust of unhallowed lucre, disappointed but not discouraged, they have at length ventured completely to subvert all property of all descriptions throughout the extent of a great kingdom. They have compelled all men, in all transactions of commerce, in the disposal of lands, in civil dealing, and through the whole communion of life, to accept as perfect payment and good and lawful tender, the symbols of their speculations on a projected sale of their plunder. What vestiges of liberty or property have they left? The tenant-right of a cabbage-garden, a year's interest in a hovel, the good-will of an alehouse, or a baker's shop, the very shadow of a constructive property, are more ceremoniously treated in our parliament than with you the oldest and most valuable landed possessions, in the hands of the most respectable personages, or than the whole body of the monied and commercial interest of your country. We entertain an high opinion of the legislative authority; but we have never dreamt that parliaments had any right whatever to violate property, to overrule prescription, or to force a currency of their own fiction in the place of that which is real, and recognized by the law of nations. But you, who began with refusing to submit to the most moderate restraints, have ended by establishing an unheard of despotism. I find the ground upon which your confiscators go is this; that indeed their proceedings could not be supported in a court of justice; but that the rules of prescription cannot bind a legislative assembly.* So that this legislative assembly of a free nation sits, not for the security, but for the destruction of property, and not of property only, but of every rule and maxim which can give it stability, and of those instruments which can alone give it circulation.

* Speech of Mr Camus,[125] published by order of the National Assembly.

When the Anabaptists of Munster,[126] in the sixteenth century, had filled Germany with confusion by their system of levelling and their wild opinions concerning property, to what country in Europe did not the progress of their fury furnish just cause of alarm? Of all things, wisdom is the most terrified with epidemical fanaticism, because of all enemies it is that against which she is the least able to furnish any kind of resource. We cannot be ignorant of the spirit of atheistical fanaticism, that is inspired by a multitude of writings, dispersed with incredible assiduity and expence, and by sermons delivered in all the streets and places of public resort in Paris. These writings and sermons have filled the populace with a black and savage atrocity of mind, which supersedes in them the common feelings of nature, as well as all sentiments of morality and religion; insomuch that these wretches are induced to bear with a sullen patience the intolerable distresses brought upon them by the violent convulsions and permutations that have been made in property?* The spirit of

* Whether the following description is strictly true I know not; but it is what the publishers would have pass for true, in order to animate others. In a letter from Toul, given in one of their papers, is the following passage concerning the people of that district: 'Dans la Revolution actuelle, ils ont résisté à touts les *séductions du bigotisme, aux persécutions et aux tracasseries* des Ennemis de la Révolution. *Oubliant leurs plus grands intérêts* pour rendre hommage aux vues d'ordre général qui ont determiné l'Assemblée Nationale, ils voient, *sans se plaindre,* supprimer cette foule d'établissemens ecclésiastiques par lesquels *ils subsistoient;* et même, en perdant leur siège épiscopal, la seule de toutes ces ressources qui pouvoit, ou plutôt *qui devoit, en tout équité,* leur être conservée; condamnés *à la plus effrayante misère,* sans avoir *été ni pu être entendus, ils ne murmurent point,* ils restent fidèles aux principes du plus pur patriotisme; ils sont encore prêts à *verser leur sang* pour le maintien de la Constitution, qui va reduire leur Ville *à la plus déplorable nullité.'* These people are not supposed to have endured those sufferings and injustices in a struggle for liberty, for the same account states truly that they had been always free; their

proselytism attends this spirit of fanaticism. They have societies to cabal and correspond at home and abroad for the propagation of their tenets. The republic of Berne, one of the happiest, the most prosperous, and the best governed countries upon earth, is one of the great objects, at the destruction of which they aim. I am told they have in some measure succeeded in sowing there the seeds of discontent. They are busy throughout Germany. Spain and Italy have not been untried. England is not left out of the comprehensive scheme of their malignant charity; and in England we find those who stretch out their arms to them, who recommend their examples from more than one pulpit, and who choose, in more than one periodical meeting, publicly to correspond with them, to applaud them, and to hold them up as objects for imitation; who receive from them tokens of confraternity, and standards consecrated amidst their rites and mysteries;* who suggest to them leagues of perpetual amity, at the very time when the power, to which our constitution has exclusively delegated the federative capacity of this kingdom, may find it expedient to make war upon them.

It is not the confiscation of our church property from this example in France that I dread, though I think this would be no trifling evil. The great source of my solicitude is, lest it should ever be considered in England as the policy of a state, to seek a resource in confiscations of any kind; or that any one description of citizens should be brought to regard any of the others, as their proper prey.† Nations

---

patience in beggary and ruin, and their suffering, without remonstrance, the most flagrant and confessed injustice, if strictly true, can be nothing but the effect of this dire fanaticism. A great multitude all over France is in the same condition and the same temper.

* See the proceedings of the confederation at Nantz.[127]

† 'Si plures sunt ii quibus improbe datum est, quam illi quibus injuste adeptum est, idcirco plus etiam valent? Non enim numero

are wading deeper and deeper into an ocean of boundless debt. Public debts, which at first were a security to governments, by interesting many in the public tranquillity, are likely in their excess to become the means of their subversion. If governments provide for these debts by heavy impositions, they perish by becoming odious to the people. If they do not provide for them, they will be undone by the efforts of the most dangerous of all parties; I mean an extensive discontented monied interest, injured and not destroyed. The men who compose this interest look for their security, in the first instance, to the fidelity of government; in the second, to its power. If they find the old governments effete, worn out and with their springs relaxed, so as not to be of sufficient vigour for their purposes, they may seek new ones that shall be possessed of more energy; and this energy will be derived, not from an acquisition of resources, but from a contempt of justice. Revolutions are favourable to confiscation; and it is impossible to know under what obnoxious names the next confiscations will be authorised. I am sure that the princi-

---

hæc judicantur sed pondere. Quam autem habet æquitatem, ut agrum multis annis, aut etiam sæculis ante possessum, qui nullum habuit habeat; qui, autem habuit amittat. Ac, propter hoc injuriæ genus, Lacedæmonii Lysandrum Ephorum expulerunt: Agin regem (quod nunquam antea apud eos acciderat) necaverunt: exque eo tempore tantæ discordiæ secutæ sunt, ut et tyranni exsisterint, et optimates exterminarentur, et preclarissime constituta respublica dilaberetur. Nec vero solum ipsa cecidit, sed etiam reliquam Græciam evertit contagionibus malorum, quæ a Lacadæmoniis profectae manarunt latius.' – After speaking of the conduct of the model of true patriots, Aratus of Sycion, which was in a very different spirit, he says, 'Sic par est agere cum civibus; non ut bis jam vidimus, hastam in foro ponere et bona civium voci subjicere præconis. At ille Græcus (id quod fuit sapientis et præstantis viri) omnibus consulendum esse putavit: eaque est summa ratio et sapientia boni civis, commoda civium non divellere, sed omnes eadem aequitate continere.' Cic. Off. 1. 2.[128]

ples predominant in France extend to very many persons and descriptions of persons in all countries who think their innoxious indolence their security. This kind of innocence in proprietors may be argued into inutility; and inutility into an unfitness for their estates. Many parts of Europe are in open disorder. In many others there is a hollow murmuring under ground; a confused movement is felt, that threatens a general earthquake in the political world. Already confederacies and correspondences of the most extraordinary nature are forming, in several countries.* In such a state of things we ought to hold ourselves upon our guard. In all mutations (if mutations must be) the circumstance which will serve most to blunt the edge of their mischief, and to promote what good may be in them, is, that they should find us with our minds tenacious of justice, and tender of property.

But it will be argued, that this confiscation in France ought not to alarm other nations. They say it is not made from wanton rapacity; that it is a great measure of national policy, adopted to remove an extensive, inveterate, superstitious mischief. It is with the greatest difficulty that I am able to separate policy from justice. Justice is itself the great standing policy of civil society; and any eminent departure from it, under any circumstances, lies under the suspicion of being no policy at all.

When men are encouraged to go into a certain mode of life by the existing laws, and protected in that mode as in a lawful occupation – when they have accommodated all their ideas, and all their habits to it – when the law had long made their adherence to its rules a ground of reputation, and their departure from them a ground of disgrace and even of penalty – I am sure it is unjust in legislature,

---

* See two books intitled, *Einige Originalschriften des Illuminatenordens. – System und Folgen des Illuminatenordens*. Munchen 1787.[129]

by an arbitrary act, to offer a sudden violence to their minds and their feelings; forcibly to degrade them from their state and condition, and to stigmatize with shame and infamy that character and those customs which before had been made the measure of their happiness and honour. If to this be added an expulsion from their habitations, and a confiscation of all their goods, I am not sagacious enough to discover how this despotic sport, made of the feelings, consciences, prejudices, and properties of men, can be discriminated from the rankest tyranny.

If the injustice of the course pursued in France be clear, the policy of the measure, that is, the public benefit to be expected from it, ought to be at least as evident, and at least as important. To a man who acts under the influence of no passion, who has nothing in view in his projects but the public good, a great difference will immediately strike him, between what policy would dictate on the original introduction of such institutions, and on a question of their total abolition, where they have cast their roots wide and deep, and where by long habit things more valuable than themselves are so adapted to them, and in a manner interwoven with them, that the one cannot be destroyed without notably impairing the other. He might be embarrassed, if the case were really such as sophisters represent it in their paltry style of debating. But in this, as in most questions of state, there is a middle. There is something else than the mere alternative of absolute destruction, or unreformed existence. *Spartam nactus es; hanc exorna.*[130] This is, in my opinion, a rule of profound sense, and ought never to depart from the mind of an honest reformer. I cannot conceive how any man can have brought himself to that pitch of presumption, to consider his country as nothing but *carte blanche*, upon which he may scribble whatever he pleases. A man full of warm speculative benevolence may wish his society otherwise constituted than he finds it; but a good patriot, and a true politician, always considers how he shall make the most of the existing materials of his country. A disposition to preserve, and an ability to improve, taken together, would be my standard of a statesman. Every thing else is vulgar in the conception, perilous in the execution.

There are moments in the fortune of states when particular men are called to make improvements by great mental exertion. In those moments, even when they seem to enjoy the confidence of their prince and country, and to be invested with full authority, they have not always apt instruments. A politician, to do great things, looks for a *power*, what our workmen call a *purchase*; and if he finds that power, in politics as in mechanics he cannot be at a loss to apply it. In the monastic institutions, in my opinion, was found a great *power* for the mechanism of politic benevolence. There were revenues with a public direction; there were men wholly set apart and dedicated to public purposes, without any other than public ties and public principles; men without the possibility of converting the estate of the community into a private fortune; men denied to self-interests, whose avarice is for some community; men to whom personal poverty is honour, and implicit obedience stands in the place of freedom. In vain shall a man look to the possibility of making such things when he wants them. The winds blow as they list. These institutions are the products of enthusiasm; they are the instruments of wisdom. Wisdom cannot create materials; they are the gifts of nature or of chance; her pride is in the use. The perennial existence of bodies corporate and their fortunes, are things particularly suited to a man who has long views; who meditates designs that require time in fashioning; and which propose duration when they are accomplished. He is not deserving to rank high, or even to be mentioned in the order of great statesmen, who, having obtained the command and direction of such a power as existed in the wealth, the discipline, and the habits of such corporations, as those which you have rashly destroyed, cannot find any way of converting it to the great and lasting benefit of his country. On the view of this subject a thousand uses suggest themselves to a contriving mind. To destroy any power, growing wild from the rank productive force of the human mind, is almost tantamount, in the moral world, to the destruction of the apparently active properties of bodies in the material.[131] It would be like the attempt to destroy (if it were in our competence to destroy) the expansive force of fixed air in nitre, or the power of steam, or of electricity, or of magnetism. These energies always existed in nature, and they were always discernible. They seemed, some of them unserviceable, some noxious, some no better than a sport to children; until contemplative ability, combining with practic skill, tamed their wild nature, subdued them to use, and rendered them at once the most powerful and the most tractable agents, in subservience to the great views and designs of men. Did fifty thousand persons, whose mental and whose bodily labour you might direct, and so many hundred thousand a year of a revenue, which was neither lazy nor superstitious, appear too big for your abilities to wield? Had you no way of using the men but by converting monks into pensioners? Had you no way of turning the revenue to account, but through the improvident resource of a spendthrift sale? If you were thus destitute of mental funds, the proceeding is in its natural course. Your politicians do not understand their trade; and therefore they sell their tools.

But the institutions savour of superstition in their very principle; and they nourish it by a permanent and standing influence. This I do not mean to dispute; but this ought not to hinder you from deriving from superstition itself any resources which may thence be furnished for the public advantage. You derive benefits from many dispositions and many passions of the human mind, which are of as doubtful a colour in the moral eye, as superstition itself. It was your business to correct and mitigate every thing which was noxious in this passion, as in all the passions. But is superstition the greatest of all possible vices? In its possible excess I think it becomes a very great evil. It is, however, a moral subject; and of course admits of all degrees and all modifications. Superstition is the religion of feeble minds; and they must be tolerated in an intermixture of it, in some trifling or some enthusiastic shape or other, else you will deprive weak minds of a resource found necessary to the strongest. The body of all true religion consists, to be sure, in obedience to the will of the sovereign of the world; in a confidence in his declarations; and an imitation of his perfections. The rest is our own. It may be prejudicial to the great end; it may be auxiliary. Wise men, who as such, are not *admirers* (not admirers at least of the *Munera Terræ*[132]) are not violently attached to these things, nor do they violently hate them. Wisdom is not the most severe corrector of folly. They are the rival follies, which mutually wage so unrelenting a war; and which make so cruel a use of their advantages, as they can happen to engage the immoderate vulgar on the one side or the other in their quarrels. Prudence would be neuter; but if, in the contention between fond attachment and fierce antipathy concerning things in their nature not made to produce such heats, a prudent man were obliged to make a choice of what errors and excesses of enthusiasm he would condemn or bear, perhaps he would think the superstition which builds, to be more tolerable than that which demolishes – that which adorns a country, than that which deforms it – that which endows, than that which plunders – that which disposes to mistaken beneficence, than that which stimulates to real injustice – that which leads a man to refuse to himself lawful pleasures, than that which snatches from others the scanty subsistence of their self-denial. Such, I think, is very nearly the state of the question between the ancient founders of monkish superstition, and the superstition of the pretended philosophers of the hour.

For the present I postpone all consideration of the supposed public profit of the sale, which however I conceive to be perfectly delusive. I shall here only consider it as a transfer of property. On the policy of that transfer I shall trouble you with a few thoughts.

In every prosperous community something more is produced than goes to the immediate support of the producer. This surplus forms the income of the landed capitalist. It will be spent by a proprietor who does not labour. But this idleness is itself the spring of labour; this repose the spur to industry. The only concern of the state is, that the capital taken in rent from the land, should be returned again to the industry from whence it came; and that its expenditure should be with the least possible detriment to the morals of those who expend it, and to those of the people to whom it is returned.

In all the views of receipt, expenditure, and personal employment, a sober legislator would carefully compare the possessor whom he was recommended to expel, with the stranger who was proposed to fill his place. Before the inconveniences are incurred which *must* attend all violent revolutions in property through extensive confiscation, we ought to have some rational assurance that the purchasers of the confiscated property will be in a considerable degree more laborious, more virtuous, more sober, less disposed to extort an unreasonable proportion of the gains of the labourer, or to consume on themselves a larger share than is fit for the measure of an individual, or that they should be qualified to dispense the surplus in a more steady and equal mode, so as to answer the purposes of a politic expenditure, than the old possessors, call those possessors, bishops, or canons, or commendatory abbots, or monks, or what you please. The monks are lazy. Be it so. Suppose them no otherwise employed than by singing in the choir. They are as usefully employed as those who neither sing nor say. As usefully even as those who sing upon the stage. They are as usefully employed as if they worked from dawn to dark in the innumerable servile, degrading, unseemly, unmanly, and often most unwholesome and pestiferous occupations, to which by the social œconomy so many wretches are inevitably doomed. If it were not generally pernicious to disturb the natural course of things, and to impede, in any degree, the great wheel of circulation which is turned by the strangely directed labour of these unhappy people, I should be infinitely more inclined forcibly to rescue them from their miserable industry, than violently to disturb the tranquil repose of monastic quietude. Humanity, and perhaps policy, might better justify me in the one than in the other. It is a subject on which I have often reflected, and never reflected without feeling from it. I am sure that no consideration, except the necessity of submitting to the yoke of luxury, and the despotism of fancy, who in their own imperious way will distribute the surplus product of the soil, can justify the toleration of such trades and employments in a wellregulated state. But, for this purpose of distribution, it seems to me, that the idle expences of monks are quite as well directed as the idle expences of us lay-loiterers.

When the advantages of the possession, and of the project, are on a par, there is no motive for a change. But in the present case, perhaps they are not upon a par, and the difference is in favour of the possession. It does not appear to me, that the expences of those whom you are going to expel, do, in fact, take a course so directly and so generally leading to vitiate and degrade and render miserable those through whom they pass, as the expences of those favourites whom you are intruding into their houses. Why should the expenditure of a great landed property, which is a dispersion of the surplus product of the soil, appear intolerable to you or to me, when it takes its course through the accumulation of vast libraries, which are the history of the force and weakness of the human mind; through great collections of antient records, medals, and coins, which attest and explain laws and customs; through paintings and statues, that, by imitating nature, seem to extend the limits of creation; through grand monuments of the dead, which continue the regards and connexions of life beyond the grave; through collections of the specimens of nature, which become a representative assembly of all the classes and families of the world, that by disposition facilitate, and, by exciting curiosity, open the avenues to science? If, by great permanent establishments, all these objects of expence are better secured from the inconstant sport of personal caprice and personal extravagance, are they worse than if the same tastes prevailed in scattered individuals? Does not the sweat of the mason and carpenter, who toil in order to partake the sweat of the peasant, flow as pleasantly and as salubriously, in the construction and repair of the majestic edifices of religion, as in the painted booths and sordid sties of vice and luxury; as honourably and as profitably in repairing those sacred works, which grow hoary with innumerable years, as on the momentary receptacles of transient voluptuousness; in opera-houses, and brothels, and gaming-houses, and club-houses, and obelisks in the Champ de Mars?[133] Is the surplus product of the olive and the vine worse employed in the frugal sustenance of persons, whom the fictions of a pious imagination raise to dignity by construing in the service of God, than in pampering the innumerable multitude of those who are degraded by being made useless domestics subservient to the pride of man? Are the decorations of temples an expenditure less worthy a wise man than ribbons, and laces, and national cockades, and petits maisons, and petit soupers, and all the innumerable fopperies and follies in which opulence sports away the burthen of its superfluity?

We tolerate even these; not from love of them, but for fear of worse. We tolerate them, because property and liberty, to a degree, require that toleration. But why proscribe the other, and surely, in every point of view, the more laudable use of estates? Why, through the violation of all property, through an outrage upon every principle of liberty, forcibly carry them from the better to the worse?

This comparison between the new individuals and the old corps is made upon a supposition that no reform could be made in the latter. But in a question of reformation, I always consider corporate bodies, whether sole or consisting of many, to be much more susceptible of a public direction by the power of the state, in the use of their property, and in the regulation of modes and habits of life in their members, than private citizens ever can be, or perhaps ought to be; and this seems to me a very material consideration for those who undertake any thing which merits the name of a politic enterprize. – So far as to the estates of monasteries.

With regard to the estates possessed by bishops and canons, and commendatory abbots, I cannot find out for what reason some landed estates may not be held otherwise than by inheritance. Can any philosophic spoiler undertake to demonstrate the positive or the comparative evil, of having a certain, and that too a large portion of landed property, passing in succession thro' persons whose title to it is, always in theory, and often in fact, an eminent degree of piety, morals, and learning; a property which, by its destination, in their turn, and on the score of merit, gives to the noblest families renovation and support, to the lowest the means of dignity and elevation; a property, the tenure of which is the performance of some duty, (whatever value you may choose to set upon that duty) and the character of whose proprietors demands at least an exterior decorum and gravity of manners; who are to exercise a generous but temperate hospitality; part of whose income they are to consider as a trust for charity; and who, even when they fail in their trust, when they slide from their character, and degenerate into a mere common secular nobleman or gentleman, are in no respect worse than those who may succeed them in their forfeited possessions? Is it better that estates should be held by those who have no duty than by those who have one? – by those whose character and destination point to virtues, than by those who have no rule and direction in the expenditure of their estates but their own will and appetite? Nor are these estates held altogether in the character or with the evils supposed inherent in mortmain.[134] They pass from hand to hand with a more rapid circulation than any other. No excess is good; and therefore too great a proportion of landed property may be held officially for life; but it does not seem to me of material injury to any commonwealth, that there should exist some estates that have a chance of being acquired by other means than the previous acquisition of money.

This letter is grown to a great length, though it is indeed short with regard to the infinite extent of the subject. Various avocations have from time to time called my mind from the subject. I was not sorry to give myself leisure to observe whether, in the proceedings of the national assembly, I might not find reasons to change or to qualify some of my first sentiments. Every thing has confirmed me more strongly in my first opinions. It was my original purpose to take a view of the principles of the national assembly with regard to the great and fundamental establishments; and to compare the whole of what you have substituted in the place of what you have destroyed, with the several members of our British constitution. But this plan is of greater extent than at first I computed, and I find that you have little desire to take the advantage of any examples. At present I must content myself with some remarks upon your establishments; reserving for another time what I proposed to say concerning the spirit of our British monarchy, aristocracy, and democracy, as practically they exist.

I have taken a review of what has been done by the governing power in France. I have certainly spoke of it with freedom. Those whose principle it is to despise the antient permanent sense of mankind, and to set up a scheme of society on new principles, must naturally expect that such of us who think better of the judgment of the human race than of theirs, should consider both them and their devices, as men and schemes upon their trial. They must take it for granted that we attend much to their reason, but not at all to their authority. They have not one of the great influencing prejudices of mankind in their favour. They avow their hostility to opinion. Of course they must expect no support from that influence, which, with every other authority, they have deposed from the seat of its jurisdiction.

I can never consider this assembly as any thing else than a voluntary association of men, who have availed themselves of circumstances, to seize upon the power of the state. They have not the sanction and authority of the character under which they first met. They have assumed another of a very different nature; and have completely altered and inverted all the relations in which they originally stood. They do not hold the authority they exercise under any constitutional law of the state. They have departed from the instructions of the people by whom they were sent; which instructions, as the assembly did not act in virtue of any antient usage or settled law, were the sole source of their authority. The most considerable of their acts have not been done by great majorities; and in this sort of near divisions, which carry only the constructive authority of the whole, strangers will consider reasons as well as resolutions.

If they had set up this new experimental government as a necessary substitute for an expelled tyranny, mankind would anticipate the time of prescription, which, through long usage, mellows into legality governments that were violent in their commencement. All those who have affections which lead them to the conservation of civil order would recognize, even in its cradle, the child as legitimate, which has been produced from those principles of cogent expediency to which all just governments owe their birth, and on which they justify their continuance. But they will be late and reluctant in giving any sort of countenance to the operations of a power, which has derived its birth from no law and no necessity; but which on the contrary has had its origin in those vices and sinister practices by which the social union is often disturbed and sometimes destroyed. This assembly has hardly a year's prescription. We have their own word for it that they have made a revolution. To make a revolution is a measure which, *prima fronte*, requires an apology. To make a revolution is to subvert the antient state of our country; and no common reasons are called for to justify so violent a proceeding. The sense of mankind authorizes us to examine into the mode of acquiring new power, and to criticise on the use that is made of it with less awe and reverence than that which is usually conceded to a settled and recognized authority.

In obtaining and securing their power, the assembly proceeds upon principles the most opposite from those which appear to direct them in the use of it. An observation on this difference will let us into the true spirit of their conduct. Every thing which they have done, or continue to do, in order to obtain and keep their power, is by the most common arts. They proceed exactly as their ancestors of ambition have done before them. Trace them through all their artifices, frauds, and violences, you can find nothing at all that is new. They follow precedents and examples with the punctilious exactness of a pleader. They never depart an iota from the authentic formulas of tyranny and usurpation. But in all the regulations relative to the public good, the spirit has been the very reverse of this. There they commit the whole to the mercy of untried speculations; they abandon the dearest interests of the public to those loose theories, to which none of them would chuse to trust the slightest of his private concerns. They make this difference, because in their desire of obtaining and securing power they are thoroughly in earnest; there they travel in the beaten road. The public interests, because about them they have no real solicitude, they abandon wholly to chance; I say to chance, because their schemes have nothing in experience to prove their tendency beneficial.

We must always see with a pity not unmixed with respect, the errors of those who are timid and doubtful of themselves with regard to points wherein the happiness of mankind is concerned. But in these gentlemen there is nothing of the tender parental solicitude which fears to cut up the infant for the sake of an experiment. In the vastness of their promises, and the confidence of their predictions, they far outdo all the boasting of empirics.

The arrogance of their pretensions, in a manner provokes, and challenges us to an enquiry into their foundation.

I am convinced that there are men of considerable parts among the popular leaders in the national assembly. Some of them display eloquence in their speeches and their writings. This cannot be without powerful and cultivated talents. But eloquence may exist without a proportionable degree of wisdom. When I speak of ability, I am obliged to distinguish. What they have done towards the support of their system bespeaks no ordinary men. In the system itself, taken as the scheme of a republic constructed for procuring the prosperity and security of the citizen, and for promoting the strength and grandeur of the state, I confess myself unable to find out any thing which displays, in a single instance, the work of a comprehensive and disposing mind, or even the provisions of a vulgar prudence. Their purpose every where seems to have been to evade and slip aside from *difficulty*. This it has been the glory of the great masters in all the arts to confront, and to overcome; and when they had overcome the first difficulty, to turn it into an instrument for new conquests over new difficulties; thus to enable them to extend the empire of their science; and even to push forward beyond the reach of their original thoughts, the land marks of the human understanding itself. Difficulty is a severe instructor, set over us by the supreme ordinance of a parental guardian and legislator, who knows us better than we know ourselves, as he loves us better too. *Pater ipse colendi haud facilem esse viam voluit.*[135] He that wrestles with us strengthens our nerves, and sharpens our skill. Our antagonist is our helper. This amicable conflict with difficulty obliges us to an intimate acquaintance with our object, and compels us to consider it in all its relations. It will not suffer us to be superficial. It is the want of nerves of understanding for such a talk; it is the degenerate fondness for tricking short-cuts, and little fallacious facilities, that has in so many parts of the world created governments with arbitrary powers. They have created the late arbitrary monarchy of France. They have created the arbitrary republic of Paris. With them defects in wisdom are to be supplied by the plenitude of force. They get nothing by it. Commencing their labours on a principle of sloth, they have the common fortune of slothful men. The difficulties which they rather had eluded than escaped, meet them again in their course; they multiply and thicken on them; they are involved, through a labyrinth of confused detail, in an industry without limit, and without direction; and, in conclusion, the whole of their work becomes feeble, vitious, and insecure.

It is this inability to wrestle with difficulty which has obliged the arbitrary assembly of France to commence their schemes of reform with abolition and total destruction.* But is it in destroying and pulling down that skill is displayed? Your mob can do this as well at least as your assemblies. The shallowest understanding, the rudest hand, is more than equal to that task. Rage and phrenzy will pull down more in half an hour, than prudence,

---

*A leading member of the assembly, M. Rabaud de St Etienne,[136] has expressed the principle of all their proceedings as clearly as possible. Nothing can be more simple: – '*Tous les établissemens en France couronnent le malheur du peuple: pour le rendre heureux il faut le renouveler; changer ses idées; changer ses loix; changer ses moeurs; ... changer les hommes; changer les choses; changer les mots ... tout détruire; oui, tout détruire; puisque tout est à recrèer.*' This gentleman was chosen president in an assembly not sitting at the *Quinze vingt,* or the *Petites Maisons;*[137] and composed of persons giving themselves out to be rational beings; but neither his ideas, language, or conduct, differ in the smallest degree from the discourses, opinions, and actions of those within and without the assembly, who direct the operations of the machine now at work in France.

deliberation, and foresight can build up in a hundred years. The errors and defects of old establishments are visible and palpable. It calls for little ability to point them out; and where absolute power is given, it requires but a word wholly to abolish the vice and the establishment together. The same lazy but restless disposition, which loves sloth and hates quiet, directs these politicians, when they come to work, for supplying the place of what they have destroyed. To make every thing the reverse of what they have seen is quite as easy as to destroy. No difficulties occur in what has never been tried. Criticism is almost baffled in discovering the defects of what has not existed; and eager enthusiasm, and cheating hope, have all the wide field of imagination in which they may expiate with little or no opposition.

At once to preserve and to reform is quite another thing. When the useful parts of an old establishment are kept, and what is superadded is to be fitted to what is retained, a vigorous mind, steady persevering attention, various powers of comparison and combination, and the resources of an understanding fruitful in expedients are to be exercised; they are to be exercised in a continued conflict with the combined force of opposite vices; with the obstinacy that rejects all improvement, and the levity that is fatigued and disgusted with every thing of which it is in possession. But you may object – 'A process of this kind is slow. It is not fit for an assembly, which glories in performing in a few months the work of ages. Such a mode of reforming, possibly might take up many years.' Without question it might; and it ought. It is one of the excellencies of a method in which time is amongst the assistants, that its operation is slow, and in some cases almost imperceptible. If circumspection and caution are a part of wisdom, when we work only upon inanimate matter, surely they become a part of duty too, when the subject of our demolition and construction is not brick and timber, but sentient beings, by the sudden alteration of whose state, condition, and habits, multitudes may be rendered miserable. But it seems as if it were the prevalent opinion in Paris, that an unfeeling heart, and an undoubting confidence, are the sole qualifications for a perfect legislator. Far different are my ideas of that high office. The true lawgiver ought to have an heart full of sensibility. He ought to love and respect his kind, and to fear himself. It may be allowed to his temperament to catch his ultimate object with an intuitive glance; but his movements towards it ought to be deliberate. Political arrangement, as it is a work for social ends, is to be only wrought by social means. There mind must conspire with mind. Time is required to produce that union of minds which alone can produce all the good we aim at. Our patience will achieve more than our force. If I might venture to appeal to what is so much out of fashion in Paris, I mean to experience, I should tell you, that in my course I have known, and, according to my measure, have co-operated with great men; and I have never yet seen any plan which has not been mended by the observations of those who were much inferior in understanding to the person who took the lead in the business. By a slow but well-sustained progress, the effect of each step is watched; the good or ill success of the first, gives light to us in the second; and so, from light to light, we are conducted with safety through the whole series. We see, that the parts of the system do not clash. The evils latent in the most promising contrivances are provided for as they arise. One advantage is as little as possible sacrificed to another. We compensate, we reconcile, we balance. We are enabled to unite into a consistent whole the various anomalies and contending principles that are found in the minds and affairs of men. From hence arises, not an excellence in simplicity, but one far superior, an excellence in composition. Where the great interests of mankind are concerned through a long succession of generations, that succession ought to be admitted into some share in the councils which are so deeply to affect them. If justice requires this, the work itself requires the aid of more minds than one age can furnish. It is from this view of things that the best legislators have been often satisfied with the establishment of some sure, solid, and ruling principle in government; a power like that which some of the philosophers have called a plastic nature; and having fixed the principle, they have left it afterwards to its own operation.

To proceed in this manner, that is, to proceed with a presiding principle, and a prolific energy, is with me the criterion of profound wisdom. What your politicians think the marks of a bold, hardy genius, are only proofs of a deplorable want of ability. By their violent haste, and their defiance of the process of nature, they are delivered over blindly to every projector and adventurer, to every alchymist and empiric. They despair of turning to account any thing that is common. Diet is nothing in their system of remedy. The worst of it is, that this their despair of curing common distempers by regular methods, arises not only from defect of comprehension, but, I fear, from some malignity of disposition. Your legislators seem to have taken their opinions of all professions, ranks, and offices, from the declamations and buffooneries of satirists; who would themselves be astonished if they were held to the letter of their own descriptions. By listening only to these, your leaders regard all things only on the side of their vices and faults, and view those vices and faults under every colour of exaggeration. It is undoubtedly true, though it may seem paradoxical; but in general, those who are habitually employed in finding and displaying faults, are unqualified for the work of reformation: because their minds are not only unfurnished with patterns of the fair and good, but by habit they come to take no delight in the contemplation of those things. By hating vices too much, they come to love men too little. It is therefore not wonderful, that they should be indisposed and unable to serve them. From hence arises the complexional disposition of some of your guides to pull every thing in pieces. At this malicious game they display the whole of their *quadrimanous* activity. As to the rest, the paradoxes of eloquent writers, brought forth purely as a sport of fancy, to try their talents, to rouze attention, and excite surprize, are taken up by these gentlemen, not in the spirit of the original authors, as means of cultivating their taste and improving their style. These paradoxes become with them serious grounds of action, upon which they proceed in regulating the most important concerns of the state. Cicero ludicrously describes Cato as endeavouring to act in the commonwealth upon the school paradoxes which exercised the wits of the junior students in the stoic philosophy.[138] If this was true of Cato, these gentlemen copy after him in the manner of some persons who lived about his time – *pede nudo Catonem*.[139] Mr Hume told me, that he had from Rousseau himself the secret of his principles of composition.[140] That acute, though eccentric, observer had perceived, that to strike and interest the public, the marvellous must be produced; that the marvellous of the heathen mythology had long since lost its effect; that giants, magicians, fairies, and heroes of romance which succeeded, had exhausted the portion of credulity which belonged to their age; that now nothing was left to a writer but that species of the marvellous, which might still be produced, and with as great an effect as ever, though in another way; that is, the marvellous in life, in manners, in characters, and in extraordinary situations, giving rise to new and unlooked-for strokes in politics and morals. I believe, that were Rousseau alive, and in one of his lucid intervals, he would be shocked at the practical phrenzy of his scholars, who in their paradoxes are servile imitators; and even in their incredulity discover an implicit faith.

Men who undertake considerable things, even in a regular way, ought to give us ground to presume ability. But the physician of the state, who, not satisfied with the cure of distempers, undertakes to regenerate constitutions, ought to shew uncommon powers. Some very unusual appearances of wisdom ought to display themselves on the face of the designs of those who appeal to no practice, and who copy after no model. Has any such been manifested? I shall take a view (it shall for the subject be a very short one) of what the assembly has done, with regard, first, to the constitution of the legislature; in the next place, to that of the executive power; then to that of the judicature; afterwards to the model of the army; and conclude with the system of finance, to see whether we can discover in any part of their schemes the portentous ability, which may justify these bold undertakers in the superiority which they assume over mankind.

It is in the model of the sovereign and presiding part of this new republic, that we should expect their grand display. Here they were to prove their title to their proud demands. For the plan itself at large, and for the reasons on which it is grounded, I refer to the journals of the assembly of the 29th of September 1789, and to the subsequent proceedings which have made any alterations in the plan. So far as in a matter somewhat confused I can see light, the system remains substantially as it has been originally framed. My few remarks will be such as regard its spirit, its tendency, and its fitness for framing a popular commonwealth, which they profess theirs to be, suited to the ends for which any commonwealth, and particularly such a commonwealth, is made. At the same time, I mean to consider its consistency with itself, and its own principles.

Old establishments are tried by their effects. If the people are happy, united, wealthy, and powerful, we presume the rest. We conclude that to be good from whence good is derived. In old establishments various correctives have been found for their aberrations from theory. Indeed they are the results of various necessities and expediences. They are not often constructed after any theory; theories are rather drawn from them. In them we often see the end best obtained, where the means seem not perfectly reconcileable to what we may fancy was the original scheme. The means taught by experience may be better suited to political ends than those contrived in the original project. They again re-act upon the primitive constitution, and sometimes improve the design itself from which they seem to have departed. I think all this might be curiously exemplified in the British constitution. At worst, the errors and deviations of every kind in reckoning are found and computed, and the ship proceeds in her course. This is the case of old establishments; but in a new and merely theoretic system, it is expected that every contrivance shall appear, on the face of it, to answer its end; especially where the projectors are no way embarrassed with an endeavour to accommodate the new building to an old one, either in the walls or on the foundations.

The French builders, clearing away as mere rubbish whatever they found, and, like their ornamental gardeners, forming every thing into an exact level, propose to rest the whole local and general legislature on three bases of three different kinds; one geometrical, one arithmetical, and the third financial; the first of which they call the *basis of territory*; the second, the *basis of population*; and the third, the *basis of contribution*. For the accomplishment of the first of these purposes they divide the area of their country into eighty-three pieces, regularly square, or eighteen leagues by eighteen. These large divisions are called *Departments*. These they portion, proceeding by square measurement, into seventeen hundred and twenty districts called *Communes*. These again they subdivide, still proceeding by square measurement, into smaller districts called *cantons*, making in all 6,400.

At first view this geometrical basis of theirs presents not much to admire or to blame. It calls for no great legislative talents. Nothing more than an accurate land surveyor, with his chain, sight, and theodolite, is requisite for such a plan as this. In the old divisions of the country various accidents at various times, and the ebb and flow of various properties and jurisdictions, settled their bounds. These bounds were not made upon any fixed system undoubtedly. They were subject to some inconveniencies; but they were inconveniencies for which use had found remedies, and habit had supplied accommodation and patience. In this new pavement of square within square, and this organisation and semiorganisation made on the system of Empedocles and Buffon,[141] and not upon any politic principle, it is impossible that innumerable local inconveniences, to which men are not habituated, must not arise. But these I pass over, because it requires an accurate knowledge of the country, which I do not possess, to specify them.

When these state surveyors came to take a view of their work of measurement, they soon found, that in politics, the most fallacious of all things was geometrical demonstration. They had then recourse to another basis (or rather buttress) to support the building which tottered on that false foundation. It was evident, that the goodness of the soil, the number of the people, their wealth, and the largeness of their contribution, made such infinite variations between square and square as to render mensuration a ridiculous standard of power in the commonwealth, and equality in geometry the most unequal of all measures in the distribution of men. However, they could not give it up. But dividing their political and civil representation into three parts, they allotted one of those parts to the square measurement, without a single fact or calculation to ascertain whether this territorial proportion of representation was fairly assigned, and ought upon any principle really to be a third. Having however given to geometry this portion (of a third for her dower) out of compliment I suppose to that sublime science, they left the other two to be scuffled for between the other parts, population and contribution.

When they came to provide for population, they were not able to proceed quite so smoothly as they had done in the field of their geometry. Here their arithmetic came to bear upon their juridical metaphysics. Had they stuck to their metaphysic principles, the arithmetical process would be simple indeed. Men, with them, are strictly equal, and are entitled to equal rights in their own government. Each head, on this system, would have its vote, and every man would vote directly for the person who was to represent him in the legislature. 'But soft – by regular degrees, not yet.'[142] This metaphysic principle, to which law, custom, usage, policy, reason, were to yield, is to yield itself to their pleasure. There must be many degrees, and some stages, before the representative can come in contact with his constituent. Indeed, as we shall soon see, these two persons are to have no sort of communion with each other. First, the voters in the *Canton*, who compose what they call *primary assemblies*, are to have a *qualification*. What! a qualification on the indefeasible rights of men? Yes; but it shall be a very small qualification. Our injustice shall be very little oppressive; only the local valuation of three days labour paid to the public. Why, this is not much, I readily admit, for any thing but the utter subversion of your equalising principle. As a qualification it might as well be let alone; for it answers no one purpose for which qualifications are established: and, on your ideas, it excludes from a vote, the man of all others whose natural equality stands the most in need of protection and defence; I mean the man who has nothing else but his natural equality to guard him. You order him to buy the right, which you before told him nature had given to him gratuitously at his birth, and of which no authority on earth could lawfully deprive him. With regard to the person who cannot come up to your market, a tyrannous aristocracy, as against him, is established at the very outset, by you who pretend to be its sworn foe.

The gradation proceeds. These primary assemblies of the *Canton* elect deputies to the *Commune*; one for every two hundred qualified inhabitants. Here is the first medium put between the primary elector and the representative legislator; and here a new turnpike is fixed for taxing the rights of men with a second qualification: for none can be elected into the *Commune* who does not pay the amount of ten days labour. Nor have we yet done. There is still to be another gradation.* These *Communes*,

---

* The assembly, in executing the plan of their committee, made some alterations. They have struck out one stage in these gradations; this removes a part of the objection: but the main objection, namely, that in their scheme the first constituent voter has no connexion with the representative legislator, remains in all its force. There are other alterations, some possibly for the better, some certainly for the worse; but to the author the merit or de-merit of these smaller alterations appear to be of no moment, where the scheme itself is fundamentally vitious and absurd.

chosen by the *Canton*, choose to the *Department*; and the deputies of the *Department* choose their deputies to the *National Assembly*. Here is a third barrier of a senseless qualification. Every deputy to the national assembly must pay, in direct contribution, to the value of a *mark of silver*. Of all these qualifying barriers we must think alike; that they are impotent to secure independence; strong only to destroy the rights of men.

In all this process, which in its fundamental elements affects to consider only *population* upon a principle of natural right, there is a manifest attention to *property*; which, however just and reasonable on other schemes, is on theirs perfectly unsupportable.

When they come to their third basis, that of *Contribution*, we find that they have more completely lost sight of their rights of men. This last basis rests *entirely* on property. A principle totally different from the equality of men, and utterly irreconcileable to it, is thereby admitted; but no sooner is this principle admitted, than (as usual) it is subverted; and it is not subverted, (as we shall presently see,) to approximate the inequality of riches to the level of nature. The additional share in the third portion of representation, (a portion reserved exclusively for the higher contribution,) is made to regard the *district* only, and not the individuals in it who pay. It is easy to perceive, by the course of their reasonings, how much they were embarrassed by their contradictory ideas of the rights of men and the privileges of riches. The committee of constitution do as good as admit that they are wholly irreconcileable. 'The relation, with regard to the contributions, is without doubt *null* (say they) when the question is on the balance of the political rights as between individual and individual; without which *personal equality would be destroyed*, and *an aristocracy of the rich* would be established. But this inconvenience entirely disappears when the proportional relation of the contribution is only considered in the *great masses*, and is solely between province and province; it serves in that case only to form a just reciprocal proportion between the cities, without affecting the personal rights of the citizens.'

Here the principle of *contribution*, as taken between man and man, is reprobated as *null*, and destructive to equality; and as pernicious too; because it leads to the establishment of an *aristocracy of the rich*. However, it must not be abandoned. And the way of getting rid of the difficulty is to establish the inequality as between department and department, leaving all the individuals in each department upon an exact par. Observe, that this parity between individuals had been before destroyed when the qualifications within the departments were settled; nor does it seem a matter of great importance whether the equality of men be injured by masses or individually. An individual is not of the same importance in a mass represented by a few, as in a mass represented by many. It would be too much to tell a man jealous of his equality, that the elector has the same franchise who votes for three members as he who votes for ten.

Now take it in the other point of view, and let us suppose their principle of representation according to contribution, that is according to riches, to be well imagined, and to be a necessary basis for their republic. In this their third basis they assume, that riches ought to be respected, and that justice and policy require that they should entitle men, in some mode or other, to a larger share in the administration of public affairs; it is now to be seen, how the assembly provides for the pre-eminence, or even for the security of the rich, by conferring, in virtue of their opulence, that larger measure of power to their district which is denied to them personally. I readily admit (indeed I should lay it down as a fundamental principle) that in a republican government, which has a democratic basis, the rich do require an additional security above what is necessary to them in monarchies. They are subject to envy, and through envy to oppression. On the present scheme, it is impossible to divine what advantage they derive from the aristocratic preference upon which the unequal representation of the masses is founded. The rich cannot feel it, either as a support to dignity, or as security to fortune: for the aristocratic mass is generated from purely democratic principles; and the prevalence given to it in the general representation has no sort of reference to or connexion with the persons, upon account of whose property this superiority of the mass is established. If the contrivers of this scheme meant any sort of favour to the rich in consequence of their contribution, they ought to have conferred the privilege either on the individual rich, or on some class formed of rich persons (as historians represent Servius Tullius[143] to have done in the early constitution of Rome); because the contest between the rich and the poor is not a struggle between corporation and corporation, but a contest between men and men; a competition not between districts but between descriptions. It would answer its purpose better if the scheme were inverted; that the votes of the masses were rendered equal; and that the votes within each mass were proportioned to property.

Let us suppose one man in a district (it is an easy supposition) to contribute as much as an hundred of his neighbours. Against these he has but one vote. If there were but one representative for the mass, his poor neighbours would outvote him by an hundred to one for that single representative. Bad enough. But amends are to be made him. How? The district, in virtue of his wealth, is to choose, say, ten members instead of one: that is to say, by paying a very large contribution he has the happiness of being outvoted, an hundred to one, by the poor for ten representatives, instead of being outvoted exactly in the same proportion for a single member. In truth, instead of benefitting by this superior quantity of representation, the rich man is subjected to an additional hardship. The encrease of representation within his province sets up nine persons more, and as many more than nine as there may be democratic candidates, to cabal and intrigue, and to flatter the people at his expence and to his oppression. An interest is by this means held out to multitudes of the inferior sort, in obtaining a salary of eighteen livres a day (to them a vast object) besides the pleasure of a residence in Paris, and their share in the government of the kingdom. The more the objects of ambition are multiplied and become democratic, just in that proportion the rich are endangered.

Thus it must fare between the poor and the rich in the province deemed aristocratic, which in its internal relation is the very reverse of that character. In its external relation, that is, its relation to the other provinces, I cannot see how the unequal representation, which is given to masses on account of wealth, becomes the means of preserving the equipoise and the tranquillity of the commonwealth. For if it be one of the objects to secure the weak from being crushed by the strong (as in all society undoubtedly it is) how are the smaller and poorer of these masses to be saved from the tyranny of the more wealthy? Is it by adding to the wealthy further and more systematical means of oppressing them. When we come to a balance of representation between corporate bodies, provincial interests, emulations, and jealousies are full as likely to arise among them as among individuals; and their divisions are likely to produce a much hotter spirit of dissention, and something leading much more nearly to a war.

I see that these aristocratic masses are made upon what is called the principle of direct contribution. Nothing can be a more unequal standard than this. The indirect contribution, that which arises from duties on consumption, is in truth a better standard, and follows and discovers wealth more naturally than this of direct contribution. It is difficult indeed to fix a standard of local preference on account of the one, or of the other, or of both, because some provinces may pay the more of either or of both, on account of causes not intrinsic, but originating from those very districts over whom they have obtained a preference in consequence of their ostensible contribution. If the masses were independent sovereign bodies, who were to provide for a federative treasury by distinct contingents, and that the revenue had not (as it has) many impositions running through the whole, which affect men individually, and not corporately, and which, by their nature, confound all territorial limits, something might be said for the basis of contribution as founded on masses. But of all things, this representation, to be measured by contribution, is the most difficult to settle upon principles of equity in a country, which considers its districts as members of an whole. For a great city, such as Bourdeaux or Paris, appears to pay a vast body of duties, almost out of all assignable proportion to other places, and its mass is considered accordingly. But are these cities the true contributors in that proportion? No. The consumers of the commodities imported into Bourdeaux, who are scattered through all France, pay the import duties of Bourdeaux. The produce of the vintage in Guienne and Languedoc give to that city the means of its contribution growing out of an export commerce. The landholders who spend their estates in Paris, and are thereby the creators of that city, contribute for Paris from the provinces out of which their revenues arise. Very nearly the same arguments will apply to the representative share given on account of *direct* contribution: because the direct contribution must be assessed on wealth real or presumed; and that local wealth will itself arise from causes not local, and which therefore in equity ought not to produce a local preference.

It is very remarkable, that in this fundamental regulation, which settles the representation of the mass upon the direct contribution, they have not yet settled how that direct contribution shall be laid, and how apportioned. Perhaps there is some latent policy towards the continuance of the present assembly in this strange procedure. However, until they do this, they can have no certain constitution. It must depend at last upon the system of taxation, and must vary with every variation in that system. As they have contrived matters, their taxation does not so much depend on their constitution, as their constitution on their taxation. This must introduce great confusion among the masses; as the variable qualification for votes within the district must, if ever real contested elections take place, cause infinite internal controversies.

To compare together the three bases, not on their political reason, but on the ideas on which the assembly works, and to try its consistency with itself, we cannot avoid observing, that the principle which the committee call the basis of *population*, does not begin to operate from the same point with the two other principles called the bases of *territory* and of *contribution*, which are both of an aristocratic nature. The consequence is, that where all three begin to operate together, there is the most absurd inequality produced by the operation of the former on the two latter principles. Every canton contains four square leagues, and is estimated to contain, on the average, 4,000 inhabitants, or 680 voters in the *primary assemblies*, which vary in numbers with the population of the canton, and send *one deputy* to the *commune* for every 200 voters. *Nine cantons* make a *commune*.

Now let us take *a canton* containing *a sea-port town of trade*, or *a great manufacturing town*. Let us suppose the population of this canton to be 12,700 inhabitants, or 2,193 voters, forming *three primary assemblies*, and sending *ten deputies* to the *commune*.

Oppose to this *one* canton *two* others of the remaining eight in the same commune. These we may suppose to have their fair population of 4,000 inhabitants, and 680 voters each, or 8,000 inhabitants and 1,360 voters, both together. These will form only *two primary assemblies*, and send only *six* deputies to the *commune*.

When the assembly of the *commune* comes to vote on the *basis of territory*, which principle is first admitted to operate in that assembly, the *single canton* which has *half* the territory of the *other two*, will have *ten* voices to *six* in the election of *three deputies* to the assembly of the department, chosen on the express ground of a representation of territory.

This inequality, striking as it is, will be yet highly aggravated, if we suppose, as we fairly may, the *several* other cantons of the *commune* to fall proportionably short of the average population, as much as the *principal canton* exceeds it. Now, as to *the basis of contribution*, which also is a principle admitted first to operate in the assembly of the *commune*. Let us again take *one* canton, such as is stated above. If the whole of the direct contributions paid by the great trading or manufacturing town be divided equally among the inhabitants, each individual will be found to pay much more than an individual living in the country according to the same average. The whole paid by the inhabitants of the former will be more than the whole paid by the inhabitants of the latter

— we may fairly assume one-third more. Then the 12,700 inhabitants, or 2,193 voters of the canton will pay as much as 19,050 inhabitants, or 3,289 voters of the *other cantons*, which are nearly the estimated proportion of inhabitants and voters of *five* other cantons. Now the 2,193 voters will, as I before said, send only *ten* deputies to the assembly; the 3,289 voters will send *sixteen*. Thus, for an *equal* share in the contribution of the whole *commune*, there will be a difference of *sixteen* voices to *ten* in voting for deputies to be chosen on the principle of representing the general contribution of the whole *commune*.

By the same mode of computation we shall find 15,875 inhabitants, or 2,741 voters of the *other* cantons, who pay *one-sixth* LESS to the contribution of the whole *commune*, will have *three* voices MORE than the 12,700 inhabitants, or 2,193 voters of the *one* canton.

Such is the fantastical and unjust inequality between mass and mass, in this curious repartition of the rights of representation arising out of *territory* and *contribution*. The qualifications which these confer are in truth negative qualifications, that give a right in an inverse proportion to the possession of them.

In this whole contrivance of the three bases, consider it in any light you please, I do not see a variety of objects, reconciled in one consistent whole, but several contradictory principles reluctantly and irreconcileably brought and held together by your philosophers, like wild beasts shut up in a cage, to claw and bite each other to their mutual destruction.

I am afraid I have gone too far into their way of considering the formation of a constitution. They have much, but bad, metaphysics; much, but bad, geometry; much, but false proportionate arithmetic; but if it were all as exact as metaphysics, geometry, and arithmetic ought to be, and if their schemes were perfectly consistent in all their parts, it would make only a more fair and sightly vision. It is remarkable, that in a great arrangement of mankind, not one reference whatsoever is to be found to any thing moral or any thing politic; nothing that relates to the concerns, the actions, the passions, the interests of men. *Hominem non sapiunt.*[144]

You see I only consider this constitution as electoral, and leading by steps to the National Assembly. I do not enter into the internal government of the Departments, and their genealogy through the Communes and Cantons. These local governments are, in the original plan, to be as nearly as possible composed in the same manner and on the same principles with the elective assemblies. They are each of them bodies perfectly compact and rounded in themselves.

You cannot but perceive in this scheme, that it has a direct and immediate tendency to sever France into a variety of republics,[145] and to render them totally independent of each other, without any direct constitutional means of coherence, connection, or subordination, except what may be derived from their acquiescence in the determinations of the general congress of the ambassadors from each independent republic. Such in reality is the National Assembly, and such governments I admit do exist in the world, though in forms infinitely more suitable to the local and habitual circumstances of their people. But such associations, rather than bodies politic, have generally been the effect of necessity, not choice; and I believe the present French power is the very first body of citizens, who, having obtained full authority to do with their country what they pleased, have chosen to dissever it in this barbarous manner.

It is impossible not to observe, that in the spirit of this geometrical distribution, and arithmetical arrangement, these pretended citizens treat France exactly like a country of conquest. Acting as conquerors, they have imitated the policy of the harshest of that harsh race. The policy of such barbarous victors, who contemn a subdued people, and insult their feelings, has ever been, as much as in them lay, to destroy all vestiges of the antient country, in religion, in polity, in laws, and in manners; to confound all territorial limits; to produce a general poverty; to put up their properties to auction; to crush their princes, nobles, and pontiffs; to lay low every thing which had lifted its head above the level, or which could serve to combine or rally, in their distresses, the disbanded people, under the standard of old opinion. They have made France free in the manner in which those sincere friends to the rights of mankind, the Romans, freed Greece, Macedon, and other .nations. They destroyed the bonds of their union, under colour of providing for the independence of each of their cities.

When the members who compose these new bodies of cantons, communes, and departments, arrangements purposely produced through the medium of confusion, begin to act, they will find themselves, in a great measure, strangers to one another. The electors and elected throughout, especially in the rural *cantons*, will be frequently without any civil habitudes or connexions, or any of that natural discipline which is the soul of a true republic. Magistrates and collectors of revenue are now no longer acquainted with their districts, bishops with their dioceses, or curates with their parishes. These new colonies of the rights of men bear a strong resemblance to that sort of military colonies which Tacitus has observed upon in the declining policy of Rome. In better and wiser days (whatever course they took with foreign nations) they were careful to make the elements of a methodical subordination and settlement to be coeval; and even to lay the foundations of civil discipline in the military.* But, when all the good arts had fallen into ruin, they proceeded, as your assembly does, upon the equality of men, and with as little judgment, and as little care for those things which make a republic tolerable or durable. But in this, as well as almost every instance, your new commonwealth is born, and bred, and fed, in those corruptions, which mark degenerated and worn out republics. Your child comes into the world with the symptoms of death; the *facies Hippocratica*[147] forms the character of its physiognomy, and the prognostic of its fate.

The legislators who framed the antient republics knew that their business was too arduous to be accomplished with no better apparatus than the metaphysics of an under-graduate, and the mathematics and arithmetic of an exciseman. They had to do with men, and they were obliged to study human nature. They had to do with citizens, and they were obliged to study the effects of those habits which are communicated by the circumstances of civil life. They were sensible that the operation of this second nature on the first produced a new combination; and thence arose many diversities amongst men, according to their birth, their education, their professions, the periods of their lives, their residence in towns or in the country, their several ways of acquiring and of fixing property, and according to the quality of the property itself, all which rendered them as it were so many different species of animals. From hence they

* Non, ut olim, universæ legiones deducebantur cum tribunis, et centurionibus, et sui cujusque ordinis militibus, ut consensu et caritate rempublicam afficerent; sed ignoti inter se, diversis manipulis, sine rectore, sine affectibus mutuis, quasi ex alio genere mortalium, repente in unum collecti, numerus magis quam colonia. Tac. Annal. 1. 14. sect. 27. All this will be still more applicable to the unconnected, rotatory, biennial national assemblies, in this absurd and senseless constitution.[146]

thought themselves obliged to dispose their citizens into such classes, and to place them in such situations in the state as their peculiar habits might qualify them to fill, and to allot to them such appropriated privileges as might secure to them what their specific occasions required, and which might furnish to each description such force as might protect it in the conflict caused by the diversity of interests, that must exist, and must contend in all complex society: for the legislator would have been ashamed, that the coarse husbandman should well know how to assort and to use his sheep, horses, and oxen, and should have enough of common sense not to abstract and equalize them all into animals, without providing for each kind an appropriate food, care, and employment; whilst he, the œconomist, disposer, and shepherd of his own kindred, subliming himself into an airy metaphysician, was resolved to know nothing of his flocks, but as men in general. It is for this reason that Montesquieu[148] observed very justly, that in their classification of the citizens, the great legislators of antiquity made the greatest display of their powers, and even soared above themselves. It is here that your modern legislators have gone deep into the negative series, and sunk even below their own nothing. As the first sort of legislators attended to the different kinds of citizens, and combined them into one commonwealth, the others, the metaphysical and alchemistical legislators, have taken the direct contrary course. They have attempted to confound all sorts of citizens, as well as they could, into one homogeneous mass; and then they divided this their amalgama into a number of incoherent republics. They reduce men to loose counters merely for the sake of simple telling, and not to figures whose power is to arise from their place in the table. The elements of their own metaphysics might have taught them better lessons. The troll[149] of their categorical table might have informed them that there was something else in the intellectual world besides *substance* and *quantity*. They might learn from the catechism of metaphysics that there were eight heads more,* in every complex deliberation, which they have never thought of, though these, of all the ten, are the subject on which the skill of man can operate any thing at all.

So far from this able disposition of some of the old republican legislators, which follows with a solicitous accuracy, the moral conditions and propensities of men, they have levelled and crushed together all the orders which they found, even under the coarse unartificial arrangement of the monarchy, in which mode of government the classing of the citizens is not of so much importance as in a republic. It is true, however, that every such classification, if properly ordered, is good in all forms of government; and composes a strong barrier against the excesses of despotism, as well as it is the necessary means of giving effect and permanence to a republic. For want of something of this kind, if the present project of a republic should fail, all securities to a moderated freedom fail along with it; all the indirect restraints which mitigate despotism are removed; insomuch that if monarchy should ever again obtain an entire ascendency in France, under this or under any other dynasty, it will probably be, if not voluntarily tempered at setting out, by the wise and virtuous counsels of the prince, the most completely arbitrary power that has ever appeared on earth. This is to play a most desperate game.

The confusion which attends on all such proceedings, they even declare to be one of their objects, and they hope to secure their constitution by a terror of a return of those evils which attended their making it. 'By this,' say they, 'its destruction will become difficult to authority, which

* Qualitas, Relatio, Actio, Passio, Ubi, Quando, Situs, Habitus.

cannot break it up without the entire disorganization of the whole state.' They presume, that if this authority should ever come to the same degree of power that they have acquired, it would make a more moderate and chastised use of it, and would piously tremble entirely to disorganise the state in the savage manner that they have done. They expect, from the virtues of returning despotism, the security which is to be enjoyed by the offspring of their popular vices.

I wish, Sir, that you and my readers would give an attentive perusal to the work of M. de Calonne,[150] on this subject. It is indeed not only an eloquent but an able and instructive performance. I confine myself to what he says relative to the constitution of the new state, and to the condition of the revenue. As to the disputes of this minister with his rivals, I do not wish to pronounce upon them. As little do I mean to hazard any opinion concerning his ways and means, financial or political, for taking his country out of its present disgraceful and deplorable situation of servitude, anarchy, bankruptcy, and beggary. I cannot speculate quite so sanguinely as he does: but he is a Frenchman, and has a closer duty relative to those objects, and better means of judging of them, than I can have. I wish that the formal avowal which he refers to, made by one of the principle leaders in the assembly, concerning the tendency of their scheme to bring France not only from a monarchy to a republic, but from a republic to a mere confederacy, may be very particularly attended to. It adds new force to my observations; and indeed M. de Calonne's work supplies my deficiencies by many new and striking arguments on most of the subjects of this Letter.*

It is this resolution, to break their country into separate republics, which has driven them into the greatest

* See L'Etat de la France, p. 363.[150]

number of their difficulties and contradictions. If it were not for this, all the questions of exact equality, and these balances, never to be settled, of individual rights, population, and contribution, would be wholly useless. The representation, though derived from parts, would be a duty which equally regarded the whole. Each deputy to the assembly would be the representative of France, and of all its descriptions, of the many and of the few, of the rich and of the poor, of the great districts and of the small. All these districts would themselves be subordinate to some standing authority, existing independently of them; an authority in which their representation, and every thing that belongs to it, originated, and to which it was pointed. This standing, unalterable, fundamental government would make, and it is the only thing which could make, that territory truly and properly an whole. With us, when we elect popular representatives, we send them to a council, in which each man individually is a subject, and submitted to a government complete in all its ordinary functions. With you the elective assembly is the sovereign, and the sole sovereign: all the members are therefore integral parts of this sole sovereignty. But with us it is totally different. With us the representative, separated from the other parts, can have no action and no existence. The government is the point of reference of the several members and districts of our representation. This is the center of our unity. This government of reference is a trustee for the *whole*, and not for the parts. So is the other branch of our public council, I mean the house of lords. With us the king and the lords are several and joint securities for the equality of each district, each province, each city. When did you hear in Great Britain of any province suffering from the inequality of its representation; what district from having no representation at all? Not only our monarchy and our peerage secure the

equality on which our unity depends, but it is the spirit of
the house of commons itself. The very inequality of
representation, which is so foolishly complained of, is
perhaps the very thing which prevents us from thinking
or acting as members for districts. Cornwall elects as
many members as all Scotland. But is Cornwall better
taken care of than Scotland? Few trouble their heads
about any of your bases, out of some giddy clubs. Most
of those, who wish for any change, upon any plausible
grounds, desire it on different ideas.

Your new constitution is the very reverse of ours in its
principle; and I am astonished how any persons could
dream of holding out any thing done in it as an example
for Great Britain. With you there is little, or rather no,
connection between the last representative and the first
constituent. The member who goes to the national assembly is not chosen by the people, nor accountable to
them. There are three elections before he is chosen: two
sets of magistracy intervene between him and the primary
assembly, so as to render him, as I have said, an ambassador of a state, and not the representative of the people
within a state. By this the whole spirit of the election is
changed; nor can any corrective your constitution-
mongers have devised render him any thing else than what
he is. The very attempt to do it would inevitably introduce a confusion, if possible, more horrid than the
present. There is no way to make a connexion between
the original constituent and the representative, but by the
circuitous means which may lead the candidate to apply
in the first instance to the primary electors, in order
that by their authoritative instructions (and something
more perhaps) these primary electors may force the two
succeeding bodies of electors to make a choice agreeable
to their wishes. But this would plainly subvert the whole
scheme. It would be to plunge them back into that tumult

and confusion of popular election, which, by their interposed gradation elections, they mean to avoid, and at
length to risque the whole fortune of the state with those
who have the least knowledge of it, and the least interest
in it. This is a perpetual dilemma, into which they are
thrown by the vicious, weak, and contradictory principles
they have chosen. Unless the people break up and level
this gradation, it is plain that they do not at all substantially elect to the assembly; indeed they elect as little in
appearance as reality.

What is it we all seek for in an election? To answer its
real purposes, you must first possess the means of knowing the fitness of your man; and then you must retain
some hold upon him by personal obligation of dependence. For what end are these primary electors compli-
mented, or rather mocked, with a choice? They can never
know any thing of the qualities of him that is to serve
them, nor has he any obligation whatsoever to them. Of
all the powers unfit to be delegated by those who have any
real means of judging, that most peculiarly unfit is what
relates to a *personal* choice. In case of abuse, that body
of primary electors never can call the representative to an
account for his conduct. He is too far removed from them
in the chain of representation. If he acts improperly at
the end of his two years lease, it does not concern him for
two years more. By the new French constitution, the best
and the wisest representatives go equally with the worst
into this *Limbus Patrum*.[151] Their bottoms are supposed
foul, and they must go into dock to be refitted. Every
man who has served in an assembly is ineligible for two
years after. Just as these magistrates begin to learn their
trade, like chimney-sweepers, they are disqualified for exercising it. Superficial, new, petulant acquisition, and interrupted, dronish, broken, ill recollection, is to be the
destined character of all your future governors. Your

constitution has too much of jealousy to have much of sense in it. You consider the breach of trust in the representative so principally, that you do not at all regard the question of his fitness to execute it.

This purgatory interval is not unfavourable to a faithless representative, who may be as good a canvasser as he was a bad governor. In this time he may cabal himself into a superiority over the wisest and most virtuous. As, in the end, all the members of this elective constitution are equally fugitive, and exist only for the election, they may be no longer the same persons who had chosen him, to whom he is to be responsible when he solicits for a renewal of his trust. To call all the secondary electors of the *Commune* to account, is ridiculous, impracticable, and unjust; they may themselves have been deceived in their choice, as the third set of electors, those of the *Department*, may be in theirs. In your elections responsibility cannot exist.

Finding no sort of principle of coherence with each other in the nature and constitution of the several new republics of France, I considered what cement the legislators had provided for them from any extraneous materials. Their confederations, their *spectacles*, their civic feasts, and their enthusiasm, I take no notice of; They are nothing but mere tricks; but tracing their policy through their actions, I think I can distinguish the arrangements by which they propose to hold these republics together. The first, is the *confiscation*, with the compulsory paper currency annexed to it; the second, is the supreme power of the city of Paris; the third, is the general army of the state. Of this last I shall reserve what I have to say, until I come to consider the army as an head by itself.

As to the operation of the first (the confiscation and paper currency) merely as a cement, I cannot deny that these, the one depending on the other, may for some time compose some sort of cement, if their madness and folly in the management, and in the tempering of the parts together, does not produce a repulsion in the very outset. But allowing to the scheme some coherence and some duration, it appears to me, that if, after a while, the confiscation should not be found sufficient to support the paper coinage (as I am morally certain it will not) then, instead of cementing, it will add infinitely to the dissociation, distraction, and confusion of these confederate republics, both with relation to each other, and to the several parts within themselves. But if the confiscation should so far succeed as to sink the paper currency, the cement is gone with the circulation. In the mean time its binding force will be very uncertain, and it will straiten or relax with every variation in the credit of the paper.

One thing only is certain in this scheme, which is an effect seemingly collateral, but direct, I have no doubt, in the minds of those who conduct this business, that is, its effect in producing an *Oligarchy* in every one of the republics. A paper circulation, not founded on any real money deposited or engaged for, amounting already to four-and-forty millions of English money, and this currency by force substituted in the place of the coin of the kingdom, becoming thereby the substance of its revenue, as well as the medium of all its commercial and civil intercourse, must put the whole of what power, authority, and influence is left, in any form whatsoever it may assume, into the hands of the managers and conductors of this circulation.

In England we feel the influence of the bank; though it is only the center of a voluntary dealing. He knows little indeed of the influence of money upon mankind, who does not see the force of the management of a monied concern, which is so much more extensive, and in its

nature so much more depending on the managers than
any of ours. But this is not merely a money concern. There
is another member in the system inseparably connected
with this money management. It consists in the means
of drawing out at discretion portions of the confiscated
lands for sale; and carrying on a process of continual
transmutation of paper into land, and land into paper.
When we follow this process in its effects, we may conceive something of the intensity of the force with which
this system must operate. By this means the spirit of
money-jobbing and speculation goes into the mass of land
itself, and incorporates with it. By this kind of operation, that species of property becomes (as it were) volatil-
ized; it assumes an unnatural and monstrous activity, and
thereby throws into the hands of the several managers,
principal and subordinate, Parisian and provincial, all the
representative of money, and perhaps a full tenth part of
all the land in France, which has now acquired the worst
and most pernicious part of the evil of a paper circulation, the greatest possible uncertainty in its value. They
have reversed the Latonian kindness to the landed property of Delos.[152] They have sent theirs to be blown about,
like the light fragments of a wreck, *oras et littora
circum.*[153]

The new dealers being all habitually adventurers, and
without any fixed habits or local predilections, will purchase to job out again, as the market of paper, or of
money, or of land shall present an advantage. For though
an holy bishop[154] thinks that agriculture will derive
great advantages from the '*enlightened*' usurers who are
to purchase the church confiscations, I, who am not a
good, but an old farmer, with great humility beg leave to
tell his late lordship, that usury is not a tutor of agriculture; and if the word 'enlightened' be understood according to the new dictionary, as it always is in your new

schools, I cannot conceive how a man's not believing in God can teach him to cultivate the earth with the least of any additional skill or encouragement. 'Diis immortalibus sero,'[155] said an old Roman when he held one handle of the plough, whilst Death held the other. Though you were to join in the commission all the directors of the two academies to the directors of the *Caisse d'Escompte*, one old experienced peasant is worth them all. I have got more information, upon a curious and interesting branch of husbandry, in one short conversation with a Carthusian monk, than I have derived from all the Bank directors that I have ever conversed with. However, there is no cause for apprehension from the meddling of money-dealers with rural œconomy. These gentlemen are too wise in their generation. At first, perhaps, their tender and susceptible imaginations may be captivated with the innocent and unprofitable delights of a pastoral life; but in a little time they will find that agriculture is a trade much more laborious, and much less lucrative than that which they had left. After making its panegyric, they will turn their backs on it like their great precursor and prototype. – They may, like him, begin by singing *'Beatus ille'* – but what will be the end?

> *Hæc ubi locutus fœnerator Alphius,*
> *Jam jam futurus rusticus*
> *Omnem relegit idibus pecuniam,*
> *Quærit calendis ponere.*[156]

They will cultivate the *caisse d'Eglise*, under the sacred auspices of this prelate, with much more profit than its vineyards or its corn-fields. They will employ their talents according to their habits and their interests. They will not follow the plough whilst they can direct treasuries, and govern provinces.

Your legislators, in every thing new, are the very first

who have founded a commonwealth upon gaming, and infused this spirit into it as its vital breath. The great object in these politics is to metamorphose France, from a great kingdom into one great play-table; to turn its inhabitants into a nation of gamesters; to make speculation as extensive as life; to mix it with all its concerns; and to divert the whole of the hopes and fears of the people from their usual channels, into the impulses, passions, and superstitions of those who live on chances. They loudly proclaim their opinion, that this their present system of a republic cannot possibly exist without this kind of gaming fund; and that the very thread of its life is spun out of the staple of these speculations. The old gaming in funds was mischievous enough undoubtedly; but it was so only to individuals. Even when it had its greatest extent, in the Mississippi and the South Sea,[157] it affected but few, comparatively; where it extends further, as in lotteries, the spirit has but a single object. But where the law, which in most circumstances forbids, and in none countenances gaming, is itself debauched, so as to reverse its nature and policy, and expressly to force the subject to this destructive table, by bringing the spirit and symbols of gaming into the minutest matters, and engaging every body in it, and in every thing, a more dreadful epidemic distemper of that kind is spread than yet has appeared in the world. With you a man can neither earn nor buy his dinner, without a speculation. What he receives in the morning will not have the same value at night. What he is compelled to take as pay for an old debt, will not be received as the same when he comes to pay a debt contracted by himself; nor will it be the same when by prompt payment he would avoid contracting any debt at all. Industry must wither away. Œconomy must be driven from your country. Careful provision will have no existence. Who will labour without knowing the amount of his pay? Who will study to encrease what none can estimate? who will accumulate, when he does not know the value of what he saves? If you abstract it from its uses in gaming, to accumulate your paper wealth, would be not the providence of a man, but the distempered instinct of a jackdaw.

The truly melancholy part of the policy of systematically making a nation of gamesters is this; that tho' all are forced to play, few can understand the game; and fewer still are in a condition to avail themselves of the knowledge. The many must be the dupes of the few who conduct the machine of these speculations. What effect it must have on the country-people is visible. The towns-man can calculate from day to day: not so the inhabitant of the country. When the peasant first brings his corn to market, the magistrate in the towns obliges him to take the assignat at par; when he goes to the shop with this money, he finds it seven per cent the worse for crossing the way. This market he will not readily resort to again. The towns-people will be inflamed! they will force the country-people to bring their corn. Resistance will begin, and the murders of Paris and St Dennis may be renewed through all France.

What signifies the empty compliment paid to the country by giving it perhaps more than its share in the theory of your representation? Where have you placed the real power over monied and landed circulation? Where have you placed the means of raising and falling the value of every man's freehold? Those whose operations can take from, or add ten per cent to, the possesions of every man in France, must be the masters of every man in France. The whole of the power obtained by this revolution will settle in the towns among the burghers, and the monied directors who lead them. The landed gentleman, the yeoman, and the peasant have, none of them, habits or inclinations, or experience, which can lead them to any share in this the sole source of power and influence now left in France. The very nature of a country life, the very nature of landed property, in all the occupations, and all the pleasures they afford, render combination and arrangement (the sole way of procuring and exerting influence) in a manner impossible amongst country-people. Combine them by all the art you can, and all the industry, they are always dissolving into individuality. Any thing in the nature of incorporation is almost impracticable amongst them. Hope, fear, alarm, jealousy, the ephemerous tale that does its business and dies in a day, all these things, which are the reins and spurs by which leaders check or urge the minds of followers, are not easily employed, or hardly at all, amongst scattered people. They assemble, they arm, they act with the utmost difficulty, and at the greatest charge. Their efforts, if ever they can be commenced, cannot be sustained. They cannot proceed systematically. If the country gentlemen attempt an influence through the mere income of their property, what is it to that of those who have ten times their income to sell, and who can ruin their property by bringing their plunder to meet it at market. If the landed man wishes to mortgage, he falls the value of his land, and raises the value of assignats. He augments the power of his enemy by the very means he must take to contend with him. The country gentleman therefore, the officer by sea and land, the man of liberal views and habits, attached to no profession, will be as completely excluded from the government of his country as if he were legislatively proscribed. It is obvious, that in the towns, all the things which conspire against the country gentleman, combine in favour of the money manager and director. In towns combination is natural. The habits of burghers, their occupations, their diversion, their business, their idleness, continually bring them into mutual contact. Their virtues and their vices are sociable; they are always in garrison; and they come embodied and half disciplined into the hands of those who mean to form them for civil, or for military action.

All these considerations leave no doubt on my mind, that if this monster of a constitution can continue, France will be wholly governed by the agitators in corporations, by societies in the towns formed of directors of assignats, and trustees for the sale of church lands, attornies, agents, money-jobbers, speculators, and adventurers, composing an ignoble oligarchy founded on the destruction of the crown, the church, the nobility, and the people. Here end all the deceitful dreams and visions of the equality and rights of men. In 'the Serbonian bog'[158] of this base oligarchy they are all absorbed, sunk, and lost for ever.

Though human eyes cannot trace them, one would be tempted to think some great offences in France must cry to heaven, which has thought fit to punish it with a subjection to a vile and inglorious domination, in which no comfort or compensation is to be found in any, even of those false splendours, which, playing about other tyrannies, prevent mankind from feeling themselves dishonoured even whilst they are oppressed. I must confess I am touched with a sorrow, mixed with some indignation, at the conduct of a few men, once of great rank, and still of great character, who, deluded with specious names, have engaged in a business too deep for the line of their understanding to fathom; who have lent their fair reputation, and the authority of their high-sounding names, to the designs of men with whom they could not be acquainted; and have thereby made their very virtues operate to the ruin of their country.

So far as to the first cementing principle.

The second material of cement for their new republic is the superiority of the city of Paris; and this I admit is strongly connected with the other cementing principle of paper circulation and confiscation. It is in this part of the project we must look for the cause of the destruction of all the old bounds of provinces and jurisdictions, ecclesiastical and secular, and the dissolution of all ancient combinations of things, as well as the formation of so many small unconnected republics. The power of the city of Paris is evidently one great spring of all their politics. It is through the power of Paris, now become the center and focus of jobbing, that the leaders of this faction direct, or rather command the whole legislative and the whole executive government. Every thing therefore must be done which can confirm the authority of that city over the other republics. Paris is compact; she has an enormous strength, wholly disproportioned to the force of any of the square republics; and this strength is collected and condensed within a narrow compass. Paris has a natural and easy connexion of its parts, which will not be affected by any scheme of a geometrical constitution, nor does it much signify whether its proportion of representation be more or less, since it has the whole draft of fishes in its dragnet. The other divisions of the kingdom being hackled and torn to pieces, and separated from all their habitual means, and even principles of union, cannot, for some time at least, confederate against her. Nothing was to be left in all the subordinate members, but weakness, disconnection, and confusion. To confirm this part of the plan, the assembly has lately come to a resolution, that no two of their republics shall have the same commander in chief.

To a person who takes a view of the whole, the strength of Paris thus formed, will appear a system of general weakness. It is boasted, that the geometrical policy has been adopted, that all local ideas should be sunk, and that the people should no longer be Gascons, Picards, Bretons, Normans, but Frenchmen, with one country, one heart, and one assembly. But instead of being all Frenchmen, the greater likelihood is, that the inhabitants of that region will shortly have no country. No man ever was attached by a sense of pride, partiality, or real affection, to a description of square measurement. He never will glory in belonging to the Checquer, No 71, or to any other badge-ticket. We begin our public affections in our families. No cold relation is a zealous citizen. We pass on to our neighbourhoods, and our habitual provincial connections. These are inns and resting-places. Such divisions of our country as have been formed by habit, and not by a sudden jerk of authority, were so many little images of the great country in which the heart found something which it could fill. The love to the whole is not extinguished by this subordinate partiality. Perhaps it is a sort of elemental training to those higher and more large regards, by which alone men come to be affected, as with their own concern, in the prosperity of a kingdom so extensive as that of France. In that general territory itself, as in the old name of provinces, the citizens are interested from old prejudices and unreasoned habits, and not on account of the geometric properties of its figure. The power and pre-eminence of Paris does certainly press down and hold these republics together, as long as it lasts. But, for the reasons I have already given you, I think it cannot last very long.

Passing from the civil creating, and the civil cementing principles of this constitution, to the national assembly, which is to appear and act as sovereign, we see a body in its constitution with every possible power, and no possible external controul. We see a body without fundamental laws, without established maxims, without respected rules of proceeding, which nothing can keep firm to any system whatsoever. Their idea of their powers is always taken at the utmost stretch of legislative competency, and their examples for common cases, from the exceptions of the most urgent necessity. The future is to be in most respects like the present assembly; but, by the mode of the new elections and the tendency of the new circulations, it will be purged of the small degree of internal controul existing in a minority chosen originally from various interests, and preserving something of their spirit. If possible, the next assembly must be worse than the present. The present, by destroying and altering every thing, will leave to their successors apparently nothing popular to do. They will be roused by emulation and example to enterprises the boldest and the most absurd. To suppose such an assembly sitting in perfect quietude is ridiculous.

Your all-sufficient legislators, in their hurry to do every thing at once, have forgot one thing that seems essential, and which, I believe, never has been before, in the theory or the practice, omitted by any projector of a republic. They have forgot to constitute a *Senate*, or something of that nature and character. Never, before this time, was heard of a body politic composed of one legislative and active assembly, and its executive officers, without such a council; without something to which foreign states might connect themselves; something to which, in the ordinary detail of government, the people could look up; something which might give a bias and steadiness, and preserve something like consistency in the proceedings of state. Such a body kings generally have as a council. A monarchy may exist without it; but it seems to be in the very essence of a republican government. It holds a sort of middle place between the supreme power exercised by the people, or immediately delegated from them, and the mere executive. Of this there are no traces in your constitution; and in providing nothing of this kind, your Solons and Numas[159] have, as much as in any thing else, discovered a sovereign incapacity.

Let us now turn our eyes to what they have done towards the formation of an executive power. For this they have chosen a degraded king. This their first executive officer is to be a machine, without any sort of deliberative discretion in any one act of his function. At best he is but a channel to convey to the national assembly such matter as may import that body to know. If he had been made the exclusive channel, the power would not have been without its importance; though infinitely perilous to those who would choose to exercise it. But public intelligence and statement of facts may pass to the assembly, with equal authenticity, through any other conveyance. As to the means, therefore, of giving a direction to measures by the statement of an authorized reporter, this office of intelligence is as nothing.

To consider the French scheme of an executive officer in its two natural divisions of civil and political – In the first it must be observed, that, according to the new constitution, the higher parts of judicature, in either of its lines, are not in the king. The king of France is not the fountain of justice. The judges, neither the original nor the appellate, are of his nomination. He neither proposes the candidates, nor has a negative on the choice. He is not even the public prosecutor. He serves only as a notary to authenticate the choice made of the judges in the several districts. By his officers he is to execute their sentence. When we look into the true nature of his authority, he appears to be nothing more than a chief of bumbailiffs, serjeants at mace, catchpoles, jailers, and hangmen. It is impossible to place any thing called royalty in a more degrading point of view. A thousand times better it had been for the dignity of this unhappy prince, that he had nothing at all to do with the administration of justice, deprived as he is of all that is venerable, and all that is consolatory in that function, without power of originating any process; without a power of suspension, mitigation, or pardon. Every thing in justice that is vile and odious is thrown upon him. It was not for nothing that the assembly has been at such pains to remove the stigma from certain offices, when they were resolved to place the person who lately had been their king in a situation but one degree above the executioner, and in an office nearly of the same quality. It is not in nature, that situated as the king of the French now is, he can respect himself, or can be respected by others.

View this new executive officer on the side of his political capacity, as he acts under the orders of the national assembly. To execute laws is a royal office; to execute orders is not to be a king. However, a political executive magistracy, though merely such, is a great trust. It is a trust indeed that has much depending upon its faithful and diligent performance, both in the person presiding in it and in all his subordinates. Means of performing this duty ought to be given by regulation; and dispositions towards it ought to be infused by the circumstances attendant on the trust. It ought to be environed with dignity, authority, and consideration, and it ought to lead to glory. The office of execution is an office of exertion. It is not from impotence we are to expect the tasks of power. What sort of person is a king to command executory service, who has no means whatsoever to reward it? Not in a permanent office; not in a grant of land; no, not in a pension of fifty pounds a year; not in the vainest and most trivial title. In France the king is no more the fountain of honour than he is the fountain of justice. All rewards, all distinctions are in other hands. Those who serve the king can be actuated by no natural motive but fear; by a fear of every thing except their master. His functions of internal coercion are as odious, as those which he exercises in the department of justice. If relief is to be given to any municipality, the assembly gives it. If troops are to be sent to reduce them to obedience to the assembly, the king is to execute the order; and upon every occasion he is to be spattered over with the blood of his people. He has no negative; yet his name and authority is used to enforce every harsh decree. Nay, he must concur in the butchery of those who shall attempt to free him from his imprisonment, or shew the slightest attachment to his person or to his antient authority.

Executive magistracy ought to be constituted in such a manner, that those who compose it should be disposed to love and to venerate those whom they are bound to obey. A purposed neglect, or, what is worse, a literal but perverse and malignant obedience, must be the ruin of the wisest counsels. In vain will the law attempt to anticipate or to follow such studied neglects and fraudulent attentions. To make men act zealously is not in the competence of law. Kings, even such as are truly kings, may and ought to bear the freedom of subjects that are obnoxious to them. They may too, without derogating from themselves, bear even the authority of such persons if it promotes their service. Louis the XIIIth mortally hated the cardinal de Richlieu; but his support of that minister against his rivals was the source of all the glory of his reign, and the solid foundation of his throne itself. Louis the XIVth, when come to the throne, did not love the cardinal Mazarin;[160] but for his interests he preserved him in power. When old, he detested Louvois;[160] but for years, whilst he faithfully served his greatness, he endured his person. When George the IId took Mr Pitt, who certainly was not agreeable to him, into his councils, he did nothing which could humble a wise sovereign.[161] But these ministers, who were chosen by affairs, not by affections, acted in the name of, and in trust for, kings; and not as their avowed, constitutional, and ostensible masters. I think it impossible that any king, when he has recovered his first terrors, can cordially infuse vivacity and vigour into measures which he knows to be dictated by those who he must be persuaded are in the highest degree ill affected to his person. Will any ministers, who serve such a king (or whatever he may be called) with but a decent appearance of respect, cordially obey the orders of those whom but the other day in his name they had committed to the Bastile? will they obey the orders of those whom, whilst they were exercising despotic justice upon them, they conceived they were treating with lenity; and for whom, in a prison, they thought they had provided an asylum? If you expect such obedience, amongst your other innovations and regenerations, you ought to make a revolution in nature, and provide a new constitution for the human mind. Otherwise, your supreme government cannot harmonize with its executory system. There are cases in which we cannot take up with names and abstractions. You may call half a dozen leading individuals, whom we have reason to fear and hate, the nation. It makes no other difference, than to make us fear and hate them more. If it had been thought justifiable and expedient to make such a revolution by such means, and through such persons, as you have made yours, it would have been more wise to have completed the business of the fifth and sixth of October. The new executive officer would then owe his situation to those who are his creators as well as his masters; and he might be bound in interest, in the society of crime, and (if in crimes there could be virtues) in gratitude, to serve those who had promoted him to a place of great lucre and great sensual indulgence; and of something more: For more he must have received from those who certainly would not have limited an aggrandized creature, as they have done a submitting antagonist.

A king circumstanced as the present, if he is totally stupefied by his misfortunes, so as to think it not the necessity, but the premium and privilege of life, to eat and sleep, without any regard to glory, never can be fit for the office. If he feels as men commonly feel, he must be sensible, that an office so circumstanced is one in which he can obtain no fame or reputation. He has no generous interest that can excite him to action. At best, his conduct will be passive and defensive. To inferior people such an office might be matter of honour. But to be raised to it, and to descend to it, are different things, and suggest different sentiments. Does he *really* name the ministers? They will have a sympathy with him. Are they forced upon him? The whole business between them and the nominal king will be mutual counteraction. In all other countries, the office of ministers of state is of the highest dignity. In France it is full of peril and incapable of glory. Rivals however they will have in their nothingness, whilst shallow ambition exists in the world, or the desire of a miserable salary is an incentive to short-sighted avarice. Those competitors of the ministers are enabled by your constitution to attack them in their vital parts, whilst they have not the means of repelling their charges in any other then the degrading character of culprits. The ministers of state in France are the only persons in that country who are incapable of a share in the national councils. What ministers! What councils! What a nation! – But they are responsible. It is a poor service that is to be had from responsibility. The elevation of mind, to be derived from fear, will never make a nation glorious. Responsibility prevents crimes. It makes all attempts against the laws dangerous. But for a principle of active and zealous service, none but idiots could think of it. Is the conduct of a war to be trusted to a man who may abhor its principle; who, in every step he may take to render it successful, confirms the power of those by whom he is oppressed? Will foreign states seriously treat with him who has no prerogative of peace or war; no, not so much as in a single vote by himself or his ministers, or by any one whom he can possibly influence. A state of contempt is not a state for a prince: better get rid of him at once.

I know it will be said, that these humours in the court and executive government will continue only through this generation; and that the king has been brought to declare the dauphin shall be educated in a conformity to his situation. If he is made to conform to his situation, he will have no education at all. His training must be worse even than that of an arbitrary monarch. If he reads, – whether he reads or not, some good or evil genius will tell him his ancestors were kings. Thenceforward his object must be to assert himself, and to avenge his parents. This you will say is not his duty. That may be; but it is Nature; and whilst you pique Nature against you, you do unwisely to trust to Duty. In this futile scheme of polity, the state nurses in its bosom, for the present, a source of weakness, perplexity, counteraction, inefficiency, and decay; and it prepares the means of its final ruin. In short, I see nothing in the executive force (I cannot call it authority) that has even an appearance of vigour, or that has the smallest degree of just correspondence or symmetry, or amicable relation, with the supreme power, either as it now exists, or as it is planned for the future government.

You have settled, by an œconomy as perverted as the policy, two* establishments of government; one real, one

* In reality three, to reckon the provincial republican establishments.

fictitious. Both maintained at a vast expence; but the fictitious at, I think, the greatest. Such a machine as the latter
is not worth the grease of its wheels. The expence is ex-
orbitant; and neither the shew nor the use deserve the
tenth part of the charge. Oh! but I don't do justice to the
talents of the legislators. I don't allow, as I ought to do,
for necessity. Their scheme of executive force was not
their choice. This pageant must be kept. The people would
not consent to part with it. Right; I understand you.
You do, in spite of your grand theories, to which you
would have heaven and earth to bend, you do know how
to conform yourselves to the nature and circumstances
of things. But when you were obliged to conform thus far
to circumstances, you ought to have carried your submission farther, and to have made what you were obliged to
take, a proper instrument, and useful to its end. That was
in your power. For instance, among many others, it was
in your power to leave to your king the right of peace
and war. What! to leave to the executive magistrate the
most dangerous of all prerogatives? I know none more
dangerous; nor any one more necessary to be so trusted.
I do not say that this prerogative ought to be trusted to
your king, unless he enjoyed other auxiliary trusts along
with it, which he does not now hold. But, if he did possess them, hazardous as they are undoubtedly, advantages
would arise from such a constitution, more than compensating the risque. There is no other way of keeping the
several potentates of Europe from intriguing distinctly
and personally with the members of your assembly, from
intermeddling in all your concerns, and fomenting, in the
heart of your country, the most pernicious of all factions; factions in the interest and under the direction of
foreign powers. From that worst of evils, thank God, we
are still free. Your skill, if you had any,[162] would be well
employed to find out indirect correctives and controls

upon this perilous trust. If you did not like those which in England we have chosen, your leaders might have exerted their abilities in contriving better. If it were necessary to exemplify the consequences of such an executive government as yours, in the management of great affairs, I should refer you to the late reports of M. de Montmorin[163] to the national assembly, and all the other proceedings relative to the differences between Great Britain and Spain. It would be treating your understanding with disrespect to point them out to you.

I hear that the persons who are called ministers have signified an intention of resigning their places. I am rather astonished that they have not resigned long since. For the universe I would not have stood in the situation in which they have been for this last twelvemonth. They wished well, I take it for granted, to the Revolution. Let this fact be as it may, they could not, placed as they were upon an eminence, though an eminence of humiliation, but be the first to see collectively, and to feel each in his own department, the evils which have been produced by that revolution. In every step which they took, or forbore to take, they must have felt the degraded situation of their country, and their utter incapacity of serving it. They are in a species of subordinate servitude, in which no men before them were ever seen. Without confidence from their sovereign, on whom they were forced, or from the assembly who forced them upon him, all the noble functions of their office are executed by committees of the assembly, without any regard whatsoever to their personal, or their official authority. They are to execute, without power; they are to be responsible, without discretion; they are to deliberate, without choice. In their puzzled situation, under two sovereigns, over neither of whom they have any influence, they must act in such a manner as (in effect, whatever they may intend) sometimes to betray the one, sometimes the other, and always to betray themselves. Such has been their situation; such must be the situation of those who succeed them. I have much respect, and many good wishes, for Mr Necker. I am obliged to him for attentions. I thought when his enemies had driven him from Versailles, that his exile was a subject of most serious congratulation – *sed multæ urbes et publica vota vicerunt.*[164] He is now sitting on the ruins of the finances, and of the monarchy of France.

A great deal more might be observed on the strange constitution of the executory part of the new government; but fatigue must give bounds to the discussion of subjects, which in themselves have hardly any limits.

As little genius and talent am I able to perceive in the plan of judicature formed by the national assembly. According to their invariable course, the framers of your constitution have begun with the utter abolition of the parliaments.[165] These venerable bodies, like the rest of the old government, stood in need of reform, even though there should be no change made in the monarchy. They required several more alterations to adapt them to the system of a free constitution. But they had particulars in their constitution, and those not a few, which deserved approbation from the wise. They possessed one fundamental excellence; they were independent. The most doubtful circumstance attendant on their office, that of its being vendible, contributed however to this independency of character. They held for life. Indeed they may be said to have held by inheritance. Appointed by the monarch, they were considered as nearly out of his power. The most determined exertions of that authority against them only shewed their radical independence. They composed permanent bodies politic, constituted to resist arbitrary innovation; and from that corporate constitution, and from most of their forms, they were well calculated to afford both certainty and stability to the laws. They had been a safe asylum to secure these laws in all the revolutions of humour and opinion. They had saved that sacred deposit of the country during the reigns of arbitrary princes, and the struggles of arbitrary factions. They kept alive the memory and record of the constitution. They were the great security to private property; which might be said (when personal liberty had no existence) to be, in fact, as well guarded in France as in any other country. Whatever is supreme in a state, ought to have, as much as possible, its judicial authority so constituted as not only not to depend upon it, but in some sort to balance it. It ought to give a security to its justice against its power. It ought to make its judicature, as it were, something exterior to the state.

These parliaments had furnished, not the best certainly, but some considerable corrective to the excesses and vices of the monarchy. Such an independent judicature was ten times more necessary when a democracy became the absolute power of the country. In that constitution, elective, temporary, local judges, such as you have contrived, exercising their dependent functions in a narrow society, must be the worst of all tribunals. In them it will be vain to look for any appearance of justice towards strangers, towards the obnoxious rich, towards the minority of routed parties, towards all those who in the election have supported unsuccessful candidates. It will be impossible to keep the new tribunals clear of the worst spirit of faction. All contrivances by ballot, we know experimentally, to be vain and childish to prevent a discovery of inclinations. Where they may best answer the purposes of concealment, they answer to produce suspicion, and this is a still more mischievous cause of partiality.

If the parliaments had been preserved, instead of being dissolved at so ruinous a change to the nation, they might have served in this new commonwealth, perhaps not precisely the same (I do not mean an exact parallel) but near the same purposes as the court and senate of Areopagus[166] did in Athens; that is, as one of the balances and correctives to the evils of a light and unjust democracy. Every one knows, that this tribunal was the great stay of that state; every one knows with what care it was upheld, and with what a religious awe it was consecrated. The parliaments were not wholly free from faction, I admit; but this evil was exterior and accidental, and not so much the vice of their constitution itself, as it must be in your new contrivance of sexennial elective judicatories. Several English commend the abolition of the old tribunals, as supposing that they determined every thing by bribery and corruption. But they have stood the test of monarchic and republican scrutiny. The court was well disposed to prove corruption on those bodies when they were dissolved in 1771.[167] – Those who have again dissolved them would have done the same if they could – but both inquisitions having failed, I conclude, that gross pecuniary corruption must have been rather rare amongst them.

It would have been prudent, along with the parliaments, to preserve their antient power of registering, and of remonstrating at least, upon all the decrees of the national assembly, as they did upon those which passed in the time of the monarchy. It would be a means of squaring the occasional decrees of a democracy to some principles of general jurisprudence. The vice of the antient democracies, and one cause of their ruin, was, that they ruled, as you do, by occasional decrees, *psephismata*.[168] This practice soon broke in upon the tenour and consistency of the laws; it abated the respect of the people towards them; and totally destroyed them in the end.

Your vesting the power of remonstrance, which, in the

time of the monarchy, existed in the parliament of Paris, in your principal executive officer, whom, in spite of common sense, you persevere in calling king, is the height of absurdity. You ought never to suffer remonstrance from him who is to execute. This is to understand neither council nor execution; neither authority nor obedience. The person whom you call king, ought not to have this power, or he ought to have more.

Your present arrangement is strictly judicial. Instead of imitating your monarchy, and seating your judges on a bench of independence, your object is to reduce them to the most blind obedience. As you have changed all things, you have invented new principles of order. You first appoint judges, who, I suppose, are to determine according to law, and then you let them know, that, at some time or other, you intend to give them some law by which they are to determine. Any studies which they have made (if any they have made) are to be useless to them. But to supply these studies, they are to be sworn to obey all the rules, orders, and instructions, which from time to time they are to receive from the national assembly. These if they submit to, they leave no ground of law to the subject. They become complete, and most dangerous instruments in the hands of the governing power, which, in the midst of a cause, or on the prospect of it, may wholly change the rule of decision. If these orders of the National Assembly come to be contrary to the will of the people who locally choose those judges, such confusion must happen as is terrible to think of. For the judges owe their place to the local authority; and the commands they are sworn to obey come from those who have no share in their appointment. In the mean time they have the example of the court of *Chatelet*[169] to encourage and guide them in the exercise of their functions. That court is to try criminals sent to it by the National Assembly, or brought before it by other courses of delation. They sit under a guard, to save their own lives. They know not by what law they judge, nor under what authority they act, nor by what tenure they hold. It is thought that they are sometimes obliged to condemn at peril of their lives. This is not perhaps certain, nor can it be ascertained; but when they acquit, we know, they have seen the persons whom they discharge, with perfect impunity to the actors, hanged at the door of their court.

The assembly indeed promises that they will form a body of law, which shall be short, simple, clear, and so forth. That is, by their short laws, they will leave much to the discretion of the judge; whilst they have exploded the authority of all the learning which could make judicial discretion, (a thing perilous at best) deserving the appellation of a *sound* discretion.

It is curious to observe, that the administrative bodies are carefully exempted from the jurisdiction of these new tribunals. That is, those persons are exempted from the power of the laws, who ought to be the most entirely submitted to them. Those who execute public pecuniary trusts, ought of all men to be the most strictly held to their duty. One would have thought, that it must have been among your earliest cares, if you did not mean that those administrative bodies should be real sovereign independent states, to form an awful tribunal, like your late parliaments, or like our king's-bench, where all corporate officers might obtain protection in the legal exercise of their functions, and would find coercion if they trespassed against their legal duty. But the cause of the exemption is plain. These administrative bodies are the great instruments of the present leaders in their progress through democracy to oligarchy. They must therefore be put above the law. It will be said, that the legal tribunals which you have made are unfit to coerce them. They are undoubtedly. They are unfit for any rational purpose. It will be said too, that the administrative bodies will be accountable to the general assembly. This I fear is talking, without much consideration, of the nature of that assembly or of these corporations. However, to be subject to the pleasure of that assembly, is not to be subject to law, either for protection or for constraint.

This establishment of judges as yet wants something to its completion. It is to be crowned by a new tribunal. This is to be a grand state judicature; and it is to judge of crimes committed against the nation, that is, against the power of the assembly. It seems as if they had something in their view of the nature of the high court of justice erected in England during the time of the great usurpation. As they have not yet finished this part of the scheme, it is impossible to form a direct judgment upon it. However, if great care is not taken to form it in a spirit very different from that which has guided them in their proceedings relative to state offences, this tribunal, subservient to their inquisition, *the committee of research*,[170] will extinguish the last sparks of liberty in France, and settle the most dreadful and arbitrary tyranny ever known in any nation. If they wish to give to this tribunal any appearance of liberty and justice, they must not evoke from, or send to it, the causes relative to their own members, at their pleasure. They must also remove the seat of that tribunal out of the republic of Paris.*

Has more wisdom been displayed in the constitution of your army than what is discoverable in your plan of judicature? The able arrangement of this part is the more difficult, and requires the greater skill and attention, not only as a great concern itself, but as it is the third cementing principle in the new body of republics, which you call

* For further elucidations upon the subject of all these judicatures, and of the committee of research, see M. de Calonne's work.

the French nation. Truly it is not easy to divine what
that army may become at last. You have voted a very
large one, and on good appointments, at least fully equal
to your apparent means of payment. But what is the
principle of its discipline? or whom is it to obey? You
have got the wolf by the ears, and I wish you joy of
the happy position in which you have chosen to place
yourselves, and in which you are well circumstanced for
a free deliberation, relatively to that army, or to any thing
else.

The minister and secretary of state for the war department, is M. de la Tour du Pin.[171] This gentleman, like his
colleagues in administration, is a most zealous assertor
of the revolution, and a sanguine admirer of the new constitution, which originated in that event. His statement
of facts, relative to the military of France, is important,
not only from his official and personal authority, but because it displays very clearly the actual condition of the
army in France, and because it throws light on the
principles upon which the assembly proceeds in the administration of this critical object. It may enable us to
form some judgment how far it may be expedient in this
country to imitate the martial policy of France.

M. de la Tour du Pin, on the 4th of last June, comes to
give an account of the state of his department, as it exists
under the auspices of the national assembly. No man
knows it so well; no man can express it better. Addressing
himself to the National Assembly, he says, 'His Majesty
has *this day* sent me to apprize you of the multiplied disorders of which *every day* he received the most
distressing intelligence. The army (le corps militaire)
threatens to fall into the most turbulent anarchy. Entire
regiments have dared to violate at once the respect due to
the laws, to the King, to the order established by your
decrees, and to the oaths which they have taken with the

most awful solemnity. Compelled by my duty to give you information of these excesses, my heart bleeds when I consider who they are that have committed them. Those, against whom it is not in my power to withhold the most grievous complaints, are a part of that very soldiery which to this day have been so full of honour and loyalty, and with whom, for fifty years, I have lived the comrade and the friend.

'What incomprehensible spirit of delirium and delusion has all at once led them astray? Whilst you are indefatigable in establishing uniformity in the empire, and moulding the whole into one coherent and consistent body; whilst the French are taught by you, at once the respect which the laws owe to the rights of man, and that which the citizens owe to the laws, the administration of the army presents nothing but disturbance and confusion. I see in more than one corps the bonds of discipline relaxed or broken; the most unheard-of pretensions avowed directly and without any disguise; the ordinances without force; the chiefs without authority; the military chest and the colours carried off; the authority of the King himself [*risum teneatis*][172] proudly defied; the officers despised, degraded, threatened, driven away, and some of them prisoners in the midst of their corps, dragging on a precarious life in the bosom of disgust and humiliation. To fill up the measure of all these horrors, the commandants of places have had their throats cut, under the eyes, and almost in the arms of their own soldiers.

'These evils are great; but they are not the worst consequences which may be produced by such military insurrections. Sooner or later they may menace the nation itself. *The nature of things requires*, that the army should never act but as *an instrument*. The moment that, erecting itself into a deliberative body, it shall act according to its own resolutions, the *government, be it what it may,* will immediately degenerate into a military democracy; a species of political monster, which has always ended by devouring those who have produced it.

'After all this, who must not be alarmed at the irregular consultations, and turbulent committees, formed in some regiments by the common soldiers and non-commissioned officers, without the knowledge, or even in contempt of the authority of their superiors; although the presence and concurrence of those superiors could give no authority to such monstrous democrative assemblies [comices.]'

It is not necessary to add much to this finished picture: finished as far as its canvas admits; but, as I apprehend, not taking in the whole of the nature and complexity of the disorders of this military democracy, which, the minister at war truly and wisely observes, wherever it exists, must be the true constitution of the state, by whatever formal appellation it may pass. For, though he informs the assembly, that the more considerable part of the army have not cast off their obedience, but are still attached to their duty, yet those travellers who have seen the corps whose conduct is the best, rather observe in them the absence of mutiny than the existence of discipline.

I cannot help pausing here for a moment, to reflect upon the expressions of surprise which this Minister has let fall, relative to the excesses he relates. To him the departure of the troops from their antient principles of loyalty and honour seems quite inconceivable. Surely those to whom he addresses himself know the causes of it but too well. They know the doctrines which they have preached, the decrees which they have passed, the practices which they have countenanced. The soldiers remember the 6th of October. They recollect the French guards. They have not forgot the taking of the King's castles in Paris, and at Marseilles.[173] That the governors in both places, were murdered with impunity, is a fact that has not passed out of their minds. They do not abandon the principles laid down so ostentatiously and laboriously of the equality of men. They cannot shut their eyes to the degradation of the whole noblesse of France; and the suppression of the very idea of a gentleman. The total abolition of titles and distinctions is not lost upon them. But Mr du Pin is astonished at their disloyalty, when the doctors of the assembly have taught them at the same time the respect due to laws. It is easy to judge which of the two sorts of lessons men with arms in their hands are likely to learn. As to the authority of the King, we may collect from the minister himself (if any argument on that head were not quite superfluous) that it is not of more consideration with these troops, than it is with every body else. 'The King,' says he, 'has over and over again repeated his orders to put a stop to these excesses: but, in so terrible a crisis *your* [the assembly's] concurrence is become indispensably necessary to prevent the evils which menace the state. *You* unite to the force of the legislative power, *that of opinion* still more important.' To be sure the army can have no opinion of the power or authority of the king. Perhaps the soldier has by this time learned, that the assembly itself does not enjoy a much greater degree of liberty than that royal figure.

It is now to be seen what has been proposed in this exigency, one of the greatest that can happen in a state. The Minister requests the assembly to array itself in all its terrors, and to call forth all its majesty. He desires that the grave and severe principles announced by them may give vigour to the King's proclamation. After this we should have looked for courts civil and martial; breaking of some corps, decimating others, and all the terrible means which necessity has employed in such cases to arrest the progress of the most terrible of all evils; particularly, one might expect, that a serious inquiry would be made into the murder of commandants in the view of their soldiers. Not one word of all this, or of any thing like it. After they had been told that the soldiery trampled upon the decrees of the assembly promulgated by the King, the assembly pass new decrees; and they authorise the King to make new proclamations. After the Secretary at War had stated that the regiments had paid no regard to oaths *prêtés avec la plus imposante solemnité* – they propose – what? More oaths. They renew decrees and proclamations as they experience their insufficiency, and they multiply oaths in proportion as they weaken, in the minds of men, the sanctions of religion. I hope that handy abridgments of the excellent sermons of Voltaire, d'Alembert, Diderot, and Helvetius, on the Immortality of the Soul, on a particular superintending Providence, and on a Future State of Rewards and Punishments, are sent down to the soldiers along with their civic oaths. Of this I have no doubt; as I understand, that a certain description of reading makes no inconsiderable part of their military exercises, and that they are full as well supplied with the ammunition of pamphlets as of cartridges.

To prevent the mischiefs arising from conspiracies, irregular consultations, seditious committees, and monstrous democratic assemblies ['comitia, comices'] of the soldiers, and all the disorders arising from idleness, luxury, dissipation, and insubordination, I believe the most astonishing means have been used, that ever occurred to men, even in all the inventions of this prolific age. It is no less than this: – The King has promulgated in circular letters to all the regiments his direct authority and encouragement, that the several corps should join themselves with the clubs and confederations in the

several municipalities, and mix with them in their feasts
and civic entertainments! This jolly discipline, it seems,
is to soften the ferocity of their minds; to reconcile them
to their bottle companions of other descriptions; and to
merge particular conspiracies in more general associations.* That this remedy would be pleasing to the soldiers,
as they are described by Mr de la Tour du Pin, I can
readily believe; and that, however mutinous otherwise,
they will dutifully submit themselves to *these* royal
proclamations. But I should question whether all this
civic swearing, clubbing, and feasting, would dispose
them more than at present they are disposed, to an
obedience to their officers; or teach them better to submit
to the austere rules of military discipline. It will make
them admirable citizens after the French mode, but not
quite so good soldiers after any mode. A doubt might well
arise, whether the conversations at these good tables,
would fit them a great deal the better for the character of
mere instruments, which this veteran officer and statesman justly observes, the nature of things always requires
an army to be.

Concerning the likelihood of this improvement in discipline, by the free conversation of the soldiers with the
municipal festive societies, which is thus officially encouraged by royal authority and sanction, we may judge
by the state of the municipalities themselves, furnished
to us by the war minister in this very speech. He con-
ceives good hopes of the success of his endeavours to-

* Comme sa Majesté y a reconnu, non une systême d'associations
particulières, mais une réunion de volontés de tous les François
pour la liberté et la prosperité communes, ainsi pour le maintien
de l'ordre publique; il a pensé qu'il convenoit que chaque regiment
prit part a ces fêtes civiques pour multiplier les rapports, et re-
serrer les liens d'union entre les citoyens et les troupes. – Lest I
should not be credited, I insert the words, authorising the troops to
feast with the popular confederacies.

wards restoring order *for the present* from the good disposition of certain regiments; but he finds something cloudy with regard to the future. As to preventing the return of confusion 'for this, the administration (says he) cannot be answerable to you, as long as they see the muncipalities arrogate to themselves an authority over the troops, which your institutions have reserved wholly to the monarch. You have fixed the limits of the military authority and the municipal authority. You have bounded the action, which you have permitted to the latter over the former, to the right of requisition; but never did the letter or the spirit of your decrees authorise the commons in these municipalities to break the officers, to try them, to give orders to the soldiers, to drive them from the posts committed to their guard, to stop them in their marches ordered by the King, or, in a word, to enslave the troops to the caprice of each of the cities or even market towns through which they are to pass.'

Such is the character and disposition of the municipal society which is to reclaim the soldiery, to bring them back to the true principles of military subordination, and to render them machines in the hands of the supreme power of the country! Such are the distempers of the French troops! Such is their cure! As the army is, so is the navy. The municipalities supersede the orders of the assembly, and the seamen in their turn supersede the orders of the municipalities. From my heart I pity the condition of a respectable servant of the public, like this war minister, obliged in his old age to pledge the assembly in their civic cups, and to enter with an hoary head into all the fantastick vagaries of these juvenile politicians. Such schemes are not like propositions coming from a man of fifty years wear and tear amongst mankind. They seem rather such as ought to be expected from those grand compounders in politics, who shorten the road to their degrees in the state; and have a certain inward fanatical assurance and illumination upon all subjects; upon the credit of which one of their doctors has thought fit, with great applause, and greater success, to caution the assembly not to attend to old men, or to any persons who valued themselves upon their experience. I suppose all the ministers of state must qualify, and take this test; wholly abjuring the errors and heresies of experience and observation. Every man has his own relish. But I think, if I could not attain to the wisdom, I would at least preserve something of the stiff and peremptory dignity of age. These gentlemen deal in regeneration; but at any price I should hardly yield my rigid fibres to be regenerated by them; nor begin, in my grand climacteric, to squall in their new accents, or to stammer, in my second cradle, the elemental sounds of their barbarous metaphysics.* *Si isti mihi largiantur ut repueriscam, et in eorum cunis vagiam, valde recusem!*[174]

The imbecility of any part of the puerile and pedantic system, which they call a constitution, cannot be laid open without discovering the utter insufficiency and mischief of every other part with which it comes in contact, or that bears any the remotest relation to it. You cannot propose a remedy for the incompetence of the crown, without displaying the debility of the assembly. You cannot deliberate on the confusion of the army of the state, without disclosing the worse disorders of the armed municipalities. The military lays open the civil, and the civil betrays the military anarchy. I wish every body carefully to peruse the eloquent speech (such it is) of Mons. de la Tour du Pin. He attributes the salvation of the municipalities to the good behaviour of some of the troops. These troops are to preserve the well-disposed part of those

* This war-minister has since quitted the school and resigned his office.

municipalities, which is confessed to be the weakest, from the pillage of the worst disposed, which is the strongest. But the municipalities affect a sovereignty and will command those troops which are necessary for their protection. Indeed they must command them or court them. The municipalities, by the necessity of their situation, and by the republican powers they have obtained, must, with relation to the military, be the masters, or the servants, or the confederates, or each successively; or they must make a jumble of all together, according to circumstances. What government is there to coerce the army but the municipality, or the municipality but the army? To preserve concord where authority is extinguished, at the hazard of all consequences, the assembly attempts to cure the distempers by the distempers themselves; and they hope to preserve themselves from a purely military democracy, by giving it a debauched interest in the municipal.

If the soldiers once come to mix for any time in the municipal clubs, cabals, and confederacies, an elective attraction will draw them to the lowest and most desperate part. With them will be their habits, affections, and sympathies. The military conspiracies, which are to be remedied by civic confederacies; the rebellious municipalities, which are to be rendered obedient by furnishing them with the means of seducing the very armies of the state that are to keep them in order; all these chimeras of a monstrous and portentous policy, must aggravate the confusions from which they have arisen. There must be blood. The want of common judgment manifested in the construction of all their descriptions of forces, and in all their kinds of civil and judicial authorities, will make it flow. Disorders may be quited in one time and in one part. They will break out in others; because the evil is radical and intrinsic. All these schemes of mixing mutinous soldiers with seditious citizens, must weaken still more and more the military connection of soldiers with their officers, as well as add military and mutinous audacity to turbulent artificers and peasants. To secure a real army, the officer should be first and last in the eye of the soldier; first and last in his attention, observance, and esteem. Officers it seems there are to be, whose chief qualification must be temper and patience. They are to manage their troops by electioneering arts. They must bear themselves as candidates not as commanders. But as by such means power may be occasionally in their hands, the authority by which they are to be nominated becomes of high importance.

What you may do finally, does not appear; nor is it of much moment, whilst the strange and contradictory relation between your army and all the parts of your republic, as well as the puzzled relation of those parts to each other and to the whole, remain as they are. You seem to have given the provisional nomination of the officers, in the first instance, to the king, with a reserve of approbation by the National Assembly. Men who have an interest to pursue are extremely sagacious in discovering the true seat of power. They must soon perceive that those who can negative indefinitely, in reality appoint. The officers must therefore look to their intrigues in that assembly, as the sole certain road to promotion. Still, however, by your new constitution they must begin their solicitation at court. This double negotiation for military rank seems to me a contrivance as well adapted, as if it were studied for no other end, to promote faction in the assembly itself, relative to this vast military patronage; and then to poison the corps of officers with factions of a nature still more dangerous to the safety of government, upon any bottom on which it can be placed, and destructive in the end to the efficiency of the army itself. Those officers, who lose the promotions intended for them by the crown, must become of a faction opposite to that of the assembly which has rejected their claims, and must nourish discontents in the heart of the army against the ruling powers. Those officers, on the other hand, who, by carrying their point through an interest in the assembly, feel themselves to be at best only second in the good-will of the crown, though first in that of the assembly, must slight an authority which would not advance, and could not retard their promotion. If to avoid these evils you will have no other rule for command or promotion than seniority, you will have an army of formality; at the same time it will become more independent, and more of a military republic. Not they but the king is the machine. A king is not to be deposed by halves. If he is not every thing in the command of an army, he is nothing. What is the effect of a power placed nominally at the head of the army, who to that army is no object of gratitude, or of fear? Such a cypher is not fit for the administration of an object, of all things the most delicate, the supreme command of military men. They must be constrained (and their inclinations lead them to what their necessities require) by a real, vigorous, effective, decided, personal authority. The authority of the assembly itself suffers by passing through such a debilitating channel as they have chosen. The army will not long look to an assembly acting through the organ of false shew, and palpable imposition. They will not seriously yield obedience to a prisoner. They will either despise a pageant, or they will pity a captive king. This relation of your army to the crown will, if I am not greatly mistaken, become a serious dilemma in your politics.

It is besides to be considered, whether an assembly like yours, even supposing that it was in possession of another sort of organ through which its orders were to pass, is fit for promoting the obedience and discipline of an army. It is known, that armies have hitherto yielded a very precarious and uncertain obedience to any senate, or popular authority; and they will least of all yield it to an assembly which is to have only a continuance of two years. The officers must totally lose the characteristic disposition of military men, if they see with perfect submission and due admiration, the dominion of pleaders; especially when they find, that they have a new court to pay to an endless succession of those pleaders, whose military policy, and the genius of whose command (if they should have any) must be as uncertain as their duration is transient. In the weakness of one kind of authority, and in the fluctuation of all, the officers of an army will remain for some time mutinous and full of faction, until some popular general, who understands the art of conciliating the soldiery, and who possesses the true spirit of command, shall draw the eyes of all men upon himself. Armies will obey him on his personal account. There is no other way of securing military obedience in this state of things. But the moment in which that event shall happen, the person who really commands the army is your master; the master (that is little) of your king, the master of your assembly, the master of your whole republic.[175]

How came the assembly by their present power over the army? Chiefly, to be sure, by debauching the soldiers from their officers. They have begun by a most terrible operation. They have touched the central point, about which the particles that compose armies are at repose. They have destroyed the principle of obedience in the great essential critical link between the officer and the soldier, just where the chain of military subordination commences, and on which the whole of that system depends. The soldier is told, he is a citizen, and has the rights of man and citizen. The right of a man, he is told, is to be his own governor, and to be ruled only by those to whom he delegates that self-government. It is very natural he should think, that he ought most of all to have his choice where he is to yield the greatest degree of obedience. He will therefore, in all probability, systematically do, what he does at present occasionally; that is, he will exercise at least a negative in the choice of his officers. At present the officers are known at best to be only permissive, and on their good behaviour. In fact, there have been many instances in which they have been cashiered by their corps. Here is a second negative on the choice of the king; a negative as effectual at least as the other of the assembly. The soldiers know already that it has been a question, not ill received in the national assembly, whether they ought not to have the direct choice of their officers, or some proportion of them? When such matters are in deliberation, it is no extravagant supposition that they will incline to the opinion most favourable to their pretensions. They will not bear to be deemed the army of an imprisoned king, whilst another army in the same country, with whom too they are to feast and confederate, is to be considered as the free army of a free constitution. They will cast their eyes on the other and more permanent army; I mean the municipal. That corps, they well know, does actually elect its own officers. They may not be able to discern the grounds of distinction on which they are not to elect a Marquis de la Fayette[176] (or what is his new name) of their own? If this election of a commander in chief be a part of the rights of men, why not of theirs? They see elective justices of peace, elective judges, elective curates, elective bishops, elective municipalities, and elective commanders of the Parisian army. — Why should they alone be excluded? Are the brave troops of France the only men in that nation who are not the fit judges of military merit, and of the qualifications necessary for a commander in chief? Are they paid by the state, and do they therefore lose the rights of men? They are a part of that nation themselves, and contribute to that pay. And is not the king, is not the national assembly, and are not all who elect the national assembly, likewise paid? Instead of seeing all these forfeit their rights by their receiving a salary, they perceive that in all these cases a salary is given for the exercise of those rights. All your resolutions, all your proceedings, all your debates, all the works of your doctors in religion and politics, have industriously been put into their hands; and you expect that they will apply to their own case just as much of your doctrines and examples as suits your pleasure.

Every thing depends upon the army in such a government as yours; for you have industriously destroyed all the opinions, and prejudices, and, as far as in you lay, all the instincts which support government. Therefore the moment any difference arises between your national assembly and any part of the nation, you must have recourse to force. Nothing else is left to you; or rather you have left nothing else to yourselves. You see by the report of your war minister, that the distribution of the army is in a great measure made with a view of internal coercion.* You must rule by an army; and you have infused into that army by which you rule, as well as into the whole body of the nation, principles which after a time must disable you in the use you resolve to make of it. The king is to call out troops to act against his people, when the world has been told, and the assertion is still ringing in our ears, that troops ought not to fire on citizens. The colonies assert to themselves an independent

* Courier François, 30 July, 1790. Assemblée Nationale, Numero 210.[177]

constitution and a free trade. They must be constrained by troops. In what chapter of your code of the rights of men are they able to read, that it is a part of the rights of men to have their commerce monopolized and restrained for the benefit of others. As the colonists rise on you, the negroes rise on them. Troops again – Massacre, torture, hanging![178] These are your rights of men! These are the fruits of metaphysic declarations wantonly made, and shamefully retracted! It was but the other day that the farmers of land in one of your provinces refused to pay some sorts of rents to the lord of the soil. In consequence of this you decree, that the country people shall pay all rents and dues, except those which as grievances you have abolished; and if they refuse, then you order the king to march troops against them. You lay down metaphysic propositions which infer universal consequences, and then you attempt to limit logic by despotism. The leaders of the present system tell them of their rights, as men, to take fortresses, to murder guards, to seize on kings without the least appearance of authority even from the assembly, whilst, as the sovereign legislative body, that assembly was sitting in the name of the nation – and yet these leaders presume to order out the troops, which have acted in these very disorders to coerce those who shall judge on the principles, and follow the examples, which have been guarantied by their own approbation.

The leaders teach the people to abhor and reject all feodality as the barbarism of tyranny, and they tell them afterwards how much of that barbarous tyranny they are to bear with patience. As they are prodigal of light with regard to grievances, so the people find them sparing in the extreme with regard to redress. They know that not only certain quitrents and personal duties, which you have permitted them to redeem (but have furnished no money for the redemption) are as nothing to those burthens for which you have made no provision at all. They know, that almost the whole system of landed property in its origin is feudal; that it is the distribution of the possessions of the original proprietors, made by a barbarous conqueror to his barbarous instruments; and that the most grievous effects of the conquest are the land rents of every kind, as without question they are.

The peasants, in all probability, are the descendants of these antient proprietors, Romans or Gauls. But if they fail, in any degree, in the titles which they make on the principles of antiquaries and lawyers, they retreat into the citadel of the rights of men. There they find that men are equal; and the earth, the kind and equal mother of all, ought not to be monopolized to foster the pride and luxury of any men, who by nature are no better than themselves, and who, if they do not labour for their bread, are worse. They find, that by the laws of nature the occupant and subduer of the soil is the true proprietor; that there is no prescription against nature; and that the agreements (where any there are) which have been made with their landlords, during the time of slavery, are only the effect of duresse and force; and that when the people re-entered into the rights of men, those agreements were made as void as every thing else which had been settled under the prevalence of the old feudal and aristocratic tyranny. They will tell you that they see no difference between an idler with a hat and a national cockade, and an idler in a cowl or in a rochet. If you ground the title to rents on succession and prescription, they tell you, from the speech of Mr *Camus*,[179] published by the national assembly for their information, that things ill begun cannot avail themselves of prescription; that the title of these lords was vicious in its origin; and that force is at least as bad as fraud. As to the title by succession, they will tell you that the succession of those who have cultivated the soil is the true pedigree of property, and not rotten parchments and silly substitutions; that the lords have enjoyed their usurpation too long; and that if they allow to these lay monks any charitable pension, they ought to be thankful to the bounty of the true proprietor, who is so generous towards a false claimant to his goods.

When the peasants give you back that coin of sophistic reason, on which you have set your image and superscription, you cry it down as base money, and tell them you will pay for the future with French guards, and dragoons, and hussars. You hold up, to chastise them, the second-hand authority of a king, who is only the instrument of destroying, without any power of protecting either the people or his own person. Through him it seems you will make yourselves obeyed. They answer, You have taught us that there are no gentlemen; and which of your principles teach us to bow to kings whom we have not elected? We know, without your teaching, that lands were given for the support of feudal dignities, feudal titles, and feudal offices. When you took down the cause as a grievance, why should the more grievous effect remain? As there are now no hereditary honours, and no distinguished families, why are we taxed to maintain what you tell us ought not to exist? You have sent down our old aristocratic landlords in no other character, and with no other title, but that of exactors under your authority. Have you endeavoured to make these your rent-gatherers respectable to us? No. You have sent them to us with their arms reversed, their shields broken, their impresses defaced; and so displumed, degraded, and metamorphosed, such unfeathered two-legged things, that we no longer know them. They are strangers to us. They do not even go by the names of our ancient lords. Physically they may be the same men; though we are not quite sure of that, on your new philosophic doctrines of personal identity. In all other respects they are totally changed. We do not see why we have not as good a right to refuse them their rents, as you have to abrogate all their honours, titles, and distinctions. This we have never commissioned you to do; and it is one instance, among many indeed, of your assumption of undelegated power. We see the burghers of Paris, through their clubs, their mobs, and their national guards, directing you at their pleasure, and giving that as law to you, which, under your authority, is transmitted as law to us. Through you, these burghers dispose of the lives and fortunes of us all. Why should not you attend as much to the desires of the laborious husbandman with regard to our rent, by which we are affected in the most serious manner, as you do to the demands of these insolent burghers, relative to distinctions and titles of honour, by which neither they nor we are affected at all? But we find you pay more regard to their fancies than to our necessities. Is it among the rights of man to pay tribute to his equals? Before this measure of yours, we might have thought we were not perfectly equal. We might have entertained some old, habitual, unmeaning prepossession in favour of those landlords; but we cannot conceive with what other view than that of destroying all respect to them, you could have made the law that degrades them. You have forbidden us to treat them with any of the old formalities of respect, and now you send troops to sabre and to bayonet us into a submission to fear and force, which you did not suffer us to yield to the mild authority of opinion.

The ground of some of these arguments is horrid and ridiculous to all rational ears; but to the politicians of metaphysics who have opened schools for sophistry, and made establishments for anarchy, it is solid and conclusive. It is obvious, that on a mere consideration of the right, the leaders in the assembly would not in the least

have scrupled to abrogate the rents along with the titles
and family ensigns. It would be only to follow up the
principle of their reasonings, and to complete the
analogy of their conduct. But they had newly possessed
themselves of a great body of landed property by confiscation. They had this commodity at market; and the market would have been wholly destroyed, if they were to
permit the husbandmen to riot in the speculations with
which they so freely intoxicated themselves. The only
security which property enjoys in any one of its descriptions, is from the interests of their rapacity with regard to
some other. They have left nothing but their own arbitrary
pleasure to determine what property is to be protected
and what subverted.

Neither have they left any principle by which any of
their municipalities can be bound to obedience; or even
conscientiously obliged not to separate from the whole,
to become independent, or to connect itself with some
other state. The people of Lyons, it seems, have refused
lately to pay taxes. Why should they not? What lawful
authority is there left to exact them? The king imposed
some of them. The old states, methodised by orders, settled the more ancient. They may say to the assembly,
Who are you, that are not our kings, nor the states we
have elected, nor sit on the principles on which we have
elected you? And who are we, that when we see the
gabelles[180] which you have ordered to be paid, wholly
shaken off, when we see the act of disobedience afterwards
ratified by yourselves, who are we, that we are not to
judge what taxes we ought or ought not to pay, and who
are not to avail ourselves of the same powers, the validity
of which you have approved in others? To this the answer
is, We will send troops. The last reason of kings, is always
the first with your assembly. This military aid may serve
for a time, whilst the impression of the increase of pay

remains, and the vanity of being umpires in all disputes is flattered. But this weapon will snap short, unfaithful to the hand that employs it. The assembly keep a school where, systematically, and with unremitting perseverance, they teach principles, and form regulations destructive to all spirit of subordination, civil and military – and then they expect that they shall hold in obedience an anarchic people by an anarchic army.

The municipal army, which, according to their new policy, is to balance this national army, if considered in itself only, is of a constitution much more simple, and in every respect less exceptionable. It is a mere democratic body, unconnected with the crown or the kingdom; armed, and trained, and officered at the pleasure of the districts to which the corps severally belong; and the personal service of the individuals, who compose, or the fine in lieu of personal service, are directed by the same authority.* Nothing is more uniform. If, however, considered in any relation to the crown, to the national assembly, to the public tribunals, or to the other army, or considered in a view to any coherence or connection between its parts, it seems a monster, and can hardly fail to terminate its perplexed movements in some great national calamity. It is a worse preservative of a general constitution, than the systasis[181] of Crete, or the confederation of Poland, or any other ill-devised corrective which has yet been imagined, in the necessities produced by an ill-constructed system of government.

* I see by Mr Necker's account, that the national guards of Paris have received, over and above the money levied within their own city, about 145,000 *l.* sterling out of the public treasure. Whether this be an actual payment for the nine months of their existence, or an estimate of their yearly charge, I do not clearly perceive. It is of no great importance, as certainly they may take whatever they please.

Having concluded my few remarks on the constitution of the supreme power, the executive, the judicature, the military, and on the reciprocal relation of all these establishments, I shall say something of the ability shewed by your legislators with regard to the revenue.

In their proceedings relative to this object, if possible, still fewer traces appear of political judgment or financial resource. When the states met, it seemed to be the great object to improve the system of revenue, to enlarge its collection, to cleanse it of oppression and vexation, and to establish it on the most solid footing. Great were the expectations entertained on that head throughout Europe. It was by this grand arrangement that France was to stand or fall; and this became, in my opinion, very properly, the test by which the skill and patriotism of those who ruled in that assembly would be tried. The revenue of the state is the state. In effect all depends upon it, whether for support or for reformation. The dignity of every occupation wholly depends upon the quantity and the kind of virtue that may be exerted in it. As all great qualities of the mind which operate in public, and are not merely suffering and passive, require force for their display, I had almost said for their unequivocal existence, the revenue, which is the spring of all power, becomes in its administration the sphere of every active virtue. Public virtue, being of a nature magnificent and splendid, instituted for great things, and conversant about great concerns, requires abundant scope and room, and cannot spread and grow under confinement, and in circumstances straitened, narrow, and sordid. Through the revenue alone the body politic can act in its true genius and character, and therefore it will display just as much of its collective virtue, and as much of that virtue which may characterize those who move it, and are, as it were, its life and guiding principle, as it is possessed of a just revenue. For from hence, not only magnanimity, and liberality, and beneficence, and fortitude, and providence, and the tutelary protection of all good arts, derive their food, and the growth of their organs, but continence, and self-denial, and labour, and vigilance, and frugality, and whatever else there is in which the mind shews itself above the appetite, are no where more in their proper element than in the provision and distribution of the public wealth. It is therefore not without reason that the science of speculative and practical finance, which must take to its aid so many auxiliary branches of knowledge, stands high in the estimation not only of the ordinary sort, but of the wisest and best men; and as this science has grown with the progress of its object, the prosperity and improvement of nations has generally encreased with the encrease of their revenues; and they will both continue to grow and flourish, as long as the balance between what is left to strengthen the efforts of individuals, and what is collected for the common efforts of the state, bear to each other a due reciprocal proportion, and are kept in a close correspondence and communication. And perhaps it may be owing to the greatness of revenues, and to the urgency of state necessities, that old abuses in the constitution of finances are discovered, and their true nature and rational theory comes to be more perfectly understood; insomuch, that a smaller revenue might have been more distressing in one period than a far greater is found to be in another; the proportionate wealth even remaining the same. In this state of things, the French assembly found something in their revenues to preserve, to secure, and wisely to administer, as well as to abrogate and alter. Though their proud assumption might justify the severest tests, yet in trying their abilities on their financial proceedings, I would only consider what is the plain obvious duty of a common finance minister, and try them upon that, and not upon models of ideal perfection.

The objects of a financier are, then, to secure an ample revenue; to impose it with judgment and equality; to employ it œconomically; and when necessity obliges him to make use of credit, to secure its foundations in that instance, and for ever, by the clearness and candour of his proceedings, the exactness of his calculations, and the solidity of his funds. On these heads we may take a short and distinct view of the merits and abilities of those in the national assembly, who have taken to themselves the management of this arduous concern. Far from any encrease of revenue in their hands, I find, by a report of M. Vernier,[182] from the committee of finances, of the second of August last, that the amount of the national revenue, as compared with its produce before the revolution, was diminished by the sum of two hundred millions, or *eight millions sterling* of the annual income, considerably more than one-third of the whole!

If this be the result of great ability, never surely was ability displayed in a more distinguished manner, or with so powerful an effect. No common folly, no vulgar incapacity, no ordinary official negligence, even no official crime, no corruption, no peculation, hardly any direct hostility which we have seen in the modern world, could in so short a time have made so complete an overthrow of the finances, and with them, of the strength of a great kingdom. – *Cedò quî vestram rempublicam tantam amisistis tam cito?*[183]

The sophisters and declaimers, as soon as the assembly met, began with decrying the ancient constitution of the revenue in many of its most essential branches, such as the public monopoly of salt. They charged it, as truly as unwisely, with being ill-contrived, oppressive, and partial.

This representation they were not satisfied to make use of in speeches preliminary to some plan of reform; they declared it in a solemn resolution or public sentence, as it were judicially, passed upon it; and this they dispersed throughout the nation. At the time they passed the decree, with the same gravity they ordered this same absurd, oppressive, and partial tax to be paid, until they could find a revenue to replace it. The consequence was inevitable. The provinces which had been always exempted from this salt monopoly, some of whom were charged with other contributions, perhaps equivalent, were totally disinclined to bear any part of the burthen, which by an equal distribution was to redeem the others. As to the assembly, occupied as it was with the declaration and violation of the rights of men, and with their arrangements for general confusion, it had neither leisure nor capacity to contrive, nor authority to enforce any plan of any kind relative to the replacing the tax or equalizing it, or compensating the provinces, or for conducting their minds to any scheme of accommodation with the other districts which were to be relieved.

The people of the salt provinces, impatient under taxes damned by the authority which had directed their payment, very soon found their patience exhausted. They thought themselves as skilful in demolishing as the assembly could be. They relieved themselves by throwing off the whole burthen. Animated by this example each district, or part of a district, judging of its own grievance by its own feeling, and of its remedy by its own opinion, did as it pleased with other taxes.

We are next to see how they have conducted themselves in contriving equal impositions, proportioned to the means of the citizens, and the least likely to lean heavy on the active capital employed in the generation of that private wealth, from whence the public fortune must be

derived. By suffering the several districts, and several of
the individuals in each district, to judge of what part of
the old revenue they might withhold, instead of better
principles of equality, a new inequality was introduced
of the most oppressive kind. Payments were regulated by
dispositions. The parts of the kingdom which were the
most submissive, the most orderly, or the most affection-
ate to the commonwealth, bore the whole burthen of the
state. Nothing turns out to be so oppressive and unjust as
a feeble government. To fill up all the deficiencies in the
old impositions, and the new deficiencies of every kind
which were to be expected, what remained to a state without authority? The national assembly called for a voluntary benevolence; for a fourth part of the income of all
the citizens, to be estimated on the honour of those who
were to pay. They obtained something more than could
be rationally calculated, but what was, far indeed, from
answerable to their real necessities, and much less to
their fond expectations. Rational people could have hoped
for little from this their tax in the disguise of a benevolence; a tax, weak, ineffective, and unequal; a tax by
which luxury, avarice, and selfishness were screened, and
the load thrown upon productive capital, upon integrity,
generosity, and public spirit – a tax of regulation upon
virtue. At length the mask is thrown off, and they are
now trying means (with little success) of exacting their
benevolence by force.

This benevolence, the ricketty offspring of weakness,
was to be supported by another resource, the twin brother
of the same prolific imbecility. The patriotic donations
were to make good the failure of the patriotic contribution. John Doe was to become security for Richard Roe.
By this scheme they took things of much price from the
giver, comparatively of small value to the receiver; they
ruined several trades; they pillaged the crown of its

ornaments, the churches of their plate, and the people of their personal decorations. The invention of these juvenile pretenders to liberty, was in reality nothing more than a servile imitation of one of the poorest resources of doting despotism. They took an old huge full-bottomed perriwig out of the wardrobe of the antiquated frippery of Louis XIV. to cover the premature baldness of the national assembly. They produced this old-fashioned formal folly, though it had been so abundantly exposed in the Memoirs of the Duke de St Simon,[184] if to reasonable men it had wanted any arguments to display its mischief and insufficiency. A device of the same kind was tried in my memory by Louis XV. but it answered at no time. However, the necessities of ruinous wars were some excuse for desperate projects. The deliberations of calamity are rarely wise. But here was a season for disposition and providence. It was in a time of profound peace, then enjoyed for five years, and promising a much longer continuance, that they had recourse to this desperate trifling. They were sure to lose more reputation by sporting, in their serious situation, with these toys and playthings of finance, which have filled half their journals, than could possibly be compensated by the poor temporary supply which they afforded. It seemed as if those who adopted such projects were wholly ignorant of their circumstances, or wholly unequal to their necessities. Whatever virtue may be in these devices, it is obvious that neither the patriotic gifts, nor the patriotic contribution, can ever be resorted to again. The resources of public folly are soon exhausted. The whole indeed of their scheme of revenue is to make, by any artifice, an appearance of a full reservoir for the hour, whilst at the same time they cut off the springs and living fountains of perennial supply. The account not long since furnished by Mr Necker was meant, without question, to be favourable. He gives a flattering view of the means of getting through the year; but he expresses, as it is natural he should, some apprehension for that which was to succeed. On this last prognostic, instead of entering into the grounds of this apprehension, in order by a proper foresight, to prevent the prognosticated evil, Mr Necker receives a sort of friendly reprimand from the president of the assembly.

As to their other schemes of taxation, it is impossible to say any thing of them with certainty; because they have not yet had their operation; but nobody is so sanguine as to imagine they will fill up any perceptible part of the wide gaping breach which their incapacity has made in their revenues. At present the state of their treasury sinks every day more and more in cash, and swells more and more in fictitious representation. When so little within or without is now found but paper, the representative not of opulence but of want, the creature not of credit but of power, they imagine that our flourishing state in England is owing to that bank-paper, and not the bank-paper to the flourishing condition of our commerce, to the solidity of our credit, and to the total exclusion of all idea of power from any part of the transaction. They forget that, in England, not one shilling of paper-money of any description is received but of choice; that the whole has had its origin in cash actually deposited; and that it is convertible, at pleasure, in an instant, and without the smallest loss, into cash again. Our paper is of value in commerce, because in law it is of none. It is powerful on Change, because in Westminster-hall it is impotent.[185] In payment of a debt of twenty shillings, a creditor may refuse all the paper of the bank of England. Nor is there amongst us a single public security, of any quality or nature whatsoever, that is enforced by authority. In fact it might be easily shewn, that our paper wealth, instead of lessening the real coin, has a tendency to increase it; instead of being a substitute for money, it only facilitates its entry, its exit, and its circulation; that is the symbol of prosperity, and not the badge of distress. Never was a scarcity of cash, and an exuberance of paper, a subject of complaint in this nation.

Well! but a lessening of prodigal expences, and the œconomy which has been introduced by the virtuous and sapient assembly, makes amends for the losses sustained in the receipt of revenue. In this at least they have fulfilled the duty of a financier. Have those, who say so, looked at the expences of the national assembly itself? of the municipalities, of the city of Paris? of the increased pay of the two armies? of the new police? of the new judicatures? Have they even carefully compared the present pension-list with the former? These politicians have been cruel, not œconomical. Comparing the expences of the former prodigal government and its relation to the then revenues with the expences of this new system as opposed to the state of its new treasury, I believe the present will be found beyond all comparison more chargeable.*

* The reader will observe, that I have but lightly touched (my plan demanded nothing more) on the condition of the French finances, as connected with the demands upon them. If I had intended to do otherwise, the materials in my hands for such a task are not altogether perfect. On this subject I refer the reader to M. de Calonne's[186] work; and the tremendous display that he has made of the havock and devastation in the public estate, and in all the affairs of France, caused by the presumptuous good intentions of ignorance and incapacity. Such effects, those causes will always produce. Looking over that account with a pretty strict eye, and, with perhaps too much rigour, deducting every thing which may be placed to the account of a financier out of place, who might be supposed by his enemies desirous of making the most of his cause, I believe it will be found, that a more salutary lesson of caution against the daring spirit of innovators than what has been supplied at the expence of France, never was at any time furnished to mankind.

It remains only to consider the proofs of financial ability, furnished by the present French managers when they are to raise supplies on credit. Here I am a little at a stand; for credit, properly speaking, they have none. The credit of the antient government was not indeed the best: but they could always, on some terms, command money, not only at home, but from most of the countries of Europe where a surplus capital was accumulated; and the credit of that government was improving daily. The establishment of a system of liberty would of course be supposed to give it new strength; and so it would actually have done, if a system of liberty had been established. What offers has their government of pretended liberty had from Holland, from Hamburgh, from Switzerland, from Genoa, from England, for a dealing in their paper? Why should these nations of commerce and œconomy enter into any pecuniary dealings with a people who attempt to reverse the very nature of things; amongst whom they see the debtor prescribing, at the point of the bayonet, the medium of his solvency to the creditor; discharging one of his engagements with another; turning his very penury into his resource; and paying his interest with his rags?

Their fanatical confidence in the omnipotence of church plunder, has induced these philosophers to overlook all care of the public estate, just as the dream of the philosopher's stone induces dupes, under the more plausible delusion of the hermetic art, to neglect all rational means of improving their fortunes. With these philosophic financiers, this universal medicine made of church mummy is to cure all the evils of the state. These gentlemen perhaps do not believe a great deal in the miracles of piety; but it cannot be questioned, that they have an undoubting faith in the prodigies of sacrilege. Is there a debt which presses them – Issue *assignats*.[187] – Are compensations to be made, or a maintenance decreed to those whom they have robbed of their freehold in their office, or expelled from their profession – *Assignats*. Is a fleet to be fitted out – *Assignats*. If sixteen millions sterling of these *assignats*, forced on the people, leave the wants of the state as urgent as ever – issue, says one, thirty millions sterling of *assignats* – says another, issue fourscore millions more of *assignats*. The only difference among their financial factions is on the greater or the lesser quantity of *assignats* to be imposed on the publick sufferance. They are all professors of *assignats*. Even those, whose natural good sense and knowledge of commerce, not obliterated by philosophy, furnish decisive arguments against this delusion, conclude their arguments, by proposing the emission of *assignats*. I suppose they must talk of *assignats*, as no other language would be understood. All experience of their inefficacy does not in the least discourage them. Are the old *assignats* depreciated at market? What is the remedy? Issue new *assignats*. – *Mais si maladia, opiniatria, non vult se garire, quid illi facere? assignare – postea assignare; ensuita assignare.*[188] The word is a trifle altered. The Latin of your present doctors may be better than that of your old comedy; their wisdom, and the variety of their resources, are the same. They have not more notes in their song than the cuckow; though, far from the softness of that harbinger of summer and plenty, their voice is as harsh and as ominous as that of the raven.

Who but the most desperate adventurers in philosophy and finance could at all have thought of destroying the settled revenue of the state, the sole security for the public credit, in the hope of rebuilding it with the materials of confiscated property? If, however, an excessive zeal for the state should have led a pious and venerable prelate[189] (by anticipation a father of the church)* to

*La Bruyere of Bossuet.[190]

pillage his own order, and, for the good of the church and people, to take upon himself the place of grand financier of confiscation, and comptroller general of sacrilege, he and his coadjutors were, in my opinion, bound to shew, by their subsequent conduct, that they knew something of the office they assumed. When they had resolved to appropriate to the Fisc,[191] a certain portion of the landed property of their conquered country, it was their business to render their bank a real fund of credit; as far as such a bank was capable of becoming so.

To establish a current circulating credit upon any *Land-bank*, under any circumstances whatsoever, has hitherto proved difficult at the very least. The attempt has commonly ended in bankruptcy. But when the assembly were led, through a contempt of moral, to a defiance of œconomical principles, it might at least have been expected, that nothing would be omitted on their part to lessen this difficulty, to prevent any aggravation of this bankruptcy. It might be expected that to render your *Land-bank* tolerable, every means would be adopted that could display openness and candour in the statement of the security; every thing which could aid the recovery of the demand. To take things in their most favourable point of view, your condition was that of a man of a large landed estate, which he wished to dispose of for the discharge of a debt, and the supply of certain services. Not being able instantly to sell, you wished to mortgage. What would a man of fair intentions, and a commonly clear understanding, do in such circumstances? Ought he not first to ascertain the gross value of the estate; the charges of its management and disposition; the encumbrances perpetual and temporary of all kinds that affect it; then, striking a net surplus, to calculate the just value of the security? When that surplus (the only security to the creditor) had been clearly ascertained, and properly vested in the hands of trustees; then he would indicate the parcels to be sold, and the time and conditions of sale; after this, he would admit the public creditor, if he chose it, to subscribe his stock into this new fund; or he might receive proposals for an *assignat* from those who would advance money to purchase this species of security.

This would be to proceed like men of business, methodically and rationally; and on the only principles of public and private credit that have an existence. The dealer would then know exactly what he purchased; and the only doubt which could hang upon his mind would be, the dread of the resumption of the spoil, which one day might be made (perhaps with an addition of punishment) from the sacrilegious gripe of those execrable wretches who could become purchasers at the auction of their innocent fellow-citizens.

An open and exact statement of the clear value of the property, and of the time, the circumstances, and the place of sale, were all necessary, to efface as much as possible the stigma that has hitherto been branded on every kind of Land-bank. It became necessary on another principle, that is, on account of a pledge of faith previously given on that subject, that their future fidelity in a slippery concern might be established by their adherence to their first engagement. When they had finally determined on a state resource from church booty, they came, on the 14th of April 1790, to a solemn resolution on the subject; and pledged themselves to their country, 'that in the statement of the public charges for each year there should be brought to account a sum sufficient for defraying the expences of the R. C. A. religion, the support of the ministers at the altars, the relief of the poor, the pensions to the ecclesiastics, secular as well as regular, of the one and of the other sex, *in order that the estates and goods which are at the disposal of the nation may be disengaged of all charges, and employed by the representatives, or the legislative body, to the great and most pressing exigencies of the state.'* They further engaged, on the same day, that the sum necessary for the year 1791 should be forthwith determined.

In this resolution they admit it their duty to show distinctly the expence of the above objects, which, by other resolutions, they had before engaged should be first in the order of provision. They admit that they ought to shew the estate clear and disengaged of all charges, and that they should shew it immediately. Have they done this immediately, or at any time? Have they ever furnished a rent-roll of the immoveable estates, or given in an inventory of the moveable effects which they confiscate to their assignats? In what manner they can fulfil their engagements of holding out to public service 'an estate disengaged of all charges,' without authenticating the value of the estate, or the quantum of the charges, I leave it to their English admirers to explain. Instantly upon this assurance, and previously to any one step towards making it good, they issue, on the credit of so handsome a declaration, sixteen millions sterling of their paper. This was manly. Who, after this masterly stroke, can doubt of their abilities in finance? – But then, before any other emission of these financial *indulgences*, they took care at least to make good their original promise! – If such estimate, either of the value of the estate or the amount of the incumbrances, has been made, it has escaped me. I never heard of it.

At length they have spoken out, and they have made a full discovery of their abominable fraud, in holding out the church lands as a security for any debts or any service whatsoever. They rob only to enable them to cheat; but in a very short time they defeat the ends both of the robbery and the fraud, by making out accounts for other purposes, which blow up their whole apparatus of force and of deception. I am obliged to M. de Calonne for his reference to the document which proves this extra-ordinary fact: it had, by some means, escaped me. Indeed it was not necessary to make out my assertion as to the breach of faith on the declaration of the 14th of April 1790. By a report of their Committee it now appears, that the charge of keeping up the reduced ecclesiastical estab-lishments, and other expences attendant on religion, and maintaining the religious of both sexes, retained or pensioned, and the other concomitant expences of the same nature, which they have brought upon themselves by this convulsion in property, exceeds the income of the estates acquired by it in the enormous sum of two mil-lions sterling annually; besides a debt of seven millions and upwards. These are the calculating powers of im-posture! This is the finance of philosophy! This is the result of all the delusions held out to engage a miserable people in rebellion, murder, and sacrilege, and to make them prompt and zealous instruments in the ruin of their country! Never did a state, in any case, enrich itself by the confiscations of the citizens. This new experiment has succeeded like all the rest. Every honest mind, every true lover of liberty and humanity must rejoice to find that injustice is not always good policy, nor rapine the high road to riches. I subjoin with pleasure, in a note, the able and spirited observations of M. de Calonne on this sub-ject.*

* 'Ce n'est point à l'assemblée entière que je m'adresse ici; je ne parle qu'à ceux qui l'égarent, en lui cachant sous des gazes séduisantes le but où ils l'entraînent. C'est à eux que je dis : votre objet, vous n'en disconviendrez pas, c'est d'ôter tout espoir au clergé, & de consommer sa ruine; c'est-la, en ne vous soupçonnant d'aucune combinaison de cupidité, d'aucun regard sur le jeu des effets publics, c'est-là ce qu'on doit croire que vous avez en vue dans la terrible opération que vous proposez; c'est ce qui doit en

In order to persuade the world of the bottomless resource of ecclesiastical confiscation, the assembly have
proceeded to other confiscations of estates in offices,
which could not be done with any common colour without being compensated out of this grand confiscation of
landed property. They have thrown upon this fund, which
was to shew a surplus, disengaged of all charges, a new
charge; namely, the compensation to the whole body of
the disbanded judicature; and of all suppressed offices and
estates; a charge which I cannot ascertain, but which unquestionably amounts to many French millions. Another
of the new charges, is an annuity of four hundred and
eighty thousand pounds sterling, to be paid (if they
choose to keep faith) by daily payments, for the interest
of the first assignats. Have they ever given themselves the
trouble to state fairly the expence of the management
of the church lands in the hands of municipalities, to
whose care, skill, and diligence, and that of their legion
of unknown under agents, they have chosen to commit
the charge of the forfeited estates, and the consequence

être le fruit. Mais le peuple que vous y intéressez, quel avantage
peut-il y trouver? En vous servant sans cesse de lui, que faites vous
pour lui? Rien, absolument rien; &, au contraire, vous faites ce
qui ne conduit qu'à l'accabler de nouvelles charges. Vous avez
rejeté, à son prejudice, une offre de 400 millions, dont l'acceptation
pouvoit devenir un moyen de soulagement en sa faveur; & à cette
ressource, aussi profitable que legitime, vous avez substitué une
injustice ruineuse, qui, de votre propre aveu, charge le trésor
public & par conséquent le peuple, d'un surcroît de depense an-
nuelle de 50 millions au moins, & d'un remboursement de 150
millions.

'Malheureux peuple, voilà ce que vous vaut en dernier résultat
l'expropriation de l'Eglise, & la dureté des décrets taxateurs du
traitement des ministres d'une religion bienfaisante; & deformais
ils seront à votre charge: leurs charités soulageoient les pauvres;
& vous allez être imposés pour subvenir à leur entretien!' – *De
l'Etat de la* France, p. 81. See also p. 92, and the following pages.

of which had been so ably pointed out by the bishop of Nancy?[192]

But it is unnecessary to dwell on these obvious heads of incumbrance. Have they made out any clear state of the grand incumbrance of all, I mean the whole of the general and municipal establishments of all sorts, and compared it with the regular income by revenue? Every deficiency in these becomes a charge of the confiscated estate, before the creditor can plant his cabbages on an acre of church property. There is no other prop than this confiscation to keep the whole state from tumbling to the ground. In this situation they have purposely covered all that they ought industriously to have cleared, with a thick fog; and then, blindfold themselves, like bulls that shut their eyes when they push, they drive, by the point of the bayonets, their slaves, blindfolded indeed no worse than their lords, to take their fictions for currencies, and to swallow down paper pills by thirty-four millions sterling at a dose. Then they proudly lay in their claim to a future credit, on failure of all their past engagements, and at a time when (if in such a matter any thing can be clear) it is clear that the surplus estates will never answer even the first of their mortgages, I mean that of the four hundred million (or sixteen millions sterling) of *assignats*. In all this procedure I can discern neither the solid sense of plain-dealing, nor the subtle dexterity of ingenious fraud. The objection within the assembly to pulling up the flood-gates for this inundation of fraud, are unanswered; but they are thoroughly refuted by an hundred thousand financiers in the street. These are the numbers by which the metaphysic arithmeticians compute. These are the grand calculations on which a philosophical public credit is founded in France. They cannot raise supplies; but they can raise mobs. Let them rejoice in the applauses of the club at Dundee,[193] for their wisdom and patriotism

in having thus applied the plunder of the citizens to
the service of the state. I hear of no address upon this
subject from the directors of the Bank of England; though
their approbation would be of a *little* more weight in
the scale of credit than that of the club at Dundee. But,
to do justice to the club, I believe the gentlemen who
compose it to be wiser than they appear; that they will
be less liberal of their money than of their addresses; and
that they would not give a dog's-ear[194] of their most rum-
pled and ragged Scotch paper for twenty of your fairest
assignats.

Early in this year the assembly issued paper to the
amount of sixteen millions sterling: What must have
been the state into which the assembly has brought your
affairs, that the relief afforded by so vast a supply has
been hardly perceptible? This paper also felt an almost
immediate depreciation of five per cent. which in little
time came to about seven. The effect of these assignats on
the receipt of the revenue is remarkable. Mr Necker found
that the collectors of the revenue, who received in coin,
paid the treasury in *assignats*. The collectors made seven
per cent. by thus receiving in money, and accounting in
depreciated paper. It was not very difficult to foresee,
that this must be inevitable. It was, however, not the less
embarrassing. Mr Necker was obliged (I believe, for a considerable part, in the market of London) to buy gold and
silver for the mint, which amounted to about twelve
thousand pounds above the value of the commodity
gained. That minister was of opinion, that whatever their
secret nutritive virtue might be, the state could not live
upon *assignats* alone; that some real silver was necessary,
particularly for the satisfaction of those, who having
iron in their hands, were not likely to distinguish themselves for patience, when they should perceive that whilst
an encrease of pay was held out to them in real money, it

was again to be fraudulently drawn back by depreciated paper. The minister, in this very natural distress, applied to the assembly, that they should order the collectors to pay in specie what in specie they had received. It could not escape him, that if the treasury paid 3 per cent. for the use of a currency, which should be returned seven per cent. worse than the minister issued it, such a dealing could not very greatly tend to enrich the public. The assembly took no notice of his recommendation. They were in this dilemma – If they continued to receive the assignats, cash must become an alien to their treasury: If the treasury should refuse those paper *amulets*, or should discountenance them in any degree, they must destroy the credit of their sole resource. They seem then to have made their option; and to have given some sort of credit to their paper by taking it themselves; at the same time in their speeches they made a sort of swaggering declaration, something, I rather think, above legislative competence; that is, that there is no difference in value between metallic money and their assignats. This was good stout proof article of faith, pronounced under an anathema, by the venerable fathers of this philosophic synod. *Credat* who will – certainly not *Judæus Apella.*[195]

A noble indignation rises in the minds of your popular leaders, on hearing the magic lanthorn in their shew of finance compared to the fraudulent exhibitions of Mr Law.[196] They cannot bear to hear the sands of his Mississippi compared with the rock of the church, on which they build their system. Pray let them suppress this glorious spirit, until they shew to the world what piece of solid ground there is for their assignats, which they have not pre-occupied by other charges. They do injustice to that great, mother fraud, to compare it with their degenerate imitation. It is not true, that Law built solely on a speculation concerning the Mississippi. He added the

East India trade; he added the African trade; he added the farms of all the farmed revenue of France. All these together unquestionably could not support the structure which the public enthusiasm, not he, chose to build upon these bases. But these were, however, in comparison, generous delusions. They supposed, and they aimed at an increase of the commerce of France. They opened to it the whole range of the two hemispheres. They did not think of feeding France from its own substance. A grand imagination found in this flight of commerce something to captivate. It was wherewithal to dazzle the eye of an eagle. It was not made to entice the smell of a mole, nuzzling and burying himself in his mother earth, as yours is. Men were not then quite shrunk from their natural dimensions by a degrading and sordid philosophy, and fitted for low and vulgar deceptions. Above all remember, that in imposing on the imagination, the then managers of the system made a compliment to the freedom of men. In their fraud there was no mixture of force. This was reserved to our time, to quench the little glimmerings of reason which might break in upon the solid darkness of this enlightened age.

On recollection, I have said nothing of a scheme of finance which may be urged in favour of the abilities of these gentlemen, and which has been introduced with great pomp, though not yet finally adopted in the national assembly. It comes with something solid in aid of the credit of the paper circulation; and much has been said of its utility and its elegance. I mean the project for coining into money the bells of the suppressed churches. This is their alchymy. There are some follies which baffle argument; which go beyond ridicule; and which excite no feeling in us but disgust; and therefore I say no more upon it.

It is as little worth remarking any farther upon all

their drawing and re-drawing, on their circulation for putting off the evil day, on the play between the treasury and the *Caisse d'Escompte*, and on all these old exploded contrivances of mercantile fraud, now exalted into policy of state. The revenue will not be trifled with. The prattling about the rights of men will not be accepted in payment for a biscuit or a pound of gunpowder. Here then the metaphysicians descend from their airy speculations, and faithfully follow examples. What examples? the examples of bankrupts. But, defeated, baffled, disgraced, when their breath, their strength, their inventions, their fancies desert them, their confidence still maintains its ground. In the manifest failure of their abilities they take credit for their benevolence. When the revenue disappears in their hands, they have the presumption, in some of their late proceedings, to value *themselves* on the relief given to the people. They did not relieve the people. If they entertained such intentions, why did they order the obnoxious taxes to be paid? The people relieved themselves in spite of the assembly.

But waving all discussion on the parties, who may claim the merit of this fallacious relief, has there been, in effect, any relief to the people in any form? Mr Bailly,[197] one of the grand agents of paper circulation, lets you into the nature of this relief. His speech to the National Assembly contained an high and laboured panegyric on the inhabitants of Paris for the constancy and unbroken resolution with which they have borne their distress and misery. A fine picture of public felicity! What! great courage and unconquerable firmness of mind to endure benefits, and sustain redress! One would think from the speech of this learned Lord Mayor, that the Parisians, for this twelvemonth past, had been suffering the straits of some dreadful blockade; that Henry the Fourth had been stopping up the avenues to their supply, and Sully[198] thundering with his ordnance at the gates of Paris; when in reality they are besieged by no other enemies than their own madness and folly, their own credulity and perverseness. But Mr Bailly will sooner thaw the eternal ice of his atlantic regions, than restore the central heat to Paris, whilst it remains 'smitten with the cold, dry, petrifick mace'[199] of a false and unfeeling philosophy. Some time after this speech, that is, on the thirteenth of last August, the same magistrate, giving an account of his government at the bar of the same assembly, expresses himself as follows: 'In the month of July 1789, [the period of everlasting commemoration] the finances of the city of Paris were *yet* in good order; the expenditure was counterbalanced by the receipt, and she had at that time a million [forty thousand pounds sterling] in bank. The expences which she has been constrained to incur, *subsequent to the revolution*, amount to 2,500,000 livres. From these expences, and the great falling off in the product of the *free gifts*, not only a momentary but a *total* want of money has taken place.' This is the Paris upon whose nourishment, in the course of the last year, such immense sums, drawn from the vitals of all France, has been expended. As long as Paris stands in the place of antient Rome, so long she will be maintained by the subject provinces. It is an evil inevitably attendant on the dominion of sovereign democratic republics. As it happened in Rome, it may survive that republican domination which gave rise to it. In that case despotism itself must submit to the vices of popularity. Rome, under her emperors, united the evils of both systems; and this unnatural combination was one great cause of her ruin.

To tell the people that they are relieved by the dilapidation of their public estate, is a cruel and insolent imposition. Statesmen, before they valued themselves on the relief given to the people, by the destruction of their revenue, ought first to have carefully attended to the solution of this problem: – Whether it be more advantageous to the people to pay considerably, and to gain in proportion; or to gain little or nothing, and to be disburthened of all contribution? My mind is made up to decide in favour of the first proposition. Experience is with me, and, I believe, the best opinions also. To keep a balance between the power of acquisition on the part of the subject, and the demands he is to answer on the part of the state, is a fundamental part of the skill of a true politician. The means of acquisition are prior in time and in arrangement. Good order is the foundation of all good things. To be enabled to acquire, the people, without being servile, must be tractable and obedient. The magistrate must have his reverence, the laws their authority. The body of the people must not find the principles of natural subordination by art rooted out of their minds. They must respect that property of which they cannot partake. They must labour to obtain what by labour can be obtained; and when they find, as they commonly do, the success disproportioned to the endeavour, they must be taught their consolation in the final proportions of eternal justice. Of this consolation, whoever deprives them, deadens their industry, and strikes at the root of all acquisition as of all conservation. He that does this is the cruel oppressor, the merciless enemy of the poor and wretched; at the same time that by his wicked speculations he exposes the fruits of successful industry, and the accumulations of fortune, to the plunder of the negligent, the disappointed, and the unprosperous.[200]

Too many of the financiers by profession are apt to see nothing in revenue, but banks, and circulations, and annuities on lives, and tontines,[201] and perpetual rents, and all the small wares of the shop. In a settled order of the state, these things are not to be slighted, nor is the skill in them to be held of trivial estimation. They are good, but then only good, when they assume the effects of that settled order, and are built upon it. But when men think that these beggarly contrivances may supply a resource for the evils which result from breaking up the foundations of public order, and from causing or suffering the principles of property to be subverted, they will, in the ruin of their country, leave a melancholy and lasting monument of the effect of preposterous politics, and presumptuous, short-sighted, narrow-minded wisdom.

The effects of the incapacity shewn by the popular leaders in all the great members of the commonwealth are to be covered with the 'all-atoning name' of liberty. In some people I see great liberty indeed; in many, if not in the most, an oppressive degrading servitude. But what is liberty without wisdom, and without virtue? It is the greatest of all possible evils; for it is folly, vice, and madness, without tuition or restraint. Those who know what virtuous liberty is, cannot bear to see it disgraced by incapable heads, on account of their having high-sounding words in their mouths. Grand, swelling sentiments of liberty, I am sure I do not despise. They warm the heart; they enlarge and liberalise our minds; they animate our courage in a time of conflict. Old as I am, I read the fine raptures of Lucan and Corneille[202] with pleasure. Neither do I wholly condemn the little arts and devices of popularity. They facilitate the carrying of many points of moment; they keep the people together; they refresh the mind in its exertions; and they diffuse occasional gaiety over the severe brow of moral freedom. Every politician ought to sacrifice to the graces; and to join compliance with reason. But in such an undertaking as that in France, all these subsidiary sentiments and artifices are of little avail. To make a government requires no great prudence. Settle the seat of power; teach obedience: and the work is done. To give freedom is still more easy. It is not necessary to guide; it only requires to let go the rein. But to form a *free government*; that is, to temper together these opposite elements of liberty and restraint in one consistent work, requires much thought, deep reflection, a sagacious, powerful, and combining mind. This I do not find in those who take the lead in the national assembly. Perhaps they are not so miserably deficient as they appear. I rather believe it. It would put them below the common level of human understanding. But when the leaders choose to make themselves bidders at an auction of popularity, their talents, in the construction of the state, will be of no service. They will become flatterers instead of legislators; the instruments, not the guides of the people. If any of them should happen to propose a scheme of liberty, soberly limited, and defined with proper qualifications, he will be immediately outbid by his competitors, who will produce something more splendidly popular. Suspicions will be raised of his fidelity to his cause. Moderation will be stigmatized as the virtue of cowards; and compromise as the prudence of traitors; until, in hopes of preserving the credit which may enable him to temper and moderate on some occasions, the popular leader is obliged to become active in propagating doctrines, and establishing powers, that will afterwards defeat any sober purpose at which he ultimately might have aimed.

But am I so unreasonable as to see nothing at all that deserves commendation in the indefatigable labours of this assembly? I do not deny that among an infinite number of acts of violence and folly, some good may have been done. They who destroy every thing certainly will remove some grievance. They who make every thing new, have a chance that they may establish something beneficial. To give them credit for what they have done in virtue of the authority they have usurped, or which can excuse them in the crimes by which that authority has been acquired, it must appear, that the same things could not have been accomplished without producing such a revolution. Most assuredly they might; because almost every one of the regulations made by them, which is not very equivocal, was either in the cession of the king, voluntarily made at the meeting of the states, or in the concurrent instructions to the orders. Some usages have been abolished on just grounds; but they were such that if they had stood as they were to all eternity, they would little detract from the happiness and prosperity of any state. The improvements of the national assembly are superficial, their errors fundamental.

Whatever they are, I wish my countrymen rather to recommend to our neighbours the example of the British constitution, than to take models from them for the improvement of our own. In the former they have got an invaluable treasure. They are not, I think, without some causes of apprehension and complaint; but these they do not owe to their constitution, but to their own conduct. I think our happy situation owing to our constitution; but owing to the whole of it, and not to any part singly; owing in a great measure to what we have left standing in our several reviews and reformations, as well as to what we have altered or super-added. Our people will find employment enough for a truly patriotic, free, and independent spirit, in guarding what they possess, from violation. I would not exclude alteration neither; but even when I changed, it should be to preserve. I should be led to my remedy by a great grievance. In what I did, I should follow the example of our ancestors. I would make the reparation as nearly as possible in the style of the building. A politic caution, a guarded circumspection, a moral rather than a complexional timidity were among the ruling principles of our forefathers in their most decided conduct. Not being illuminated with the light of which the gentlemen of France tell us they have got so abundant a share, they acted under a strong impression of the ignorance and fallibility of mankind. He that had made them thus fallible, rewarded them for having in their conduct attended to their nature. Let us imitate their caution, if we wish to deserve their fortune, or to retain their bequests. Let us add, if we please, but let us preserve what they have left; and, standing on the firm ground of the British constitution, let us be satisfied to admire rather than attempt to follow in their desperate flights the aëronauts of France.

I have told you candidly my sentiments. I think they are not likely to alter yours. I do not know that they ought. You are young; you cannot guide, but must follow the fortune of your country. But hereafter they may be of some use to you, in some future form which your commonwealth may take. In the present it can hardly remain; but before its final settlement it may be obliged to pass, as one of our poets says, 'through great varieties of untried being,'[203] and in all its transmigrations to be purified by fire and blood.[204]

I have little to recommend my opinions, but long observation and much impartiality. They come from one who has been no tool of power, no flatterer of greatness; and who in his last acts does not wish to belye the tenour of his life. They come from one, almost the whole of whose public exertion has been a struggle for the liberty of others; from one in whose breast no anger durable or vehement has ever been kindled, but by what he considered as tyranny; and who snatches from his share in the endeavours which are used by good men to discredit opulent oppression, the hours he has employed on your affairs; and who in so doing persuades himself he has not departed from his usual office: they come from one who desires honours, distinctions, and emoluments, but little; and who expects them not at all; who has no contempt for fame, and no fear of obloquy; who shuns contention, though he will hazard an opinion: from one who wishes to preserve consistency; but who would preserve consistency by varying his means to secure the unity of his end; and, when the equipoise of the vessel in which he sails, may be endangered by overloading it upon one side, is desirous of carrying the small weight of his reasons to that which may preserve its equipoise.

FINIS.

NOTES

These notes are set in the text as superior numbers,
the footnotes within the text being set in asterisk,
dagger, etc.

(Where the versions of classical texts and translations used are not otherwise indicated, they are those of the Loeb Classical Library.)

1. See Introduction, pp. 14–15. This original answer to de Pont was probably actually written in November 1789. Much less heated, and more paternal in tone than the *Reflections*, it was offered as advice 'not in the taste of this enlightened age and indeed ... no better than the late, ripe fruit of mere experience.'

2. The Society for Constitutional Information was founded in 1780 by Major Cartwright and became most active after 1790, under the leadership of Horne Tooke, and on the principles of Tom Paine, who was a member. It did not survive the arrest and prosecution of its leaders in 1794. See E. P. Thompson, *The Making of the English Working Class* (Pelican Book). The Revolution Society had been founded in 1788 to commemorate the centenary of the English revolution of 1688. Its chairman was Earl Stanhope (see n.6). E. J. Payne, a nineteenth-century editor of Burke, has an interesting comment on the changing connotation of the term 'revolution' in English. 'It is not insignificant that this use of the term *in bonam partem* [favourably, as in 'The Revolution Society'] which was still in vogue, though in its decline, at the time of the French Revolution, from that time wholly disappears from the English language' (Burke, *Select Works*, 1875, vol. II, p. 295). It has cropped up again since, occasionally.

3. 'Never wholly seperate in your mind the merits of any Political Question from the Men who are concerned in it' (*Letter to de Pont*; *Corr.* VI, p. 47).

4. Don Quixote.

5. Richard Price (1723–91) was at this time an eminent dissenting preacher. His 'Discourse on the love of our country', preached at the Old Jewry, 4 November 1789, provided the immediate stimulus for the *Reflections*, when Burke read it in January 1790 (*Correspondence*, Vol. VI, ed. Cobban and Smith, p. 81). It had been published by the Revolution Society together with the Congratulatory Address referred to above and the letters constituting the Assembly's reply

(see *Reflections*, p. 93). Price was attached to Lord Shelburne, Rockingham's rival, whom Burke detested. (See n.9 below.) Jean de Dieu-Raymond de Cucé Boisgelin, (1732–1804) Archbishop of Aix, was elected President of the National Assembly in November 1789 and subsequently charged by the Assembly with the task of replying to the London address. A serious reforming churchman, he was compelled later to break with the Revolution and fled into exile in England. Louis Alexandre, duc de la Roche-Guyon et de la-Rochefoucauld d'Anville (1743–92) was one of the first of the nobility to unite with the Third Estate. A friend of Lord Stanhope (see n.6 below), he acted as intermediary in conveying the London Revolution Society's address to the National Assembly and initiated the Assembly's grateful acknowledgement of it. He was stoned to death at Gisors in 1792. For the duc de la Rochefoucauld-Liancourt, also one of the first of the nobility to support the new order, and elected President of the National Assembly on 20 July 1789, see n.97. Both noblemen are referred to currently as 'duc de la Rochefoucauld'.

6. Charles, third Earl Stanhope (1753–1816) chairman of the Revolution Society (1788), whose address of congratulation on the capture of the Bastille he forwarded to Paris. Published in 1790 an answer to Burke's speech on the French Revolution. Vacated his parliamentary seat (acquired by favour of Lord Shelburne – see n.9 below) in 1795 after being 'in a minority of one' on his motion against interfering in the internal affairs of France. He was a noted scientist and inventor of calculating machines, and ill-treated and disinherited all his children. He represented a type of humanity especially antipathetic to Burke: 'The bear loves, licks and forms her young; but bears are not philosophers.' (*Letter to a member of the National Assembly*, 1791, *Works* II, pp. 519–58.)

7. Demosthenes said that the Delphic Oracle was *philippizing* – meaning that the prophecies served the secular interests of Philip of Macedon. The phenomenon is a recurring one, under varied forms.

8. Hugh Peters (1598–1660), independent minister, and chaplain in the Parliamentary army; at the restoration executed on a charge of concerting the King's death.

9. The first reference is to Augustus Henry Fitzroy, third Duke of Grafton (1735–1811), Chancellor of the University of Cambridge and author of *Hints Submitted to the Serious Attention of the Clergy, Nobility and Gentry, by a Layman* (1789). He was attacked by Junius (the eighteenth-century pseudonymous political polemicist now believed to have been Sir Philip Francis, the enemy of Warren Hastings, see nn. 31 and 63) for stealing wood and also 'for what

could not be gainsaid, his connexion with Nancy Parsons' (*D.N.B.*) Burke probably also had in mind his *bête noire*, William Petty, first Marquis of Lansdowne, better known as Lord Shelburne (1737–1805), one of the leading political figures of the time, who patronized dissenters and favoured conciliation with France. He had his critics: 'A Catiline and a Borgia were his models in an age when half their wickedness would have suited his purposes better' (Walpole); 'If Lord Shelburne was not a Catiline or a Borgia in morals, it must not be ascribed to anything but his understanding.' (Burke.)

10. *Seekers*, a 17th century sect of independents, most of whose leaders later joined the Society of Friends (Quakers), believing that they had found what they had sought.

11. A collection of dried plants.

12. *Mess-John* or *Mas John*: familiar term for a Scottish Presbyterian Minister; 'mess' is a corruption of 'magister'.

13. Juvenal, *Satires* IV, 150. 'I wish he had devoted to nonsense all the time he had to spare for violence'.

14. Horace, *Epistles* I, i, 12.

> I search and search, and when I find I lay
> The wisdom up aganist a rainy day. – *Conington*

15. The term Declaration of Right is more usually applied to the instrument by which William and Mary were declared King and Queen in February of 1689, which was, as Macaulay has pointed out, strictly speaking a revolutionary document, the Convention by which it was drafted and adopted being an extra-legal body and the Declaration itself never having received royal sanction. Its provisions were subsequently embodied in the Bill of Rights and became law at the end of the year. It is clear from the context that Burke is here referring to the statute.

16. Maxim of Roman law: the sense is indicated by Burke in the preceding sentence.

17. James II's son by his second marriage, afterwards the Old Pretender, was reputed by his father's enemies to be a supposititious child smuggled into Saint James's Palace in a warming-pan.

18. John, Baron Somers (1651–1716), the Whig statesman, counsellor of William III and Lord Chancellor.

19. 'From the common engagement of the state' (Ed.): the phrase has not been traced to a classical source. 'It was possibly invented by Burke to express his meaning with the more weight.' (Payne.)

20. Under Roman law, inheritance was *per stirpes*, each lineal

branch of descendants taking only the portion which their parent would have taken had he been living – instead of *per capita*, under which all lineal descendants standing in an equal degree from a common ancestor share equally. Here 'by the heir per capita Burke means the eldest and most worthy of the same blood' (Payne).

21. Virgil, *Georgics* IV, 208, on bees:

> The immortal line in sure succession reigns:
> The fortune of the family remains,
> And grandsires' grandsires the long list contains
>   – Dryden.

22. *De tallagio non concedendo*: 25 Edw. 1 (1297), relied on as constitutional authority for the doctrine that there can be no taxation except by parliament. *The Petition of Right* (1628): that Statute of Charles I binding the King not to raise money without the consent of Parliament, imprison except in due course of law or impose courts martial. The reader will be familiar with the doctrine of *habeas corpus*.

23. *istaec commemoratio quasi exprobratio est* (Terence, *Andria*, I, i, 17) 'Such a reminder is almost a rebuke ...' Burke, as often quotes from memory. He also at times amends the text to suit his context. The notes to Payne's edition demonstrate how much of Burke's English echoes the classics, often word for word.

24. Titles used by the Papacy. See Burke's earlier allusion to the 'deposing power' of the Pope.

25. The medieval kings of Aragon were obliged to submit any differences with the Aragonese nobility to the arbitration of the *Justicia* (Chief Justice).

26. *Justum est bellum ... quibus necessarium* (Livy, IX, i, 10) 'War is just for those to whom it is necessary.' (Ed.)

27. Sir Edward Coke (1552–1634), judge and law writer. His *Reports* and *Institutes* (especially the first part, 'Coke upon Littleton') have exercised a profound influence on English Law. 'The key to his whole life' according to his biographer in the *D.N.B.*, 'is his veneration for the law, for its technicalities as well as for its substance, and the belief that on its rigorous maintenance and the following of precedents depended the liberty of England.' Sir William Blackstone (1723–80), judge and law writer, edited Magna Charta (1759). His *Commentaries on the Laws of England* (1765–9), considered to have shaped the course of legal education both in England and America, have been criticized for their flattery of English institutions and their extreme conservatism.

28. John Selden (1584–1654), jurist, counsel for Hampden, and M.P. for Oxford University in the Long Parliament.

29. Emmanuel-Joseph Sieyès ('or, as he preferred to sign himself Sieys', J. M. Thompson, *op. cit.*) (1748–1836), priest, publicist and politician, played a leading part in the early stages of the Revolution and drew up, for the Constituent Assembly, the *Reconnaissance et exposition des droits de l'homme et du citoyen* (July 1789).

30. 'It cannot at this time be too often repeated; line upon line; precept upon precept; until it comes into the currency of a proverb, – *to innovate is not to reform*' (*Letter to a Noble Lord; Works* V, p. 120.

31. Philip Francis took particular exception to this proposition, which he thought 'likely to fill the minds of common readers with doubt and surprise'. See Introduction.

32. Maroon slaves – fugitive slaves.

33. Burke's main practical preoccupation at this time was the conduct of the impeachment of Warren Hastings. See the *Reflections*, concluding paragraph, 'endeavours ... to discredit opulent oppression ...'

34. Sir Henry Rich, first Earl of Holland (b. 1590), courtier and politician; vacillated between king and parliament; beheaded 1649. Burke takes him as the prototype of noblemen of his own time who toyed with French Revolutionary ideas, and whose frivolity and inconsequence he attacks repeatedly, notably in the *Letter to a Noble Lord*.

35. Waller, *Panegyric to my Lord Protector* (presented 1655). He later wrote a panegyric on Charles. A similar feat was performed in our times by Paul Claudel, who wrote an ode to Pétain (1940) and one to de Gaulle (1944).

36. Burke's horror of regicide does not prevent him from seeing merits in Cromwell: 'Cromwell had delivered England from anarchy. His government, though military and despotic, had been regular and orderly. Under the iron, and under the yoke, the soil yielded its produce.' (*Letter to a member of the National Assembly*, *1791; Works* II, p. 544.)

37. Leaders in the French wars of religion in the sixteenth century. The reference to the 'Richlieus' following concerns Louis XIII's minister, the Cardinal, but also evokes contemporary French noblemen of that surname of whose conduct and politics Burke disapproved; see nn. 95, 96.

38. Maximilien de Béthune, duc de Sully (1560–1641), soldier, statesman and counsellor of Henri IV.

39. In his writings on the Revolution Burke's frequent references to Jews are almost invariably slighting or hostile, but he distinguishes between classes of Jews: 'We have in London very respectable persons of the Jewish nation, whom we will keep, but we have of the same tribe others of a very different description – housebreakers and receivers of stolen goods, and forgers of paper currency, more than we can conveniently hang.' (*Letter to a member of the National Assembly*, *Works* II p. 529.)

40. Jean-Sylvain Bailly, for whom see further n.67.

41. The Apocrypha originally designated those books of the Old Testament found in the Greek, but not in the Hebrew, the most parts of which were included by Jerome in the Latin Vulgate.

42. Commenting on this passage Gladstone wrote, 'There is a saying of Burke's from which I must utterly dissent, "Property is sluggish and inert." Quite the contrary, Property is vigilant, active, sleepless; if ever it seems to slumber be sure that one eye is open' (Morley, *Gladstone*, III, p. 469).

43. Dr Joseph Priestley (1733–1804), theologian and scientist; appointed (1772–80) librarian to Shelburne (see n.9 above) on the recommendation of Price. The passage quoted is the conclusion to his *History of the Corruptions of Christianity* (1782).

44. Virgil, *Aeneid*, I. 140:

> His power to hollow caverns is confined:
> There let him reign the jailor of the wind,
> With hoarse commands his breathing subjects call,
> And boast and bluster in his empty hall – *Dryden*.

45. Stormy east wind.

46. Horace, *de Arte Poetica*, 465, 466:

> deus immortalis haberi
> dum cupit Empedocles, ardentem frigidus Aetnam
> insiluit. Sit ius liceatque perire poetis.

'Empedocles, wishing to be thought a god, in cold blood leapt into blazing Etna. Suffer poets to destroy themselves if they choose ...' (Blakeney). See Matthew Arnold, *Empedocles on Etna*.

47. 'mercury sublimate: a violent passion; 'cantharides': the Spanish or blistering fly, employed for their stimulant, diuretic and supposed aphrodisiac properties.

48. Juvenal, *Satires*, VII, 151: 'While the crowded class is killing off the cruel tyrants' (Ed.): a reference to a routine exercise in rhetoric.

49. Unidentified.

50. See n.8 – Burke himself visibly triumphs, with this deadly *argumentum ad hominem*.

51. Seat of a Jesuit mission to the Indians, south of Lake Ontario.

52. In the first edition this read: 'There they sit, after a gang of assassins had driven away all the men of moderate minds and moderating authority amongst them, and left them as a sort of dregs and refuse, under the apparent lead of those in whom they do not so much as pretend to have any confidence.' After a conservative member, M. de Menonville, had protested, Burke corrected the passage and made amends in his *Letter to a Member of the National Assembly*, (1791). *Works* II, pp. 519–58. See also *Corr.* VI, p. 162–9.

53. Gaius Cornelius Cethegus, a fellow-conspirator of Catiline's.

54. 'Explode', the opposite of 'applaud'.

55. Lucan, *Pharsalia*, IX, 207: *nec color imperii nec frons erit* [Burke: *erat*] *ulla Senatus*: the preceding words show how Burke understood this ambiguous passage.

56. Date of the revolutionary removal of the king and queen from Versailles to Paris.

57. Remark attributed to Antoine-Joseph-Marie-Pierre Barnave, a member of the National Assembly, on learning of the lynching of Foullon and Berthier in July 1789 (see n.67 below). Barnave was later to become the *confidant* of the court and the champion of the Queen.

58. Burke assumes that Price's words – 'their king led in triumph, etc.' referred to the events of 6 October. Price, in the preface to the fourth edition of his sermon, claims that he was referring to the events of 14 July (fall of the Bastille).

59. *Io Paean*: from the words of the chorus of the Greek hymn to Apollo, now generalized in English as 'paean' with the meaning, 'a song of triumph'.

60. The misspelt French is part of the text of the seventh edition as reprinted under the editorship of William B. Todd and represents one of those 'peculiarities repeatedly condoned by the author' referred to by Mr Todd in his preface.

61. The Fifth Monarchy is the last of the five great empires in Daniel, ii.44 and was identified with the Millennium of the Apocalypse by the chiliastic English seventeenth-century sect, the Fifth Monarchy Men.

62. Trophime Gérard, Marquis de Lally-Tollendal (1758–1830), the legitimized son of the ill-fated general, the Comte de Lally, who

was executed by Louis XV. Emigrated in 1790; returned to France in 1792 to try to rescue the King; honoured at the Restoration. Burke's feelings about him changed. See *Corr.* VI, pp. 321–2.

Jean-Joseph Mounier (1758–1806), a talented constitutional lawyer and, as a young man, a hero of the pre-revolutionary protest movements which led to the summoning of the States-general; elected President of the Constituent Assembly in 1789, he was subsequently obliged to take refuge in Switzerland in the circumstances here described.

63. The famous passage beginning here irritated one of its first and most attentive readers: 'In my opinion all that you say of the Queen is pure foppery. If she be a perfect female character, you ought to take your ground upon her virtues. If she be the reverse, it is ridiculous in any but a Lover, to place her personal charms in opposition to her crimes ...' (Francis to Burke, 19 February 1790: *Corr.* VI, pp. 86–7.) Burke was hurt: 'The contrast ... did draw Tears from me and wetted my Paper.' ... 'Am I obliged to prove judicially the Virtues of those I shall see suffering every kind of wrong, and contumely, and risk of Life before I endeavour to interest others in their sufferings?' (Burke to Francis, 20 February 1790: *Corr.* VI, pp. 88–92.) A correspondent of Burke's later reported to him that the passage had been brought to the attention of Marie Antoinette in her captivity: 'who before she had read half the Lines she Burst into a Flood of Tears and was a long Time before she was sufficiently composed to peruse the remainder.' (E. Jeringham to Burke, before 18 January 1791; *Corr.* VI, pp. 203–4.)

64. Horace, *De Arte Poetica*, 99. 'It is not enough for poems to be fine; they must charm' (Blakeney).

65. Andrew Marvell put this more succinctly:

> The same arts that did gaine
> A power must it maintain
> (*A Horatian Ode upon Cromwell's
> Return from Ireland*).

66. The indefinite article is important. Burke's opponents quoted him as referring to 'the swinish multitude' – thereby implying that swinishness was the inherent character of the multitude. This was the principal theme of popular demonstrations against his book. Burke, however, may have been referring to a particular type of multitude, with a particular occasion in mind. (See asterisked note on p. 173; also n.67 below.)

67. Jean-Sylvain Bailly (1736–93) astronomer and politician, pre-

sided over the Tennis-court session and was the first to take the Oath. As mayor of Paris he tried to save the lives of Foullon and Berthier (see below) on the occasion which Burke seems to have had in mind. He was executed, in unusually atrocious circumstances, on 21 Brumaire of the Year II (12 November 1793).

Jean-Antoine Nicolas de Caritat, marquis de Condorcet (1743–94) scientist, economist and politician; voted against the death of the king, and against the constitution of 1793; committed suicide in prison, 9 Germinal of the Year II (29 March 1794).

Joseph-François Foullon, an unpopular landlord and army contractor, who had tried to save himself by the macabre stratagem of circulating a false report of his own death, was lynched by the mob on 23 July 1789, together with his son-in-law, Berthier de Sauvigny, Intendant of Paris.

68. Virgil, *Aeneid*, III. 105: *gentis cunabula nostrae*: 'the cradle of our people'.

69. David Garrick (1717–79), the famous actor-manager and member of Dr Johnson's circle, to whom Burke refers again in the 4th *Letter on a Regicide Peace* (1795) as follows:

I remember, in a conversation I once had with my ever dear friend Garrick, who was the first of actors, because he was the most acute observer of nature I ever knew, I asked him, how it happened, that, whenever a senate appeared on the stage, the audience seemed always disposed to laughter? He said the reason was plain: the audience was well acquainted with the faces of most of the senators [as what we call 'extras' – Ed.] and it was of course that the contrast of the vileness of the actors with the pomp of their habits naturally excited ideas of contempt and ridicule. (*Works* V, p. 386.)

Sarah Siddons (1755–1831): 'probably the one great tragedy queen that Britain ever produced' (Harvey, *Oxford Companion to English Literature*).

70. Johann Reinhold Patkul (1660–1707), Livonian politician and agitator, executed for treason by Charles XII.

71. Gian Renaldo Monaldischi (d. 1657), impoverished Italian nobleman, murdered at Fontainebleau on the orders of the exiled Queen Christina of Sweden.

72. Lord George Gordon (1751–93), agitator, prosecuted in connexion with the anti-popery riots in London of 5–6 June, 1780 (in which Burke's house and person were endangered). After a later conviction for libel, Gordon was imprisoned in Newgate in 1788, and died there in 1793, after singing the '*Ça ira*'.

73. 'Such masters, such scholars. Who ever dreamt of Voltaire and Rousseau as legislators? The first has the merit of writing agreeably; and nobody has ever united blasphemy and obscenity so happily together. The other was not a little deranged in his intellects, to my almost certain knowledge. But he saw things in bold and uncommon lights, and he was very eloquent –. But as to the rest!' (Burke to Unknown, January 1790; *Corr.* VI, pp. 78–81.) See also *Letter to A Member of the National Assembly*, 1791.

74. Claude-Adrien Helvétius (1715–71), French *philosophe*; his book *De l'Esprit* (1758) was condemned by Clement XIII, and widely read.

75. Anthony Collins (1676–1729), friend of Locke, author of *Discourse of Freethinking* (1713), had the misfortune of attracting the ridicule of both Bentley and Swift; John Toland (1670–1722), author of *Christianity Not Mysterious* (1696), the first shot in the English controversy between deist and orthodox; Matthew Tindal (1657–1733), author of *The Rights of the Christian Church Asserted* (1706), which was burnt by order of the House of Commons; Thomas Chubb (1679–1747), deist and tallow-chandler: Leslie Stephen observes of Chubb that he 'has long been a name, though the name was frequently used to communicate a certain plebeian flavour to catalogues of contemptible deists' (*English Thought in the Eighteenth Century*, 1876); Thomas Morgan (d. 1743), also involved in the deist controversy, but 'never obtained much notice' (*D.N.B.*); Henry St John, Viscount Bolingbroke (1678–1751), the tory statesman and author of *The Idea of a Patriot King* (1738), was parodied in one of Burke's first books, *A Vindication of Natural Society* (1756).

76. Mary Wollstonecraft comments: 'It is a well-known fact that when *we*, the people of England, have a son whom we scarcely know what to do with – *we* make a clergyman of him' (*A Vindication of the Rights of Men*, London 1790). See also n. 83.

77. Burke's claim to write as a representative English Protestant irritated some of his contemporaries: note Mary Wollstonecraft's use (n.76 above) of the italicized *we*. The claim, made by Burke on their behalf, that English Protestants no longer 'violently condemned' Roman Catholicism was not calculated to appease such critics.

78. Burke's reference does not correspond to the existing standard text, where the passage occurs at II.vii; his text also departs from standard in minor details. The following is the Loeb English version:

So in the very beginning we must persuade our citizens that the gods are the lords and rulers of all things, and that what is done is done by their will and authority; that they are likewise great bene-factors of man, observing the character of every individual, what he does, of what wrong he is guilty, and with what intentions and with what piety he fulfills his religious duties; and that they take note of the pious and the impious. For surely minds which are imbued with such ideas will not fail to form true and useful opinions.

79. 'Art is man's nature' – *Appeal from the New to the Old Whigs* (1791). *Works* III, p. 86.

80. Lucan, *Pharsalia*, V. 260: ... 'whatever offence is committed by many goes unpunished.'

81. Mary Wollstonecraft comments: 'The only way in which the people interfere in government, religious or civil, is in electing representatives.... Are these *holy* nominations? Where is the booth of religion? Does she mix her awful mandates, or lift her persuasive voice in those scenes of drunken riot and beastly glut-tony?' (*Vindication*.)

82. *Cicero, de Republica*, VI. xiii. (For to that supreme God who made the Universe, there is nothing on earth more acceptable than these gatherings and orderly societies of men, called States' (Blake-ney).

83. Mary Wollstonecraft comments: 'The little respect paid, in great houses, to tutors and chaplains proves, Sir, the fallacy of your reasoning.... They sometimes are only modern substitutes for the jesters of Gothic memory, and serve as whetstones for the blunt wit of the noble peer who patronizes them' (*Vindication*.)

84. Here, 'education'; the *O.E.D.* gives no examples of this use later than 1790.

85. The channel between the island of Euboea and the mainland of Greece, remarkable for the force of its current and its frequent changes of direction.

86. *Palais Royal*, residence of the duc d'Orléans (Philippe Egalité); its gardens were a centre of agitation in the early part of the Revolu-tion. *Jacobins*, the famous political club, which sat in the monastery of the 'Jacobins' (Dominicans) in the Rue St Honoré. The term *Jacobins* was first applied to its members in ridicule, and was not formally accepted by them until 1792 ('*Société des Jacobins, amis de la liberté et de l'égalité*').

87. *jus retractus*, right of recovery. Under the laws of the *ancien régime* in France a lord could at any time compulsively repurchase alienated lands which had once formed part of his fief; and the

heirs of a landowner could similarly repurchase any part of their ancestors' estates which he had alienated. In modern times the poet Yeats admired laws of the latter type enacted under the Third Reich. (Hone, *Yeats*, p. 467.)

88. There were at this time actually *five* 'Académies', learned societies holding letters patent, to which this reference might apply: the Académie française, founded by Richelieu in 1634, the Académie des Beaux-Arts, founded by Mazarin in 1648, Colbert's Académies des Inscriptions et Belles-Lettres (1663), and des Sciences (1666), and the Académie royale de musique (1671); the four first-named are now incorporated in the present Institut de France.

The Encyclopédie is the outstanding literary undertaking of the philosophic spirit of the eighteenth century; conceived as a dictionary of the arts and sciences, which would establish a rational explanation of the universe and discourage superstition, and under the general direction of Diderot with such collaborators as Voltaire, Montesquieu and Rousseau, its influence on the intellectual life of the time was immense (in spite of the hostility of the orthodox), as was, incidentally, its financial success. Its promoters and supporters, the '*encyclopédistes*' and '*philosophes*', did in fact form a brotherhood of a sort as here described, bound together, if only loosely, by a real community of purpose and interests.

89. Burke visited Paris in January–February, 1773 and was in touch with intellectual society there (Madame du Deffand, Abbé Morellet and others). Unfortunately such of his letters as have been preserved do not record his immediate impressions of this society. For some of their impressions of him see *Corr.* II, p. 425.

90. Frederick the Great.

91. Anne-Robert-Jacques Turgot (1727–81), the reforming Controller General of Finance 1774–76; author of *Réflexions sur la formation et la distribution de la richesse* (1766), he was the associate of the *philosophes*, esteemed by Voltaire, and contributed to the *Encyclopédie*; in economics he is considered in some respects a precursor of Ricardo.

92. Nineteenth-century editors take the Laborde in question to be Jean-Joseph Dart (1724–94) a wealthy banker, created Marquis of Laborde by Louis XV. There was another wealthy contemporary Laborde, however, François-Louis-Joseph, Marquis de Laborde-Méréville (d. 1801), financier and politician; formerly keeper of the royal treasury, he became an active member of the Constituent Assembly; in 1790 he was one of the commissioners for the receipt of patriotic gifts of church silver. It is possible that as in the case of the

Aiguillons and Rochefoucaulds (see nn.95–7 below) Burke is aiming at more than one person of the name.

93. The National Assembly, in November 1789, confiscated all Church lands. The Archbishop of Paris was Antoine-Eléonore-Léon Leclerc de Juigné (1728–1811), widely known for his charitable disposal of the considerable revenues of his charge. In or about this time he abandoned his office and went into exile.

94. Étienne-François, duc de Choiseul (1719–85), minister of Louis XV. He died heavily in debt. Burke lived to regret this reference; he agreed to correct the French edition at the request of Choiseul's widow (*Corr.* II, pp. 234–7, 285, 337).

95. Emmanuel-Armand de Vignoret duPlessis-Richelieu, duc d'Aiguillon (1720–88), governor of Upper Alsace, tried for abuse of power in 1770. The case was closed by order of Louis XV. Burke's shaft is aimed at his son. See n.96 below.

96. Louis-Marie, vicomte de Noailles (1756–1804) proposed in the National Assembly, on 4 August 1789, the abolition of feudal dues and privileges. This proposal, which was carried, was seconded by Armand-Désiré Vignoret duPlessis-Richelieu, duc d'Aiguillon (1761–1800), son of the duke to whom Burke refers.

97. For the duc de la Rochefoucauld d'Anville see n.5. Burke has no mercy on the noblemen who helped in the early stages of the French Revolution, or on those whom he considers their English political equivalents. See *Letter to a Noble Lord* (1796).

E. J. Payne takes the reference here to be to François Alexandre Frédéric, duc de la Rochefoucauld-Liancourt (1747–1827); an enthusiastic reforming economist and anglophile, the friend of Louis XVI, President of the National Assembly (1789); the duke was subsequently forced into exile, returned to take an active part in public life under Napoleon, and died under Charles X having been a focus of opposition to the Bourbon government since the Restoration. If his are the estates in question, it may be noted that they were restored to him by Napoleon after their forfeiture under the provisions relating to the property of *émigrés*.

98. Dominique de la Rochefoucauld (1713–1800), Archbishop of Rouen and cardinal, protested from the beginning against the principles of the Revolution and emigrated after the fall of the monarchy (10 August 1792). He came from a poor and obscure branch of the family.

99. *crudelem illam hastam*: 'that cruel spear' – the spear stuck in the ground at public auctions in ancient Rome; the phrase is approximately from Cicero (*De Officiis*, II. viii. 29: *hastam illam*

cruentam), who was alluding to the sales under the confiscations of Sulla.

100. Sir John Denham (1615–69) was a friend of Charles I.

101. Jacques Necker (1732–1804), the Genevan banker appointed Director General of Finance in succession to Turgot (see n.91) by Louis XVI; he held that office successively 1776–81, 1788–9 and 1789–90; his probity and moral courage were generally acknowledged, but his statesmanship is open to criticism. He was the father of Madame de Staël.

102. See n.5.

103. The *assignats*, notes issued on the security of the church and crown lands confiscated to the state; as Burke foresaw, the *assignat* system enriched a class of speculators.

104. The Caisse d'Escompte.

105. The *parlements*, judicial bodies with administrative and regulating functions, were abolished at the revolution.

106. See n.75; Bolingbroke's *style* – 'that rapid torrent of an impetuous and overbearing eloquence' ... (*Works* I, p. 229) – had left a channel.

107. Tahmasp Quli Khan, later Nadir Shah (1736–47).

108. The *généralités* were the territorial units of financial administration, for each of which an *intendant* was responsible.

109. Charles–Alexandre de Calonne (1734–1802), one-time minister of Louis XVI, his work, *L'État de la France*, was published in London in 1790. The politics of the counter-revolution were soon to bring Burke and Calonne into close contact. See *Corr.* VI.

110. The *Orsini*, Guelf nobles famous for their destructive feuds with the Ghibelline *Colonnas* from the twelfth to the fifteenth century; *Vitelli*, fifteenth-century *condottieri*; *Mamelukes*, military class who ruled in Egypt and Syria from the thirteenth to the sixteenth century; *Nayres*, military caste of Malabar, crushed by Hyder Ali in the 1760s.

111. Officious = helpful.

112. Voltaire, however, was thrashed by the lackeys of the Chevalier de Rohan. The implications of Burke's remark, for the behaviour of the *English* upper classes of his day, are of interest. The Victorian editor, E. J. Payne, notes here: 'a form of outrage never very uncommon in this country'. (Burke, *Select Works* II, p. 366).

113. Cicero, *pro Sestio*, IX. 21: 'all of us good citizens always love a lord' (Ed.). Cicero was of course a favourite of Burke's.

114. Mackintosh (*Vindiciae Gallicae*) thus answered all this part:

We are not considering the demerit of citizens whom it is fit to punish, but the spirit of a body which it is politic to dissolve. We are not concluding that the Nobility and Clergy were in their private capacity bad citizens, but that they were members of corporations which could not be preserved with security to civil freedom.

115. Spenser, *Faerie Queene*, II. c.7, st. 14.

116. The play was *Charles IX* by Marie-Joseph de Chénier (1764–1811), a brother of André de Chénier (1762–94). Banned in 1787, it was a great hit in November 1789.

117. The house of Guise, a cadet branch of the house of Lorraine, played a spectacular and stormy part over three generations in the politics of France, civil and ecclesiastical. They were held to have dynastic pretentions to the throne. The Cardinal of Lorraine here referred to, whose name is associated with the Massacre of St Bartholomew, was Louis de Guise (1555–88), the third member of the family to hold that eminence.

118. See n.93.

119. François de la Mothe-Fénelon (1651–1715), Archbishop of Cambrai, renowned for piety, learning, eloquence and gentleness. See Ronald Knox, *Enthusiasm*. (Oxford, 1950).

120. Auxerre; *Corr*. II, pp. 421–2. The bishop, Jean-Baptiste-Marie Champion de Cicé (1725–1806), was to become an *émigré* and be helped by the Burkes. He was a brother of the Visconte de Cicé (1745–1815), who corresponded with Burke. (See *Corr*. VI, pp. 206–8; Also Introduction, pp. 52–3.)

121. Not mentioned in relevant contemporary letter. (*Corr*., p. 421–2.)

122. Here used generally; but the implication 'independence from Rome' would occur to Burke's readers, and favour his argument.

123. Gilbert Burnet (1643–1715), Bishop of Salisbury under William III; the quotation is from his *History of His Own Times* (1723–34).

124. Jean Domat (1625–96), author of *Les Lois civiles dans leur ordre naturel* (1689).

125. Armand Gaston Camus (1740–1804), Jansenist lawyer and member of the Constituent Assembly: drew up the civil constitution of the clergy.

126. Levelling and millenary sect.

127. The 'Patriotic Society' of Nantes was a correspondent of the Revolution Society. See n.2.

128. *De officiis*, II. xxii. 79–xxiii. 80–83:

Thus even though they to whom property has been wrongfully awarded be more in number than they from whom it has been unjustly taken, they do not for that reason have more influence; for in such matters influence is measured not by numbers but by weight. And how is it fair that a man who never had any property should take possession of lands that had been occupied for many years or even generations, and that he who had them before should lose possession of them?

Now, it was on account of just this sort of wrong-doing that the Spartans banished their Ephor Lysander, and put their King Agis to death – an act without precedent in the history of Sparta. From that time on – and for the same reason – dissensions so serious ensued that tyrants arose, the nobles were sent into exile, and the state, though most admirably constituted, crumbled to pieces. Nor did it fall alone, but by the contagion of the ills that, starting in Lacedaemon, spread widely and more widely, it dragged the rest of Greece down to ruin.... That is the right way to deal with one's fellow-citizens, and not, as we have already witnessed on two occasions, to plant the spear in the forum and knock down the property of citizens under the auctioneer's hammer. But yon Greek, like a wise and excellent man, thought that he must look out for the welfare of all. And this is the highest statesmanship and the soundest wisdom on the part of a good citizen, not to divide the interests of the citizens, but to unite all on the basis of impartial justice. (Tr. W. Miller, Loeb Classical Library.)

129. The works in question are about the supposed conspiracy of the *Illuminati*, a quasi-masonic society.

130. 'This saying should be engraved everywhere in the halls of princes, *You have obtained Sparta, adorn it* ...' (*The Adages of Erasmus*, tr. Phillips.)

131. Compare the passage in the *Appeal from the New to the Old Whigs* (1791) about a 'true natural aristocracy'. (Works III, pp. 85–7.)

132. 'Gifts of Earth' (Ed.), i.e. material as opposed to spiritual benefits: Horace, *Odes*, II.xiv.10.

133. Scene of Revolutionary commemorative rallies.

134. The condition of property held inalienably by a corporation.

135. Virgil, *Georgics*, I. 120. 'God himself decreed that the farmer's way should not be easy'. (Ed.)

136. Jean-Paul Rabaut St Etienne (b. 1743), Protestant pastor, later a member of the Girondin group in the Convention; guillotined 1793.

137. *Quinze-vingts*, an ancient foundation for the blind; *petites maisons*, a lunatic asylum.

138. Cicero, *Pro Murena*, XXIX–XXXI.

139. Horace, *Epistles*, I, xix. 12–14: *Quid? siquis voltu torvo ferus et pede nudo Exiguaeque togae simulet textore Catonem, Virtutemne repraesentet moresque Catonis?* 'If someone looks fierce and goes round in bare feet and poor clothes to be like Cato, does he really display the virtue and morality of Cato?' (Ed.)

140. Rousseau was helped by Hume in England, 1766–7, and quarrelled with him.

141. Empedocles, Greek philosopher of the fifth century B.C., derived all things from a mixture of the four elements in varying proportions. The French naturalist Georges-Louis Leclerc, comte de Buffon, (1707–88) should really be Burke's ally, not his target: no true *philosophe*, he prized 'experience'.

142. Pope, *Moral Essays*, Ep. iv.l.129.

143. Servius Tullius (578–534 B.C.), an early king of Rome supposed to have divided the Romans into 'centuries' or groups of 100.

144. cf. Martial *Epigrams*, X.iv.10: *Hominem pagina nostra sapit*: 'My page smacks of man' (Ed.). Also 'All Human Life is There' (*News of the World*).

145. It would not be long before Burke would find the centralized France of the Convention more alarming than the 'variety of republics' had been.

146. 'For the days had passed when entire legions – with tribunes centurions, privates in their proper centuries – were so transplanted as to create, by their unanimity, and their comradeship, a little commonwealth. The settlers now were strangers among strangers; men from totally different maniples; leaderless; mutually indifferent; suddenly, as if they were anything in the world except soldiers, massed in one place to compose an aggregate rather than a colony.' (*tr*. J. Jackson.)

147. The physician Hippocrates (fifth century B.C.) gave the classical account of the facial appearance of the dying.

148. Charles Louis de Secondat, baron de Montesquieu (1689–1755), political philosopher, author of the *Lettres persanes* (1721) and the *Esprit des Lois* (1748). He admired the British constitution and Burke admired him.

149. Troll – anything round, a roll, repetition. E. J. Payne could not believe that Burke could have penned 'this trivial repartee' and thought that the whole paragraph was the work of his son Richard.

The touch of pedantry in it is consistent with this hypothesis. The ten categories are Aristotle's (*The Organon*).

150. See n.109.

151. In scholastic theology a place in the underworld, neither heaven nor hell, where the virtuous of the Old Dispensation stayed until Christ's 'harrowing' of hell. It was distinct from the *limbus infantum*, residence of unbaptized children. Burton (*Anatomy of Melancholy*) dismissed 'all that subterranean geography'.

152. Delos, the legend went, had been a floating island until Latona there gave birth to Apollo and Diana, and Jupiter made the island fast.

153. 'Round shores and coasts.' (Aeneid III, 75.)

154. Talleyrand, bishop of Autun.

155. Cicero, *de Senectute* VII. 25: 'I sow for the immortal Gods': supposedly the farmer's reply when questioned why he labours.

156. Horace, *Epode* II: 'So saying the moneylender Alphius, who was always thinking about becoming a farmer, called in all his money in the middle of the month, to put it out at interest again at the beginning of the next'. The third line of the Latin should read *Omnem redegit. . . .*

157. Famous eighteenth-century financial crashes. See also n.196.

158. Milton, *Paradise Lost*, II.592:

> *A gulf profound as that Serbonian Bog*
> *Betwixt Damiata and mount Casius old,*
> *Where armies whole have sunk:*

This paragraph of Burke brings to mind Marx's reflections at the beginning of the *Communist Manifesto*; see Introduction, p. 11.

159. Archetypal law-givers, of Athens and Rome respectively.

160. Cardinal Mazarin (1602–61), successor of Richelieu; François Michel Le Tellier, Marquis de Louvois (1641–91), Louis XIV's Minister of War.

161. Pitt had been critical of the king for allowing his Hanoverian concerns to influence his policy for England.

162. Burke did not long remain so contemptuous of the intellectual resources of the Revolution. Within a year he was warning against under-estimating the Jacobins: 'Oh let those who would restore the good in that country be careful how they despise their enemy !' (11 August 1791; *Sheffield papers*.) Later he wrote 'I have a good

opinion of the general abilities of the Jacobins: not that I suppose them better born than others; but strong passions awaken the faculties; they suffer not a particle of the man to be lost. The spirit of enterprise gives to this description the full use of all their native energies'. (First *Letter on a Regicide Peace*, 1796, *Works* V, p. 191.)

163. Armand Marc, Comte de Montmorin-de Saint Hérem (1745–1792) was minister for foreign affairs; the occasion Burke refers to was one on which the Assembly, by attaching a humiliating condition to a proposed agreement (*Pacte national*) with Spain, presented Pitt with a diplomatic victory. Montmorin was forced to resign after the flight to Varennes and perished in the September massacres.

164. Juvenal, *Satires* X. 284: The idea is that he was ruined by his own popularity.

165. See n.105.

166. A hill near Athens where the council of elders met.

167. By Louis XV's Chancellor, René-Nicolas de Maupéou (1714–92).

168. Decrees of the assembly of the citizens of Athens, which had the force of law.

169. After the capture of the Bastille the Constituent Assembly decided that certain royalists should be tried by the old Paris court of the Châtelet for the crime of *lèse-nation*.

170. The *comité des recherches*, a committee of the National Assembly formed to discover conspiracies against the nation.

171. Jean Frédéric, Comte de la Tour du Pin (1727–94), head of the military committee of the Assembly, guillotined in 1794.

172. 'You're not supposed to laugh.'

173. The Governor of the Bastille, Bernard-René-Jourdan de Launey (1740–89), was murdered by the crowd on the day the fortress fell; in April, 1790 the forts at Marseilles were taken over by the *garde nationale* and the Chevalier de Bausset was murdered.

174. Cicero, *de Senectute*, XXIII.83. 'If these people should offer me the chance of becoming a child again, and crying in a cradle of theirs, I should certainly refuse.' Burke's text is slightly modified.

175. Burke did not live to see the fulfilment of this prophecy, which occurred on the 18th Brumaire 1799, two years after his death.

176. Marie-Joseph Motier, Marquis de La Fayette (1757–1834), at this time Commandant of the *garde nationale*. In June, 1890 the

Assembly abolished hereditary titles and the Marquis became, in theory, plain Monsieur Motier.

177. Probably either the *Courrier de Versailles à Paris et de Paris à Versailles*, or its successor, the *Courrier des 93 Départements*, both edited by Antoine-Joseph Gorsas (1752–93), whose execution was witnessed by the young Wordsworth.

178. See C. L. R. James, *The Black Jacobins* (New York 1963).

179. See n.125.

180. The salt tax, one of the most unpopular under the *ancien régime*.

181. The systasis was the temporary defence union of the Cretan cities when attacked by a common enemy; Poland for most of its history was a loose confederation of semi-independent fiefs.

182. Théodore Vernier, comte de Mont-Orient (1731–1818), one of the Assembly's principal financial experts.

183. Naevius, the poet, quoted by Cicero, *De Senectute*, VI.xx: 'How did you manage to ruin your great country so quickly?' The answer is: *Proveniebant oratores novi, stulti adulescentuli*: 'New orators coming forward, foolish young men.'

184. Louis de Rouvroy, Duc de Saint-Simon; his famous *Mémoires* cover the period 1694–1723.

185. *Change*: here the London Stock Exchange; Westminster Hall: long the chief of the great law courts of England. In it Burke prosecuted Warren Hastings.

186. See n.109.

187. See n.103.

188. Dog-latin, in imitation of Molière's *La Malade Imaginaire*.

189. Talleyrand: Burke did not disdain the heavier forms of irony. See Introduction, pp. 43–5.

190. Jean de la Bruyère (1645–96), essayist and aphorist; Jacques-Bénigne Bossuet (1627–1704), Bishop of Meaux, the great preacher and controversalist who opposed Fénelon (see n.119) in the struggle over Quietism.

191. The Treasury or Exchequer; in other contexts the Department of Inland Revenue.

192. Anne-Louis Henri de la Fare (1752–1829) refused to take the oath of the Civil Constitution of the clergy and emigrated. He was made Archbishop of Sens at the Restoration, and Cardinal. He preached the coronation sermon of Charles X.

193. The Dundee 'Friends of Liberty'.

194. This phrase confused Burke's French translator.

195. Horace, *Satires* I.v.100: *credat Iudeaus Apella, non ego*: 'Let

the Jew Apella believe it (not me)'. Burke turns the phrase round, in one of his frequent gibes at the Jewish financiers whom he regarded as among the principal beneficiaries of the Revolution.

196. John Law (1671–1729), Scottish financier who became controller-general of finance in France under the Regent and, as creator of the Mississippi Company, virtual sovereign of Louisiana. He persuaded the government to issue paper currency. The fury of financial speculation by the public which attended his operations brought about his ruin and he died in Venice. See n.157.

197. See n.67.

198. Maximilien de Béthune, Duc de Sully (1560–1641), companion in arms and superintendent of finances to Henri IV.

199. The mace of death in *Paradise Lost* x.293.

200. On this passage Mary Wollstonecraft comments: 'This is contemptible hard-hearted sophistry, in the specious form of humility, and submission to the will of Heaven.' (*Vindication*.)

201. Lotteries on groups of lives.

202. Marcus Annaeus Lucanus (A.D. 39–65), Roman poet; Pierre Corneille (1606–84), dramatist.

203. Addison, *Cato*, Act V, scene 1:

> *Eternity! thou pleasing dreadful Thought!*
> *Through what Variety of untry'd Being,*
> *Through what new Scenes and Changes must we pass!*

204. The tone of detachment assumed by Burke in this penultimate paragraph recalls Matthew Arnold's comment in *The Function of Criticism at the Present Time* (1864) on a similar but more marked disengagement at the conclusion of Burke's *Thoughts on French Affairs* (1791; *Works* III, pp. 392–3.): 'That return of Burke's upon himself has always seemed to me one of the finest things in English literature, or indeed in any literature. That is what I call living by ideas: when one side of a question has long had your earnest support, when all your feelings are engaged, when you hear all round you no language but one, when your party talks this language like a steam-engine and can imagine no other, – still to be able to think, still to be irresistibly carried, if so it be, by the current of thought to the opposite side of the question, and, like Balaam, to be unable to speak anything *but what the Lord has put in your mouth*. I know nothing more striking, and I must add that I know nothing more un-English'. We may suppose Yeats to have something like this in view when in *On the Boiler* he so surprisingly attributes to the Irish mind the characteristic of a 'cold, detonating impartiality'.

BIBLIOGRAPHICAL NOTE

By kind permission of Dr William B. Todd and his publishers, the text of the *Reflections* in this edition follows that of Dr Todd's edition, published by Holt, Reinhart & Winston in New York, 1959 (second printing, 1962). Dr Todd's text superseded all previous texts of this work generally available. It is based on James Dodsley's 'Seventh Edition' (or tenth and final 1790 impression: 'the last attended and revised by the author'). Dr Todd notes that this edition, like the predecessors, contains 'inconsistencies in spelling, mis-quotations from the Latin, and false accenting in French'; he has preserved these 'as peculiarities repeatedly condoned by the author.'

The footnotes appended to the text are Burke's from the Seventh Edition, with the addition of a number of notes added by Dr Todd from the 1803 edition: 'supposedly representing marginalia which Burke entered in his copy of the 1792 *Works*' (Todd). All these are indicated thus: (1803). Dr Todd observes that the footnote which in this edition is on page 173 'appears to be from another source'. The remaining five – which in this edition are on pages 212, 213, 215, 216 and 250 – are 'of the author's composition' (Todd).

The references, in the Introduction and in the editor's notes at the end of the book, to *Burke's Works*, are to the edition in eight volumes published in Bohn's Standard Library, fifth edition, 1883–90. There is at present no modern edition of Burke's works. As the present edition of the *Reflections* goes to press, students of Burke hope that the editors of the monumental edition of Burke's *Correspondence* (see below) may be persuaded to undertake the definitive edition of the *Works*.

The references, in the Introduction and editor's notes, to Burke's *Correspondence*, are to the edition published by the Cambridge University Press and the University of Chicago Press, under the general editorship of Professor Thomas W. Copeland. I have drawn particularly heavily on Volume VI, *July 1789–December 1791*, edited by Professor Alfred Cobban and Robert A. Smith. For correspondence later than 1791 I have referred, under the designation 'Sheffield papers', to the collection of papers in the famous 'Burke factory' at the Sheffield Central Library. Papers later than 1791 had not been published in the collected *Correspondence* at the time when this edition of the *Reflections* was in preparation. The Sheffield collection includes, as well as the largest collection of Burke's private papers – in the Fitzwilliam MSS – also collected by the editors of the *Correspondence*, duplicates of all known Burke letters of which the originals are elsewhere. See also 'Acknowledgements'.

RECOMMENDED READING

Cobban, Alfred: *Edmund Burke and the Revolt Against the Eighteenth Century* (London, 1960).

Cobban, Alfred: *The Debate on the French Revolution 1789–1900* (London: second edition, 1960). Contains a section, 'The Intervention of Burke', with many interesting extracts having a bearing on the *Reflections*.

Cone, Carl B.: *Burke and the Nature of Politics*. Vol. 1 *The Age of the American Revolution*. Vol. 2 *The Age of the French Revolution*. (University of Kentucky Press, 1957 and 1964). This is the first biography to make extensive use of the Burke papers, in the Fitzwilliam collection and elsewhere.

Copeland, Thomas W.: *Edmund Burke: Six Essays* (London, 1960).

Hughes, A. M. D.: *Edmund Burke: Selections* (Oxford, 1928). Contains a useful little anthology of comments on Burke by Hazlitt, Coleridge, De Quincey, Macaulay and others.

Magnus, Sir Philip: *Edmund Burke: A Life* (London, 1939). Although superseded in many respects by Cone's more modern and detailed work (above) this remains a useful, concise biography.

Payne, E. J.: *Burke: Select Works*. Three vols., (Oxford 1874, 1875, 1878). The second volume contains the *Reflections*, copiously annotated. The present editor has reason to be grateful to this predecessor, particularly for his unerring identification of Burke's classical tags. The third volume consists of the *Letters on a Regicide Peace* (1796–7) which contain some of Burke's most splendid writing. Readers with access to a good library will be able to read these letters in Payne's edition.

Reference to a number of other works with some reference to the *Reflections* are scattered through the Introduction and notes. Omission from the above 'recommended' list should not of course be taken as implying any kind of censure. Many of the works concerned – like Wecter's study of the Burke finances – are specialized works, and the above short list is not intended for specialists.